Beowulf as Children's Literature

EDITED BY BRUCE GILCHRIST
AND BRITT MIZE

UNIVERSITY OF TORONTO PRESS
Toronto Buffalo London

© University of Toronto Press 2021
Toronto Buffalo London
utorontopress.com
Printed in the U.S.A.

ISBN 978-1-4875-0270-6 (cloth)   ISBN 978-1-4875-1585-0 (EPUB)
                                   ISBN 978-1-4875-1584-3 (PDF)

Library and Archives Canada Cataloguing in Publication

Title: Beowulf as children's literature / edited by Bruce Gilchrist and Britt Mize.
Names: Gilchrist, Bruce D., editor. | Mize, Britt, editor.
Description: Includes bibliographical references and index.
Identifiers: Canadiana (print) 20210170417 | Canadiana (ebook) 20210170611 |
    ISBN 9781487502706 (cloth) | ISBN 9781487515843 (PDF) | ISBN
    9781487515850 (EPUB)
Subjects: LCSH: Beowulf – Adaptations. | LCSH: Children's literature –
    History and criticism. | LCSH: Children – Books and reading – History.
Classification: LCC PR1585 .B46 2021 | DDC 829/.3–dc23

University of Toronto Press acknowledges the financial assistance to its
publishing program of the Canada Council for the Arts and the Ontario Arts
Council, an agency of the Government of Ontario.

Contents

Illustrations

Acknowledgments

Together we wish to express profound gratitude to Marijane Osborn, whose scholarship lighted the way for this project, and without whose early involvement, and even gifts of some books from her collection, it would never have become a reality. We are very grateful as well to Suzanne Rancourt at the University of Toronto Press for her encouraging belief in this book's worth throughout its long development.

Britt would like to thank his colleagues at Texas A&M, especially Claudia Nelson, the students in his *Beowulf*'s Afterlives graduate and undergraduate seminars, and all participants in the Medieval Studies Working Group and the Critical Child Studies Working Group. Thank you also to Ruby Perry-Mize for being an actual child – and one willing to provide incisive commentary on many, many youth versions of *Beowulf*. Generous support for this project has been provided by Stanford Text Technologies, and by Texas A&M University through its Department of English and the Melbern G. Glasscock Center for Humanities Research.

Bruce wishes to acknowledge foremost Anna Smol, whose 1994 essay, "Heroic Ideology and the Children's *Beowulf*," is the first serious critical appraisal of the breadth and cultural work of adaptations of the poem for children. Her research of the holdings at the Osborne Collection of Early Children's Books at the Toronto Public Library proves how vital archives of physical books are for understanding our reception of the past. Following her work, I then built my own collection, which was happily shared with my son Oscar in a great many bedtime readings of Grendel stealing towards Heorot and the dragon being pushed into the ocean. I also must acknowledge the extraordinary patience of our chapter contributors on the lengthy whale-road to publication, and, most deeply, my co-editor, Britt Mize, for his quietly compelling this book into the world with persistence and grace.

BEOWULF AS CHILDREN'S LITERATURE

Introduction: *Beowulf* in and near Children's Literature

BRITT MIZE

Recycling *Beowulf* is a booming business, in output if not always in commercial or aesthetic profit. At least eleven feature-length films have been *Beowulf*-themed, with more doubtful claims made for others. There are dozens of songs and musical compositions, many original poetic treatments, a slew of novels and shorter fiction (including representatives of the sci-fi, cyberpunk, and fantasy genres), around twenty graphic novel or comics versions, several video games, and three published board games.[1] But the single largest category of *Beowulf* representation and adaptation, outside of direct translation of the poem into modern languages, is children's literature: as Bruce Gilchrist's bibliography in this volume attests, *Beowulf* has been remade for the consumption of young readers well over a hundred times in English alone. Almost from the moment the Old English epic found its way into print for adults, adults have been refashioning it for youth, first in Danish, then in English and German, and more recently in Afrikaans, Chinese, Dutch, French, Greek, Italian, Japanese, Korean, Polish, Portuguese, Russian, Slovenian, Spanish, and Swedish, to give a partial list.[2] This essay collection examines the history and processes of remaking *Beowulf* for young readers. For greatest coherence we focus on the mainstay forms of children's literature – picture books, illustrated storybooks, and youth novels – while certain other materials, like curricular aids, illustrated full translations of the poem, and songs, will enter discussion where they link closely to the historical and theoretical dimensions of bringing *Beowulf* to child audiences.[3]

Reworkings of *Beowulf* for children cover a full gamut of style and register. Some are graceful and sophisticated:

> Through the dark night a darker shape slid. A sinister figure shrithed
> down from the moors ... toward the timbered hall, huge and hairy and
> slightly stooping ... Then it grasped the great ring-handle and swung open

the door, the mouth of Heorot ... Grendel saw the knot of sleeping warriors and his eyes shone with an unearthly light.[4]

Others come across as ponderously archaizing:

Dead the monster sank to the ground, and Beowulf ... saw at his feet the lifeless carcase of his foe ... He strode thither, and, seizing the corpse by the hideous coiled locks, shore off the head to carry to earth again.[5]

And a few embrace silliness:

"Wow! Not *the* Beowulf? The winner of Best Warrior in West Denmark three years in a row?" marvelled the Dane.
   Beowulf smiled and buffed his nails on his chain-mail shirt.
   "Not the Beowulf who ... was named Most Gorgeous Geat by *Midgard Maiden Magazine*?"
   "'Tis I!" Beowulf struck a heroic pose.[6]

Every stylistic choice, every illustration program, every enveloping paratext reflects decision-making about what kind of work a new version of the story should do for (and upon) young readers, in particular times and places, situated within their ecologies of opportunity, ability, and desire. Do children's presentations of *Beowulf* educate? Entertain? Awe? Invite young people into more grown-up discourses? Do they encourage curiosity and exploration? Promote fixed values? Teach systems of social relations that adults find agreeable? Do they address children as they are presumed already to be, or urge young people to aspire to something unattained?

The answer to all of these questions is "yes" in a holistic view of the corpus, although the nature of the specific instance is always inflected by larger forces that shape adult investment: trajectories of nationalism; reforms in education like those in nineteenth-century Denmark and the twentieth-century United States; epoch-making trends and events in popular literary culture like the Tolkien phenomenon and Heaney's *Beowulf* translation. Nor has the production of children's *Beowulf* engagements, though large in volume, had a constant rate, and its ebbs and flows prove that the motivation to make a youth adaptation in the first place is no less responsive to its social moment than are the strategies used in doing so. Every aspect of the practice of accommodating such a monument of traditional literary history to youth readers, both in its chronological rhythms and its methods, deserves serious investigation.

But scholarly interest in children's adaptations of canonical literature has not matched the market and library presence of such adaptations. As Anja Müller points out in her introduction to the only whole book dedicated to the remaking of venerated adult literature for younger readers, the studies that do exist have tended to focus narrowly on individual cases rather than taking up larger questions of theory and method.[7] Yet adaptations of works originally intended for adults are hardly a negligible part of the landscape of children's literature. Bookstores stock an ample selection, and the catalogues of most publishers of youth literature include some retellings of "classics," if not a whole series of them. The disparity of production and public demand with critical acknowledgment could imply merely a prevailing scholarly opinion that the adaptation of adult literature does not normally result in high-quality children's books. Such a view may also be joined with a valid scepticism, among thoughtful observers of cultural and educational paradigms, as to whether perpetuating an old-fashioned literary canon is a project children's literature should invest in.

I suspect, however, that another reason this area of study has not gained more traction is a perception that children's adaptations of long-appreciated literature will be *only* subtractive and attenuating, instrumental in purpose, and therefore analytically uninteresting. Publishers reinforce such a perception when they stress the authority of the antecedent work and represent an adaptation of *Beowulf*, or the *Iliad*, or a Shakespeare play, as an uncoloured transmission of it. But even the most conservative retelling for a new audience requires imagination and creativity, inevitably endowing it with its own character; and the status of the resulting narrative as a new cultural object is all the more obvious when multimedia complexity is introduced through illustrations and other features of visual design. As to the instrumentality of children's adaptations, if they are more instrumental than original children's literature – which is not self-evident, although adaptations sometimes work less hard to conceal it – extratextual goals are themselves an eligible target of analysis, with paratexts and educational rhetoric furnishing evidence for crucial critical enquiry into what such works communicate and do. A few valuable articles on children's *Beowulf* adaptations have appeared,[8] and of course children's literature as a genre, medievalism as an impulse, and adaptation as a practice each has its own vast critical literature; but this book is the first to bring together a group of scholars, and even some creators, of *Beowulf* reflexes for young audiences in order to address many of the most important issues of transmuting the Old English poem into textual and pictorial forms that appeal to children, past and present – and to the adults who in any era influence their access to literature.

Beowulf books for children represent a wide spectrum of material characteristics and quality of manufacture, with everything that the physical aspects of a codex imply about the social work of its text. At one extreme are cheaply produced, almost disposable paperbacks, such as might pass through many hands in a classroom set and be treated carelessly with little liability against a purchaser's small expense.[9] At the other are beautiful, richly illustrated large-format volumes good for savouring with family members in a peaceful domestic setting, or else in privacy: books designed for a lap or a clean, uncluttered table.[10] These books' material features encourage a reader to treasure them and to seek again and again the captivating sensory experiences they offer, much like objet d'art presentations of *Beowulf* made for adults.[11] Free-standing *Beowulf* presentations of this type project around themselves an idealization of social space implying affluence and tranquillity, a message for the parents and librarians who buy them as much as for any child readers.

Inclusion of the *Beowulf* story in larger literary bundles, like anthologies and subscription series for children, has also been frequent for more than a century, making its incorporation into superstructures of cultural value an explicit part of its physical and conceptual presence for young readers. Here, variety in material presentation is less an indication of difference in anticipated use than an effort to assert *Beowulf*'s importance through marketplace channels that allow different levels of expenditure on books. Among the home libraries that might be acquired as sets or serially, for example, the magazine-like *Books for the Bairns* ("price one penny" for issue 51, containing "The Story of Beowulf") stand alongside the luxurious tomes of *Journeys through Bookland*.[12] Single-volume anthologies for home or school that include a version of *Beowulf* have a similar canon-making and -sustaining effect, in that they present the story as part of a fabric of institutionally endorsed culture, dissociation from which is resisted by its integration with other works of recognized literary status.[13]

Material format and physical context thus carry messages about *Beowulf*, but the retellings the books embody also carry messages about the world and others in it. Words and pictures can powerfully attract young readers to templates for perception of what is normal, good, or admirable; what factors appropriately define groups; what roles within and outside of one's own group should be sought; and what social structures ensure that the right types of people thrive. Such messages, though designed for children, often must first speak successfully to adults with their own preformed beliefs about not only these matters, but also about what children should encounter or are capable of understanding. Thus children's books inherently have an ideological dimension, one that is difficult to analyse without simultaneous acknowledgment of the genre's didactic involvements. These involvements may be official (as in educational settings) or unofficial, and they may either affirm or challenge systemic lines of force like beliefs about ontological inequality, assumptions about gender identity and roles, and perceptual cues to cooperation, sympathy, or antagonism.[14]

This collection was nearing its final form when the long entanglement of medieval studies as a discipline (just as much as creative medievalism) with histories of personal and institutional racism became a foregrounded issue to many academics who until recently were comfortable referring to themselves as "Anglo-Saxonists."[15] Those discussions, and the shifts in perspective that they have prompted, speak broadly to the importance of this book's subject matter, given the textual and visual power of children's literature to contribute to the formation of categorical perceptions. Supposed racial histories implied or sometimes directly traced by paratexts are frequent in children's versions of *Beowulf*, especially from the nineteenth and earlier twentieth centuries. In images, the more human the hero's adversaries are made to appear, the more their monstrosity is expressed visually as something like racialization. Both phenomena are less common now than they once were in children's literature, but recent books are not devoid of racially loaded assertions to child readers that *Beowulf* represents their own people's heritage – meaning the heritage of white English or Northern European people, extended to other regions through colonial settlement. A fully theorized, historicizing study of race and racism in *Beowulf* adaptations for children remains to be written; several of the essays here will join previously published scholarship in laying crucial groundwork for that endeavour, revealing much about specific moments and movements in the long history of claimed ownership through presumed racial heritage.[16]

Ideological messages, like other attributes of children's books, are tuned to the anticipated age and experiences of the readership. Only one reformulation of *Beowulf* for the extremely young has yet appeared[17] – even John Green's colouring book is not for preschoolers, with its closely drawn lines and detailed captions[18] – but a handful of versions seem designed for children in the lower grades of primary school to enjoy.[19] Retellings for higher primary or middle-grades audiences abound, some of them keeping a storybook-like format and a continuous program of artwork but pairing this visual elaboration with text appropriate to fairly advanced readers, and others for the same age groups novelizing the narrative in unillustrated or little-illustrated formats. Of course, the generalized correlation of age and reading ability used by educational entities and book publishers is far from absolute. For readers who follow a presumptive path towards high proficiency as they mature, "children's literature" shades into simply "literature," with a transition zone of books that were not conceived primarily for pre-adult readers but might either attract their interest (with enticements like Leonard Baskin's pictures accompanying Burton Raffel's full translation of *Beowulf*), or else might be put into their hands institutionally (like translation extracts in high school readers, or John Gardner's *Grendel*, used in some college-preparatory English classes).[20]

Some adapters of *Beowulf* consider precisely the developmental position of readers who are moving out of childhood, or contemplate a readership whose age, abilities, and experience may mix elements regarded as typical of "childhood" and "adulthood." In the preface to his *Beowulf: A New Verse Translation for Fireside and Classroom*, William Ellery Leonard states that he intends it for "mainly the first two years of college, but without embarrassing, I hope, the needs of the high school or even the junior high school," and signals which parts of the text he considers less suitable for the younger segments of his audience: "Presumably the high school student should skip those portions ... which I have enclosed in brackets; and presumably the college student should attend to them."[21] Leonard marks for exclusion passages that lack linearity with the main narrative, such as the Finnsburh episode, sometimes explaining the reason for omission in the teacherly commentary he interjects between sections of the poem.[22] My guess is that Leonard's stilted diction and cumbersome couplets were always more forbidding to teenage readers than an embedded tale of revenge,[23] but setting aside his specific judgments, his text is interesting in suggesting alternative realizations for an audience he imagines to span the boundary of childhood. Marney Worden's unique and creative rendering of *Beowulf*, written entirely in short, basic sentences of a kind not often found in a pictureless book of 126 pages, is for audiences that she describes as "young" but also, more broadly, as "inexperienced" readers:

> That night there was a feast. King Hrothgar welcomed the coming of Beowulf and his men.

> Everybody came. There was wine to drink. There was deer meat to eat –
> with fish and rabbit, too.[24]

Amy Hager extols simplicity, identifying it as something she herself has longed for in the *Beowulf* story, and makes it the guiding principle of her unillustrated retelling, never stating that she has a youth audience in mind.[25] Cases like these reward awareness of vagueness at the edges of "children's literature" as a category.

The genre's boundaries can also be both defined and complicated by conventions of topical acceptability and the frankness with which socially delicate subject matter is treated. In this frame of reference, children's literature verges into young adult (YA) literature, which caters to aspirational grown-ups at a stage of increasingly perceptive encounter with such issues as gender identity, sexual activity, chemical substance abuse, mental illness or disability, and mortality and grief. In YA literature so defined, non-incidental interactions with *Beowulf* are limited to A.E. Kaplan's *Grendel's Guide to Love and War* and *The Boneless Mercies* by April Genevieve Tucholke, two well-written novels that maturely address death, grief, trauma, and less prominently some of the other topics listed above.[26] Several of the comic books and graphic novels that riff on *Beowulf* contain eroticized imagery, typically enmeshed with regressive gender politics or worse;[27] most do not depart from the modes of titillation common to works in this media form marketed to young teen boys.[28] Closer to what is usually understood as a YA treatment of sexuality is the *Grimm Fairy Tales* magazine's *Beowulf* foray, in which Wulf, approximately college age, makes out with classmates at two academies for future heroes,[29] and a couple of the graphic novels portray some kind of sexual contact overtly.[30] But none of the *Beowulf* comics or graphic novels takes a nuanced approach to sex or any of the other potentially fraught topics that YA literature has proved capable of exploring.

Something the few YA *Beowulf* novels and the more numerous graphic novels and comics have succeeded at, though, is owning their autonomy as reimaginings of the Old English poem or isolated components of it. A view of *Beowulf* as an open resource that a later creator may draw upon or manipulate freely is less common in works readily classified as children's literature, which usually follow the poem's main plot structure, even if elaborating greatly or exercising much freedom in the realization of characters and events. However, adaptational activity less constrained by the received story does exist among children's books. Some novels for middle-grades audiences retain the contours of a portion of *Beowulf* while building around it a wider original narrative, or use the events of *Beowulf* as a background against which some other, foregrounded new story unfolds.[31] Others, in an approach similar to that of the YA novels by Kaplan and Tucholke, detach certain threads or iconic elements from their connections in *Beowulf* to use as raw material for recombination and development according to wholly new creative visions.[32]

Such freedom brings up two major theoretical issues for a critic of engagements with *Beowulf* in children's literature.[33] First, radically inventive treatments strain at the boundaries of "adaptation" by many definitions of that term: when can a highly creative interaction with *Beowulf* still be considered a version of *Beowulf*, and when does it cease to be, notionally, "*Beowulf*" in a meaningful way? In this matter children's works deriving from the poem are not separated from the larger field of *Beowulf*'s manifestations in popular culture, or from concerns of adaptation theory broadly. Preoccupation with naming does not seem helpful to me (is it *Beowulf*? is it *an adaptation*?); more useful is a critical focus on the activity of working from earlier materials to create new ones. Even the most fragmented and transformational appropriation of *Beowulf* for a young audience, if that appropriation can be recognized, is a legitimate part of the Old English poem's cascading presence through the field of cultural productions for children and can be analysed as such.[34]

The other issue is endemic to children's literature as a genre with its own social realities. Although informed literary critics have abandoned the belief that fidelity to the antecedent work is prerequisite to an adaptation's quality or interest, the entanglement of children's literature with education keeps the question of fidelity near the surface for many who create, publish, buy, or recommend children's reworkings of canonical texts. The degree of commitment to fidelity by any of these adults rests on assumptions about the purpose of an adaptation for youth. If a children's *Beowulf* is a surrogate for or representation of the Old English poem, much as a traditional translation might be, then a teacher, librarian, or parent is not unreasonable to hope that it tells approximately the same story. On the other hand, if it is solely for entertainment, whether it follows a thousand-year-old text matters little, and the character's name might as well be "Beowulf" as anything else.

Between these two possibilities lies the wish to provide young people with reading material they like that will stimulate the imagination, broaden interests, and encourage ongoing learning, and most *Beowulf* adaptations for children are designed to combine pleasure with intellectual enrichment in some proportion.[35] At a theoretical level we know that "fidelity" is a red herring: any act of adaptation involves countless choices to privilege some aspects of the original for reproduction while sacrificing others. Remaking *Beowulf* for child readers amplifies that truth with the additional need for calibration not just to a modern audience, but to a young one, often in a mixed textual/pictorial format that demands profound creativity. Yet none of this changes the fact that reader judgments will be based on aesthetic appreciation blended with a desired sense (at least among many adults) that notional "*Beowulf*" has survived the transformation, and those judgments have stakes for all parties.

While each chapter that follows treats in some way both the development of *Beowulf* adaptation for children and the technical or conceptual nature of that adaptational activity, the essays are grouped by emphasis into a series more focused on history followed by a series more focused on method and message.

The earliest stages of this history are elucidated by Mark Bradshaw Busbee and Renée Ward. Busbee examines in detail the first attempt to bring *Beowulf* to child audiences, N.F.S. Grundtvig's Danish translation and its subsequent repackagings and derivations, taking account of Grundtvig's many other writings on *Beowulf* and on educational theory. Never clearer than in this case is the entwinement of *Beowulf* as children's literature with institutional goals: the initial failure of Grundtvig's *Bjowulfs Drape* was reversed by its later prominence in the public schools he founded, where it entered the standard curriculum in the form of extracts and songs. For many decades *Bjowulfs Drape* influenced Danish national consciousness, and its echoes extended also to Germany (in the youth drama of Otto Bruder) and England (in J.R.R. Tolkien's ideas about the poem).

Ward identifies for the first time the earliest children's adaptation of *Beowulf* in English – E.L. Hervey's tale "The Fight with the Ogre," in her 1873 book *The Children of the Pear-Garden* – which preceded by eight years the next documented version for English-speaking children. In a thorough consideration of Hervey's treatment of the story, including its sources in *Beowulf* retellings meant for adults, Ward reveals the continuity of this children's adaptation with adaptations more generally and with the literary and ideological tastes of Victorian England. The chapter concludes by presenting readers with a perplexing mystery of publication history to solve, one borne of an illustration in Hervey's book.

Amber Dunai and Carl Edlund Anderson look at important moments in the twentieth-century development of *Beowulf* engagements in books read by young people. J.R.R. Tolkien, who cared greatly about children's reading but disdained the idea of literature *for* children, thought that authors should write so as to include young people in a general community of readers; Dunai measures Tolkien's theory against his practice in several of his *Beowulf*-related writings. Working from Tolkien's concept of "faërie" and his beliefs about the desirable narrative trajectory for stories fitting that category, Dunai finds that *The Hobbit* (popular among many audiences), the song "The Lay of Beowulf" (which Tolkien sang to his own children), and the story *Sellic Spell* (which never reached readers during Tolkien's lifetime) reflect complexly the author's philosophy of literature that is well suited for child and adult audiences alike.

Anderson too focuses on the middle part of the twentieth century to identify the emergence of a new mode of interaction with *Beowulf* among children's writers. He argues that during this era authors felt newly free to draw upon elements of *Beowulf* in ways not closely tethered to the Old English poem's narrative. After surveying several examples that illustrate the difference he proposes between "retellings" and "reuses" of *Beowulf*, Anderson reads one of each type by the same author, Rosemary Sutcliff, as a closer study in this distinction. Sutcliff's *Beowulf: Dragon Slayer*, a fairly conservative adaptation of *Beowulf*, is well known; less widely read now is her youth novel *The Shield Ring*, which (like Tolkien's *Hobbit*) borrows from *Beowulf* and refracts elements of the poem creatively to integrate them into a new story. Anderson describes systematically for the first time the mid-century expansion of possibilities for *Beowulf*'s presence in literature for young audiences, coinciding with a period of dynamic change in both *Beowulf* adaptation more broadly and the history of children's literature.

Bruce Gilchrist's chapter is the collection's fulcrum between the historical emphasis of its first several chapters and the emphasis of the next several on matters of technique and theme. Gilchrist traces pictorial representation of female characters in *Beowulf* from Victorian times to the present, on the premise that illustration history constitutes its own record of emphasis, priorities, and flavouring of the story's gender politics for child audiences. Sets of artistic choices, he shows, can group pictorial representations into four broad periods, each with its own patterns of implication about the presence and importance of regal women and Grendel's mother. Gilchrist finds, perhaps surprisingly, that in visual art the trend has been to increasingly displace and de-emphasize the poem's female figures despite some social and textual movements in the opposite direction.

Janet Schrunk Ericksen's topic, manipulations of perspective, complements Gilchrist's study of pictures by examining narrative techniques used in the story's telling to implicitly situate a reader with a specific vantage point on a scene. Ericksen selects Beowulf's fight with Grendel's mother as an especially informative episode, given that the poem's isolation of the hero in that scene establishes an a priori limitation of perspectival options to which adapters must respond creatively. In a sampling of books for both younger and more advanced readers, Ericksen finds complex interplay among perspective, perceived risk, and probable audience sympathy in representations of a violent confrontation.

My own essay proceeds from one of the major tenets of adaptation theory: that adaptation creates a fully dialogic relationship between the new work and its antecedent. This chapter analyses features of a recent Chinese children's book, whose representation of *Beowulf* differs in some important ways from those familiar in the European/American tradition, to discover how its creators' choices can prompt new perspectives on the Old English poem itself.

Robert Stanton surveys the use in children's *Beowulf* versions of a staple strategy in much children's literature: the incorporation, narratively and pictorially, of animal characters in more and less anthropomorphic realizations. Working from the insights of critical animal studies, Stanton's close analysis of several examples – including ones by Rudyard Kipling and "Dr. Seuss" (Theodor Seuss Geisel) that are not widely recognized as having *Beowulf* connections – sheds light on how the narrative and visual reimagining of *Beowulf* characters as animals relates to ideologies of humanness and power in the contexts of these works' creation.

Yvette Kisor examines the textual and graphic design features of several *Beowulf* versions that she argues are meant for the "new Tolkien generation": an appellation by which Kisor refers to young people in the first decade of the 2000s whose aesthetics and tooth for medievalism were shaped in part by the CGI-enhanced Peter Jackson films adapting Tolkien's fiction to the screen. Kisor links several *Beowulf* books to these films and the demographic group they were designed to attract. She suggests that the 2007 Robert Zemeckis *Beowulf* film, publicized in part through an "educational program" or "study guide" sent out to teachers, responded to the same demographic, but that unlike the books' creators with their variously thoughtful efforts to stimulate learning and imagination, the film's promoters took a much more exploitative view of schools and students.

In the penultimate chapter I interview author Rebecca Barnhouse and author and artist James Rumford, two accomplished creators of *Beowulf* engagements for child audiences.[36] Barnhouse and Rumford both provide generous insight into their methods and goals in bringing *Beowulf* to children, and their comments return to many of the issues raised in the collection's introduction and other chapters.

Prior bibliographies of *Beowulf*-related materials are either spotty in their coverage of children's books, being more focused on *Beowulf* scholarship,[37] or are now outdated.[38] The final chapter of this collection, Gilchrist's cumulative bibliography of *Beowulf* books for children, gives the fullest documentation to date in one chronological listing.

NOTES

1 Short treatments exist of single or small groups of works in these genres and media forms. At the larger scale, some of these materials have recently been or are now being studied in Veronika Traidl, *Telling Tales about Beowulf: The Poem and the Films* (Munich: Herbert Utz, 2016); Kathleen Forni, *Beowulf's Popular Afterlife in Literature, Comic Books, and Film* (New York: Routledge, 2018); and an essay collection in progress, edited by David F. Johnson and Britt Mize. The *Beowulf's Afterlives Bibliographic Database* (beowulf.dh.tamu.edu), made public in a pilot form in 2018, will eventually be the most complete record of *Beowulf* representations, versions, and adaptational engagements.

2 Not including the bilingual ramifications of Henriette Barkow, *Beowulf*, illus. Alan Down (London: Mantra Lingua, 2004), which pairs Barkow's English version with a translation into any of seventeen languages (according to usa.mantralingua.com as of 15 August 2019). In the present collection, Mark Bradshaw Busbee studies the earliest *Beowulf* presentations for children, in Danish; Renée Ward identifies what now becomes the earliest known example in English; and my essay analyses perhaps the first monolingual Chinese *Beowulf* for children.

3 Less well represented types for young audiences include drama (e.g., David Calcutt, *Beowulf: A Play Based on the Anglo-Saxon Epic Poem* [Cheltenham, Gloucestershire: Nelson Thornes, 2001]), animated retellings (e.g., Yuri Kulakov, dir., *Animated Epics: Beowulf* [Bright Spark Productions, 1998]), a colouring book (John Green, *Beowulf* [Mineola, NY: Dover Publications, 2007]), and a recent series of stories written and illustrated *by* children (3EB [children of Canary Wharf College, Glenworth], *Battles & Beasts: A Collection of Beowulf Stories* [London: 3EB, 2018]). We do not attempt systematic treatment of comics and graphic novels – a media

form with its own genres and established critical discourse, and having a complex relationship to children's literature per se – but examples will be mentioned from time to time, and those most clearly designed for child audiences are listed in Gilchrist's bibliography of children's versions. *Beowulf*-themed serial comics include Michael Uslan (text) and Ricardo Villamonte (art), *Beowulf: Dragon Slayer*, six issues (New York: DC Comics, 1975–6); Brian Augustyn (text), Joshua Ortega (text), Dub (art), Attila Adorjany (art), Jeff Lemire (art), Pierre Andre Dery (art), and Jim Mahfood (art), *Beowulf: Gods and Monsters*, seven issues (Toronto: Speakeasy Comics, 2005–6); and Pat Shand (text), David Lorenzo (art), Ryan Best (art), and Maria Laura Sanapo (art), "Beowulf," in *Grimm Fairy Tales* 109–10 (2015). *Beowulf*-themed graphic novels include Jerry Bingham, *Beowulf* (Chicago: First Comics, 1984); David Hutchison, *Beowulf*, 3 vols. issued serially (San Antonio: Antarctic Press, 2006; reissued 2007 without colour in a single volume retitled *BIOwulf*); and Erik Evensen, *The Beast of Wolfe's Bay* (Bemidji, MN: Evensen Creative, 2013).

4 Kevin Crossley-Holland, *Beowulf*, illus. Charles Keeping (Oxford: Oxford University Press, 1982), 17.

5 M.I. Ebbutt, "Beowulf," illus. J.H.F. Bacon, in *Hero Myths and Legends of the British Race* (London: George G. Harrap and Co., 1910), 1–41, at 26.

6 Julia Golding, *Beowulf and the Beast*, illus. Victor Rivas Villa (Harlow, Essex: Pearson Education, 2012), 22.

7 Müller, "Introduction: Adapting Canonical Texts in and for Children's Literature," in *Adapting Canonical Texts in Children's Literature*, ed. Anja Müller (London: Bloomsbury Academic, 2013), 1–8, at 3. Müller's collection does include a chapter on *Beowulf* (Łukasz Neubauer, "Adapting an Old English Epic: The Case of Rosemary Sutcliff's *Beowulf: Dragonslayer*," 113–26), but it exemplifies the problems Müller describes.

8 Excluding circumscribed studies of individual works, the main contributions have been Anna Smol, "Heroic Ideology and the Children's *Beowulf*," *Children's Literature* 22 (1994): 90–100; Lise Jaillant, "'A Fine Old Tale of Adventure': *Beowulf* Told to the Children of the English Race, 1898–1908," *Children's Literature Association Quarterly* 38 (2013): 399–419; Janice Hawes, "Beowulf as Hero of Empire," in *Teaching Medieval and Early Modern Cross-Cultural Encounters*, ed. Karina F. Attar and Lynn Shutters (New York: Palgrave Macmillan, 2014), 179–96; and Daniel Pinti, "Thus Did Hearth-Companions Grieve Their Lord's Fall: Death, Mourning, and the Children's *Beowulf*," in *Global Perspectives on Death in Children's Literature*, ed. Lesley D. Clement and Leyli Jamali (New York: Routledge, 2015), 23–34. Chapters or sections surveying several *Beowulf* adaptations for children are contained in Rebecca Barnhouse, *The Middle Ages in Literature for Youth: A Guide and Resource Book* (Lanham, MD: Scarecrow Press,

2004); Velma Bourgeois Richmond, *Chivalric Stories as Children's Literature: Edwardian Retellings in Words and Pictures* (Jefferson, NC: McFarland, 2014); and Forni, *Beowulf's Popular Afterlife*.

 9 E.g., Thomas O. Jones, *Lord of the Geats* (Unionville, NY: Royal Fireworks Press, 1995); Brian Patten, *Beowulf and the Monster*, illus. Chris Riddell (London: Scholastic, 1999), "a story to read or tell for just £1" (front cover); M.A. Roberts, ed., *Beowulf* (Clayton, DE: Prestwick House, 2005).

10 E.g., Strafford Riggs, *The Story of Beowulf*, illus. Henry C. Pitz (London: D. Appleton-Century, 1933); J.L. Herrera, *Beowulfo*, illus. Julio Castro (Madrid: Aguilar, 1965); Nicky Raven, *Beowulf: A Tale of Blood, Heat, and Ashes*, illus. John Howe (Cambridge, MA: Candlewick Press, 2007).

11 A category in which I include fine limited editions like William Morris, trans. and designer, *The Tale of Beowulf Sometime King of the Folk of the Weder Geats* (Hammersmith: Kelmscott Press, 1895) and Shirley Jones, trans. and illus., *Scop Hwilum Sang* ([Llanhamlach, UK]: Red Hen Press, 1983); but also economically accessible yet sensuous presentations like Marijane Osborn, Raymond Oliver, and Randolph Swearer, *Beowulf: A Likeness* (New Haven, CT: Yale University Press, 1990), and John Porter, trans., and Anke Eißmann, illus. and designer (using text from E.V.K. Dobbie's *ASPR* edition), *Beowulf: Beowulf and the Dragon* (Zurich: Walking Tree, 2009).

12 W.T. Stead, ed., "The Story of Beowulf" [called on the front cover "Beowulf and the Dragon"], in *Tales of Long Ago*, illus. Brinsley Le Fanu, *Books for the Bairns* 51 (London: "Review of Reviews" Office, [1900]), price stated on front cover; Charles H. Sylvester, "Beowulf and Grendel," illus. D.A. Petersen, Milo Winter, and Frank H. Young, in *Journeys through Bookland*, ed. Charles H. Sylvester, 10 vols. (Chicago: Bellows-Reeve, 1909), 3:478–94.

13 E.g., Ebbutt, "Beowulf"; Barbara Leonie Picard, "Beowulf," in *Tales of the British People*, illus. Eric Fraser (New York: Criterion Books, 1961), 51–72; Antonio Urrutia Raspall, *Leyendas Nórdicas*, illus. Vicente B. Ballestar (Barcelona: Instituto de Artes Gráficas, 1963), 133–71; [no author named], "Beowulf," illus. Brian Froud, in *The Magic of Words: The 1975 Childcraft Annual* (Chicago: Field Enterprises Educational Corporation, 1975), 76–81.

14 The essays below by Janet Schrunk Ericksen, Robert Stanton, and Bruce Gilchrist address *Beowulf* adaptations' inducements to children to see the story, and by extension the world, in particular ways.

15 For many, the centrality of this issue emerged at the July–August 2019 conference of the International Society of Anglo-Saxonists (ISAS) in Albuquerque, New Mexico, where Adam Miyashiro delivered a keynote address entitled "Mythmaking the 'Anglo-Saxon': Settler Colonialism, White Supremacy, and Medieval Heritage Politics." Earlier commentary on racism as a component of past and present fascination with the Middle Ages, of which there had been much especially in social media but also

in topical conference sessions, had not been as universally acknowledged throughout the discipline. Ensuing discussions and an eventual vote resulted in the organization's changing its name to the International Society for the Study of Early Medieval England (ISSEME) in late November 2019, shortly before this book's submission in December.

16 Especially Mark Bradshaw Busbee's chronicle of a Danish nationalist enterprise to popularize *Beowulf*, Renée Ward's study of an early Victorian children's *Beowulf* enmeshed with Orientalism, and Carl Edlund Anderson's essay situating Rosemary Sutcliff's *Beowulf* engagements within mid-century English longing for an idealized "Anglo-Saxon" past. See also Jaillant, "'A Fine Old Tale of Adventure.'"

17 Melissa Niemann, *Beowulf* (Maricopa, AZ: Little Literary Classics, 2016).

18 For example: "Not long after, Grendel's mother, a frightening fiend in her own right, arrived to take revenge for the death of her son. Seizing one of Hrothgar's favourite warriors, she rushed back to her lair in the misty mere" (Green, *Beowulf*, 14).

19 E.g., Tessa Potter, *Beowulf and the Dragon*, illus. Simon Noyes (Crystal Lake, IL: 1996); Patten, *Beowulf and the Monster*; Eric A. Kimmel, *The Hero Beowulf*, illus. Leonard Everett Fisher (New York: Farrar, Straus, and Giroux, 2005).

20 Raffel, trans., *Beowulf*, illus. Leonard Baskin (Amherst: University of Massachusetts Press, 1971); Gardner, *Grendel*, illus. Emil Antonucci (New York: Alfred A. Knopf, 1971). Gilchrist's chapter on illustrations of *Beowulf* includes works such as Raffel's alongside books designed for children. Amber Dunai's essay below scrutinizes J.R.R. Tolkien's blurring of the category of children's literature in relation to his own *Beowulf*-related creative works.

21 Leonard, *Beowulf: A New Verse Translation for Fireside and Classroom* (New York: Century, 1923); quotations from pp. v and v–vi.

22 In one such headnote Leonard writes of the Finnsburh tale that "many wise men of today have striven to puzzle it out ... but ... they despise one another grievously for their differences of opinion. Now ... I suggest that we don't listen to 'The Woe of Hildeburh' at all – lest we too fall to quarreling over its meaning" (47–8). He prompts readers to skip instead to his translation of *The Fight at Finnsburh*, which follows *Beowulf* as an appendix.

23 The greater longevity of Leonard's translation has been with adult audiences, for whom it was reset twice in deluxe illustrated formats: Leonard, *Beowulf*, illus. Rockwell Kent (New York: Random House, 1932); and Leonard, *Beowulf*, illus. Lynd Ward (New York: Heritage Press, 1939). Oddly, both include the brackets but not the preface explaining their presence, and the 1932 version also removes the translation of *The Fight at Finnsburh* to which Leonard's headnote already cited (see previous note) still refers readers.

24 Worden, *Beowulf*, ed. John R. Olson (Silver Spring, MD: National Association of the Deaf, 1973); quotations from pp. iii and 34.

25 Hager, *A Modern Scop Tells Beowulf* (Coral Springs, FL: Llumina Press, 2007), i.

26 Kaplan, *Grendel's Guide to Love and War* (New York: Alfred A. Knopf, 2017); Tucholke, *The Boneless Mercies* (New York: Farrar Straus Giroux, 2018). The status of the latter as a gender-flipped *Beowulf* interaction is asserted in its marketing but may be less evident from the novel itself. Another highly creative recent *Beowulf* adaptation (Maria Dahvana Headley, *The Mere Wife* [New York: MCD/Farrar, Straus and Giroux, 2018]), though by an author who has previously written YA fiction, is pitched more to adult readers.

27 To give one case in point: Tony Bedard (text) and Jesus Saiz (art), "Beowulf," in the DC Comics magazine *Sword of Sorcery* 0–3 (Nov. 2012–Feb. 2013), is set up as a coming-of-age story centred on Wiglaf, with whom many features of the presentation encourage an audience of boys to identify. When Wiglaf and Beowulf confront Grendel's mother, an eroti-cized cyber-woman who has attacked no one, she offers no threat to them other than that which is assumed to inhere in her power and superior knowledge: she herself has already confined Grendel, reveals valuable information, and shows no aggression toward Beowulf. Nevertheless, Beowulf's willingness to listen to her explanations rather than kill her makes Wiglaf increasingly anxious until the boy attacks her himself, con-firming his manhood through violence against an exaggerated female body. The episode is in issue 3, pp. [26]–[31].

28 Par for the course are the warrior woman Nan-Zee in Uslan and Villamonte, *Beowulf: Dragon Slayer*, and the ambiguously nude, Angelina Jolie–inspired Grendel's mother in the graphic novel ancillary to the 2007 Zemeckis film (Chris Ryall [text], Gabriel Rodriguez [art], and Jay Fotos [art], *Beowulf*, 4 vols. issued serially [San Diego: IDW Publishing, 2007]).

29 Shand et al., in *Grimm Fairy Tales* 102 (one of the instalments in which Wulf is present before the start of the "Beowulf" story proper) and 109.

30 In one, Freawaru and Beowulf are understood through most of the book to be sexual partners and are twice shown having intercourse (Stephen L. Antczak [text], James C. Bassett [text], and Andy Lee [art], *Beowulf: The Legend* [Decatur, GA: VLE Comics, 2006], 37 and 135); and amid the hyper-bolic violence of another, Grendel is depicted with an erection, fondles the naked Beowulf as he pretends to sleep, and ejaculates profusely on him during their fight (Santiago García and David Rubín, *Beowulf* [Bilbao: Astiberri Ediciones, 2014], [44]–[46]).

31 E.g., Rebecca Barnhouse, *The Coming of the Dragon* (New York: Random House Children's Books, 2010); Charles A. Brady, *The King's Thane*, illus.

Henry [C.] Pitz (Garden City, NY: Doubleday, 1961); Nancy Farmer, *Sea of Trolls* (New York: Atheneum Books for Young Readers, 2004).

32 E.g., James Rumford, *Beo-Bunny* (Honolulu: Mānoa Press, 2012); N.D. Wilson, *Boys of Blur* (New York: Random House, 2014); Rick Barba, *The Massively Multiplayer Mystery* (New York: Aladdin, 2006).

33 The following two paragraphs' comments on principles of adaptation and its analysis have several points of contact with Linda Hutcheon, *A Theory of Adaptation*, 2nd ed. with contributions by Siobhan O'Flynn (New York: Routledge, 2013) – not always in full agreement, but in ways that do not require debate here. In a field that has tended to bog down in taxonomy, Hutcheon redirects attention to analytical implications of the unique relationship between works that emerges through adaptation, and hers is the best holistic treatment of adaptation as a creative mode. Hutcheon does not address children's literature; O'Flynn's "Epilogue" (new to the 2nd ed.) briefly discusses digital adaptation of works that started out as children's books (201–5).

34 Carl Edlund Anderson's essay below carries out such an analysis in tracing the increasing freedom exercised by mid-twentieth-century children's authors.

35 A wish felt keenly and addressed very thoughtfully by some creators of children's books, as is clear in Rebecca Barnhouse's and James Rumford's interview below, and to which writers and illustrators respond more and less successfully, as Yvette Kisor's chapter shows.

36 Barnhouse, *The Coming of the Dragon* (with a sequel, *Peaceweaver* [New York: Random House Children's Books, 2012], less closely tied to *Beowulf*); Rumford, *Beowulf: A Hero's Tale Retold* (Boston: Houghton Mifflin, 2007), and *Beo-Bunny*.

37 Donald K. Fry, *Beowulf and The Fight at Finnsburh: A Bibliography* (Charlottesville: University Press of Virginia, 1969); Stanley B. Greenfield and Fred C. Robinson, *A Bibliography of Publications on Old English Literature to the End of 1972* (Toronto: University of Toronto Press, 1980).

38 Marijane Osborn's trailblazing work established *Beowulf* adaptations as having their own interest: Osborn, "Translations of *Beowulf* (and 'The Fight at Finnsburg')," appendix to Chauncey B. Tinker, *The Translations of Beowulf: A Critical Bibliography* (1903), rev. ed. (Hamden, CT: Archon Books, 1974), 151–80; updated informally in Osborn, *Annotated List of Beowulf Translations* (2003), formerly published online by the Arizona Center for Medieval and Renaissance Studies, but removed in 2019, and now appearing as a reprint in *Medieval Perspectives* 35 (2021).

1 "A Little Shared Homer for England and the North": The First *Beowulf* for Young Readers

MARK BRADSHAW BUSBEE

The tradition of adapting *Beowulf* for young readers began in 1820, when the Danish priest, poet, politician, and educator (and much else), N.F.S. Grundtvig (1783–1872),[1] wrote that *Beowulf* is

> det eneste gamle Digt, man med glad Sikkerhed kan lade Børn læse ... da man vist inderlig maatte ønske Børn livlige Riim-Krøniker istedetfor dødt Meel-Pap, og dog har saa ondt ved at finde Bøger, som med den nødvendige Livlighed og Trohjertighed forene den ikke mindre nødvendige Reenhed og Ærbarhed.

> [one of the very few old poems that people would happily allow children to read, (that is) if they want them to read lively rhyme chronicles instead of dead pulp fiction; and it is very difficult to find books that with the necessary liveliness and honour unite no less needed purity and honesty.[2]

The remark appeared in the introduction to *Bjowulfs Drape: Et Gothisk Helte-Digt fra forrige Aar-Tusinde* [Beowulf: A Gothic hero-poem from the previous millennium], which was the first complete translation of the poem into a modern language.[3] Like the translation, the idea was unprecedented: no one had before suggested that *Beowulf* might be suitable for children.[4] Some early scholars had deemed it rude and barbaric and therefore inappropriate reading for polite society; others thought it little more than a curiosity, a historical artifact not worth translating. But Grundtvig argued that *Beowulf*'s poetry contained living words bearing forth undying historical truths; the poem itself is an example of "the Word's fight to victory,"[5] not the "dull and stupid trash which some English writers of no small name have chosen to suppose."[6] Instead, it was "shaped and adapted to be a little shared Homer for England and for the North"[7] and should therefore "be found in all homes and become a reader for all children, yes, become for Scandinavia ... what the *Iliad* and the *Odyssey* were for the Greeks."[8] As the self-proclaimed prophet of modern Denmark,[9] he intended to made "a living use of it all" in order "to amuse and secretly enlighten both children and parents."[10] And he did, by writing extensively about its hidden meanings and by repurposing its heroes and monsters for his own poetic recreations – all with the aim of awakening the people to a cultural heritage different from classical "Homerisk" and German traditions dominating education and thought in Denmark.

However, despite his efforts, *Bjowulfs Drape* was, on its own, not a successful version for young readers. Like his adaptations of Saxo Grammaticus's *Gesta Danorum* and Snorri Sturluson's *Heimskringla*,[11] when *Bjowulfs Drape* was published in 1820 few people bought the translation and fewer actually read it. Grundtvig admitted that the book fell dead from the press, that "for many years it was hardly read outside [his] own house," and that he himself carried a copy to the British Library in 1829.[12] The main problem was that it was a hybrid text produced without the slightest consumer awareness.[13]

But from the late 1820s on, as the Danish School Reform Act of 1814 promoted popular literacy, as children's literature came into its own as a genre in Denmark, and as Grundtvig began making educational and political use of *Beowulf*, his followers, who called themselves "Grundtvigians," began excerpting selections of *Bjowulfs Drape* in children's textbooks, readers, and songbooks.[14] As a result, the translation became a text in Grundtvig-inspired Friskoler [Free Schools] and Folkhøjskoler [People's High Schools], Grundtvigian educational leaders, artists, and children's writers constructed adaptations for children upon Grundtvig's translation and interpretation, and Grundtvigian ideas about the hero and the monsters quietly found their way abroad into adaptations and interpretations of the poem for young readers.

A Skald in the Childhood of Art

Grundtvig's interpretations and adaptations of *Beowulf* for his countrymen between 1815 and 1820 were inspired by German Romanticism and the integration of "children's with adult literature into a national literature."[15] The godfather of German Romanticism, Johann Gottfried von Herder (1744–1803), had called ancient traditional poetry "the language in its childhood" and a *"living expression"* of "human nature." The old poems were not like modern ones, which relate "arbitrary *dead ideas*."[16] Adam Oehlenschläger (1779–1850), the Danish poet Grundtvig admired most, modelled Herder-inspired recreations of Norse legends and myths in his *Nordiske Digte* [Norse poems].

Oehlenschläger wrote that it wasn't "a Homeric exhilaration" that had inspired him but "the Nordic character itself, these mountains … with their rich metals and diamonds that only need to be polished to shine with an incredible radiance." It must be remembered, he added, "that the diamond can only be polished in its own dust."[17]

Grundtvig declared himself of the same mind as Oehlenschläger,[18] and by 1815, when the Icelandic-born Danish scholar Grímur Jónsson Thorkelin (1752–1829) published the *editio princeps* of *Beowulf*,[19] Grundtvig was prepared to exalt the Northern character in *Beowulf*.[20] Thorkelin had discovered the poem in October of 1786, when Grundtvig was a small boy, and had returned from England with the transcripts of it in spring of 1791. Waiting eagerly for its publication, Grundtvig wrote that the edition would no doubt "shed a splendid light" over the people of the North.[21] Later, knowing its history – that the unique manuscript was nearly destroyed by fire in 1731 and that the transcripts were nearly destroyed in 1807, when the British navy bombed Copenhagen – Grundtvig attributed a salvific quality to the poem, calling it "a brand from the fire":[22] a phrase lifted from the Old Testament, where the prophets Amos (4:11) and Zechariah (3:2) remind the people that God had saved them from destruction. *Beowulf* had twice been saved providentially, and now it called for interpretation. It was Grundtvig's calling, as the prophet of modern Denmark, to relate its divine messages about kingship and community and remind his countrymen, young and old, of the spiritual gift they had received. He immersed himself – allowed himself to be trained "like a child"[23] – in the language, so that he might "learn the whole poem by heart."[24] Of his first encounter, he later wrote, "Feeling the warmth that only those who know what it's like to love from childhood the literature, the past and the Fatherland, I sat myself down and listened to the old song whose language the hand of time had so sorely crippled."[25]

Assuming childlike openness, Grundtvig "wrote himself to clarity"[26] and became the first modern person to understand the plot of the poem, identifying some fifteen characters Thorkelin had misunderstood or overlooked, explaining significant events such as Scyld's ship burial and the Finnsburg episode, and making the only historical connection in the poem: the association of Beowulf's King Hygelac with Chochilaicus in Geoffrey of Tours' *Gesta Francorum*.[27] He made a few mistakes, too – at first, he refused to acknowledge the first, Danish Beowulf (Beow, at l. 18)[28] – and his imagination led him into a few wild misreadings, such as the idea that "the text mentions a deity's, presumably Hilda's, revelation in a golden airship, promising the hero both to protect him and to guard his ships."[29] Throughout, he attended closely to the poem's illustrations of ancient Denmark. *Beowulf* was like "a distant close relative that we have never seen" speaking to him across time,[30] helping him to see rich interpretative possibilities in Scyld Scefing and, most influentially to twentieth-century scholars like J.R.R. Tolkien, the monsters.

Grundtvig claimed that *Beowulf* was written by "a skald in the childhood of art,"[31] a notion that fit within his broader idea that the stages of the life of man match the progression of history. It was composed at a turning point in history, a time of childhood and youth when "man gives free reign to his imagination."[32] Scyld's mysterious arrival from the sea as a child, his formation into a powerful, beloved king, his magnanimous reign, and his equally mysterious return in death over the seas – these events unfolded, in Grundtvig's view, like a providential prophecy of "Nordisk" destiny. The Scyld episode constituted "the most superb part of the poem ... a prediction of the incorruptibility of the Skjoldung stock [i.e., the Danish line of kings]."[33]

To correct Thorkelin's Latin mistranslation of the crucial fifty-two line passage about Scyld Scefing, Grundtvig offered what he admitted was a speculative rendition in the mother tongue,[34] in order "to provide readers with a picture of the poem's singularity"; he announced a plan to illustrate it "through a quiet contemplation of the whole" in "a rhymed translation for those of [his] countrymen who do not have the opportunity to become acquainted with the original language."[35] The following excerpt represents the style and tone of his 1815 rendering of lines 43–4 of the original, the arrival and passing of Scyld ("Skjold" in Grundtvig's version):

> Udstyre Man vilde
> Den Herre fra Land,
> Med Gaver saa gilde,
> Som da over Strand
> Han underlig drevet
> Af Herren var blevet
> Til Dannemarks Land.[36]

> [This lord they would send / Equipped from the land, / With gifts so worthy, / As when, over the sea, / Miraculously he / Was driven by God / To Dannemark's land.][37]

The translation might better be termed a paraphrase due to its departure from the form of the original. Like all of Grundtvig's verse translations of *Beowulf*, the lines demonstrate a balancing act: they attempt not to "diverge from the words of the text but ... to allow its spirit to express itself in another language, not only in other words but also in other expressions."[38] The translation keeps with the fashion of the day of lineating the poem's half-lines independently; it dispenses with allit-eration, preferring instead ballad form with varying rhyme. Patterned after the folk-speech of Grundtvig's boyhood nanny Malene Jensdatter (1732–1810) when she told him folktales as a child,[39] it often maintains features of spoken narration. Grundtvig adds oral fillers like *ja* (yes) and *dog* (well) and subjective touches like emotive or evaluative ad-jectives: for example, Skjold faces death with "graanende Haar" (1820, 3) [greying hair] and "danske Adels-Blod" (1820, 14) [Danish royal blood] trails from Heorot after Grendel's attacks. The additions often steer narration in directions of the translator's choosing. The result is that Grundtvig is omnipresent as background storyteller. Flemming Lundgreen-Nielsen observes that this was the first time anyone from high literary circles tried to use popular speech when dealing with prestigious materials. "Thus," Lundgreen-Nielsen writes, "Grundtvig anticipated Hans Christian Andersen's stylistic experiments in his fairy tales for children from 1835 onwards."[40]

An example of how Grundtvig steers the narrative through choices in translation can be seen in his treatment of Heorot. He explains that Hrothgar's hall is called "*Hjort* ... partly because *heorth* is 'home' and partly – it seems clear ... that *Hjort* [hart; deer] is in any case stated to be the hall's poetic name, presumably from the word *hiorta* (merry, cheerful)."[41] Heorot, like the modern Danish state, "is the physical heart-muscle that distributes and guides the spiritual streams that em-anate from the larger heart of civil society"; it is where the people are protected and provided justice, where they celebrate their culture and a shared reason for being.[42] In a translation of lines 76b–81a, Heorot is im-agined as *hyggeligt* (cosy) and symbolic of Hrothgar's relationship to his people, stylized as a sort of King Arthur's court with its round table.[43] Grundtvig writes, "There was strength in the King's words. [Hrothgar] called the Fortress 'Heart.' He benched his fighters around the table and gave them what they had earned. Yes, he filled their hands with silver and gold. He gave them from his heart."[44] Like Frederik VI (r. 1808–39), Grundtvig's king and benefactor, Hrothgar gifts the people "not just with gold and shiny jewels but with the most honorable and rarest stones in the crown: fervent love."[45] His magnanimity extends to other Northern peoples, especially to the "Goth" Beowulf before he departs for Gothland. Lines 1870–3 are adapted to amplify the close relationship of Denmark with the other peoples of the north:

Se Taarerne runde
Den Gubbe paa Kind,
Ei dølge han kunde

Bevægede Sind,
Tog Bjovulf i Arme,
Som Ven tager Ven,
Og kysde med Varme
Den herlige Svend.[46]

[See, the tears flowed down / On the old man's cheeks. / He could not
conceal / His deeply moved mind, / Embraced Beowulf, / As friend hugs
his friend, / And kissed him with warmth, / The glorious lad.][47]

To this idealized Danish community, the monsters offer for Grundtvig a violent contrast, a threat that elevates the poem's meaning. They
demonstrate the poet's "Barn-Dommen" [child-like judgement] and
love of "æventyr" [folktale] (both terms quoted from *Bjowulfs Drape*,
liv), so, naturally, Grundtvig appeals to Danish superstition and folklore, calling Grendel a troll, his mother a *Hex* (witch), and the dragon by
the name "Stærkhjort,"[48] and suggesting that Grendelsmere is located
in "Trumholt Skov," which in Jutland is called "the witch's meeting
place."[49] Choices like these allow a dual focus to emerge. The monsters
must be vividly portrayed for young readers, but like all compelling
stories for children, they must also contain images intriguing to adults
reading (and buying) books for their children. In his longest essay on
Beowulf, Grundtvig offers the following explanation of the meaning of
the monsters and the hero: "The stories about Grendel and the dragon
make up the chief content of the poem, as a continuation of the warfare
that the devil and the old giants waged against God, a fight which, carried on by trolls and the like, interpenetrates the historical matter of the
poem and is meant to give to this matter a higher meaning."[50]

The monster fights "can be seen to shadow forth in the double adventure" of mankind. That double adventure is revealed in "falsehood's
hostility to truth ... partly in history and partly in nature."[51] Beowulf
is not only the "Helten er Gothernes, det Nordiske Kaempe Folks"
[hero of the Goths, the Scandinavian warrior-people], he is also God's
agent who "afvæbner Mørkets Magt og redder med Kraft det døende
Folke-Liv" [disarms the powers of the dark and rescues by force the
dying people's life] (*Bjowulfs Drape*, li–lii, li). *Bjowulfs Drape* makes this
existentialist meaning understandable to the child by having "Trolden
Grendel" cast sleep upon the "drunken, snoring" warriors before devouring them.[52] Beowulf explains the problem to his Danish hosts:

Saa vidt han sig formaster,
Han kommer vaabenløs,

Kun Søvn han paa jer kaster,
Jer Helsot er en Døs!   (*Bjowulfs Drape*, 56)

[So far as he presumes to, / He comes weaponless. / He only casts sleep
upon you, / Your wasting disease is a stupor.]

The proposal amplifies dual interpretive potential for Grendel: he is a
bogeyman who attacks people when they are asleep and most vulnerable – the stuff of childhood nightmares; for adults he is an intellectual and spiritual or moral problem that goes "nær til Hjerte" (*Bjowulfs
Drape*, 14) [close to the heart]. Endnotes explain how Grundtvig's reading solves a crux at line 600,[53] but the translation fits Grendel's actions
into broader meanings for the poem as a whole. Grendel is a "Hed-
ning Sjæl," "Gud forhadt" (*Bjowulfs Drape*, 79, 67) [heathen soul, hated
by God]; for adults he also plays a metaphorical role akin to that of
Jean-Paul Sartre's *angoisse*: he is the lie preventing modern Danes from
dragging themselves out of *le visqueux* (the mud) or *le néant* (the void)
of paganism and national lethargy.[54] He is the force inhibiting national
self-awareness and growth and a symbol of "discontinuity in human
existence, particularly in the struggle between the forces of life and
death."[55]

Skjold and the Monsters as Allegorical Figures

Between 1815 and his first interpretations of the poem, and 1820 when
Bjowulfs Drape was published, Grundtvig repurposed the heroes and
monsters of *Beowulf* in ways that can be seen as a subtext for later Danish adaptations for young readers. An early retelling of the first fifty-two
lines of the poem – Scyld Scefing's arrival and departure over the sea –
shows Grundtvig working Scyld Scefing into the better-known story of
the Danish King Skjold, already well-known through Saxo Grammaticus's *Gesta Danorum*. In the poem "Danne-Virke," Skjold's body is sent
out over the waves, but rather than drifting into the unknown, it lands
again on Danish soil. His death represents the unfortunate historical
loss of a uniquely Danish form of spirituality, during a period of national decline and depression. And the poet calls Skjold back to help the
Danes when they need him.[56]

   This poem anticipated Grundtvig's evolving thoughts about the role
of the *Beowulf* interpreter and about the meanings of the monster fights,
thoughts that reach new levels in 1817 during the three-hundred-year
jubilee for the Reformation. His poem "Ragna-Roke, (et dansk Æmter)"
was published in Grundtvig's journal *Danne-Virke*,[57] alongside his

longest essay on *Beowulf*, "Om Bjovulfs Drape." In the second of five scenes imagined as dialogues between the Northern spirit and the legendary folk hero Holger Danske, the poet Cædmon says,

Jeg drømde, jeg drømde,
Kong David jeg saae,
Han gav mig i Hænde
Sin Harpe saa prud,
Strængene gyldne
Slog jeg med Vælde,
End vel i Midgard
Mindes mit Kvad.
Jeg bøied mit Øre
Til Bogen hin gamle,
Dens Tale fik Tone,
Og Tungen fik Røst,
Billeder høie
Blikket opdaged,
Venlig jeg skiænked
Skriften mit Prud.
"Us is riht micel
Dhæt ve rodera-veard
Vereda vuldor-cining
Vordum herigen!"
Toner som disse
Tør jeg vel haabe,
Sank ei i Tidens
Skummende Bølger.
Jeg Øre og laande
Til Oldtidens Sagn,
I Krands jeg dem fletted,
Med Konst jeg dem bandt,
Som svaiende Kviste
Man sanker og binder,
Og skaber et Lysthuus
I Skoven saa vild.
"Hvæt ve gar-dena
In gear-dægum,
Theod-cyninga
Thrym gefrunon,"
End vil jeg haabe
Hrodgar og Bjovulf

> Kvæde i Salen
> Kæmpernes Priis.
> Saa jeg paa Harpen
> Hævede Sandsagn,
> Adled til Epos
> Oldtidens Digt,
> Stridige Stykker
> Snild jeg forbandt:
> Yndig blev Sandhed,
> Og Æmter sandsynligt.   ("Ragna-Roke," 340–2)

[I dreamed, I dreamed, / I saw King David. / He put into my hand / his beautiful harp. / Golden strings / I struck with might. / Then well in Middle-earth / my song will be remembered. / I bent my ear / to the ancient book. / Its speech received tone, / and the tongue, a voice; / noble images / flashed before my eyes. / I paid my respects / to the writing. / "For us, it is an important duty / that we praise the protector of heaven / king over armies / with our words." / Tones such as these / I dare hope / never sink in time's / foam-bearing waves. / I lent an ear / to the myths of ancient times, / I wove them into garlands, / with art I bound them, / as swaying twigs / one collects and binds / and builds an arbour / in the forest so wild. / "Listen! We of the Spear-Danes / in days of yore, / of the folk-kings, / glory have heard." / Yet will I hope / Hrothgar and Beowulf / sing together in the hall / the heroes' praise. / So with the harp / I raised up true tales, / ennobled them to epics, / the poetry of former times, / difficult pieces / cleverly I mixed: / lovely became truth, / and fairy tales possible.]

Within this recreation, Luther's reform of the Catholic Church is reconceived in terms of Beowulf's fight with Grendel. The Northern Spirit says,

> Lad høit mig dig berømme,
> Du Helt, som kiæk og bold,
> Trods Ild og Edder-Strømme,
> Lemlæsted Romas Trold!
> Ja, feig fra Kampens Bulder
> Alt fra sin Arm og Skulder
> Som Grændel flygted han.
>
> Endnu, ak, gaaer hans Moder
> Ved Midnat ud paa Rov,
> Ja, Hrodgars Vaaben-Broder
> Hun kvalde mens han sov;

Den Hex saa leed sig skjuler
I Fjeldets dybe Huler,
Paa Nykke-Havets Bund.   ("Ragna-Roke," 327)

[Let me praise you / you hero [Luther], who brave and bold, / in spite
of fire and poison streams, / mutilated the Roman troll! / Yes, cowardly
from the battle din, / from his arm and shoulder, / Grendel carried
himself away. / Yet, oh, his mother goes / at midnight out on the hunt; /
Yes, Hrothgar's brother-in-arms / she killed while he slept; / the witch
then sought to hide herself / in the deep caves / at the bottom of the
monster-mere.]

And later, Christ's harrowing of hell is imagined in terms of Beowulf's
fight with Grendel's mother:

Da, som de Toner klinge,
Skal Helten brat opspringe
Alt af sin Himmelseng.
Til Lue-Skoven haster
Den Helt som ei kan døe,
Og dristig han sig kaster
Alt i den sorte Søe.
Hans Byrnje aldrig bugner,
Og Sværd med Oldtids Runer,
Til Brug er ham beredt.
Naar vældig han det svinger,
Faaer Jesabel sin Løn,
Og hovedløs nedspringer
Til Helhjem hendes Søn;
Med Hoved og med Hjalte
Skal Bjovulf og de *Talte*,
For Hrod-Gar stædes ind.   ("Ragna-Roke," 328–9)

[Then, as the bells ring, / the hero shall spring up / out of his heavenly
bed. / To the terrible forest [where Grendel lives] rushes / the hero
who cannot die, / and valiantly he casts himself / into the dark lake. /
His armour never bends, / and a sword with ancient runes / has been
prepared for him. / When powerfully he swings it, / Jezebel gets what she
deserves / and jumps headless down / to Hell, her son; / With head and
with hilt, / shall Beowulf and *the chosen ones* / be brought before Hrothgar.]

The sword in the Christ-like hero's hands has double significance. On
a literal level, it is the sword Beowulf finds in his fight with Grendel's

mother, the hilt from which Hrothgar seems to read before making his famous sermon (*Beowulf*, ll. 1698–1795). On a metaphorical level, the sword might also be the poem *Beowulf* itself, if Grundtvig is considering the Old English and Old Icelandic meanings of the word in his metaphor for the poem as a "*Brand* udrevet af Ilden" [*sword* pulled from the fire].[58] The hero, whether he be Christ, Luther, Beowulf, or Grundtvig himself, uses the message of the poem to defeat spiritual lethargy.

This message was redirected into political channels after the July Revolutions in France in 1830 and Denmark's 1848 war with Prussia over the Schleswig-Holstein region, which bordered Prussia to the south.[59] In an 1841 essay, Grundtvig writes that "as soon as the troll manages to send [Denmark] to sleep, as so often happens, she sinks down to become a German slave-maiden."[60] In 1850, he writes,

> One sees easily at once what the old skald could then have either dreamed or thought, that the troll Grendel and his mother are the most fitting picture that one could wish for of the Germans in Denmark. One can see only shame, much like what Grendel and his mother brought ... It is also now high time that we make for ourselves a good omen, as the old Norse heroic poem gives us a glimmering victory over Denmark's arch-enemies.[61]

And in 1864, he reimagines Grendel's sleeping spell as a metaphor for the German language – Grendel's "*Trolde-Sorg*" [troll-sorrow] does damage to children's ears; the hero restores "*Barne-Glæde*" [childhood joy] by telling them the old Danish songs.[62]

Associations like these form a powerful political subtext for Danes encountering *Beowulf* through Grundtvig's translation. And why not interpret the poem this way? In 1817, he had regarded it as "a golden harp from Heathen times, with broken strings and with its stem melted by the heat."[63] It could be refashioned according to the truth, "a melting oven" in which "everything shall be cast"; that "which is left unscathed will be seen as truth, but whatever the fire melts is the lie."[64] The times called for political readings. And so, "the old forgotten poem" is given "new clothes, new money, and lessons in modern speech so that it might get along in the new world."[65]

Bjowulfs Drape as Source Text for Educational Readers and Patriotic Songbooks

Before the 1830s, Grundtvig's translation, interpretations, and adaptations of *Beowulf* fell on deaf ears. Grundtvig attributed the fact that nobody bothered to read *Bjowulfs Drape* to the indifference of the people of Denmark at the time.[66] It could be said that the public did not begin to regard *Bjowulfs Drape* as a text for young readers until 1829, when Grundtvig used his first pedagogical experiment, *Krønike-Riim til Børn-Lærdom* [Chronicle rhymes for the education of children], as a vehicle for his ideas. *Krønike-Riim* was a school reader in Danish that included the history, folklore, myth, and legend of the North. Its poems, including one titled "Angel-Sachsener," were originally written by Grundtvig for his own children in folk-style poetry so that they might more readily enjoy and identify with them. Grundtvig reintroduces *Beowulf* as the "Sagn og Æventyr / ... / Harpen kaldte, under Kors, / Heden-Old tilbage, / Bragende om Grændel Trold, / Bjovulf, Hengst, og Hnæf og Skjold, / Norden i det Hele!" [song and fairy tale / ... / of heathen times / (that) the harp called back, under the sign of the cross, / (including) heroic songs about Grendel the troll, / Beowulf, Hengst, and Hnæf and Skjold, / and the entire North!].[67]

Krønike-Riim coincided with Grundtvig's "long descent from the high-level 'scholarship of clarification' to the activity of *folkoplysning* (enlightenment of the people)."[68] He had made three consecutive summer research trips to England (1829–31) and had returned with a refined interest in education and how *Beowulf* might fit into a plan of enlightenment. "This early Gothic Homer," he proclaimed to English-speaking scholars, deserves "the attention and admiration of cultivated minds."[69] In *Nordens Mythologie* (1832), possibly his most famous work, he proclaimed that books from the Middle Ages like *Beowulf* were "suffering the same fate as its castles, that is, they lie in ruins."[70] He complained that "scholars preferred to bury these treasures in the ground and brood over them like dragons until the end of the world rather than make them fruitful for life by developing a comprehensive humane education."[71]

Bjowulfs Drape grew in popularity alongside Grundtvig's ideas and the development and spread of the People's High Schools, for which Grundtvig has been called the "Father of Western Adult Education."[72] In 1831, a follower of Grundtvig named Christian Flor (1792–1875) published *Danske Læsebog til Brug i de laerde Skoler* [Danish reader for use in schools], which reproduced the main storyline of the first part of *Beowulf* (pp. 8–62 of *Bjowulfs Drape*) and titled it "Grendels Uvæsen i Hjorteborg – Gothen Bjovulf" [Grendel's attack in Heorot – the Goth Beowulf].[73] A few years later, when Hans Christian Andersen began publishing his *Eventyr* [Fairy tales], Danish scholars began to take children's literature seriously. P.M. Møller (1794–1838) published an article titled "Om at fortælle Børn Eventyr" [On telling children fairy tales] that stirred debate about how practical contemporary children's stories

should be and what narration style is best; one of the background dis-
cussants was Søren Kierkegaard (1813–55).[74] In an 1837 journal entry,
Kierkegaard describes contemporary children's literature as "poetic
dross" ("poetisk Skyllevand"); it is overly didactic, hackneyed, and te-
dious. What matters is that the stories should "bring the poetic to bear
on their lives in every way, to exert a magical influence."[75] Often opposed to Grundtvig's ideas, Kierkegaard reflects the evolving support
amongst scholars, even among his fiercest ideological opponents, for
Grundtvigian presentations of old poems like *Beowulf*.[76]

After 1838, Grundtvig began to make public proclamations that
Beowulf is suitable as a "reader for all children" and that it would become
"what the *Iliad* and the *Odyssey* were for the Greeks."[77] By 1847, *Beowulf*
became squarely part of Grundtvig's educational program when his
Græsk og Nordisk Mythologi for Ungdommen [Greek and Nordic mythology
for the youth] was commissioned for use in schools.[78] The anthology of
stories includes sections on "Skjold og Fredegod" (248–52) [Skjold and
Fredegod], in which Skjold is described (and illustrated) as "Danmarks
Skytsaand" (248) [Denmark's guardian spirit]; "Rodgar og Grændel"
(252–3) [Hrothgar and Grendel], in which "en afskyelig Trold ... kastede
Søvn paa hans Kæmper" (252) [the monstrous troll [Grendel] ... casts
sleep on Hrothgar's warriors]; and "Bjovulf og Stærkhjort" (257–9)
[Beowulf and Strong-Heart [the dragon]], in which the hero "frelste det
indsovede Danmark" (257) [frees a sleeping Denmark]. The message is
that *Beowulf* and the Eddic poems are "folkehistoriske Myther udtryk-
ker en historisk Sandhed" (251) [folk-historic myths expressing historic
truth], shared by all nations of the north as a common heritage (252).

Grundtvig's followers were listening. Between the two wars with
Prussia in 1848 and 1864, numerous editions of Danish patriotic songbooks appeared that included excerpts from *Bjowulfs Drape*.[79] Carl
Joachim Brandt's *Rim og Sange til Fædrelandets Historie* [Rhymes and
songs of the fatherland's history], volume 1, was the first to use selections from *Bjowulfs Drape* as part of a compilation of heroic songs
of Denmark.[80] The anthology includes excerpts from it titled "Trolden
Grændel" (38–9) [The troll Grendel], "Bjovulfs Pris" (40–3) [Beowulf's
worth], and "Rodgars Tak" (44–5) [Hrothgar's thanks]. Brandt provides
short explanations before each selection that demonstrate his (and his
readers') acceptance of Grundtvig's interpretation of *Beowulf*. For example, Brandt discusses Grundtvig's attribution of magic to Grendel's
terrorizing of Heorot before providing the corresponding selection
from *Bjowulfs Drape* (38).

In 1865, Kristian Køster's *Et Hundrede Danske Sange* [One hundred
Danish songs] reproduced Grundtvig's poem "Skjold" as a song, titled

"Skjold kommer til Danmark" (no. 51, pp. 100–1) [Skjold comes to Denmark].[81] The poem-turned-song incorporates Old Testament images of Moses's arrival and the Lion of Judah (Gen. 49:9 and Rev. 5:5) as well as traditions from Norse myth – of the goddess Freya's beauty and of Odin's role as All-father. The first stanza dramatizes Denmark in a time of need by gesturing to conditions of contemporary post-war Denmark:

> I gamle dage det var en gang,
> at danske folk var i kongetrang;
> de gode græd, og de onde lo,
> hvor ingen hegner, kun torne gro!
> Da kom en snekke for fulde sejl
> med løvehoved og hjertespejl,
> med guld og våben og stads om bord,
> men ikke en sjæl ved mast og ror,
> dog var der liv, for en lille dreng
> alene lå i store seng,
> en neg var bundet med aks og strå,
> den hviled drengen sit hoved på,
> og hvor han sov både spæd og spag,
> dér vajed over et kongeflag,
> så liljehvidt og så rosenrødt,
> som kun hos Freja på kinden mødt.

[In the old days there was a time / when the Danish folk required a king; / the good cried and the evil laughed – / without a hedge, thorns upspring! / Then came a boat with its sail full, / with lion-head and heart-mirror,[82] / with gold and weapons and robes on board, / but not a soul by the mast and oar, / Yet was there life, for a little boy / alone lay in the big ship-bed, / a sheaf was bound with wheat and straw, / on which he rested his little head, / and where he slept both small and weak, / there waved over him a royal flag, / so lily white and so rose red, / as only on Freya's cheek are at play.][83]

The people wonder if the boy is a gift from Odin, the news spreads with clash of arms, and the skalds of Denmark sing the Skjold's praises.

A Grundtvigian composite image of Skjold/Scyld was already present as early as 1847 in David Jacobsen's illustration that accompanied Grundtvig's retelling of the event for young readers in *Græsk og Nordisk Mythologi for Ungdommen* (see fig. 1.1). The illustration blends anachronistic imagery – the sailed vessel, tunics, winged helmets – to give the scene a timeless quality, and it begins a long tradition of illustrations and paintings of this scene in Denmark.[84]

Figure 1.1. Skjold/Scyld, by David Jacobsen, from N.F.S. Grundtvig, *Græsk og Nordisk Mythologi for Ungdommen*. Copenhagen: Bing & Søn, 1847, p. 248.

During the final quarter of the nineteenth century, Grundtvig's version of *Beowulf*, which appeared in a second edition in 1865, became a mainstay of the People's High School tradition. Ludvig Schrøder, a follower of Grundtvig, published *Om Bjovulfs-drapen: Efter en række foredrag på folkehöjskolen i Askov* [The heroic poem of Beowulf: From a series of lectures at the People's High School in Askov][85] based on lectures Schrøder had given at Askov, a heavily politicized People's High School located just north of Denmark's border with Prussia. Schrøder's book relied greatly upon Grundtvig's 1820 translation,[86] and it revived and extended many of Grundtvig's readings of the poem, particularly his theme of awakening. Robert Bjork writes that Schrøder's work "emerged, after all, in the context of Grundtvig's educational program in the People's High Schools that Grundtvig founded in Denmark, and *Beowulf* was being used by Schrøder as the nationalistic reader Grundtvig had hoped it would be."[87] Drawing upon Grundtvig's interpretation of Grendel as a symbol of the Roman Catholic Church in "Ragna-Roke, (et dansk Æmter)," where Grundtvig had called the Pope "the troll of Rome," and his interpretation of Beowulf as a figure of Luther,

Schrøder identifies Pope Leo X's selling of indulgences to build St. Peter's in Rome as one of the causes of the Reformation. As such, Pope Leo's building of St. Peter's is similar to Hroðgar's building of Heorot. Beowulf, like Luther, had to fight to overcome the lethargic self-satisfaction that follows such a proud enterprise. Like Grundtvig, Schrøder finds other broad allegorical possibilities in the poem: Beowulf's sword symbolizes heroic action, gold symbolizes happiness, and fire symbolizes evil and anger.[88]

Most influential in bringing Grundtvig's *Beowulf* into the hands of Danish young people were the songbooks used in the People's High Schools. Poul Dam notes that, collectively, the songs adapted from the poem might be thought of as collectively constituting a third edition of Grundtvig's translation.[89] The development of the songbook tradition is informative: it could be said that, in its relationship to *Beowulf*, the roots of the tradition reach back to a series of lectures Grundtvig gave in 1838 that inspired books like Brandt's 1848 collection, *Rim og Sange til Fæderlandets Historie*, which included poems from Grundtvig's 1820 translation. The tradition grew and gained momentum in books like H. Nutzhorn and Ludvig Schrøder's *Historiske Sange* [Historical songs] in 1872, which featured thirty-five of Grundtvig's historical poems, fourteen of which were imported directly from the second edition of Grundtvig's *Beowulf* from 1865 (retitled *Bjovulfs-Drapen, et Høinordisk Heltedigt fra Anguls-Tungen*) [Beowulf's death, a High Norse heroic poem from the tongue of the Angles].[90] It seems clear that *Historiske Sange* effectively reintroduced Grundtvig's *Beowulf* to future generations and paved the way for the first People's High School songbooks, such as Jens Bek and N. Johan Laursen's *Sangbog for den danske folkehøjskole* [Songbook for the Danish People's High School], published in 1888 and, most influentially, Nutzhorn's *Sangbog for Højskoler* [Songbook for High Schools] in 1894.

Konstantin-Hansen and Skovgaard's Grundtvigian *Bjovulf* for Children

By the early twentieth century, schoolchildren, young Danes attending People's High Schools, even regular citizens – that is, nearly everyone – had been exposed to *Bjowulfs Drape* through the collective effort of Grundtvigians and the ubiquitous *Folkehøjskolens Sangbog*, and most people took it for granted that "Grundtvig had attempted to express what he saw in the poem in a creative manner."[91] Popular artists followed Grundtvig's lead, too: in 1899, Valdemar Rørdam's free translation *Bjovulf: Et Digt* [Beowulf: A poem] seems to have fully trusted

Bjowulfs Drape as its source text.[92] Rørdam accepts Grundtvig's nationalist readings, even some of his early, questionable ones. For example, in Rørdam's version we learn that

Om Natten er Grændel Jætte
Hersker paa Skjoldungestol.
Han Kastede Søvn på Vagten
Og åd den for Kongens Dør.
At Trold over Mand fik Magten
Ved Søvn, det så man før.[93]

[at night Grendel the giant / ruled on the Skjoldung throne. / He cast sleep on the watchmen / and ate them before the king's door. / That the troll gained power over men / with sleep, that has been seen before.]

The full flowering of a Grundtvigian version of *Beowulf* for children came in 1914 with *Bjovulf: Et Angelsaksisk Heltedigt* [Beowulf: An Anglo-Saxon heroic poem] by Thora Konstantin-Hansen (1867–1954), with illustrations by Niels Kristian Skovgaard (1858–1938).[94] The writer and the artist were reared in Grundtvigian households and were inculcated by followers of Grundtvig from their youth. Konstantin-Hansen grew up within the walls of Vartov, the church-school compound where Grundtvig preached until his death in 1872. It is likely that she was christened by Grundtvig and that, from a very young age, she read and sang portions of *Bjowulfs Drape* from Flor's and Brandt's readers and Køster's songbook. In the summer of 1882, when she was fifteen, she spent a summer at Askov Højskolen, where Ludvig Schrøder had presented and published his Grundtvig-inspired *Beowulf* lectures seven years earlier. (He was still headmaster when she attended.) Later in life Konstantin-Hansen claimed that the basis for her world view was the Grundtvigian Free School.[95] Niels Skovgaard's upbringing was similarly Grundtvigian. Like Konstantin-Hansen, Skovgaard's father was a close friend of Grundtvig's. He was educated in "Gregersens Skole," a Grundtvigian basic school in Copenhagen, where he, too, likely read widely in Grundtvig's writings, and where he became close friends with Grundtvig's son Frederik Lange Grundtvig and frequented his home.[96]

Their collaboration provides a rich commentary on *Bjowulfs Drape*. In the foreword to her children's version, Konstantin-Hansen writes,

Danske Lærde og Digtere har udgivet, forklaret og oversat det angelsaksiske Digt i sin Helhed længe før nogen anden, ikke engang Englænderne selv ... Især har N. F. S. Grundtvig Æren af at have gjort opmærksom paa dets Værd og gjort det tilgængeligt for os paa Dansk.

Det var hans Ønske, at Bjovulfsdrapen "maatte findes i alle Huse og blive Læsebog for alle Børn, ja, blive for Norden efter fattig Lejlighed hvad Iliaden og Odysseen var for Grækerne."

Denne Bog, som kun er en forkortet fri Gengivelse, skulde gerne give danske Børn Lyst til, naar de bliver ældre, at læse Grundtvigs Gengivelse af Bjovulfsdrapen i smukke og morsomme danske Vers. Senere kunde de saa have Udbytte af at læse Adolf Hansens Oversættelse i en Versform, der kommer den gamle angelsaksiske saa nær som muligt, og af at læse hvad A. Olrik i "Danmarks Heltedigtning I" har at fortælle om Bjovulfsdrapen og dens Forhold til Skjoldsagnene. Kunde denne lille Bog blive Begyndelsen til en saadan Læserække, var den i alt Fald Udgivelsen værd. (5)

[Danish scholars and poets have published, explicated, and translated the Anglo-Saxon poem in its entirety long before anyone else, even the English themselves ... N.F.S. Grundtvig particularly has the honour of having called attention to its worth and making it available to us in Danish.

It was his wish that *Bjovulfsdrapen* "might be found in all houses and become a reading book for all children, yes, become for the North through practice what the *Iliad* and the *Odyssey* were for the Greeks."

This book, which is only an abridged free paraphrase, is intended to spark desire in Danish children, when they get older, to read Grundtvig's version of *Beowulf* in beautiful and entertaining Danish verse. Later, they could then have the benefit of reading Adolf Hansen's translation in a verse form that comes as close as possible to the old Anglo-Saxon, and to read what Olrik, in *Danmarks Heltedigtning I*, has to say about *Bjovulfsdrapen* and its relation to the Skjoldung sagas. Should this little book be the beginning of such a reading lineup, then its publication would be worth the work.]

These remarks are dated March 1914, a month before the First World War began. Denmark had assumed neutrality but memories of the humiliation of defeat by Prussia in 1864 certainly lingered.

The prose translation gives the whole of the Danish part of the poem, ending where Grundtvig said it should have ended.[97] Konstantin-Hansen's translation follows the shape of *Bjowulfs Drape* by mirroring Grundtvig's fifteen "songs" instead of the original text's twenty-eight sections (including the proem) in the Danish half of the poem. The poem's allusion to the biblical creation story, the Finnsburg episode, and the allusion to Sigemund are omitted, and the portions of the poem that Grundtvig emphasized and that had been adapted for the *Folkhøjskole Sangbog* are amplified and savoured. Here is Konstantin-Hansen's opening:

Vi har hørt meget fortælle om Danernes Færd i gamle Dage, om Kongernes Stordaad og Heltenes Sejre. En af de bedste Fortællinger er dog den om Kong Skjold, ham der blev fundet som et hjælpeløst Barn, men havde Lykken med sig og steg saaledes i Magt og Hæder, at alle omboende Folk derovre paa den anden Side af Havet maatte adlyde ham og give ham Skat. Han styrede sit Rige godt. (9)

[We have often heard stories about the Danes' deeds in the old days, about the kings' great deeds and the heroes' victories. One of the best-known stories is one about King Skjold, he who was found as a helpless child, but was so fortunate and grew so great in might and honour, that all surrounding peoples over on the other side of the sea were forced to obey him and give him treasure. He ruled his kingdom well.]

The narration omits the Danish Beowulf/Beow (at line 56 in the original) and reports instead about Halfdan's three sons Hjorgar, Hrodgar, and Helge and a daughter "Elan," who married the warlike Skjoldung Anganthiov.[98] Following Grundtvig, Hrothgar's hall is called "Hjorthal," and the king "skænkede Ringe og Smykker til alle, der samledes i Hallen" (11) [gave rings and treasures to all who were gathered in the hall]. But harmony is broken by the troll Grendel. We are told that Grendel "spejded ind gennem Gluggen og saa, hvorledes Hirdmændene havde lagt sig til Hvile efter Gildet og nu sov sødelig uden at ane Fare" (12) [spied in through the window and saw how the warriors had lain down to rest after the feast and now slept soundly without knowing danger].

The facing page illustration (see fig. 1.2) provides a distinctly Grundtvigian subtext to the narrative. Grendel is a shadowy creature who blends into the landscape and the sky. Behind him, the clouds assume human shapes as though the monster is part of a greater, more ominous invasion, one that readers in March of 1914 were likely to discern quite clearly as suggesting German aggression.

The brave "Gøte" [Goth] Beowulf hears about "denne tunge Sorg paa Kongens Hjerte" [the heavy sorrow upon [Hrothgar's] heart] through the "Sange fra Mund til Mund vidt ud i Verden" (15) [songs sung mouth to mouth wide over the world]. In the subsequent sections, Konstantin-Hansen's narrative follows *Bjowulfs Drape* closely, though she omits Beowulf's claim that Grendel casts sleep on the Danes and quite conspicuously amplifies Wealhthow's (Valtjov's) part, providing

Figure 1.2. Grendel spying into Hjorthal, by Niels Skovgaard, from Konstantin-Hansen, *Bjovulf: Et Angelsaksisk Heltedigt*, p. 13.

the queen's speeches in their entirety. Beowulf's fight with Grendel also follows the general storyline of *Bjowulfs Drape*, though, as in Grundt-vig's version, Beowulf awaits the monster with his men positioned around him on the floor. And the narrator adjusts the tone of the scene slightly, adding that even though Beowulf's men were afraid and doubted that they would ever leave Heorot, "Snart faldt de dog alle i Sövn undtagen een" (33) [they all quickly fell asleep, all except one]. The fight scene as illustrated by Skovgaard (see fig. 1.3) suggests that he and Konstantin-Hansen were attending to the analogous scene in

Figure 1.3. Beowulf fighting Grendel, by Niels Skovgaard, from Konstantin-Hansen, *Bjovulf: Et Angelsaksisk Heltedigt*, p. 34.

Grettirs saga, which she had translated in 1912. In the scene, the hero Grettir realized that it would be useless to struggle with the undead Glam any longer so he "satte samtidig Foden mod en stor, jord-fast Sten ved Døren" [set his foot against a large, earth-bound stone by the door].[99] Skovgaard has Beowulf fight Grettir-like, leveraging himself against the doorframe.

When Grendel's mother comes for revenge, Beowulf tells Hrothgar to be strong. The narrator adds that they "var et dygtigt og rask Folk, de danske!" (43) [were a doughty and tough people, the Danes!], and we hear hints of Konstantin-Hansen's feminist outlook when she has the narrator sarcastically speculate that "det var jo dog kun en Kvinde, der ikke i Mod og Kraft kan maale sig med Mænd" (44) [[Grendel's mother] was sure enough only a woman, who in courage and power could not measure up with a man]. With her defeat, the Danes can "sove i Fred" (59) [sleep in peace]. As Beowulf sets out to depart for "Folk og Fædreland" (62) [[his] people and fatherland], Hrothgar tells him that he has "fuldbyrdet Freden mellem Gøter og Daner" (63) [fulfilled his duty to bring peace between the Goths and Danes]; then, as the king says his farewells, "Taarerne randt ned ad hans Kinder" (64) [tears ran down his cheeks]. The story ends not with the departure of the hero over the sea, in a way that would mirror Scyld's departure, but with Beowulf's joy-filled return to Gothland, where he tells his tale and thanks God for his victory.

Grundtvigian Echoes in Bruder and Tolkien

Grundtvig's pioneering belief that the poem bears forth modern-day truths found its way into the currents of influence in German and English traditions of *Beowulf* for young readers. In 1927, the German Otto Bruder published a "Laienspiel" titled *Beowulf: Ein heldisches Spiel* [Beowulf: A heroic play].[100] Intended to be performed as an inspirational piece for the German youth movement, its theme is the awakening of a people from lethargy. The plot of the play is relatively simple: each night shieldbearers stand watch, but one by one they succumb to fatigue and are devoured by a formless beast who takes them "in Ermattungszauber, / Und reißt und schlingt die Männer ein zum Fraß" (9) ["in a spell of weariness. / He snatches up and devours those men for food" (23)]. A prophecy says that the solution to this problem will come in the form of a hero resistant to the torpor, for "Wer wachend bleiben kann, bricht das Verhängnis" (12) ["he who can stay awake will break the spell" (25)]. Then, midway through the play, Beowulf arrives. The hero is an outsider, but he is still a German Everyman of sorts. Seeing the shieldbearers fall, Beowulf asks, "Wie aber halt ich meinen Groll zurück! / Ist deine Jugend matt wie welkes Gras, / Mein Volk?" (21) ["How can I calmly curb my anger? Youths / Bending as weakly as the grass in autumn – / My people" (34)]. In the end, Beowulf resists the monster's spell, becomes the people's "Kettende" (36) ["Saviour" (47)], and inspires them as a model. "Sind wache Herzen vor mir aufgetan?" (38) ["Can it be hearts awakening here before me?" (49)], Beowulf asks. The narrator issues a challenge to Beowulf: "Denn wem ... dir und den Gefährten, / Geziemt es wach zu sein, die Schatten drohen" (42) ["On you and your companions now will fall / The task of waking when the shadows threaten" (52)].

It is unknown if Bruder read Grundtvig's translation or commentaries or if he accessed Grundtvig's idea of awakening via Grundtvigian readers, songbooks, or essays by educators like Schrøder or even children's books like Konstantin-Hansen's. Marijane Osborn has proposed that Bruder "knew Danish well enough to translate poetry from that language," that he had "expressed youthful fascination with Scandinavian writers," and that he could have "received the idea second-hand."[101] It is worth noting that after he "awakens" the people from their lethargy, Beowulf devises for them "unser Spruch" ["our password"]: "Des Dochtes Dienst ist brennen! Wagt den Brand!" (41) ["The work of the brand is burning. Dare to burn!" (51)], a detail that seems to indicate Bruder's attention to Grundtvig's famous comparison of *Beowulf* to a "brand pulled from the fire."[102] If so, it is clear that Bruder gave the idea a more aggressive tone and that his version must be read in relation to growing fascism in Germany.

Influence of Grundtvig's ideas is more certain in the case of J.R.R. Tolkien, Bruder's contemporary. Michael Drout states that "the great synthesizing works" of Grundtvig were "well known to Tolkien," and Tom Shippey adds that "Grundtvig was the 'Beowulfian' whom Tolkien admired the most."[103] Tolkien certainly knew *Bjowulfs Drape*: he wrote about it and its author in his two drafts for his 1936 lecture "*Beowulf*: The Monsters and the Critics."[104] Central points of the lecture were also Grundtvig's: that the "monsters are not an inexplicable blunder of taste; they are essential, fundamentally allied to the underlying ideas of the poem," and that the hero meets the monsters in "a contest on the fields of time," in a "battle between the soul and its adversaries."[105] Some of Tolkien's other points, too, sound Grundtvigian: Grundtvig's metaphor of the castle in ruins, his naming of the dragon, his close attention to king and community – all of these resurface in Tolkien's work. More than anything else, though, it is the willingness to adapt the message of *Beowulf* into new forms comprehensible to young audiences that makes Tolkien's work resemble Grundtvig's so closely.[106] Consider this poem that appears in Tolkien's unfinished story *The Lost Road*:[107]

> The ship came shining to the shore driven
> and strode upon the strand, till its stem rested
> on sand and shingle. The sun went down.
> The clouds overcame the cold heavens.
> In fear and wonder to the fallow water
> sadhearted men swiftly hastened
> to the broken beaches the boat seeking,
> gleaming-timbered in the grey twilight.
> They looked within, and there laid sleeping
> a boy they saw breathing softly:

his face was fair, his form lovely,
his limbs were white, his locks raven
golden-braided.   (ll. 19–31)

[S]trung with silver
a harp of gold neath his hand rested;
his sleeping head was soft pillowed
on a sheaf of corn shimmering palely
as the fallow gold doth from far countries
west of Angol. Wonder filled them.   (ll. 34–9)

Lord they called him;
king they made him, crowned with golden
wheaten garland, white his raiment,
his harp his sceptre. In his house was fire,
food and wisdom; there fear came not.
To manhood he grew, might and wisdom.
Sheave they called him, whom the ship brought them,
a name renowned in the North countries
ever since in song.   (ll. 94–102)

Tolkien seems to share Grundtvig's vision of the episode as part of a common Northern heritage. In an additional set of lines to his poem, Tolkien touches upon King Sheave's lineage, particularly how his offspring "named and founded" the Northern kingdoms of "Sea-danes and Goths, Swedes and Northmen, / Franks and Frisians, folk of the islands, / Swordmen and Saxons, Swabes and English, / and the Langobards" (ll. 144, 146–9).

Like Grundtvig's "Skjold," this poem was meant to be sung. Consider also Tolkien's prose retellings of *Beowulf* in *Sellic Spell* – in both Modern and Old English – and his verse retellings in "The Lay of Beowulf," which Christopher Tolkien remembers his father singing to him when he was seven or eight years old.[108] In style, content, and effort, Tolkien's recreations resemble Grundtvig's versions of *Beowulf*.

Whether or not Tolkien consciously modelled his approach on Grundtvig's, as generations of Danish writers did, his approach legitimizes Grundtvig's vision for *Beowulf* as suitable for young readers and his progressive ideas about educating children according to their interests and abilities. Tolkien's and Grundtvig's shared literary outlook came to place them among the authors most read by twentieth-century Danish schoolchildren.[109] Through them, *Beowulf* became "a little shared Homer for England and the North."

NOTES

1 Grundtvig's achievements are described by A.M. Allchin, *N.F.S. Grundtvig: An Introduction to His Life and Work*, 2nd ed. (Aarhus: Aarhus University Press, 2015); Kaj Thaning, "Grundtvig, an Introduction," *Grundtvig-Studier* (1973): 68–84; and Kaj Thaning, *N.F.S. Grundtvig: An Introduction to His Life and Work* (London: Darton, Longman, & Todd, 1997). Anthologies about Grundtvig's influence are Christian Thodberg and Anders Pontoppidan Thyssen, eds., *N.F.S. Grundtvig: Tradition and Renewal* (Copenhagen: Det Danske Selskab, 1983); Allchin, *Grundtvig: An Introduction*; and John A. Hall, Ove Korsgaard, and Ove K. Pedersen, eds., *Building the Nation: N.F.S. Grundtvig and Danish National Identity* (Copenhagen: Djøf, 2015). For translations of key documents from his life, see S.A.J. Bradley, ed. and trans., *N.F.S. Grundtvig: A Life Recalled* (Aarhus: Aarhus University Press, 2004); of his poetry, hymns, and songs, Edward Broadbridge, trans., *Living Wellsprings: The Hymns, Songs and Poems of N.F.S. Grundtvig* (Aarhus: Aarhus University Press, 2015); and of his educational writings, Edward Broadbridge, trans., *School for Life: N.F.S. Grundtvig on the Education for the People* (Aarhus: Aarhus University Press, 2011).

2 N.F.S. Grundtvig, trans., *Bjowulfs Drape: Et Gothisk Helte-Digt fra forrige Aar-Tusinde af Angel-Saxisk paa Danske Riim* (Copenhagen: Seidelin, 1820), p. LII; hereafter cited parenthetically. For translations or creative renderings of *Beowulf* in Danish (including their introductory matter, as in this case) by Grundtvig or others, I will quote the Danish in the main text followed by translation. For critical or theoretical comments in Danish, I will give an English translation as primary and subordinate the original Danish to a footnote. Except as otherwise noted, English translations are my own and were prepared for this essay. Citations will be given where I reproduce my own or other scholars' previously published translations.

3 For discussions of Grundtvig's translations of *Beowulf*, see Kemp Malone, "Grundtvigs oversættelse af *Beowulf*," *Grundtvig-Studier* (1960): 7–25; S.A.J. Bradley, "Det er hvad jeg kalder at oversætte Digte: Grundtvig as translator," *Grundtvig-Studier* (2000): 36–59; and Mark Bradshaw Busbee, "The First Complete Translation of *Beowulf* into a Modern Language," in *Translating the Past: Essays on Medieval Literature in Honor of Marijane Osborn*, ed. Jane Beal and Mark Bradshaw Busbee (Tempe, AZ: ACMRS, 2012), 37–58.

4 Grundtvig never defined what he meant by *Børn* (children) in these contexts, though it can be assumed that he is thinking about reading-age children: ages six and older, following Kunze's identification of the age ranges of nineteenth-century German books for children (Horst J. Kunze, "German Children's Literature from Its Beginnings to the Nineteenth

Century: A Historical Perspective," *The Arbuthnot Lectures, 1980–1989* [Chicago: American Library Association, 1990], 1–12, at 3–4).

5 "Ordets Kamp til Seier" (N.F.S. Grundtvig, "Om Bjovulfs Drape eller det af Hr. Etatsraad Thorkelin 1815 udgivne angelsachsiske Digt," *Danne-Virke* 2 [1817]: 207–89, at 273).

6 N.F.S. Grundtvig, *Bibliotheca Anglo-Saxonica. Prospectus, and Proposals of a Subscription, for the Publication of the Most Valuable Anglo-Saxon Manuscripts, Illustrative of the Early Poetry and Literature of Our Language. Most of Which Have Never Yet Been Printed* (London: Black, Young & Young, 1830), 4.

7 "[S]kabt og skikket til at være en lille fælles Homér for England og Norden," a comment made in a lecture given in 1838 at Borch's Collegium and posthumously published (N.F.S. Grundtvig, *Mands Minde, 1788–1838. Foredrag over det sidste halve Aarhundredes Historie, holdte 1838* [Copenhagen: Karl Schønbergs Forlag, 1877], 460).

8 "[F]indes i alle Huse og blive Læsebog for alle Børn, ja, blive for Norden ... hvad Iliaden og Odysseen var for Grækerne" (N.F.S. Grundtvig, "Bjovulfs Drape eller det Oldnordiske Heltedigt," *Brage og Indun, et nordisk Fjaerdingaarskrift, udgivet, med Bistand af Dansk, Svenske og Normaend* 4 [1841]: 481–538, at 482).

9 Grundtvig had declared himself the prophet of modern Denmark in 1815, in the introductory poem of his sample translations of Saxo and Snorri (pp. ix–xiii, stanzas 17–29; cited from Holger Begtrup, ed., *N.F.S. Grundtvigs Udvalgte Skrifter*, 10 vols. [Copenhagen: Gyldendalske Boghandel Nordisk Forlag, 1907–14], 4:11–13). By 1824, Grundtvig was so convinced of his role as prophet that he threatened to leave Denmark and take the spirit of the people with him (*Nyaars-Morgen: Et Rim*, p. 132, stanza 264; cited from Begtrup, *Grundtvigs Udvalgte Skrifter*, 4:329).

10 "[G]øre levende Brug af det Altsammen ... hemmelig oplyse baade Børn og Forældre" (N.F.S. Grundtvig, *Statsmæssig Oplysning/Et udkast om sam-fund og skole*, ed. K.E. Bugge and Vilhelm Nielsen [Nyt Nordisk Forlag, 1983], 23–78, at 40); trans. Broadbridge, *School for Life*, 91.

11 N.F.S. Grundtvig, trans., *Danmarks Krønike af Saxo Grammaticus* (Copenhagen: Bekostet for Menig-Mand af Krønikens Danske og Norske Venner. Schulziske Officin, 1818–22); N.F.S. Grundtvig, trans., *Norges Konge-Krønike af Snorri Sturlesøn* (Copenhagen: Bekostet for Menig-Mand af Krønikens Danske og Norske Venner. Schulziske Officin, 1818–22). Less than half of the three thousand copies of the Saxo translation sold; the rest were given away in connection with the fiftieth anniversary of King Frederik VI's reign (see Bradley, *A Life Recalled*, 114).

12 N.F.S. Grundtvig, *Beowulfes Beorh eller Bjovulfs-Drapen, det Old-Angelske Heltedigt, paa Grund-Sproget* (Copenhagen: Karl Schønbergs Forlag, 1861),

xix–xx; quotation: "i mange Aar kun læst meget lidt uden for mite get Huus."

13 Jacob Grimm gave *Bjowulfs Drape* a positive review, but he complained that Grundtvig "has here delivered a poem which neither corresponds to the demands of the present nor offers a true picture of the old poem" (180) ["hat hier gleichwohl ein gedicht geliefert, das den forderungen der gegenwart weder entspricht noch ein treues bild des alten liedes aufstel"]: Grimm, "Bjowulfs Drape. et gothisk helte-digt fra forrige aartusinde af angel saxisk paa danske riim ved Nik. Fred. Sev. Grundtvig, präst. Kopenhagen" (1823), reprinted in *Kleinere Schriften*, Recensionen und Vermischte Aufsätze 1 (Berlin: Ferd. Dümmlers Verlagsbuchhandlung, 1869), 178–86. One early anonymous Danish reviewer suggested that *Bjowulfs Drape* might meet "the same particularly unfortunate reception" (799) ["Ganske ufortient Behandling"] that Grundtvig's patriotic translation of Saxo Grammaticus had ([rev. of *Bjowulfs Drape*], *Nyeste Skilderie af Kjøbenhavn* 20, no. 50 [1823]: 798–800).

14 The purpose of the reform was to instil children with "the knowledge and skills that are necessary for them to become useful citizens of the state," but the religious reasons are retained, primarily to make children "good, upright people in accordance with the teachings of evangelical Christianity" (Ove Korsgaard, "Grundtvig's Philosophy of Enlightenment and Education," in Broadbridge, *School for Life*, 13–35, at 27).

15 Kunze, "German Children's Literature," 4.

16 Johann Gottfried von Herder, *Philosophical Writings*, trans. Michael Forster (Cambridge: Cambridge University Press, 2002), 59, emphasis in original.

17 "[H]omerisk Begeistring ... Nei, det var Nordens Karakter selv, disse Fielde selv, der rige Metalaarer, med deres Diamanter, der blot behøvede at slibes, for at skinne i eiendommelig Glands. Men jeg forglemte ei, at Diamanten kun lader sig slibe i sit eget Støv" (Adam Oehlenschläger, *Nordiske Digt* [Copenhagen: Seidelin, 1807], 34).

18 See Georg Christensen and Stener Grundtvig, eds., *Breve fra og til N.F.S. Grundtvig*, 2 vols. (Copenhagen: Nordisk Forlag, 1924), 1:79, no. 56.

19 Thorkelin, ed. and trans., *De Danorum rebus gestis secul. III & IV: Poema Danicum dialect Anglosaxonica* [Of events concerning the Danes in the third and fourth centuries: A Danish poem in the Anglo-Saxon dialect] (Kobenhavn: Rangel, 1815). For information about the edition and accompanying Latin paraphrase see J.R. Hall, "The First Two Editions of *Beowulf*: Thorkelin's (1815) and Kemble's (1833)," in *Editing Old English Texts: Proceedings of the 1990 Manchester Conference*, ed. Donald K. Scragg and Paul E. Szarmach (Cambridge: D.S. Brewer, 1996), 239–50; and Robert E. Bjork, "Grímur Jónsson Thorkelin's Preface to the First Edition of *Beowulf*, 1815," *Scandinavian Studies* 68, no. 3 (1996): 291–320.

20 T.A. Shippey offers a brief account of the reception of Thorkelin's edition
and Grundtvig's first encounter with it in 1815 ("Introduction," in *Beowulf:
The Critical Heritage*, ed. T.A. Shippey and Andreas Haarder [Routledge,
1998], 1–55, at 8–18). Grundtvig wrote two 1815 essays about *Beowulf*: "Et
Par Ord om det nys udkomne angelsaxsiske Digt" [A few words about
the recently published Anglo-Saxon poem], *Nyeste Skilderie af Kjøbenhavn*
(1815): p. 60 cols. 945–52, p. 63 cols. 998–1002, p. 64 cols. 1009–15, p. 65 cols.
1025–30, and p. 66 cols. 1045–7; and "Nok et Par Ord om Bjovulfs Drape"
[A few more words about *Beowulf*], *Nyeste Skilderie af Kjøbenhavn* (1815):
p. 70 cols. 1105–9, p. 71 cols. 1121–5, and p. 72 cols. 1139–45. For translations of both, see Mark Bradshaw Busbee, trans., "A Few Words about
the Recently Published Anglo-Saxon Poem, the First Edition of *Beowulf*,"
Grundtvig-Studier (2015): 7–36, and Mark Bradshaw Busbee, trans., "A Few
More Words about *Beowulf*," *Grundtvig-Studier* (2016): 25–46.

21 "[O]pgaa et herligt Lys" (N.F.S. Grundtvig, *Nordens Mytologi eller Udsigt
over Eddalæren for dannede Mænd der ei selv ere Mytologer* [Copenhagen:
Gehubothes Forlag, 1808], 130; cited from Begtrup, *Grundtvigs Udvalgte
Skrifter*, 1:327).

22 "[S]om en Brand af Ilden" (Grundtvig, "Et Par Ord," 60 col. 945); trans.
from Busbee, "A Few Words," 8. From 1815 to 1820 Grundtvig
would refer to *Beowulf* repeatedly in these terms: in 1820 with the same
wording as given here (*Bjowulfs Drape*, xxx); and in 1817 as "en Brand
udrevet af Ilden" ("Om Bjovulfs Drape," 270).

23 "[S]om et Barn" (Grundtvig, "Nok et Par Ord," 70 col. 1106); trans. from
Busbee, "A Few More Words," 28.

24 "[A]t lære hele Digtet udenad" (Grundtvig, *Beowulfes Beorh*, xviii).

25 "Med en Varme, som kun den kiender, der veed hvad det er, fra
Barnsbeen at elske boglig Konst, Fortid og Fædreneland, satte jeg mig
hen at lytte til det gamle Kvad, hvis Tunge Tidens Haand saa saare havde
lammet" (Grundtvig, "Om Bjovulfs Drape," 208–9).

26 Thaning, "Grundtvig, an Introduction," 74.

27 See Grundtvig, "Et Par Ord," 65 col. 1030, and Grundtvig, "Om Bjovulfs
Drape," 284–8. For a discussion of the implications of and controversy
surrounding this discovery, see Franklin D. Cooley, "Contemporary
Reaction to the Identification of Hygelac," *Philologica: The Malone
Anniversary Studies*, ed. Thomas A. Birby and Henry Bosley Woolf
(Baltimore: University of Maryland Press, 1949), 269–74.

28 *Beowulf* references are to R.D. Fulk, Robert E. Bjork, and John D. Niles,
eds., *Klaeber's Beowulf and The Fight at Finnsburg*, 4th ed. (Toronto:
University of Toronto Press, 2008), and are cited parenthetically.

29 "[H]er staaer talt om en Guddoms, ventelig Hildas, Aabenbarelse i et
gyldent Luftskib og at hun lovede Helten baade at beskjærme ham og

vogte Skibene" (Grundtvig, "Et Par Ord," 63 col. 1000); trans. from
Busbee, "A Few Words," 17–18. Grundtvig recognized the presence of the
Danish Beow in his second essay about the poem ("Nok et Par Ord," 72
col. 1139). He never repeated his idea about the appearance of Hilda.

30 "[S]om en nær Paarørende vi aldrig har seet" (Grundtvig, "Om Bjovulfs
Drape," 208).

31 "[E]n Skjald i Konstens Barndom" ("Et Par Ord," 65 col. 1028); trans.
from Busbee, "A Few Words," 29.

32 Kemp Malone, "Grundtvig's Philosophy of History," *Journal of the History
of Ideas* 1, no. 3 (1940): 281–98, at 286.

33 "[D]et Ypperste af hele Digtet ... en Forjættelse om Skjoldungestammens
Uforkrænkelighed" (Grundtvig, "Et Par Ord," 60 col. 952); trans. from
Busbee, "A Few Words," 15.

34 Grundtvig, "Et Par Ord," 60 col. 952 n. 3; Busbee, "A Few Words," 15, for
translation of the relevant passage.

35 "[D]en Forstandige et bedre Billede af Digtets Eiendommelighed"; "gjen-
nem en stille Beskuelse af det Hele ... i en rimet Oversættelse skal stræbe
at gjøre muelig for dem af mine Landsmænd, hvis Leilighed det ikke er
at trænge ind i Grundsproget" (Grundtvig, "Et Par Ord," 65 col. 1027);
trans. from Busbee, "A Few Words," 29.

36 Grundtvig, "Et Par Ord," 60 col. 951.

37 Busbee, "A Few Words," 14.

38 "[A]t gaae fra Texten, men ... at lade dets Aand udtrykke sine
Forestillinger i et andet Sprog, ei blot da i andre Ord men og i andre
Vendinger" (N.F.S. Grundtvig, "Stykker af Skjoldung-Kvadet eller
Bjovulfs Minde," *Danne-Virke* 4 [1819]: 234–62, at 236).

39 See Flemming Lundgreen-Nielsen, "The Special Case of Grundtvig: Poet,
Philosopher, Educator," in *The Nordic Languages: An International Handbook
of the History of the North Germanic Languages*, vol. 1, ed. Oscar Bandle et
al. (De Gruyter, 2002), 494–502, esp. 494. In *Nyaars-Morgen* Grundtvig calls
Malene Jensdatter his "Language Mistress" ("Sprog-Mesterinde"; cited
from Begtrup, *Grundtvigs Udvalgte Skrifter*, 4:285).

40 Lundgreen-Nielsen, "Special Case of Grundtvig," 497.

41 "Hjort ... deels er jo heorth en Hjemstavn (Heerde) og deels synes det
mig klart at Hjort i al Fald siges at være Hallens poetiske Navn, ventelig
af Ordet hiorta (lystig, munter)" (Grundtvig, "Et Par Ord," 63 col. 999);
trans. from Busbee, "A Few Words," 16.

42 Uffe Jonas, "On the Church, the State, and the School: Grundtvig as
Enlightenment Philosopher and Social Thinker," in *Building the Nation*,
ed. Hall, Korsgaard, and Pedersen, 169–91, at 176.

43 In "Et Par Ord," 63 col. 999, Grundtvig concluded that the word
"Hjorte" was cognate with "Hjerte" and was therefore meant to operate

symbolically. "Hjerte-Borgen" reappears in Grundtvig's later patriotic versions.

44 "[D]er var Kraft i Kongens Ord, / Han kaldte Borgen Hjerte. / Han bænked Kæmper trindt om Bord, / Og lod dem vel beværte, / Ja Haanden fuld / Med Sølv og Guld, / Han gav dem af sit Hjerte" (Grundtvig, "Stykker af Skjoldung-Kvadet," 239). In 1820, he altered the lines to: "Her Kæmper sad om breden Bord, / Og Kraft der var i Kongens Ord: / Han kaldte Borgen Hiorte, / Og, venne-huld, / Han skifted Guld" (*Bjowulfs Drape*, 9) [Here the warriors sat around the broad table / and there was power in the king's word: / he called the fortress "Hjorte," / and, happily, / he distributed gold].

45 "[E]i blot med Guld og skinnende Klenodier, men med den herligste og sjeldneste Ædelsteen i Kongekronen: inderlig Kjærlighed" (Grundtvig, "Et Par Ord," 64 col. 1012); trans. from Busbee, "A Few Words," 23.

46 Grundtvig, "Et Par Ord," 64 col. 1012.

47 Busbee, "A Few Words," 23.

48 Grundtvig, "Om Bjovulfs Drape," 254–5. Grundtvig mistakes the compound adjective "stearcheort" [strong-hearted] at *Beowulf*, ll. 2288 and 2552, for a name.

49 "Hexens Samlingsplads" (Grundtvig, "Om Bjovulfs Drape," 241 and n. 33).

50 "[S]taae Eventyrene om Grændel og Dragen som digtets Hoved-Indhold, som en Fortsættelse af Djavelens og de gamle Geganters Kamp imod Gud, der som Trolddom griber ind i Historien, og skal derved give den en høiere Betydning" (Grundtvig, "Om Bjovulfs Drape," 278).

51 "[K]an siges at skygge i det dobbelte Eventyr ... Løgnens fiendlige forhold mod Sandheden viser sig ... deels i Historien, og deels i Naturen" (Grundtvig, "Om Bjovulfs Drape," 279).

52 "[F]ordrukne, snorkende" (Grundtvig, *Beowulfes Beorh*, xxxi).

53 See Mark Bradshaw Busbee, "The Case for a Sleeping Spell in *Beowulf*," *Medieval Perspectives* 29 (2014): 121–32, for an explanation of how Grundtvig arrived at this interpretation through a unique reading of *Beowulf*, l. 600a.

54 J.A. Cuddon defines *angoisse* as "a species of metaphysical and moral anguish" (*The Penguin Dictionary of Literary Terms and Literary Theory*, 4th ed. [London: Penguin, 1999], 295). Grendel's abode is aptly described in *Beowulf* as "moras" and "fen" (ll. 103b, 104a) [moors, fen].

55 D.J. Sneen, "Hermeneutics of N.F.S. Grundtvig," *Interpretation* 26 (1972): 42–61, at 47.

56 Grundtvig, "Danne-Virke," *Danne-Virke* 1 (1816): 1–15; collected in Begtrup, *Grundtvigs Udvalgte Skrifter*, 1:308–16.

57 Grundtvig, "Ragna-Roke, (et dansk Æmter)," *Danne-Virke* 3 (1817): 301–82, hereafter cited parenthetically.

58 Grundtvig, "Om Bjovulfs Drape," 270.

59 For a discussion of how Denmark (and Grundtvig) was affected
by war with Prussia, see Hans Kuhn, "Grundtvig and the War that
Changed Danish Identity," *Grundtvig-Studier* (2000): 190–202. W. Carr,
Schleswig-Holstein, 1815–1848: A Study in National Conflict (Manchester:
Manchester University Press, 1963), gives an account of the Schleswig-
Holstein conflict, and Shippey ("Introduction," 16–17) explains reasons
for the conflict and its effect on early *Beowulf* studies.

60 "Saasnart det lykkes Trolden, som saa tit, at kaste Sövn paa hende,
nedsynker hun til en *Tydsk Slavinde*" (Grundtvig, "Bjovulfs Drape eller
det Oldnordiske Heltedigt," 524); translation from T.A. Shippey, trans.,
"N.F.S. Grundtvig 1841," in *Beowulf: The Critical Heritage*, ed. Shippey and
Haarder, 233–6, at 235.

61 "[S]eer man nemlig strax, at hvad saa end den gamle Skjald kan have
enten drømt eller tænkt, saa er Trolden Grændel og hans Moder det
mest træffende Billede, man kan ønske sig paa Tysken i Danmark, naar
den bare kan saae Skam, ligesom Grændel og hans Moder fik ... [D]et
nu ogsaa er paa den høie Tid, at vi tilegner os det gode Varsel, som det
oldnordiske heltedigt giver os om glimrende Seier over Danmarks Arve-
fjende" (N.F.S. Grundtvig, "Trolden Grændel og hans Moder i Danmark,"
Danskeren, et Ugeblad 3, no. 15 [1850]: 225–40, at 227).

62 N.F.S. Grundtvig, *Budstikke i Høinorden* (Copenhagen: Karl Schønbergs
Forlag, 1864); references given from Begtrup, *Grundtvigs Udvalgte Skrifter*,
10:523, 524.

63 "[E]n Guld Harpe fra Hedenold, hvis Strænge sprang, og hvis Skruer
smelteede i Luen" (Grundtvig, "Om Bjovulfs Drape," 271).

64 "[E]n Smelte-ovn ... i den skal kastes alt har Sandhed bygget sig ... men
hvad Iden fortærer, det er Løgn" (N.F.S. Grundtvig, *Udsigt over Verdens-
Krøniken fornemmelig i det Lutherske Tidsrum* [Copenhagen: Andreas
Seidelin, 1817], 550; also found in Begtrup, *Grundtvigs Udvalgte Skrifter*,
3:679).

65 "[D]et forgiemte og forglemte Digt ... nye Klæder, nye Penge og
Underviisning in Dagens Talebrug, saa de kunde begaaet sig i den ny
Verden" (Grundtvig, *Beowulfes Beorh*, xix).

66 See Grundtvig, *Mands Minde*, 476. His frustrations with his fellow Danes
had been growing for some time, and by 1824 he began to see it as vanity
"to wrestle with the old troll-witch whose true name is indifference" ("at
brydes med denne gamle Trold-Hex, hvis rette Navn er Lige-Gyldighed")
(*Nyaars Morgen*, cited from Begtrup, *Grundtvigs Udvalgte Skrifter*, 4:245).
Closer to the truth is that people weren't buying books like *Bjowulfs
Drape* for children at all because children's literature as a genre was
still in its infancy, and because Grundtvig's combative public persona

had hampered the spread of his ideas and work. In 1825, Grundtvig
had engaged in heated polemical exchanges with church superiors and
was banned from public appearances and censored for twelve years;
he retreated into what he called his "inner exile" and later emerged a
more powerful and influential figure: see Uffe Østergaard, "The Nation
as Event: The Dissolution of the Oldenburg Monarchy and Grundtvig's
Nationalism," in *Building the Nation*, ed. Hall, Korsgaard, and Pedersen,
110–34, at 127.

67 N.F.S. Grundtvig, "Angel-Sachserner," in *Krønike-Riim til Børn-Lærdom*
(Copenhagen: Wahlske Boghandling, 1829), 58–61; quotation from 60.

68 Bent Christensen, *About Grundtvig's Vidskab: An Inquiry into N.F.S.
Grundtvig's View of the Knowledge Aspect of the Commitment to Life That
Is a Necessary Part of Christianity* (Copenhagen: Gads Forlag, 1998), 17.
A few Grundtvig scholars date Grundtvig's turn to education as early
as 1824 (see Anders Pontoppidan Thyssen, "Grundtvig's Ideas on the
Church and the People up to 1824," in *Tradition and Renewal*, ed. Christian
Thodberg and Anders Pontoppidan Thyssen [Copenhagen: Det Danske
Selskab, 1983], 226–94; Jørgen Elbek, "Grundtvigs atten prøvår," *Kritik* 31
[1974]: 35–40). Most, following Kaj Thaning, date the shift in Grundtvig's
attitude towards pragmatism after Grundtvig's first trip to England in
1829 (see Thaning, "Grundtvig, an Introduction"). For early discussion of
Grundtvig's change in outlook during this period, see Otto Borchsenius,
"Grundtvig paa Vendepunktet i sit Liv (1838–39)," *Fra Fyrrerne. Litterære
Skizzer* 2 (1880): 101–25.

69 Grundtvig, *Bibliotheca Anglo-Saxonica*, 4.

70 "[O]mtrent som med dens Borge, at de ligge i Gruset" (N.F.S. Grundtvig,
Nordens Mythologi eller Sindbilled-Sprog [J.H. Schubothes Boghandling,
1832], cited from Begtrup, *Grundtvigs Udvalgte Skrifter*, 5:413); trans. from
Broadbridge, *School for Life*, 70.

71 "[V]ilde heller nedgrave disse Skatte i Jorden og som Drager ruge over
dem til Verdens Ende, end giore dem frugtbare for Livet og udvikle en
fuldstaendig, mennekelig Oplysning" (Grundtvig, *Statsmæssig Oplysning*,
45); trans. from Broadbridge, *School for Life*, 94.

72 Max Lawson, "N.F.S. Grundtvig," *Prospects* 23, no. 3 (1993): 613–23. The
standard edition covering Grundtvig's educational thought is K.S. Bugge,
ed., *Grundtvigs skole verden*, 2 vols. (Copenhagen: Gads Forlag, 1968).

73 Christian Flor, "Grendels Uvaesen i Hjorteborg – Gothen Bjovulf,"
in *Danske Laesebog til Brug i de laerde Skoler* (Kiel: Kongelige
Skolebogtrykkerie, 1831), 546–55.

74 Poul Martin Møller, "Om at fortælle Børn Eventyr," in *Skrifter i
Udvalg*, ed. Vilhelm Rasmus Andreas Andersen (Copenhagen: G.E.C.
Gad, 1930), 94–8. Joakim Garff, "'Altså: At stå – Ene ved en Andens

Hjælp!' – Kierkegaards pædagogiske Paradoks," *Foredrag på Vartov* 28 (2013): 50–73, discusses Møller's article and how it affected Kierkegaard.

75 "[A]t bringe det Poetiske paa alle Maader i Forhold til deres Liv, at udøve en Tryllemagt" (Kierkegaard, cited from Niels Jørgen Cappelørn, et al., eds., "Journalen BB:37," *Søren Kierkegaards Skrifter*, online at sks.dk [accessed 3 October 2019]).

76 See Grethe Kjaer, *Barndommens ulykkelige elsker. Kierkegaard om barnet og barndommen* (Copenhagen: C.A. Reitzel, 1996), 127.

77 "Læsebog for alle Börn ... hvad Iliaden og Odysseen var for Grækerne" (Grundtvig, "Bjovulfs Drape eller det Oldnordiske Heltedigt," 482).

78 N.F.S. Grundtvig, *Græsk og Nordisk Mythologi for Ungdommen* (Copenhagen: Bing & Søn, 1847); cited parenthetically.

79 See Hans Kuhn, "Romantic Myths, Student Agitation, and International Politics: The Danish Intellectuals and Slesvig-Holsten," *Scandinavica* 27, no. 1 (1988): 5–19, for a discussion of this movement and Grundtvig's central role in it.

80 C.J. Brandt, *Rim og Sange til Fædrelandets Historie, samlede og den Danske Ungdom tilegnede* (Iversen, 1848); cited parenthetically.

81 Kristian Køster, *Et Hundrede Danske Sange* (Karl Schønberg, 1865). The earliest version of Grundtvig's poem appeared in quite different form in "Den Danske Rim-Krønike," *Den Nordiske Kirke-Tidende, et Uge-Skrift for Kirken og Skolen* 35 (1834): cols. 584–91. Brandt included another version, titlted "Skjold kommer til Danmark" [Skjold comes to Denmark], in *Rim og Sange*, pp. 4–5. The version in *Rim og Sange* was partly based on the Scyld Scefing passage in *Beowulf*, ll. 4–52, but in the version provided here Grundtvig draws upon other sources, like ones in the Icelandic tradition that have Skjold as Odin's son. See Broadbridge, *Living Wellsprings*, 195–6, for a translation. See Marijane Osborn and Bent Christensen, "'Skjöld': A Song by N.F.S. Grundtvig," *ANQ* 20:3 (2007): 36–43, for translation, notes, commentary, and musical score for the song.

82 Broadbridge explains: "A lion's head adorns the bow of a Viking ship, while on a broad ship the mirror is the rear side that can be mirrored in the water and reflect the ship's name. The 'heart-mirror' here symbolizes that the ship is bringing a King of love and peace – as well as the Lion of Judah, perhaps" (*Living Wellsprings*, 195n166).

83 The Danish flag, which has a white cross on a red base, is compared to the red cheeks of the goddess Freya.

84 See, for example, Lorenz Frølich's "Skjold tages til Konge," in *Danske Heltesagn*, ed. Axel Olrik (Copenhagen: Gads, 1901), 5; and Anne E. Munch's postal stamp image "Kong Skjold kommer til Danmark Grænseforeningen" (c. 1905), an example of which belonging to Per Sørensen can be seen at http://www.piaper.dk/postkortkunstnere/

Postkortkunstnere/Anna_E_Munch/Anna_E_Munch.htm (accessed 3 October 2019).

85 Ludvig Schrøder, *Om Bjovulfs-drapen: Efter en række foredrag på folkehöjskolen i Askov* (Copenhagen: Karl Schønberg, 1875).

86 Shippey, "Introduction," 45.

87 Robert E. Bjork, "Nineteenth-Century Scandinavia and the Birth of Anglo-Saxon Studies," in *Anglo-Saxonism and the Construction of Social Identity*, ed. Allen Frantzen and John D. Niles (Gainsville: University of Florida Press, 1997), 110–32, at 125.

88 Schrøder, *Om Bjovulfs-drapen*, 43.

89 Poul Dam, *Grundtvig-Tekster i Sangbøgerne, med særligt henblik på højskolesangen. En bibliografisk oversight* (Århus: Aros, 1992), 30. The name of this book can be confusing to non-Danes. Through its first ten editions, the songbook was titled simply "Songbook." From the eleventh through the sixteenth editions, it was called the *Folkhøjskolens Sangbog*. Its name changed again with the eighteenth edition to the *Højskolesangbogen*.

90 H. Nutzhorn and Ludvig Schrøder, *Historiske Sange* (Copenhagen: Schønberg, 1872). The volume attends only to scenes in *Beowulf* that occur in Denmark, drawing directly from pp. 17–131 of *Bjovulfus-Drapen*.

91 "Gr[undtvig] har forsøgt at sige livlig hvad han så i kvadet, er der naturligvis ingen tvivl om" (Rønning 1885, 178).

92 Valdemar Rørdam, *Bjovulf* (Copenhagen: Den Nordisk Forlag, 1899).

93 Rørdam, *Bjovulf*, 17. The trend was not absolute, of course. Adolf Hansen's scholarly translation (*Bjovulf* [Copenhagen and Kristiania, 1910], published posthumously by Hansen's brother Oskar) resists Grundtvigian influence. Malone, "Grundtvigs oversættelse af *Beowulf*," offers a comparison of Hansen's and Grundtvig's translations.

94 Thora Konstantin-Hansen, *Bjovulf: Et Angelsaksisk Heltedigt*, illus. Niels Skovgaard (Copenhagen: Gyldendalske Boghandel Nordisk Forlag, 1914); hereafter cited parenthetically. For much of the further information in this paragraph, I am indebted to Liselotte Larsen, the Head Librarian at the Grundtvig Library at the Vartov, and to Kim Arne Pedersen in the Faculty of Theology at the University of Copenhagen.

95 Thora Constantin-Hansen, *Et Skoleliv i Strid og Fred* (Copenhagen: Povl Branners Forlag, 1935), 156.

96 As young adults, Konstantin-Hansen and Skovgaard, along with other artists, left the mainstream Grundtvigian congregation for the "Københavns Valgmenighed," a congregation for "left-wing" Grundtvigians desiring to support modern emancipation movements, *reformpædagogik* (reformed educational theories), and Brandes-inspired non-religious humanism. However, the religious engagement or the nationalistic heritage from Grundtvig was never weakened. See

Constantin-Hansen, *Skoleliv i Strid og Fred*. Along with her educational writings – she translated Maria Montessori's *Il segreto dell'infanzia* [The secret of childhood] into Danish and is said to have started the Montessori movement in her Copenhagen apartment – she collaborated on translations of *Nial's Saga* (Olivia Holm-Møller, Thora Konstantin-Hansen, and Sigurður Sigtryggsson, trans., *Nials Saga* [Copenhagen: Hagerup, 1911]) and *Grettir's Saga* (Sigurður Sigtryggsson and Thora Konstantin-Hansen, trans., *Sagaen om Gretter den Stærke* [Copenhagen: H. Hagerup, 1912]). Skovgaard's output was less outwardly activist, though heavily invested in Scandinavian culture, and aptly, his drawings of trolls became internationally known when they appeared in Axel Olrik's *Danske Sagn og Aeventyr fra Folkemunde* (Copenhagen: Thieles Bogtrykkeri, 1923).

97 Grundtvig, "Om Bjovulfs Drape," 251.

98 Grundtvig decided in 1817 ("Om Bjovulfs Drape," 219n2) that the word must be "Ela," the name of Halvdan's daughter. In his 1820 translation, he does not name her, but calls her "den favre Pige" [the favoured girl] and suggests again in his notes that she might be called "Ela" (*Bjowulfs Drape*, 7, 267).

99 Sigurður and Konstantin-Hansen, *Sagaen om Gretter*, 31. Note the 1912 date visible in the illustration; Skovggard's illustrations for Konstantin-Hansen's *Bjovulf* are individually dated 1912, 1913, and 1914.

100 I cite the German text by page number from a 1933 reprint (Otto Bruder, *Beowulf: Ein heldisches Spiel* [Munich: Chr. Kaiser Verlag, 1933]) and give translations from Marijane Osborn, trans., "Bruder's *Beowulf: Ein Heldisches Spiel*," *In Geardagum* 26 (2006): 19–52, also cited by page number. Osborn translates from a 1931 reprint of the 1927 play.

101 Marijane Osborn, "Bruder's *Beowulf*: A Critical Preface by the Translator," *In Geardagum* 26 (2006): 5–18, at 11.

102 See n. 23 above and associated discussion.

103 Michael Drout, ed., *Beowulf and the Critics by J.R.R. Tolkien* (Tempe, AZ: ACMRS, 2002), 238; T.A. Shippey, *The Road to Middle Earth: How J.R.R. Tolkien Created a New Mythology* (New York: Mariner Books, 2003), 347.

104 For a comparison of Grundtvig's and Tolkien's interpretations of *Beowulf*, see Mark Bradshaw Busbee, "Grundtvig and Tolkien on *Beowulf*: A Comparative Analysis," *Grundtvig-Studier* (2010): 12–30.

105 J.R.R. Tolkien, *Beowulf: The Monsters and the Critics*, 2nd ed. (Oxford: Oxford University Press, 1958), 17, 20.

106 For detailed consideration of Tolkien's *Beowulf*-derived writings in relation to Tolkien's own ideas about children's literature and "fairy story," see Amber Dunai's essay in this volume.

107 J.R.R. Tolkien, *The Lost Road and Other Writings: Language and Legend before The Lord of the Rings*, ed. Christopher Tolkien (Boston: Houghton Mifflin, 1987), 87–91. Cited parenthetically by line number.

108   J.R.R. Tolkien, *Beowulf: A Translation and Comentary, Together with Sellic Spell*, ed. Christopher Tolkien (Boston: Houghton Mifflin, 2014), 416. *Sellic Spell* is presented elsewhere in the same volume in both Modern and neo-Old English.

109   A 1974 survey of Danish seventh-graders showed Grundtvig to be the most read Danish author, followed by Adam Oehlenschläger, and put internationally known H.C. Andersen in fourth position (Torben Weinreich, *Børnelitteratur: En Grundbog*, 2nd ed. [København: Høst & Søn, 2008], 126). See also Anette Øster, *Læs! – les – läs: læsevaner og børnebogskampagner i Norden* (Frederiksberg: Roskilde Universitetsforlag, 2004). This two-part report is based on a study of the reading habits of the nine- to fifteen-year-olds in Denmark, Norway, and Sweden, with the Danish part of the study conducted in 2000–1. My thanks to Anna Karlskov Skyggebjerg at Aarhus University for sharing this information with me.

2 The Adaptational Character of the Earliest *Beowulf* for English Children: E.L. Hervey's "The Fight with the Ogre"

RENÉE WARD[1]

Although a "forgotten and neglected" author,[2] one relatively unknown to readers in the twentieth and twenty-first centuries, Eleanora Louisa (née Montagu) Hervey (1811–1903) was a prolific Victorian children's writer popular especially in the middle decades of the nineteenth century. She had an expansive and successful literary career that stretched from her early twenties until her late seventies, and, overall, her corpus includes half a dozen collections of poems and short stories, several novels, and several original songs, as well as countless poems published in magazines and periodicals. Further, much of Hervey's corpus engages in medievalism: her works draw heavily upon a range of medieval sources, from Norse sagas and Eddic poetry to Chaucer's *Canterbury Tales*, historical records, and saints' lives.[3] Yet despite the recent trend in scholarly fields to recover lost or forgotten female writers and their works, Hervey remains absent from seminal volumes on Victorian women and female writers. She is also overlooked in the field of children's literature, even as the canon and critical materials expand to include more works by women and to recognize increasingly the significance of adaptations and retellings for children, particularly those of medieval narratives or those with connections to medieval literature.[4]

This chapter introduces to modern audiences the short story "Roderic's Tale: The Fight with the Ogre," which appears in Hervey's volume *The Children of the Pear-Garden* (1873).[5] This previously unrecognized and unexamined adaptation of *Beowulf* may, in fact, be the earliest one for English children, as it predates more widely recognized early examples like those found in W.S.W. Anson's *Epics and Romances of the Middle Ages* (1883), Mara L. Pratt's *Stories from Old Germany* (1895), and Clara Linklater Thomson's *The Adventures of Beowulf* (1899). Further, Hervey's story demonstrates the highly intertextual nature of adaptations, especially those for children. Quite a few earlier adaptations for adults of the Old English tale circulated in the mid- to late-nineteenth century in Britain, and the content of "The Fight with the Ogre" makes explicit use of one of these, the prose version by Eustace Hinton Jones published in *Popular Romances of the Middle Ages* (1871) – a volume Jones and George W. Cox prepared for adult readers[6] – while also showing Hervey's awareness of other previous print versions, particularly Henry Morley's "A Primitive Old Epic" (1858).[7]

Despite a heavy reliance upon Jones as her main source, Hervey makes a number of significant edits in "The Fight with the Ogre" that render her retelling unique, several of which anticipate – influence even – trends popular in later adaptations for children of the Old English tale. She reduces much of the direct speech found in both her source and the original poem, creating a primarily action-driven tale; eliminates the opening Scyld episode and other similar genealogies, including Beowulf's; amplifies the narratorial attention given to the female antagonist especially;[8] and cuts entirely the final third of the narrative, reworking her ending in a manner that emphasizes both Beowulf's status as an instrument of God and the security of Hrothgar's realm. She also, in this revised ending, highlights her intended audience of younger readers, gesturing to the generic shift of her adaptation.

As I demonstrate, these moves ultimately serve the ideological purposes of her adaptation, both cultural and generic. Hervey's "The Fight with the Ogre" speaks directly to the nineteenth century's heightened concern for heritage, history, and empire, and Beowulf himself epitomizes the period's understandings of martial prowess and masculinity. The volume's story-telling framework, which is heavily shaped by Victorian Orientalism, positions the male child as the precursor to the adult patriarchal head and provides instruction on how he should rule himself and his household, while the introduction and combination of male and female narrators gestures to Victorian reading practices, suggesting that all readers, regardless of gender or age, can learn from the content. Additionally, the binding and presentation of *Children of the Pear-Garden* illustrates the commercialization that heavily characterizes the children's literature industry during the Victorian era. Finally, the story includes an illustration by the renowned Victorian artist and writer Kate Greenaway. This illustration, which presumably represents Grendel, complicates interpretations of the narrative and presents a bibliographic conundrum for readers.

"The Fight with the Ogre" opens with an introduction to Hrothgar, King of the Danes, who "took it into his mind to build a great palace in his chief city; a palace wherein his warriors and councillors might feast and drink mead, they and their children for ever, and make themselves glad and rejoice, and be thankful because of the riches which God had given them" (57). Once she establishes the idyllic setting of Hrothgar's community and hall, Hervey turns to Grendel's attacks, which are followed by a brief introduction to Beowulf and his men and a synopsis of their journey. From there, the narrative quickly moves into an account of Beowulf's battle with Grendel, the ensuing and rather truncated celebrations, and the retaliation of Grendel's mother. It then describes Beowulf's descent to the underwater hall and his defeat of Grendel's mother, and concludes with the second celebratory feast at Heorot.

Initially, Hervey's tale does not strike one as notably different from Jones's *Beowulf*. In fact, large sections of "The Fight with the Ogre" are taken verbatim from the source text, so much so that a modern reader familiar with present-day understandings of plagiarism might feel uncomfortable. The story even retains the accent marks, typically over long vowels, present in Jones's text and reminiscent of contemporary editions of the Old English original.[9] Following Jones, Hervey eliminates much of the original poem's framework or narratorial digressions – the genealogies and contextual tales such as the battle at Finnsburh, the creation story, and the Sigemund episode all disappear.[10] She identifies Grendel as a ravenous force that wreaks continual havoc upon Hrothgar's hall and people, and emphasizes the antagonist's otherness by repeating Jones's omission of the original poem's evocations of his ties to humanity.[11] She also similarly aligns the outcast firmly with places understood as dark and sinister, such as fens and borderlands, as well as with the long-standing adversaries of God: Jötuns, Orks, and Giants.[12]

Hervey likewise retains two prominent thematic features of Jones's text that eventually become instrumental to her own revisions. The first feature concerns the construction of the hero as an instrument of God and as the epitome of martial prowess and masculinity. Hrothgar's initial encounter with Beowulf emphasizes these qualities: when he sees the Geats, standing out among them is "one towering tall above the rest, god-like, in his shining arms, and the dazzling war-net of mail worn by the armourer" (60). The "towering" Beowulf is physically impressive, but he is also, in this passage, deified. Descriptions of the warrior as "shining" and "dazzling" suggest that the light of God shines from or within him. This illumination of his figure starkly contrasts the "deep darkness" (58) associated with Grendel and his mother, and firmly establishes the dichotomy between them, as agents of evil versus an agent of good. When Hrothgar realizes that the warrior he sees is indeed Beowulf, he attributes his existence and presence to divine intervention: "Then Hrothgár knew that it was Beówulf and he only, Beówulf, the mighty-handed one, raised up of God to be a champion for him against Grendel the evil spirit" (60).

The protagonist's arrival is thus, in both texts, a direct act of divine power. Indeed, after defeating Grendel's mother, Beowulf recognizes that his victory is God's will. He declares, "God and my strong hand prospered me and gave me the victory. I have wrested away the sword wherewith the giants before the Flood defiled the Eternal God! I have overcome the enemies of God, who have battled against Him, and were not subdued for countless years" (66). He links his battles directly to the cosmic struggle between good and evil, and recognizes that divine power ultimately contributes to his victories over dark forces. His reference to God three times in as many lines also highlights the importance of divine will in these events.

The second key feature Hervey retains concerns the female antagonist. Both Jones and Hervey render Grendel's mother as a considerably more cunning and malevolent character than she is in the Old English poem. In their texts, the attack on Heorot becomes more than just the desire to render whole a dead son's body – more even than an eye-for-an-eye exchange or act of revenge. Grendel's mother, in fact, purposefully draws out her prey and controls the terms of their engagement, giving herself the advantage of their exchange taking place within her own space. Her attack on Heorot is a ploy, and the murder of Æschere purposeful. Æschere, one could say, is the bait. Hervey describes how, for instance, once Grendel's mother returns to the underwater hall, she "lay in wait" (65), implying that she anticipates, desires even, Beowulf's incursion into her home, and that she waits for him as would a predatory animal (a wolf, perhaps?) that has set a trap for its prey.[13] Further, Hervey retains one of Jones's significant modifications to the battle sequence between Grendel's mother and Beowulf. In the poem, the victorious warrior departs the underwater hall with two trophies: the hilt of the giants' sword and Grendel's severed head. In Jones's and Hervey's texts, though, Beowulf takes Grendel's mother's head, rather than Grendel's, back to the surface as his battle trophy.[14] This act confirms her formidable nature, and signifies her elevated status as an opponent. The decapitated head is, after all, the key signifier of the hero's success, and his decapitation of the enemy transfers any power or meaning it had to himself.[15]

Yet despite her reliance upon Jones's narrative, Hervey renders the story her own in several significant ways. One of the most striking edits she makes is the drastic elimination of almost all instances of direct speech, a crucial element of the original poem and Jones's text alike.[16] Only a mere 16 per cent (440 words) of Hervey's tale relays direct speech. Wealtheow and Hrothgar, for instance, speak only once each. Wealtheow congratulates Beowulf during the gift-giving scene after his defeat of Grendel, highlighting his success and resultant fame. As she endows the warrior with a jewel-encrusted ring and a lavishly decorated robe, she tells him, "Enjoy these well-earned gifts, dear warrior, for thou hast cleansed the mead-hall of the realm; and for thy prowess fame shall gather to thee wide as the inrolling sea that comes from all the corners of the world to circle round our windy walls" (63). While Jones similarly minimizes the queen's presence and links her primarily with cup-bearing and gift-giving, Hervey limits her presence to this single scene, rendering her almost incidental to the narrative. She exists only to highlight Beowulf's accomplishments.

Hrothgar's speech occurs after Grendel's mother's attack on Heorot and the murder of Æschere. He briefly bemoans the loss of his beloved retainer, but quickly moves on to the attacker, exclaiming, "who shall say whose blood this new wolf-fiend shall glut herself with?" (64). Hrothgar's choice of the word "glut" suggests that he believes or expects Grendel's mother to be as carnivorous as her son, and the word itself evokes excessive hunger and satiation.[17] The expectation is that she will be as gluttonous as Grendel in her desire for human flesh and blood. The king then describes the corrupt space Grendel's mother occupies and beseeches Beowulf to avenge their loss. Significantly absent from Hervey's tale (yet present in her source, as in the original) is Hrothgar's famous speech to Beowulf on the sin of pride. This omission suggests that Hervey interprets the warrior as flawless, and reinforces the characterization of him that she carries through from Jones, as a being divinely wrought.

Beowulf himself has only three short speeches, but all three reinforce his characterization: upon his arrival at Heorot, he outlines his successes against previous foes; after Hrothgar's description of Grendel's mother's home, he declares that he will undertake the second task and that those with justice on their side should not concern themselves with fate; and, after his defeat of Grendel's mother, he confirms that Heorot is once again safe. His final speech has particular significance for Hervey's adaptation. In Jones's text, after identifying his victory as God-given, Beowulf tells Hrothgar, "Wherefore fear not King Hrothgár, for thou and thine may sleep secure in Heorot" (391). Hervey, however, expands this line to "thou and thy counsellors and thy warriors, and *thy children and thy children's children*, shall sleep in safety and in peace in Heorot" (66, emphasis added). Her inclusion of generations of children here evokes the title of the volume within which her story sits, and points towards her intended younger readers.[18] The addition is a clear marker for readers with previous knowledge of the tale that her version has a specific purpose connected to its audience. Overall, then, although heavily reduced, the extant examples of direct speech draw attention to the protagonist and female antagonist, reinforcing their established prowess and alterity, respectively, while simultaneously highlighting the uniqueness of Hervey's text in relation to other adaptations.

The reduction of Wealtheow's role and voice in the text serves another purpose, too, for it increases the narrative's amplification of the female antagonist. Hervey reverses Jones's focus on the male antagonist, giving considerably more narrative space to Grendel's mother than to her son.[19] Combined, the passages concerning the second attack on Heorot and the underwater battle between Beowulf and Grendel's mother are more than double the length of the passages on Grendel, and, if one includes Hrothgar's initial speech in which he describes Grendel's mother and her home, this variance increases.[20] Hervey also modifies the scene in which Grendel's mother enters Heorot and seizes Æschere. Jones outlines how she snatches the Dane and "tare him in his sleep" (389), but Hervey includes an extra word – "piecemeal" – which specifically evokes the idea of separating a whole into smaller, "separate pieces," often slowly and sometimes for the purpose of ingestion.[21] Such additions draw the reader's attention to the predatory behaviour and unnatural acts in which these border-walkers engage, especially the devouring of human flesh and blood, and the emphasis here on this devouring nature resonates in Hrothgar's use of the word "glut." While these characterizations may be present in the original poem and in Jones's text, Hervey foregrounds them, rendering the female antagonist – the most prominent female figure of the narrative – a more gruesome foe.[22]

This amplification inextricably links to Beowulf's prowess, as the heightened ferocity of Grendel's mother increases the status of the protagonist. More importantly, Beowulf's battle against Grendel's mother, in Hervey's tale, is also the climax of the tale, and contributes to Hervey's reworking of her source's ending. While Jones's version is reduced, it retains the last section of the original poem in which Beowulf returns home and eventually faces his demise in battle against the dragon. It also concludes with a passage highly evocative of the poem's closing lines, when it describes the warrior-king as "most gracious to his people and the most jealous for glory" (398).[23] In short, Jones's text includes both the death of the hero and the complex closing lines that gesture to his fallible nature and link back to Hrothgar's speech concerning pride.

Hervey's decision to end the story after the defeat of Grendel's mother thus sets her version apart from her source, providing for her readers a story in which the life, strength, and power of the hero persist. The elimination of the final sequence reshapes the protagonist as a figure of perpetual victory rather than presenting him as a glorious figure who eventually, like his pagan culture, succumbs to decline. The link here to Beowulf's origins is key, for Hervey takes steps in several places in the tale to diminish his pagan past. Much like the original poem, Jones's tale highlights Beowulf's illustrious lineage. His version describes the warrior as "a thane, kinsman to Hygelác the Geátish chief, and nobly born, being son of Ecgtheow the Wægmunding, a war prince who wedded with the daughter of Hrethel the Geát" (384). Similarly, when Hrothgar first sights Beowulf, the narrative reinforces familial connections: "Hrothgar looked upon the Geátish warriors, chief of whom Hygelác's servant, the mighty son of Ecgtheow, towered tall above the rest" (385). Beowulf's social and familial identities are absent in Hervey's text, and while she notes that he is a war prince (thus shifting this description of Ecgtheow onto his son), she places greater emphasis on his connection to divine power and his role as an instrument of God.

Moreover, Hervey's text bears no religious ambiguities of the original poem, some of which even Jones maintains in his descriptions of the Danes, Geats, and their cultures.[24] Hervey's text at no point makes any allusion to the narrative's complex interlacement of aspects of Christian and pagan faiths, and never once suggests that a pagan past exists. Hervey goes so far as to remove Beowulf's instructions to Hrothgar on what to do with his body and his mail coat should he fall, simultaneously eliminating the possibility that he might not succeed along with the reference to Weland the Smith, the ambiguous figure with ties to Norse mythology whom Beowulf identifies as the maker of his mail coat.[25] The removal of the reference to Weland suggests that Hervey wishes to eradicate even the slightest suggestion that her hero might have roots in a pagan past. What remains are a character and culture grounded wholly in Western monotheism.

Hervey also subverts what Marijane Osborn identifies as the original poem's distinctions between the "heroic and cosmic frames" that divide the secular world of the poem from the Christian world of its audience, for her hero has access to scriptural history that his predecessor does not.[26] When Beowulf explains to Hrothgar that he achieved victory over Grendel's mother because he "wrested away the sword wherewith the giants before the Flood defied Eternal God" (66), he demonstrates his biblical knowledge. No narratorial interpretation is needed; he already recognizes the diluvian history inscribed upon it.[27] His link to God thus grants him greater wisdom than those he protects. Further, this evocation of the Old Testament narrative concerning God's eradication of the giants becomes a parallel for Beowulf's defeat of Grendel and his mother. Beowulf is equal to the flood itself, purging Heorot of its ills. Wealtheow's earlier albeit limited speech now takes on greater meaning, especially when the protagonist declares that he has "cleansed" Heorot, echoing the queen's choice of verb after the first battle.

Beowulf and Wealtheow's words about cleansing, of eradicating the non-normative other, link both the hero and the hall explicitly to notions of racial purity and national security, the latter especially through the return of the hall to the centre of society. Hervey ends her tale with the feast scene in Heorot that follows Beowulf's defeat of Grendel's mother, describing a world restored to order and the promise of stability: "Then was there great joy in Heorot, the shining palace. And when Night with her dusky mantle covered the land, the warriors laid them down in peace and safety beneath the lofty arches rich with gold. No foe came more near that lordly dwelling-place; for Heorot was fully purged" (66–7). These lines cement the idea of cleansing through the final word "purged" and simultaneously recall the tale's opening, in which the narrator describes how Heorot will provide for the Danes and their children "for ever" (57), as well as Beowulf's remark to Hrothgar that he has secured the hall for future generations. Coupled with the elision of the dragon sequence, these features suggest that Hervey positions her narrative in a kind of stasis. Heorot returns to its former glory and promise of sustenance, security, and permanence now that the monstrous and pagan other has been overcome, a condition of peaceful perpetuity if you will, but this condition lacks the progression or futurity of the original poem or even of her source text.

Hervey ultimately, then, renders her hero a floating signifier, one she can appropriate and redefine as a figure that epitomizes a specific type of masculinity, one informed by Christian values. In doing so, she participates in a popular understanding of English heritage, one that returns to the past in order to construct a cohesive "national character" that unites society in the present.[28] Indeed, such a return provides a myth of racial and cultural continuity that appealed greatly to Victorians. The values perpetuated through Anglo-Saxonism, especially through retellings of *Beowulf*, confirmed the quality of the nation.[29] As Clare A. Simmons notes, "By the 1850s it was frequently claimed that the virtues of the modern-day English, such as truth, courage, justice, and simplicity, were inherited through their Saxon blood."[30] Connecting contemporary society to a historical (purified) race and culture created the illusion of stability and continuity that countered the turbulence not only of industrial change but also of social change and international conflict that characterized the century. It also contributed to the justification of expansionist military activities.[31] According to Anna Smol, in one broad stroke, the alignment of Victorian culture with a reimagined past demonstrated that despite the Norman conquest, the "Anglo-Saxon" spirit persisted, while Beowulf, as a martial figure, "illustrates the qualities of strength and bravery that were being glorified for future soldiers of the Empire."[32] Hervey's Beowulf, then, is a more ideal or more appropriate figure for her audience. In her version he retains the idealized qualities that appealed to the Victorians, but loses the pagan associations of his medieval predecessor. Further, the image of the restored medieval kingdom and the persistence of the hero offer reassurance to readers facing the major upheavals of their own time.

The most innovative aspect of Hervey's work, however, is her adaptation of the story specifically for younger readers. This is not to say that children were previously unexposed to or unfamiliar with *Beowulf*, but rather that no previous English edition or translation had clearly identified children as the target audience. Editions and translations of the Old English original appeared increasingly as the century progressed. Sharon Turner's *History of the Anglo-Saxons* (1805) brought the poem into literary and philological discussions, and, from there, it was taken up by scholars in Scandinavia, Germany, Great Britain, and the United States of America, with translations being made in Latin, Danish, and German, as well as English.[33] In 1826, J.J. Conybeare included selected passages, translated into English, in his *Illustrations of Anglo-Saxon Poetry*, but in 1837 John Kemble provided the first full-text English translation.[34] As R.M. Liuzza points out, "In the following decades the poem was translated a dozen times."[35] Occasionally, versions of the poem were serialized in newspapers, although more frequently versions of the poem were anthologized, appearing alongside other "medieval stories with introductions outlining current theories of epic, myth, or race," and Beowulf himself quickly gained status as "the original English role model."[36] Family reading practices often meant that mixed audiences engaged with texts, especially those published in periodicals.[37]

The possibility exists that some of Hervey's edits to her source have a relationship to one of these earlier, serialized versions. More specifically, they may in fact be influenced by Henry Morley's criticism of the Old English poem, which appears in the preamble to his own version of the tale, "A Primitive Old Epic," published in Dickens's *Household Words* in 1858.[38] Morley writes, "When told as we read it, in an Anglo-Saxon poem of more than six thousand lines, it was an ancient tale that, as many of its repetitions show, had often been sung *piecemeal* over the mead cup. Divested of much repetition, reduced in its scale, and shortened by omission of the introduced lays and digressions, the tale of Beowulf is in the next few pages told again."[39] The greatly reduced nature of Hervey's narrative suggests that the tale could indeed be responding to Morley's critique on what he sees as the unnecessary length of the original. Hervey renders the 3,182-line poem into a 2,746-word prose narrative driven by action. If nothing else, Hervey's pointed addition of the word "piecemeal" may signal a relationship between the texts, and such a relationship, while conjectural, is not improbable. For the decade of its publication (1850–9), *Household Words* was one of the most widely circulating and inexpensive periodicals, with "as many as 100,000 purchasers" and the low price of a tuppence.[40] Further, its contents, which often advocated for progressive social policies, resonated with issues similarly emphasized by another prominent publication, *The Athenaeum*, of which Hervey's husband Thomas Kibble Hervey was the editor from 1846 to 1853.[41] Given Hervey's immersion in a wide literary circle informed by progressive policies, it is likely that she knew Morley's adaptation and was possibly influenced by his wording.

As seen, Hervey's narrative draws upon Beowulf's identity as the pinnacle of just and heroic behaviour, and both her story and the larger text in which it appears emphasize these behaviours in their didacticism. She includes "The Fight with the Ogre" in *The Children of the Pear-Garden*, a Christmas book aimed at child readers. This collection of tales, much like the anthologies of heroes and myths aimed at older readers, places *Beowulf* in the midst of a number of tales about heroic mythological and historical figures, including King Arthur, Charlemagne, and Roland. The frame narrative's speaker, however, highlights the didactic purpose of the tales as she simultaneously draws a parallel between the household and the nation, and foregrounds the importance of history and empire.

The opening voice is that of Aunt Bertie, who presents herself as both caregiver and teacher, much like the Mother Goose figure prevalent in children's texts.[42] She introduces those in her charge to a ritual in which she and her siblings engaged as youth, but which reaches back generations in another culture and gestures to the volume's broader concerns with empire and its overt Orientalism. They gather in the orchard, she tells her students, much like the children of the Pear Garden, those who participated in an ancient Chinese festival in which children gathered to recite "wonderful stories ... in a pavilion ... under the pear-trees in the royal orchard" (5). The festival, she explains, was an event organized by Emperor Sing-Song to honour his Empress Yungk-Wifie, as a reward "for her devotion and constancy" (4). Aunt Bertie also explains that the Empress embodies the quality all good rulers share: they are, she says, "those who have learned that to be entirely happy they must be as industrious as the very humblest of their subjects" (4).

The mocking names of the Emperor and Empress (cringeworthy and offensive for modern readers) belie their playful tone, and also the more ideologically serious program of Orientalism of Hervey's text and frame narrative, which draw upon the traditions and origins of Chinese opera, positioning Britain as the contemporary equivalent of an ancient empire as Aunt Bertie and the children engage in a type of "orientalist entertainment."[43] The title, *Children of the Pear-Garden*, is a direct reference to a Chinese term that identifies opera actors, as well as the story of the early schools in which they trained. Both thrived especially under the rule of T'ang Dynasty emperor Ming Huang (685–762), who became known as "The Brilliant Emperor" because he "established a college known as the 'Pear Garden,' or *Li Yuan* ... where hundreds of young men were trained as vocalists, musicians, and dancers."[44] An elaborate mythology comprises part of the college's history, and details the Emperor's celestial travels along with the entertainments he created "to amuse his favorite concubine, the famed Yang Keui-fe."[45] Hervey draws explicitly upon this mythology. First, in the opening sequence of *Children of the Pear-Garden*, Aunt Bertie relays to her audience another myth she claims has a Chinese heritage, the story of magpies, who join wings on the seventh day of the seventh month to "form a long bridge [and] completely span the Milky-Way" (3). The celestial references here recall the stories of Ming Huang's own supposed journey to the moon. Further, the similarity of the beloveds' names (wife or mistress) in both accounts suggests that Hervey was indeed familiar with the origins of the Pear Garden and Chinese opera. Ming Huang's concubine Yang Keui-fe sounds suspiciously like "Yungk-Wifie," while the Emperor's name is of itself a suggestion of his connection to the school.

The use of an ancient Chinese festival and figures is not out of step with Victorian sensibilities.[46] Creating a parallel between the cultures, but one in which British culture is imagined as progressive and Chinese culture is imagined as stagnant, contributes to the justification of military incursions and imperialism. A link between *Beowulf* and such forms of Orientalism was well established by the time Hervey undertook her project, and it was quite pronounced in her source text. As John Hill notes, a connection between the Old English poem and Orientalism surfaces as early as Conybeare's *Illustrations of Anglo-Saxon Poetry*, in which he draws parallels between early English and classical and/or Eastern literary traditions (the elision between classical and Eastern cultures was common), and in which Indo-European migrations are understood as the root of philological connections between Sanskrit and

Germanic languages.[47] G.W. Cox's introductory material on *Beowulf* in *Popular Romances in the Middle Ages* similarly participates in this trend, identifying the foe Beowulf fights as akin to the enemies of light in the Sanskrit tradition, and identifying the hero himself as "a counterpart of the great son of Alkmênê," that is, of Heracles, son of Alcmene and Zeus.[48] Hervey, then, participates in a literary technique prevalent in her period.[49] Through Aunt Bertie, she links orchard, household, and empire, as their small orchard and storytelling community of siblings emulates the royal garden and household of her story. The ideas of continuity and tradition become significant parts of their activity, and the present storytelling becomes a reward for good behaviour. Aunt Bertie also suggests that this good behaviour is required (and rewarded) at the household level as well as at the national level. To be a good member of society is to be a good member of one's family, and both practices require industry and humility.[50]

The link between past and present surfaces again through Aunt Bertie's explanation of how the storytelling will proceed, and how it emulates her own childhood experiences. The group of storytellers from her past are, in fact, the namesakes of the children gathered around her, and they, like those at her feet, took turns telling tales. The current children – Dick, Sophy, Roderic, Ernest, Mary, and Lucy – all deliver one or two stories each, while Old Corney, another household member, tells an additional tale. Aunt Bertie positions Roderic as the authority figure:

> Then there was my eldest brother, Roderic, who, upon my word, my dears, was very well named, for he ruled us with a rod of iron; and whom you, Roderic, are called after. He had a queer fancy that the world was growing old, losing its strength and vigour, and that we were all weaklings together. His great delight was in stories of long ago, which he would have it were full of pith and marrow, bone and muscle, like the people that lived and told them centuries ago. He loved, too, stories of magic. (6)

Bertie thus identifies Roderic's namesake, and by extension Roderic, as the leader of the group. The original Roderic's interest in stories, particularly stories that valourize the past and highlight strength of body and spirit – here aligned with strength of culture – operates as an exemplum for the current group of children and suggests that these stories should inspire them to return to the values and behaviours outlined within. The emphasis on Roderic as leader reinforces patriarchal structures – thus countering the feminized (Orientalist) frame and narrative voice (Aunt Bertie) – as it simultaneously draws attention to the tales he tells, stories of two of the greatest warriors in literature, Beowulf and Charlemagne, who epitomize the masculine behaviours that uphold patriarchal systems. It suggests that the other children, and thus readers, should pay particular attention to these stories.

Ultimately, Aunt Bertie inextricably links the history of one's family to notions of empire, just rule, and appropriate behaviour at home and in society. More importantly, "The Fight with the Ogre" offers its primary audience of child readers a moral and behaviour model. The story establishes the past as an example for proper conduct in the present, and teaches readers that if they are good Christians, God will reward them for their faith; that they should honour and protect their superiors; and that they should protect society from destructive, deviant beings. Bravery, courage, and steadfastness – all qualities Hervey's Beowulf displays – are qualities to emulate.

Hervey thus exemplifies, at an even earlier date, trends that have been recognized in later adaptations for children of *Beowulf*: a reduced or simplified narrative; an action-driven story structured around the hero's battles with his enemies; a moralization of the tale that foregrounds the desired behaviours the protagonist epitomizes; an emphasis on history and heritage, and the notion of racial superiority; continuity from the past to the present through both race and empire; and the importance of Christian piety in one's life and actions. Smol points to these characteristics, for example, in her study of later adaptations by Henrietta E. Marshall, *Stories of Beowulf, Told to the Children* (1908); Thomas Cartwright, *Brave Beowulf* (1908); and John Harrington Cox, *Beowulf: The Anglo-Saxon Epic, Translated and Adapted for School Use* (1910);[51] Smol concludes that "*Beowulf* could be seen as a guide to and justification for behavior" by writers who "believed that they could 'make heroes in the present'" through their adaptation of the poem.[52]

Hervey especially foreshadows Andrew Lang's later division of the narrative into two separate tales in his *Red Book of Animal Stories*: "The Story of Beowulf, Grendel, and Grendel's Mother," which covers Beowulf's battles against Grendel and his mother; and "The Story of Beowulf and the Fire Drake," which covers the warrior's fatal battle against the dragon.[53] Lang's decision to break the narrative between the second and third battle episodes raises the question of whether or not he was aware of and/or influenced by Hervey's decision to emphasize only the fights against Grendel and Grendel's mother. Additionally, his inclusion of these tales in a volume of animal stories rather than in, say, the later volumes *The Red Book of Heroes* (1909) or *The Book of Saints and Heroes* (1912) also suggests that he follows the narratorial patterns of both fully dehumanizing and foregrounding the antagonists.[54] Quite possibly, Hervey's tale likewise influenced Mary Augusta Ward's version, which similarly employs a storytelling frame narrative (with oral tales told to children as entertainment on a rainy day) and places greater emphasis on the first two battle sequences between Beowulf and Grendel and then Grendel's mother. While Ward's adaptation includes information of the hero's demise in battle against the dragon, this section of the narrative appears as an afterthought to the larger narrative, brought up in dialogue between the characters. It is heavily condensed and separated from the larger story.[55]

Another aspect of early Beowulf adaptations for children that has been fruitfully explored is the "bibliographic code" of the volumes in which the stories appear. In an examination of Cartwright's *Brave Beowulf*, Marshall's *Stories*, and A.J. Church's "The Story of Beowulf" (1898), Lise Jaillant argues that "the heroic and nationalistic ideology of these early versions is anchored in ... typefaces, bindings, book design, page format and layout, and other aspects of a book which give physical information about it."[56] Material elements of Hervey's work participate in such a bibliographic code that likewise reinforces the volume's message and, as with the thematic and rhetorical strategies we have seen, provide an earlier example of the bibliographic code that has been associated with the Edwardian editions.

Early editions of *Children of the Pear-Garden* had plain cloth covers blocked in blind; the one used for this study is blue, with the title and the Home Circle Library logo blocked in gold.[57] The design recalls that of a stained glass window, with inset frames decorated with flowers and vines. The spine is similarly decorated, and includes a miniature engraving – a young girl sitting on a bench below a tree – taken from the frontispiece image, *The Pear Tree*. Beneath the engraving, the spine notes that the volume is also "Illustrated," signalling to potential buyers and/or readers that its contents, like the cover, are embellished.[58] Within, elaborate headers and footers bookend each chapter. At the start of each section appears a bar across the top of the page with images that interlace animals and foliage, again in a style highly evocative of medieval art, especially tapestry. At the close appears a foliated lintel-like image, much like what one might see atop a cathedral column. The primary title of each tale ("Roderic's Tale" or "Sophy's Tale," for example) is printed in Black Gothic. The physical appearance of the volume thus reinforces the emphasis on the past presented in its contents, while the publication of the book at Christmas further asserts its worth as an artefact of value and Christian symbolism.

Hervey's "Roderic's Tale: The Fight with the Ogre," considered in its rich and complex context, participates in the well-established tradition of literary adaptations of the Victorian period. More specifically, its medievalism, greatly concerned with issues of heroism and martial endeavours, racial purity, and nation and empire, reflects dominant tendencies of its time and place. Given that Hervey's tale is likely the earliest *Beowulf* adaptation in English specially created for child readers, it deserves our attention. While Hervey's text is greatly influenced by its sources, it likewise may have influenced subsequent tales, and it most certainly anticipates many features of the turn-of-the-century explosion of children's versions of *Beowulf*.

Coda: A Bibliographic Mystery

In an essay concerned with the incompletely documented beginnings of children's *Beowulf* adaptations, perhaps it is appropriate to end with a bibliographic mystery raised by my work on Hervey, in hopes that some reader will be able to solve it.

Although marketed as an illustrated volume, *Children of the Pear-Garden* includes only four images: the frontispiece discussed above, an image for "Old Corney's Tale: The Fortunes of Penro," an image for Roderic's version of *Beowulf*, and an image for "Mary's Tale: Holy of the Golden Hair," the last of which was created by Walter Crane.[59] The illustration that accompanies "The Fight with the Ogre" is of particular interest as it problematizes a reading of Hervey's tale as especially emphasizing and increasing the dehumanization of Grendel. It appears as an insert between pages 58 and 59 and is titled *The Ogre of the Marshes* (see fig. 2.1).[60] This image greatly contrasts the gruesome description of Grendel found within the tale.[61] It certainly is not what one would expect for a depiction of a cannibalistic ogre. Instead, the pen and ink image shows a distinctly human, if oversized, male figure, lying asleep in an open field, his head resting on a hillock, with his arms relaxed, one across his stomach and the other at his side. The profile of a tree in the far right corner, which appears diminutive in contrast, emphasizes his gargantuan physique. The juxtaposition of this peaceful image with the text's descriptions of Grendel creates a tension that harks back to the blurred boundaries of the original text and certainly – through visual signs – evokes the Old English poem's identification of Grendel and his mother as descendants of Cain. Even the use of the word "ogre" in the image title (as well as the story title) reinforces this tension, as it fits Hervey's repeated use of the words "Jötun" and "ogre" to describe Grendel. The image, then, while maintaining a link between Hervey's version and the original poem, simultaneously reduces the threat of Grendel's character, rendering him visually as less terrifying or monstrous than the text suggests.

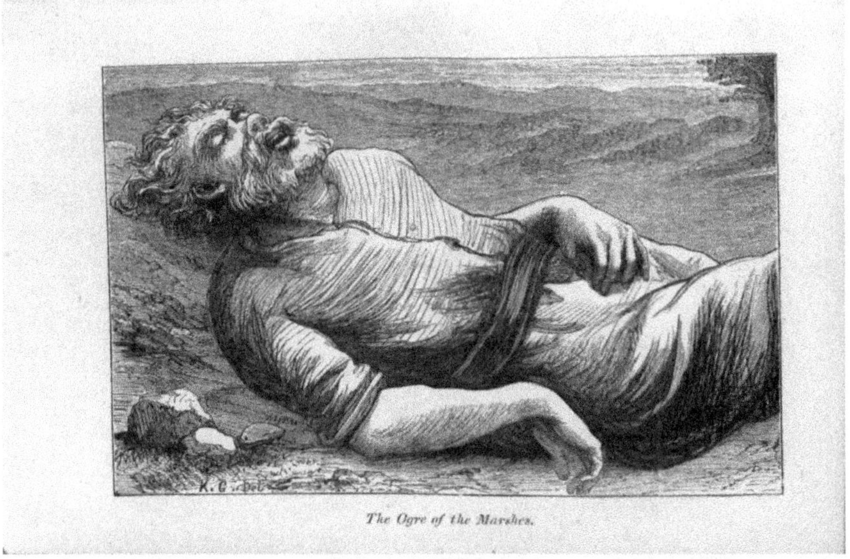

Figure 2.1. *The Ogre of the Marshes*, by Kate Greenaway, from Hervey, *The Children of the Pear-Garden*, facing p. 58.

The inclusion of the image presents a conundrum, as its known provenance does not align with the publication dates of Hervey's text. A number of reviews and advertisements confirm the initial publication date of *Children of the Pear-Garden* as 1873. The volume appears, for instance, under the "List of New Books" in the 25 October 1873 issue of *The Athenaeum* and was listed as published in the 1873 *Supplement to Allibone's Critical Dictionary of English*.[62] In late January 1874, *The Athenaeum* also printed a highly favourable review of the text.[63] Unfortunately, the only internationally catalogued copies of the volume, including the copy held by the British Library upon which this discussion is based, all list a date of 1878,[64] but this date is not a publication date. The British Library's copy has two identical stamps, examples of Type 2, Figure 2 of their stamping records: both stamps are oval in shape, note that the volume is property of the British Museum, and include an *acquisition date* of 14 February 1878.[65] So, the copy of Hervey's tale upon which this discussion rests was published in or after late 1873 but sometime before early 1878. This is likely true of the other two copies held in special collections – one at the University of Liverpool library, the other at the University of Leicester library – as

Figure 2.2.   "The giant lay sleeping on the ground," by Kate Greenaway, from Zimmern, *Tales from the Edda*, frontispiece.

their volumes are identical to that held by the British Library and were dated according to the latter's catalogue.[66]

The key feature of the image is the signature, which appears in the lower left corner of the frame and states "K. G. ~del." That is, Kate Greenaway "drew" this picture. As Greenaway's biographer Rodney Engen records, this specific image appears in fuller form in a text by the German-born author and translator Helen Zimmern (1846–1934), specifically in her 1882 volume, *Tales from the Edda*, where it was titled "The giant lay sleeping on the ground" (see fig. 2.2).[67] Further, Thomas E. Schuster and Engen, in *Printed Kate Greenaway*, list the 1882 publication of Zimmern's volume as a "first edition,"[68] and the contextual evidence suggests that Greenaway did indeed prepare the image with that text in mind. There, it appears as an illustration for the story "How Thor Was Deceived by the Giants," which recounts the journey of Thor and Loki to Jötunheim, their encounters with the giant Skrymir, the giant's trickery, and Thor's repeated attacks, with his hammer Mjolnir, upon the sleeping giant.[69] The full image in Zimmern's text reveals, in the right-hand corner of the frame, the figure of Thor, his mighty hammer raised just prior to one of his attacks upon Skrymir. A comparison of the two images reveals that the version included in Hervey's text is actually a cropped version of the larger image in Zimmern's text. Therein lies the conundrum. How does an image, noted by scholars as created for a text originally published in 1882, make its way into a text published sometime between 1873 and early 1878?

Perhaps Zimmern's text had an original publication date that precedes the noted 1882 publication with Swan and Sonnenschein, but this seems unlikely given the amount of scholarship extant on Greenaway and her works. If such a volume or earlier illustration exists, it has not yet been noted. The only other possible explanations for the dating issue would be that the dating of Hervey's text, which includes the image, is incorrect, or that Kate Greenaway's image was not initially created for Zimmern's text, and appeared in another, earlier volume (whether it be Hervey's text or another collection of Northern tales). The first scenario is highly unlikely given the evidence of the printed reviews and the acquisition stamps. It is also unlikely that Hervey herself had any connection to the appearance of this specific image in her volume, so I doubt the tension created by the juxtaposition of the image to text derives from authorial intent. As Lorraine Janzen Kooistra indicates, publishers and engravers, rather than artists or poets, typically managed gift book production, and the division of labour required for their production typically meant that only in rare instances did an author and artist collaborate in order to create a shared vision of the final product.[70] In most instances, poets would not see the illustrations included alongside their works "until the book was published."[71] Given the extensive control publishers had over gift book production, my suspicion is that the image has an earlier creation date than 1882 (for either another as-yet-unidentified text or for an earlier version of a work by Zimmern) and was repurposed by the publisher for Hervey's text.[72] This is an issue, then, that requires further investigation, and one modern readers should keep in mind when considering how they (and even perhaps how contemporary audiences) would or should interpret this image's inclusion in the volume.

NOTES

1 Support for this essay was provided by the Wilfrid Laurier University Faculty of Arts Research Support Grant, the University of Lincoln's College of Arts' Research Resources Allocation Fund (RRAF) and Research Leave Schemes, and the British Library.

2 Alan Lupack and Barbara Tepa Lupack use this expression to describe numerous female writers "who never achieved canonical status or whose

Arthurian works, by deviating from convention, place them outside the main tradition" (Lupack and Lupack, eds., *Arthurian Literature by Women* [New York: Garland, 1999], 3). They include Hervey in this category because of her innovative retelling of the Tristan and Iseult story in *King Arthur's Court; or, The Feasts of Camelot: With the Tales That Were Told There* (1863; reprinted 1877). The full text of Hervey's Arthurian collection is available at *The Camelot Project* published by the Robbins Library, University of Rochester: http://d.lib.rochester.edu/camelot/text /ward-hervey-feasts-of-camelot. I wish to thank Alan Lupack for introducing me to Hervey's Arthurian text, and for his continued support of my research on Hervey's corpus. Without his work, this study would not exist.

3 In addition to her innovative take on the Tristan and Iseult story and her adaptation of *Beowulf*, Hervey wrote, for instance, two progressive and proto-feminist adaptations of the medieval Griselda story, for adult and child readers, respectively; see Renée Ward, "Giving Voice to Griselda: Radical Reimaginings of a Medieval Tale," *Studies in Medievalism* 26 (2017): 87–116.

4 Key studies of medievalism – Victorian and modern – include those by Alice Chandler, *A Dream of Order: The Medieval Ideal in Nineteenth-Century English Literature* (Lincoln: University of Nebraska Press, 1971); Michael Alexander, *Medievalism: The Middle Ages in Modern England* (New Haven, CT: Yale University Press, 2007); Clare Broom Saunders, *Women Writers and Nineteenth-Century Medievalism* (New York: Palgrave Macmillan, 2009); Velma Bourgeois Richmond, *Chivalric Stories as Children's Literature: Edwardian Retellings in Words and Pictures* (Jefferson, NC: McFarland, 2014) and *Chaucer as Children's Literature: Retellings from the Victorian and Edwardian Eras* (Jefferson, NC: McFarland, 2004); Elizabeth Emery and Richard Utz, eds., *Medievalism: Key Critical Terms* (Woodbridge, Suffolk: D.S. Brewer, 2014); David Williams, *Medievalism: A Critical History* (Woodbridge, Suffolk: D.S. Brewer, 2015); and Louise D'Arcens, ed., *The Cambridge Companion to Medievalism* (Cambridge: Cambridge University Press, 2016).

5 "Roderic's Tale: The Fight with the Ogre," *The Children of the Pear-Garden and Their Stories* (London: Frederick Warne and Co., 1873). Citations will be parenthetical.

6 George W. Cox and Eustace Hinton Jones, *Popular Romances of the Middle Ages* (London: Longmans, Green, and Co., 1871). Jones collaborated on the volume but Cox contributed the bulk of the content: according to the preface, Jones contributed "the stories of Merlin, Tristrem, Bevis, Guy of Warwick, Roland, Olger, Havelock and Beowulf" (vii). The volume's contents suggest an adult readership, even a critical readership, as the first eighty pages offer detailed histories and discussions of the tales. The table

of contents for the prefatory material (two full pages) also outstrips the section that lists the tales themselves (one page). A volume for younger readers would be unlikely to include such an extensive introduction.

7 Henry Morley, "A Primitive Old Epic," *Household Words* 17 (1 May 1858): 459–64.

8 Hervey's corpus suggests she has a specific interest in female figures, and she reworks several medieval narratives with this concern in mind. Her revisions of the Griselda story and her focus on Grendel's mother suggest that she has an interest especially in mothers, a detail likely connected to her own status as a single parent after the death of her husband in 1859.

9 The feature of the retained editorial accents suggests that despite the younger audience targeted by *Children of the Pear-Garden*, Hervey is cognizant of the double readership of children's literature and therefore retains an aspect of her source that would speak to more sophisticated readers, those familiar with various editions of the original poem.

10 These episodes or digressions are substantial. In the Old English poem, the story of Sigemund, for instance, occupies ll. 867–915 and the battle at Finnsburh ll. 1063–1158. *Beowulf* is cited from R.D. Fulk, Robert E. Bjork, and John D. Niles, eds., *Klaeber's Beowulf*, 4th ed. (Toronto: University of Toronto Press, 2008), and translations given from R.M. Liuzza, trans., *Beowulf*, 2nd ed. (Peterborough, ON: Broadview, 2013).

11 In the Old English poem, Grendel is linked to humanity by being identified repeatedly (e.g., ll. 104b–7a and 1265b–66b) as a descendant of Cain, the progenitor of fratricide. Extensive debates exist about the poem's references to Cain/Cam and about how to read authorial or scribal intent in the emendations to the manuscript, but agreement exists that Grendel (and his mother) are both somehow connected to Cain and his progeny. See, for example, Leonard Neidorf, "Cain, Cam, Jutes, Giants, and the Textual Criticism of *Beowulf*," *Studies in Philology* 112 (2015): 608; T.A. Shippey, "The Case of Beowulf," *European Studies* 26 (2008): 223–39; Andy Orchard, *Pride and Prodigies: Studies in the Monsters of the Beowulf Manuscript* (Cambridge: D.S. Brewer, 1995), 58–85; and Ruth Mellinkoff, "Cain's Monstrous Progeny in *Beowulf*, Part I: Noachic Tradition," *Anglo-Saxon England* 8 (1979): 143–62, and "Cain's Monstrous Progeny in *Beowulf*, Part II: Post-Diluvian Survival," *Anglo-Saxon England* 9 (1980): 183–97.

12 Given Hervey's heavy use of Jones's text, when the material is closely related I cite only her tale. Here, Hervey writes, "But far off in the deep darkness where dwell the Jötuns, and Orks, and Giants which war with God, there abode a mighty evil spirit, a Jötun terrible and grim, called Grendel, who haunted the marshes and dank and fenny places" (58). Her retention of not one but three evil races (Jötuns, Orks, and Giants) is another sign of her awareness of the diversity of her potential audience;

that is, she anticipates at least some readers will be sophisticated enough to grapple with these categories. However, this list likewise reveals that Hervey (and Jones) may miss or be less concerned with the linguistic subtleties of the Old English poem: *Jötunn* is merely the Norse-derived form of the same word as OE *eoten* "giant."

13 This detail sharply contrasts the Old English text (see ll. 1292a–95b), where Grendel's mother's approach is stealthy, in hopes of sneaking into Heorot and retrieving her son's arm unnoticed. The attack on Æschere is reactionary, occurring only because she is startled and discovered.

14 This detail appears in later adaptations, suggesting that Jones's and Hervey's texts influenced the tale's transmission. For example, Thomas Cartwright's Edwardian version *Brave Beowulf* (illus. Patten Wilson [London: William Heinemann, 1908]) includes a lush illustration of the hero swimming to the mere's surface with Grendel's mother's head (opp. p. 57; the caption reads "Beowulf's return with Grendel's head," but Wilson's image clearly depicts the mother's).

15 Regina James explains that the severed head is important "for the sake of a power [it] confers and continues to possess even after it is severed, a power that can be appropriated, possessed, and transferred to the taker … [T]he head [is] a sign of the warrior's success relative to other warriors" (*Losing Our Heads: Beheadings in Literature and Culture* [New York: New York University Press, 2005], 15). On the significance of decapitation in medieval literature and culture, see further Larissa Tracy and Jeff Massey, eds., *Heads Will Roll: Decapitation in the Medieval and Early Modern Imagination* (Leiden: Brill, 2012).

16 In the original poem, "Upward of 1300 lines are devoted to speeches," which "serve to advance the action" (Fulk, Bjork, and Niles, *Klaeber's Beowulf*, lxxxvi–lxxxvii). Although Jones reduces direct speech, it still constitutes approximately 30% of his adaptation, or just under five full pages of the total sixteen. Texts geared towards younger readers typically have less direct speech overall.

17 The *Oxford English Dictionary Online* [*OEDO*] (www.oed.com, accessed 6 July 2019), s.v. *glut, v.1*, lists as definition 1.a., "To feed to repletion; to indulge (appetite) to the utmost)," and as 2.a., the figurative explanation, "To gratify to the full (in earlier use, a sense or appetite of any kind, now, esp., a ferocious or lustful desire)." Both understandings work, although in Hrothgar's mind the second is most fitting.

18 The original poem does not highlight children here, although Beowulf does suggest that "þegna gehwylc … / duguðe ond iogoþe" [every thane, young and old] may sleep in peace (ll. 1673a–74a).

19 In Jones's text, content on Grendel spans six pages, while content on his mother spans three.

20 Hrothgar's description of Grendel's mother and her home is 127 words,
    while the other two passages combined equal 459 words. In total, then,
    Hervey dedicates 586 words, or 21 per cent, of her narrative to the female
    antagonist, a sharp contrast to the 228 words, or 8 per cent, of the text ded-
    icated to Grendel.

21 See *OEDO*, s.v. *piecemeal, adv., n.,* and *adj.* (accessed 6 July 2017). Hervey's
    adjustment shifts the details found in the original poem of Grendel's
    cannibalistic attack upon Hondscio (ll. 741b–45a) to the episode with
    Grendel's mother, further increasing her ferocity.

22 Hervey also modifies passages concerning Grendel, even though he
    receives less narrative space than his mother. Jones, for instance, explains
    that Grendel invades Heorot to "prey" upon the Danes (383), but Hervey
    expands this passage, stating that Grendel is there "to feed like a beast
    of prey upon their carcases" (58). Likewise, her descriptions of Grendel's
    abduction of Danish warriors expands Jones's "[he] carried them away to
    slay and tear them" (384) to he "carried them away to slay and to feast on
    them" (58).

23 The original states, "cwædon þæt he wære wyruldcyninga / manna mild-
    est ond monðwærust, / leodum liðost ond lofgeornost" [they said that he
    was of all the kings of the world / the mildest of men and the most gentle,
    / the kindest to his folk and the most eager for fame] (ll. 3180a–82b).

24 The tension between pagan and Christian elements and/or origins
    of the Old English poem has been fertile ground for discussion and
    debate, although most modern scholars agree that the poet is Christian,
    albeit someone with respect for the pagan past. See, for example, M.B.
    McNamee, "*Beowulf*: An Allegory of Salvation?" *Journal of English and
    Germanic Philology* 59 (1960): 190–207; Charles Moorman, "The Essential
    Paganism of *Beowulf*," *Modern Language Quarterly* 28 (1967): 3–18; J.G.
    Ogilvy and Donald Baker, *Reading Beowulf* (Norman: University of
    Oklahoma Press, 1993), 180–1; Christine Fell, "Paganism in *Beowulf*:
    A Semantic Fairy-Tale," in *Pagans and Christians: The Interplay between
    Christian Latin and Traditional Germanic Cultures in Early Medieval Europe*,
    ed. T. Hofstra et al., *Mediaevalia Groningana* 16 (1995): 9–34; Fred C.
    Robinson, "The Language of Paganism in *Beowulf*: A Response to an
    Ill-Omened Essay," *Multilingua* 18, nos. 2–3 (1999): 173–84; and Andy
    Orchard, *A Critical Companion to Beowulf* (Woodbridge: Brewer, 2003),
    130–7.

25 Jones's text follows the Old English poem here, when Beowulf requests of
    Hrothgar, "send back to Hygelác the war-shroud which Wayland forged
    to guard my breast" (385). In the original, Beowulf describes his "beadu-
    scruda betst" [best battledress] (l. 453a) as "Welandes geweorc" [the work
    of Weland] (l. 455a). For more on Weland's complex and ambiguous

nature, see Janet B.T. Christie, "Reflections on the Legend of Wayland the Smith," *Folklore* 80, no. 4 (1969): 286–94; and James Bradley, "Sorcerer or Symbol? Weland the Smith in Anglo-Saxon Sculpture and Verse," *Pacific Coast Philology* 25, no. 1–2 (1990): 39–48.

26   See Marijane Osborn, "The Great Feud: Scriptural History and Strife in *Beowulf*," in *The Beowulf Reader*, ed. Peter S. Baker (New York: Garland, 2000), 112 [article orig. pub. 1978]. Osborn also notes that much of the heroic frame exists within the digressions concerning feuds that constitute a large portion of "the second half of the poem" (111). Hervey's extensive reductions of the text, then, drastically reduce this frame overall while simultaneously amplifying the cosmic one through the deification of Beowulf.

27   This detail comes from Jones, but Hervey's amplification of her hero's divine status make this detail play a greater role in her text.

28   Peter Mandler explains how, in the Victorian period, "history was now seen as central to a proper understanding of the national character and its propagation as a crucial glue for social and political cohesion" (*History and National Life* [London: Profile Books, 2002], 45).

29   For a brief history of the term "Anglo-Saxonism," see Allen J. Frantzen and John D. Niles, "Introduction: Anglo-Saxonism and Medievalism," in *Anglo-Saxonism and the Construction of Social Identity*, ed. Allen J. Frantzen and John D. Niles (Gainesville: University Press of Florida, 1997), 1–14; for a larger study of the term, see Allen J. Frantzen, *Desire for Origins: New Language: Old English, and Teaching the Tradition* (New Brunswick, NJ: Rutgers University Press, 1990).

30   Clare A. Simmons, "Anglo-Saxonism, the Future, and the Franco-Prussian War," *Medievalism in England II*, ed. Leslie J. Workman and Kathleen Verduin, *Studies in Medievalism* 7 (1995): 132.

31   As Andrew Sanders points out, for Victorians the medieval past justified contemporary action, and the present required a fitting past: "Because England, and by extension, Great Britain, had attained world power by 1848, therefore its history must prove right. The Norman Conquest of England has been undone by the conquest of the world by England ... Having been unwillingly forced into an alien empire it has responded by building an empire of its own in its own image" ("'Utter Indifference'?: The Anglo-Saxons in the Nineteenth-Century Novel," in *Literary Appropriations of the Anglo-Saxons from the Thirteenth to the Twentieth Century*, ed. Donald Scragg and Carole Weinberg [Cambridge: Cambridge University Press, 2000], 169).

32   Anna Smol, "Heroic Ideology and the Children's *Beowulf*," *Children's Literature* 22 (1994): 98.

33   A number of studies provide detailed accounts of *Beowulf*'s history as an edition or translation, in various periods and regions, the most

comprehensive being T.A. Shippey and Andreas Haarder, *Beowulf: The Critical Heritage* (London: Routledge, 1998). Other worthwhile studies include John Hill, "*Beowulf* Editions for the Ancestors: Cultural Genealogy and Power in the Claims of Nineteenth-Century English and American Editors and Translators," in *Constructing Nations, Reconstructing Myths: Essays in Honour of T.A. Shippey*, ed. Andrew Wawn, with Graham Johnson and John Walter (Turnhout: Brepols, 2007), 53–69; Shippey, "The Case of *Beowulf*"; J.R. Hall, "Anglo-Saxon Studies in the Nineteenth Century: England, Denmark, America," in *A Companion to Anglo-Saxon Literature*, ed. Philip Pulsiano and Elaine Treharne (Oxford: Blackwell, 2001), 434–54; and R.M. Liuzza, "Lost in Translation: Some Versions of *Beowulf* in the Nineteenth Century," *English Studies* 83 (2002): 281–95.

34 J.J. Conybeare, *Illustrations of Anglo-Saxon Poetry*, ed. William Daniel Conybeare (London: Harding & Lepard, 1826); John M. Kemble, *A Translation of the Anglo-Saxon Poem of Beowulf* (London: William Pickering, 1837).

35 Liuzza, "Lost in Translation," 286–7.

36 Smol, "Heroic Ideology and the Children's *Beowulf*," 90, 93.

37 Although readers of periodicals and newspapers were originally understood to be male, female and family readership increased as the century progressed, and publications responded accordingly through the inclusion first of sections dedicated to these readers and then through the creation of entire publications aimed at these audiences. For instance, family readership was expected for *The Family Economist* (1848–60), as it was much later for *The Home Circle* (1901–14), which published initially as *Home Sweet Home: A Journal of Stories & Pictures for Everybody* (1893–1901) and included a "crowded frontispiece" representing "every conceivable stage in family life" as participants in the reading process (Hilary Fraser, Stephanie Green, and Judith Johnston, *Gender and the Victorian Periodical* [Cambridge: Cambridge University Press, 2003], 59; for a detailed discussion of periodical readership, see esp. Fraser, Green, and Johnston's chapter 2, "The Gendered Reader," 48–76).

38 Critics previously identified John Earle as the author of this adaptation; more recently, Nicholas Howe convincingly attributed it to a staff writer for *Household Words*, Henry Morley (Howe, "*Beowulf* in the House of Dickens," in *Latin Learning and English Lore: Studies in Anglo-Saxon Literature for Michael Lapidge*, ed. Katherine O'Brien O'Keeffe and Andy Orchard, 2 vols. (Toronto: University of Toronto Press, 2005), 1:421–39.

39 Morley, "Primitive Old Epic," 459 (emphasis added). Morley's comment here about the length of the poem counts the a and b verses of each line as full lines. Most modern editions of the text recognize the poem's length as 3,182 lines.

40 Howe, "*Beowulf* in the House of Dickens," 422–3.
41 Howe notes that *Household Words* often included content advocating for
    "education, public health and sanitation, improved housing, municipal
    planning, prison reform, opposition to capital punishment, factory safety,
    and the rights of workers" ("*Beowulf* in the House of Dickens," 424). For
    more on the progressive politics of *The Athenaeum* and Hervey's literary
    community, see Ward, "Giving Voice to Griselda," 107–9.
42 The Mother Goose figure has long-standing traditions with fables, but
    in the nineteenth century becomes linked especially to children's litera-
    ture and to the pantomime tradition. See, for instance, Perry Nodelman,
    "The Nursery Rhymes of Mother Goose: A World without Glasses,"
    in *Touchstones: Reflections on the Best in Children's Literature*, ed. Perry
    Nodelman (West Lafayatte, IN: Scarecrow Press/Children's Literature
    Associaton, 1987), 183–201; Marina Warner, "Mother Goose Tales: Female
    Fiction, Female Fact?" *Folklore* 101, no. 1 (1990): 3–25; and Ryoji Tsurumi,
    "The Development of Mother Goose in Britain in the Nineteenth Century,"
    Folklore 101, no. 1 (1990): 28–35.
43 Drawing upon Edward Said's description of political and cultural con-
    structs of the "Orient" as "the distant and the exotic" or "the Asiatic East as
    a whole" (Said, *Orientalism* [New York: Pantheon Books, 1978], 74), Edward
    Ziter uses the term "orientalist entertainment" to describe entertainments
    especially in the Victorian period that exploited exoticized interpretations
    of the East (from northern Africa to Asia). He writes, "Throughout the
    nineteenth century, British audiences marveled at depictions of desert
    storms and harem dances as well as Nile steamers and colonial armies
    at theatres, panoramas, and exhibition rooms" (Ziter, *The Orient on the
    Victorian Stage* [Cambridge: Cambridge University Press, 2003], 3).
44 Josephine Huang Hung, "Introduction," in *Children of the Pear-Garden: Five
    Plays from the Chinese Opera*, trans. and ed. Josephine Huang Hung (Taipei:
    Heritage Press, 1961), 5.
45 Huang Hung, "Introduction," 6.
46 Jennifer L. Hargrave, for instance, notes that despite the repeated military
    conflicts between China and Britain during the nineteenth century – the
    Anglo-Chinese Wars, frequently referred to as the Opium Wars, spanned
    two significant periods of the nineteenth century, 1839–42 and 1856–60 –
    early Chinese culture was often considered to have provided "numerous
    cultural advancements" even if it had since become stagnant ("Romantic
    Pretexts: Victorian Literary Appropriations in Anglo-Sino Discourse,"
    Nineteenth-Century Contexts 37, no. 1 [2015]: 24).
47 Hill, "*Beowulf* Editions for the Ancestors," 59. John M. Ganim remarks
    that this connection originates with "Sir William Jones' reconstruction
    of Sanskrit" and suggests that "since the late eighteenth century, the

Medieval and the Orient have been paired, as aesthetic styles, as points
of linguistic origin, and, increasingly, as stages of cultural development"
(*Medievalism and Orientalism: Three Essays on Literature, Architecture and
Cultural Identity* [2005; Basingstoke: Palgrave Macmillan, 2008], 84–5).
Hervey's association of both the medieval and the Orient with children
and children's storytelling settings, along with her reduction of the names
of the Chinese figures to alliterative and homophonic names similar to
what one might expect in nursery rhymes, infantilizes the original narratives in a manner similar to what takes place when folk tales not originally
for children are assumed to be most appropriate for a child audience.
Amber Dunai's essay in this volume, for instance, explores J.R.R. Tolkien's
views on the conflation of fairy story with children's literature.

48 G.W. Cox, "Introduction," 78. An advertisement in the final pages of
Popular Romances in the Middle Ages reveals that Cox authored or edited
numerous texts on Greek, Persian, Latin, and other literary and cultural
traditions, including a volume on race: *The Mythology of the Aryan Nations*
(London: Longmans, Green & Co., 1870).

49 Hervey participates in Orientalism more explicitly through a larger volume of armchair travel in which she provides for the reader extensive
details of her time on "barbarian soil." See Mrs. Hervey, *The Adventures of a
Lady in Tartary, Thibet, China, and Kashmir*, 3 vols. (London: Hope and Co.,
1853); quoted phrase from 1.iv.

50 Aunt Bertie's descriptions of the children's namesakes echo details of the
Emperor and his wife. She tells her audience, for instance, that the Emperor
rewards "Yungk-Wifie" with the operatic celebrations for her steadfastness,
"devotion and constancy" (4), and then similarly emphasizes the "devotion
and self-sacrifice" of her nephew Dick (7).

51 Smol, "Heroic Ideology and the Children's *Beowulf*." See also Anna Smol,
"The Child, the Primitive, and the Medieval: Making Medieval Heroes
in the Nineteenth and Early Twentieth Centuries," in *The Hero Recovered:
Essays on Medieval Heroism in Honor of George Clark*, ed. Robin Waugh and
James Weldon (Kalamazoo, MI: Medieval Institute Publications, 2010),
208–27.

52 Smol, "Heroic Ideology and the Children's *Beowulf*," 98. Although Beowulf
was the pinnacle example, other early medieval exemplars appeared frequently in children's texts, including Hereward the Wake and King Alfred
the Great. See Velma Bourgeois Richmond, "Historical Novels to Teach
Anglo-Saxonism," in *Anglo-Saxonism and the Construction of Social Identity*,
ed. Allen J. Frantzen and John D. Niles (Gainesville: University of Florida
Press, 1997), 173–201.

53 Andrew Lang, ed., *The Red Book of Animal Stories* (London: Longmans,
Green, and Co., 1899).

54 Andrew Lang, ed., *The Red Book of Heroes by Mrs. Lang* (London: Longmans, Green, and Co., 1909) and *The Book of Saints and Heroes* (London: Longmans, Green, and Co., 1912).

55 See "Beowulf," in *Milly and Olly; Or, a Holiday among the Mountains* (London: Macmillan, 1881), 167–8.

56 Lise Jaillant, "'A Fine Old Tale of Adventure': *Beowulf* Told to the Children of the English Race, 1898–1908," *Children's Literature Association* 38 (Winter 2013): 400.

57 The version used for this study is held by the British Library. I base my assertion that early editions of Hervey's text were so embellished upon the various copies catalogued and held by UK libraries and upon the copy in my personal library, which is similarly blocked in blind, although the cloth cover is dark red rather than blue.

58 Hervey's text embodies standard publishing practices of the mid- to late century. Indeed, Ruari McLean describes the 1860s as "the greatest period of Victorian gift book design ... the climax of monochrome wood-engraved illustrations, when such books were actually planned and commissioned by the great wood-graving firms of Dalziel, Swain, and Evans. This was also the culmination of the gold-blocked cloth binding" (*Victorian Publishers' Book-Bindings in Cloth and Leather* [London: Gordon Fraser, 1974], 14).

59 The 1878-stamped edition of *Children of the Pear-Garden* does not make it clear that the artist responsible for the image accompanying "Mary's Tale" is Walter Crane, as the image is cropped so that the artist's signature is excluded. However, a posthumous and retitled reprint of the text includes the plate in full and reveals the signature in the lower right hand corner. See E.L. Hervey, *Told in the Orchard* (London: Frederick Warne, c. 1906). The date cited here is based upon the seller's dating of a copy of *Told in the Orchard* in my personal collection; the text itself does not include a publication date. However, the interior of the volume also includes a book plate and an inscription with the hand-written date of "Feb. 18th 1907." A similar copy listed on Ebay noted that a prize label on the interior included a date of 1904, so turn of the century or first decade of the century as a publication date is likely accurate.

60 The image presented here is from the British Library's copy of the text. My personal copy (and the first version of the image that I saw) has actually been coloured with what looks like felt-tip pens, presumably by a younger reader. Interestingly, this image is also the only image in my copy that has been treated this way, suggesting that it might have been of particular interest to the reader.

61 It was not uncommon for artists to create an image that did not precisely fit the narrative. In fact, many illustrators remained ignorant of the

material for which they created images. For instance, famous *Punch* illustrator Richard Doyle (1824–83) was notorious for ignoring the demands of the author, the tale, or even the printer, a habit which grew out of his early training at home, where his father encouraged the Doyle children to "draw from their own visual imaginations, and from memory." Likewise, Paul Gustave Doré (1832–83), who provided illustrations for Tennyson's *Idylls of the King*, has been criticized for never actually reading the poems for which he created works. See Juliet McMaster and Natalie McIntyre, "Introduction," in Richard Doyle, *Dick Doyle's Journal*, vol. 3, ed. Juliet McMaster, Amy Stafford, et al. (Sydney: Juvenilia Press, 2009), xv; and Barbara Tepa Lupack and Alan Lupack, *Illustrating Camelot* (Woodbridge, Boydell & Brewer, 2008), 17.

62 See "List of New Books," *The Athenaeum* 25 October 1873, issue 2400, p. 528, which lists Hervey's text as "Children of the Pear-Garden 12 mo. 2/cl"; and John Foster Kirk, *A Supplement to Allibone's Critical Dictionary of English Literature and British and American Authors*, 2 vols. (London: J.B. Lippincott Company, 1891), 2:814.

63 "[N]o other word than 'capital' is applicable to Mrs. Hervey's batch of stories called 'The Children of the Pear-Garden.' From the first page, in which we hear of the magpies gathering together once a year from all parts of the world, to the last, in which we are left uncertain whether the Emirs and Bashaws are still spinning round or have come to a stop, the interest does not cease. The prose is graceful and the flashes of poetry are such as might be expected from Mrs. Hervey's practised hand. Her name is among the names of story-tellers that will be dear to children" (review, *"The Children of the Pear-Garden, and their Stories*. By Eleanora Louisa Hervey – Messrs. Warne & Co," *The Athenaeum* no. 2414, 31 January 1874, 158). Given Hervey's status as the widow of *The Athenaeum*'s former editor, it is unlikely she would receive anything less than a glowing review.

64 According to WorldCat (https://www.worldcat.org), only three catalogued copies exist, all in the UK.

65 For more on the stamps employed by the British Museum and the British Library in their collection, see http://britishlibrary.typepad.co.uk/collectioncare/2013/09/a-guide-to-british-library-book-stamps.html.

66 Both libraries confirmed this detail via personal correspondence with the author in December 2016. Liverpool's copy includes an inscription – "To dear Dora, From Gertie Oct 30th 1[damaged]5" – but the illegible date does not resolve any issues concerning publication. I am grateful to the librarians at both institutions for their assistance.

67 See Rodney Engen, *Kate Greenaway: A Biography* (London: Macdonald, 1981), 232; and Helen Zimmern, *Tales from the Edda Told by Helen Zimmern with Illustrations by Kate Greenaway & Others* (London: W. Swan and

Sonnenschein & Co, 1882). The Zimmern text is stamped similarly to the Hervey text, with a Type 2 oval British Museum stamp and a 21 February 1883 date of acquisition. It was later stamped with a variation, Type 2, Figure 5, which was used after 1929. The image in the Zimmern text also includes the name of the printer Edmund Evans, with whom Greenaway had an exclusive relationship: "Greenaway never allowed anyone other than Evans to engrave and print her illustrations, clearly recognizing how much Evans's interpretative skills and ability to match medium to style contributed to the final appearance of her work" (Ruari McLean, "Evans, Edmund [1826–1905]," *Oxford Dictionary of National Biography*, online ed. [Oxford University Press, 2004], http://www.oxforddnb.com/view/article /33035; accessed 18 February 2017).

68 Thomas E. Schuster and Rodney Engen, *Printed Kate Greenaway: A Catalogue Raisonné* (London: T.E. Schuster, 1986), 99.

69 Zimmern's text decidedly humanizes Skrymir: "They had not gone far before they found *a man* of enormous bulk lying fast asleep on the ground" (*Tales from the Edda*, 33, emphasis added).

70 Kooistra lists "Dickens, Trollope, Thackeray, or Carroll" as examples of the rare instances in which authors worked closely with illustrators. See *Poetry, Pictures, and Popular Publishing: The Illustrated Gift Book and Victorian Visual Culture, 1855–1875* (Athens: Ohio UP, 2011), 17, 22. One could also include Greenaway's relationship with Evans in this category.

71 Kooistra, *Poetry, Pictures, and Popular Publishing*, 22.

72 I recently gave a talk entitled "Roderic's Tale," after which a new colleague suggested that the Greenaway image itself may have been modified: mismatches in the engraved lines surrounding the figure of Thor could reveal that Thor was a later addition to an already existing image. This is a possibility I will now pursue. My thanks to John Morrison of Lincoln's School of History and Heritage for this observation.

3 Tolkien, *Beowulf*, and Faërie: Adaptations for Readers Aged "Six to Sixty"

AMBER DUNAI

Eighty years have passed since the publication of the children's novel that would propel the medievalist and linguist J.R.R. Tolkien into the public spotlight: *The Hobbit* (1937). Indeed, following the successful three-part film adaptation of *The Lord of the Rings* (2001–3) and the subsequent capitalization on the earlier trilogy's success in the three-part *Hobbit* film series (2012–14), Tolkien's spotlight has certainly not dimmed. Renewed interest in his oeuvre has created a market for reprints and fresh editions (not to mention antique copies) of the professor's creative works, most of which were released posthumously. Tolkien fans, having exhausted the available publications on Middle-earth, might find themselves perusing Tolkien's lesser-known children's stories, such as *The Father Christmas Letters* (1976), *Mr. Bliss* (1982), and *Roverandom* (1998). While these works never achieved the popularity of *The Hobbit*, they, like the famous fantasy novel, sprang in large part from the yarns with which Tolkien entertained his children at home.

Given the immense popularity of *The Hobbit* and the plentitude of his other publications intended for young audiences, it may come as a surprise to some readers that Tolkien did not necessarily think of himself as a writer for children. In a 1959 drafted response to Walter Allen of the *New Statesman*, who had invited Tolkien to participate in a symposium that would be published in the magazine's Children's Book Supplement (an invitation that Tolkien turned down), he states outright that children's literature "has no special interest to me," and refers Allen to his lecture-based essay "On Fairy-Stories" in order to read "all that I have to say about writing for children."[1] He drives home the point that he writes in the mode of fairy story – a genre that will be explored in detail below – "not because I wish to address children ... but because I wish to write this kind of story and no other."[2] Indeed, this sentiment, that Tolkien prefers and perhaps favours an adult audience over a younger one, is repeated throughout his correspondences, and it presented me with a puzzle as I approached the task of writing about Tolkien as an adaptor of *Beowulf*s for children: namely, how does Tolkien reach his conclusions about the suitability of his works, particularly his fairy stories, for a particular audience? And do Tolkien's notions about suitable audiences for his fairy stories hold true for readers who do not approach those fairy stories through the lens of Tolkien's theory of the genre?

It is my aim in this chapter to follow the development of Tolkien's approaches to *Beowulf* as well as children's literature through analysis of three early *Beowulf*-influenced works: *The Hobbit*, *The Lay of Beowulf*, and *Sellic Spell*.[3] I will discuss these works in chronological order in the interest of tracing the development and expression of Tolkien's relevant scholarly ideas in them. My aim is to demonstrate that these pieces represent a developing interest in the folklore elements of *Beowulf* over approximately one decade, a focus which features very little in *The Lay of Beowulf*, but which grows substantially by the time of *Sellic Spell*'s composition. This interest in folklore, or as Tolkien often puts it, "fairy story," is linked but not strictly tied (as far as Tolkien himself is concerned) to a young readership, although his earliest *Beowulf*s are associated with an audience of children. I am therefore interested in what each adaptation can tell us about Tolkien's attitudes towards writing for young audiences, and how those beliefs might imply an ideal readership for his adaptions regardless of whether a given work is considered to be written for a particular age group or not. Accordingly, I will conclude this chapter by discussing the extent to which Tolkien's increasingly entrenched views on the ideal audience of fairy stories can or should drive a twenty-first-century reader's reception of these (arguably) *children's Beowulf*s.

In his essay "On Fairy-Stories" (originally delivered on 8 March 1939 as an Andrew Lang lecture and first published in the 1947 volume *Essays Presented to Charles Williams*), Tolkien laments the bowdlerization of traditional tales for young readers, citing "The Juniper Tree" as an exemplar of the kind of story whose horror "children are now too often spared in mollified versions of Grimm."[4] Taking as evidence his own frightening but ultimately benign childhood encounters with similar stories, he considers the scrubbing of dark elements from fairy stories to be their ruination, barring the reader from using the tale as a door to an "Other Time," or perhaps to a space "outside Time itself."[5]

On the other hand, Tolkien questions the popular assumption of his day, that fairy tales are particularly appropriate to younger audiences. Taking issue with (and offence at) "such waggeries as: 'this book [of fairy stories] is for children from the ages of six to sixty,'" Tolkien first identifies children as "normal, if immature, members of a particular family, and of the human family at large." He compares the limited modern audience of fairy stories to the confinement of old-fashioned furniture to the nursery: they are cast off and allowed to be ruined through rough, inexpert handling.[6] While children ought not to be prohibited from reading fairy stories, Tolkien clearly expresses his view that they are not likely to benefit from reading the tales as much as an adult. This is not simply because adults are more sophisticated readers than children, but chiefly because adults have had more time to experience traumas, both major and minor, which might be assuaged by the four chief qualities of the fairy story identified by Tolkien: Fantasy, Recovery, Escape, and Consolation.[7] Indeed, for a member of the generation initiated to adulthood by the horrors of the First World War (which Tolkien experienced first-hand at the Battle of the Somme), these aspects of Faërie must have held a poignant significance. Verlyn Flieger notes of Tolkien's "sudden joyous 'turn'" leading to a happy ending,[8] which Tolkien calls *eucatastrophe* (coining the term by attaching the prefix *eu-*, or "good," to *castastrophe*), that "those values cannot but have had a special and timely value not just to Tolkien but to his audience in relation to the two world wars – the one so recently over and the next about to start."[9]

Tolkien's construction of the fairy story genre is further characterized by his inclusion of decidedly "adult" stories in the genre (that is to say, stories which are typically read in their original form by adults, and which undergo some measure of adaptation if they are to be enjoyed by young children). Tolkien includes among those texts that deal in the realm of Faërie the Middle English alliterative poem *Sir Gawain and the Green Knight*[10] and the Old English epic *Beowulf*. Tolkien's Oxford University lecture notes on *Beowulf* repeatedly touch upon what he perceived as its folkloric/fairy story origins,[11] contending that "Beowulf the bear-man, the giant-killer comes from a different world [than does Beow]: *fairy-story*."[12] He goes to great lengths to separate out the historical aspects of the poem from its fictional/fairy story elements; for example, he distinguishes Beowulf's strength of thirty men as a folkloric attribute,[13] but finds in his assignment of Ecgtheow as a father an attempt by the poet(s) to graft the Beowulf folktale onto a historical tradition in a coherent way.[14] In Unferth he locates a "composite character" who is "balanced precisely" between the folkloric and the historical.[15]

Tolkien identifies *Beowulf* and *Sir Gawain and the Green Knight* as medieval texts bearing significant fairy story elements both because of what they are and what they are not. First, they involve forays into

Faërie, or the "Perilous Realm":[16] the mysterious Green Chapel, the monster-infested mere. They fulfil a desire "to survey the depths of space and time" and "to hold communion with other living things."[17] Perhaps as importantly, they do *not* belong to the categories of travellers' tales; tales that take place solely within dreams and have no significant bearing on the waking world; or beast fables – all varieties of stories that Tolkien argues do not have to do sufficiently with the Perilous Realm to be considered fairy stories proper.[18]

The Lay of Beowulf

I classify Tolkien's *The Lay of Beowulf* as a children's *Beowulf* based upon the main audience (indeed, perhaps the only early audience) of the piece: his own children. Christopher Tolkien recalls hearing the lay sung at age seven or eight, which would date the composition to the early 1930s, although he points out that the lay may have existed well before he heard it sung.[19] Dimitra Fimi identifies the tune to which the lay was sung as that of the English folk song "The Fox Went out on a Winter's Night" and also points out that *The Lay of Beowulf* shares the same rhyming scheme and metre as the "Stone Troll" song that Sam performs in *The Fellowship of the Ring*.[20] This song thus links Tolkien's creative work with his scholarly pursuits in an interesting (although not uncharacteristic) way.

The lay exists in two forms, identified as *Beowulf and Grendel* (I) and *Beowulf and the Monsters* (II) in the manuscript containing them. Christopher Tolkien suggests that *Beowulf and Grendel* is the older of the two, and believes that this is the version he heard sung aloud by his father in the early 1930s. He also remarks that *The Lay of Beowulf* is mentioned nowhere else in his father's writings.[21] For this reason, I think it safe to conclude that Tolkien was not actively seeking a larger audience for the lay beyond his own immediate family.

Compared to Tolkien's later *Beowulf* adaptations, one finds a significant difference in narrative focus and concentration of "fairy story" content in *The Lay of Beowulf*. Unlike *Sellic Spell* but like its Old English source, *The Lay of Beowulf* begins with Heorot and the Grendel attack rather than with Beowulf. It preserves the poem's dark insinuations regarding the burning of Heorot and also records the hero's death following the dragon encounter. Original names, such as Beowulf, Hrothgar, and Ecgtheow, are preserved. These features point to an emphasis on what Tolkien identifies as the "historical" aspect of the poem (or, at the very least, a rejection of potential fairy story–inspired revisions, such as the consoling happy ending). Tolkien does include the folklore-inspired bear-man Beowulf in the lines "As bear aroused from his mountain lair / Beowulf wrestled with Grendel there."[22] This detail, however, provides but a meagre hint of the Faërie-dominated revisions with which Tolkien would infuse *Sellic Spell*, and, to a large extent, the *Beowulf* allusions in *The Hobbit*.

What stands out in *The Lay of Beowulf* is Tolkien's ability to pare down a complex Old English poem to its simplest elements, and to structure those elements in a narratively satisfying and metrically consistent little song. While the lay is far from comprehensive, it is clear, coherent, and easy enough for a child to follow and enjoy. Of the two versions of the lay, *Beowulf and Grendel* is the tighter and more concise. This version reduces *Beowulf* to two halves: Grendel and the Dragon. This organization is consistent with Tolkien's reading of the poem in his 1936 lecture "*Beowulf*: The Monsters and the Critics" as one which juxtaposes youth and age (thereby portraying the tragedy of human mortality).[23]

What is ingenious about this organization of the narrative is the way in which Tolkien revises the story in order to link youth and age, and victory and defeat, in an explicit manner. This is accomplished by means of a curse. As Grendel lies dying, he makes a request of Beowulf:

> "O! Ecgtheow's son" he then dying said,
> "Forbear to hew my vanquished head,
> or hard and stony be thy death-bed,
> > and a red fate fall on Heorot!"   (ll. 25–8)

Beowulf, of course, does not comply, and the monster's head is hewed and hung. In order to drive home the cause-and-effect relationship between Grendel's curse and Heorot's burning and Beowulf's death, Tolkien closes the lay with an imagery-rich reminder of Grendel's words:

> The demon's head in the hall did hang
> and grinned from the wall while minstrels sang,
> till flames leapt forth and red swords rang,
> > and hushed were the harps of Heorot.
> And latest and last one hoar of head,
> as he lay on a hard and stony bed,
> and venom burned him and he bled,
> > remembered the light of Heorot.   (ll. 49–56)

The original poem makes no explicit link between Grendel's fall and the destruction of Heorot or the death of Beowulf. By putting Grendel's curse in line with death and destruction, Tolkien is able to bring to life his famous interpretation of the poem as a story of the tragedy of mortality, in which "the wages of heroism is death."[24]

Beowulf and Grendel also links, as in the "Monsters and the Critics" lecture, monsters with the realization of this grand theme of tragic mortality, presenting through their use as organizing points of action a subtle argument for the legitimacy of their presence in the poem, which Tolkien had felt compelled to defend in his scholarship. Indeed, if Christopher Tolkien has dated the lay correctly, it can be read as an artefact representing his father's developing ideas about the poem during the late twenties and early thirties, the period leading up to the 1936 lecture.[25] The status of the monsters as "enemies of God" that need to be fought even if doing so means being on the losing side represents, for Tolkien, the merging of "Northern courage"[26] (that is, pagan courage) and Christian ideology in the poem; because this transition is not completed, the poem is concerned "primarily with *man on earth*, rehandling in a new perspective an ancient theme: that man, each man and all men, and all their works shall die."[27] This is achieved through a progression between "two great moments in life, rising and setting; an elaboration of the ancient and intensely moving contrast between youth and age, first achievement and final death."[28]

Accordingly, *Beowulf and Grendel* is divided between two monster-fights, with the beginning and end of Beowulf's career linked by his first fight with Grendel and Grendel's curse. Of the seven stanzas in the lay, four are occupied with the introduction and elimination of Grendel's immediate threat, two with the happy aftermath of Beowulf's victory, and one with the destruction of Heorot and Beowulf's death. What is interesting about the aftermath of Grendel's death is that the monster never fully disappears from the narrative. In the fifth stanza his trophy head is mentioned again:

> The moon gleamed in through the windows wan;
> as Beowulf drank he looked thereon,
> and a light in the demon's eyes there shone
> > amid the blaze of Heorot.   (ll. 37–40)

This stanza describes Hrothgar's lavish gift-giving, but the hostile visage of death and destruction still leers over the festivities in a grim memento mori. Additionally, Tolkien's cleverly worded description of "the blaze of Heorot" bears a double meaning; the cheerful fire will later be replaced by a destructive one. The stage is already set for Grendel's vengeance.

What does *The Lay of Beowulf* tell us about Tolkien's approach to children's literature? One might point to his comments in "On Fairy-Stories" about the unfortunate sanitization of folktales in adaptations for younger audiences; there is certainly no shortage of grim imagery or dark philosophy in the lay, although it should also be noted that nineteenth- and early twentieth-century adaptors of *Beowulf* were also not in the habit of redacting Beowulf's death at the end of the poem, or even the gore that accompanied his struggle with Grendel in the mead hall. However, what Tolkien adds to his adaptation that is not necessarily present in others is an overwhelming sense of fatalism and doom driven by his professional analysis of the source. That he considered it appropriate for his children to hear (set to the tune of a jolly old folk song) tells us something more about Tolkien's views regarding children's literature: Tolkien is bothered that young readers are shielded not only from prurient or violent imagery (as is typically the goal today when it comes to "age-appropriate" reading), but also from deeper, "adult" concepts that they may not necessarily understand upon initial exposure. Did young Christopher understand that his father's structural organization of the lay had at its roots a tradition of Germanic pessimism that refused to die in the face of England's ongoing Christianization? Probably not, but in his father's opinion that is no reason to eliminate it from the text (or to remove the text from him). The idea that children's writing ought not to be simplified or children "talked down to" is a running theme in several of Tolkien's letters; in a letter to his aunt, Jane Neave, for instance, Tolkien remarks that while *The Lord of the Rings* was not written for a young audience, he is pleased to hear that some children "read or listen to it eagerly," even though he thinks that they "must fail to understand most of it." He adds a hope that the young audience will expand their vocabularies through their exposure to the novel.[29] In order to grow, children must be challenged. If they are "fed" only literature that they can completely understand, their intellectual growth will be inhibited. And after all, "Children are meant to grow up, and not to become Peter Pans."[30]

These comments confirm the implication in *The Lay of Beowulf* that the "happy ending" consolation of Tolkien's other, more folkloric *Beowulf* adaptations are not motivated by a desire to remove mortality and loss from the view of the younger reader. These changes, where they are found, are motivated by conventions of genre. The happy conclusion of *Sellic Spell* (to be discussed below) is appropriate for readers of all ages because fairy stories, as Tolkien understands them, are meant to console the audience, whether old or young. *The Lay of Beowulf* is something different; it is characterized not by Faërie but by a combination of "historical" elements. In order for Tolkien to adhere to this frame of reference, he cannot exclude death and slaughter. As we shall see in the next section, hints of the eucatastrophic rely on a departure from this historical *Beowulf* and movement towards the folkloric aspects of the tale.

The Hobbit

When discussing the influence of *Beowulf* on Tolkien's 1937 bestselling children's book, *The Hobbit*, it is more appropriate to talk in terms of allusion than full adaptation.[31] Tolkien names *Beowulf* "among [his] most valued sources" for *The Hobbit*, although he also claims that the Old English poem "was not consciously present to the mind in the process of writing."[32] For the purposes of this chapter, I will focus on these *Beowulf* allusions as they manifest in the skin-changer Beorn.[33] Beorn as Beowulf analogue has already been discussed at great length elsewhere, and so my main focus will be to draw him into the analysis of Tolkien's approach to children's *Beowulf*s and the adaptational patterns that accompany them.

In *The Hobbit*, we find a *Beowulf*-influenced text that is firmly identified (by young Rayner Unwin, aged ten at the time) as holding appeal for "all children between the ages of 5 and 9."[34] Tolkien does not question its status as a children's book and consistently discusses it as such. In his letter to Walter Allen, referenced earlier, he takes himself to task for stylistic choices that he considers to be demeaning to "intelligent children of good taste"; these flaws, he argues, are in "mode of expression and narrative method" that he perceives to target and condescend to a young audience.[35] No specific examples are cited, but these flaws are apparently linked to "whimsical" aspects of the story. One possible example of this regretted frivolity can be found in the characterization of the Stone-trolls at the beginning of the story; Tolkien later finds himself obliged to clear up a reader's misconception regarding the troll William's "pity" for Bilbo (when William calls Bilbo a "poor little blighter" and hesitates to allow his companions to eat the hobbit). Tolkien chides himself both for naming the troll "William" and for having him refer to Bilbo as a "poor little blighter," identifying these humorous stylistic choices as mistakes that might have been avoided had "*The Hobbit* been more carefully written."[36] This light-hearted style of writing is much subdued in *The Lord of the Rings*, although, as Wayne G. Hammond and Christina Scull note in their companion to the novel, some touches of whimsy can be located in the early Hobbiton portion of the novel, such as the roguish reference to Bilbo's "eleventy-first" birthday.[37] Tolkien continues by urging Allen not to "write down to Children or to any-body" and asserting that young and adult readers alike "only are really moved by what is at least in some point or aspect above [them], above [their] measure, at any rate before [they] have read it and 'taken it in.'"[38]

Tolkien's discussion and criticism of *The Hobbit* also provides some interesting evidence that his theory of fairy stories, first presented two years after the publication of the children's novel, had not completely permeated his creative writing practices in time for *The Hobbit*'s publi-cation, at least by his own reckoning. That is, Tolkien habitually blames the supposed deficiencies in style on his mistaken belief at the time that "there was a real and special connection between children and fairy-stories."[39] Presumably, these "defects" would not have occurred if he had not been writing for a young audience alone. Even the inclusion of the Beowulf analogue, Beorn, in *The Hobbit* can be traced to Tolkien's original child audience: his sons. John D. Rateliff argues convincingly that one of the main motivating reasons for the character's creation was the boys' avid interest in bears, which is also reflected in the prominent bear characters of *Mr. Bliss* and *The Father Christmas Letters*.[40] Given that *The Hobbit* was being drafted in the early 1930s, it is quite feasible that the ideas expressed in Tolkien's 1939 lecture may not have been fully formed, let alone adopted into his writing practices, in time for its pub-lication.[41] Keeping this in mind, in what follows I will suggest that some developing aspects of Tolkien's theory of fairy story manifest early in his children's novel, despite the limitations he perceived in it. *The Hob-bit* thus marks a transitional point between the historically dominated *Lay of Beowulf* and the thoroughly folklorized *Sellic Spell*.

In the relatively minor character Beorn, one finds a reimagining of Beowulf that is also blended with Norse features. His name is taken from the Old English poetical term *beorn*, which refers to a "warrior" or simply "man" and which is related to the Old Norse cognate *bjorn*, or "bear." The *Oxford English Dictionary* suggests that *beorn*'s signification as "warrior" or "man" (and never "bear") in Old English is in keeping with the poetic context in which it is always used; for warriors to be lik-ened to a fierce and dangerous animal is not an unusual linguistic de-velopment, and therefore the metaphor-driven semantic shift is taken by many philologists as a satisfactory explanation for the discrepancy between its English and Norse ranges of meaning.[42] The fact that Beorn the skin-changer is, in fact, both a human warrior and a bear depending on the form he takes allows Tolkien to build into the character's name a sly linguistic wink.

Beorn the bear-man can be linked to two specific sources: *Beowulf* and the *Saga of Hrólfr Kraki*. As Tom Shippey explains, the *Beowulf* connection is made through the common translation of Beowulf as "bee's wolf," a kenning-like riddle of a name that can be interpreted as "bear."[43] Appropriately, we learn that Beorn (who is apparently vegetarian and a friend of animals) keeps bees and enjoys their honey. An earlier version of the character was named "Medwed," Russian for "honey-eater,"[44] a name that links the character even more explicitly to the "bees' wolf" of the Old English poem. Regarding the Norse saga, Beorn is likened to Böthvarr Bjarki, whose name means "little bear" and who is a shape-shifter, or "were-bear," himself.[45] As Douglas A. Anderson notes, Tolkien was quite familiar with this saga, and his student Stella Mills translated and later published it under the supervision of Tolkien's colleague E.V. Gordon.[46] Thus, both the English and Norse influences on Beorn's character are likely.

Beorn's likeness to the Norse *berserkr*, or "bearshirt" warrior, has also been frequently noted.[47] Under the bear-man's initial gruffness (upon meeting Gandalf's troop of thirteen dwarves and a hobbit) is revealed a potential for great destructive violence, happily directed towards the villains of the piece – the goblins and wargs that had earlier pursued the company – rather than towards the protagonists themselves. Beorn's deep hatred for these monstrous antagonists might be likened to Beowulf's own combativeness towards the supernatural creatures of his story: the ogres, dragons, and more obscure *niceras*. His home, evocative of a Germanic mead hall with its boards and trestles and central hearth (and, indeed, drawn exactly like such a historical hall in Tolkien's illustration for *The Hobbit*, "Beorn's Hall"),[48] presents a neat and comforting picture of order and safety in contrast with the hostile creatures and environs encountered earlier in the story, down to the tame animal servants who attend the company. Like Beowulf, Beorn battles against chaotic and antisocial elements and instills order in their place. His mead hall draws to mind Hrothgar's Heorot after its cleansing, and the goblin's head and warg skin that he carries back to his home after taking bear form and hunting his enemies are reminiscent of the grisly trophies that Beowulf presents to his Danish host following the battles with Grendel and his mother. His final appearance during the Battle of Five Armies is particularly Beowulfian; he arrives in berserker's bear form and crushes the goblin leader, Bolg, recalling Beowulf's killing of Dæghrefn. As Marjorie Burns puts it, Beorn is a character of dualities: "both ruthless and kind, bear and man, homebody and wanderer, berserker and pacifist in one."[49] Burns argues that Tolkien's blending in Beorn of familiar (to the reader) English qualities with pagan, Norse ones reflects the same clash of cultures found in many medieval texts, including *Sir Gawain and the Green Knight* and *Beowulf*; this makes Beorn a particularly effective Beowulf analogue, internalizing all the pagan/ Christian tension of the Old English poem.

The appearance of Beorn at the battle also ties him to the point of eucatastrophe, the moment when almost certain defeat is turned to victory.[50] He arrives in the last hour of battle and finds the dwarves making their last stand. After rescuing the mortally wounded Thorin and his surviving men, Beorn rushes into the goblin host in such a wrath "that nothing could withstand him, and no weapon seemed to bite upon him."[51] After he dispatches Bolg, the remaining goblins scatter in fear of Beorn's berserker fury, and the day is won. Thus, Beorn's part in *The Hobbit* demonstrates that Tolkien's characteristic use of the eucatastrophe has been well assimilated into his storytelling style by the time of of the novel's publication.

Sellic Spell

The Lay of Beowulf and *The Hobbit*, as I have demonstrated above, can be easily tied to young audiences. The case of *Sellic Spell*, however, is more complex. This tale, which Tolkien wrote in alternative Old English and Modern English forms, was intended for an adult audience and is not known to have reached any audience at all. Christopher Tolkien dates *Sellic Spell* to the early 1940s.[52] In the edition containing *Sellic Spell*, Christopher Tolkien includes what he identifies as his father's only general statement about the text, which describes *Sellic Spell* as "an attempt to reconstruct the Anglo-Saxon tale that lies behind the folk-tale element in *Beowulf*."[53] In his analysis of *Sellic Spell* as fairy story,[54] Paul Acker posits there may very well be a connection between Tolkien's revision of "On Fairy-Stories" in 1943 and the composition of *Sellic Spell*, pointing out that in Flieger and Anderson's edition of the essay, Tolkien's notes for the Andrew Lang lecture state that *Beowulf* "should be retold as fairy-story" after dwelling briefly on the lack of fairy story *Beowulf*s in Lang's collections of tales and elsewhere. Flieger and Anderson suggest that this note may represent the "germ" of Tolkien's *Sellic Spell*, also dated to the early 1940s.[55]

The title *Sellic Spell*, which can be interpreted as "strange story" or "wondrous story," is taken from line 2109 of *Beowulf* during Beowulf's recounting of his adventures to his king, Hygelac.[56] Tolkien acknowledges that there are departures from the original story, particularly as a result of eliminating the historical in favour of approximating an earlier folkloric tale form. Perhaps most intriguingly, he claims that his initial composition of the story in Old English was done in order to imbue the subsequent Modern English version with a "Northern cast of expression."[57]

This stylistic choice has the effect of producing a text marked by simplified diction with a heavy reliance on words of Old English origin. Although Tolkien's prose "translation" of his folktale may seem eccentric, it is worth noting that he is not the only scholar to have translated the *Beowulf* story into an Old English prose retelling. Famous philologist Henry Sweet had provided his own prose version of the *Beowulf* story in *First Steps in Anglo-Saxon*, a teaching text which offers the prose rendering "Bēowulfes sīþ" for students to cut their teeth on.[58] Interestingly, Tolkien also saw teaching potential in his creation,[59] noting in his commentary on *Beowulf*, "See my 'reconstruction' or specimen *Sellic Spell* which I hope to read later."[60] This note pertains to Tolkien's assertion in the commentary that he believes it likely that Beowulf met Grendel along with companions or competitors in an earlier version of the story.

Like many other *Beowulf* adaptors, Tolkien follows the pattern of eliminating the more tangential portions of the poem in favour of focusing on the major conflicts that characterize it for most modern readers.[61] Grendel and his mother (referred to as Grinder and his dam in the story) take centre stage in *Sellic Spell*, and the dragon is eliminated altogether. The pseudo-historical references and juxtaposed tales that characterize the Old English poem are not eliminated from *Sellic Spell* for the sake of simplicity alone, but because, as discussed above, Tolkien wants to separate the historical aspect from *Beowulf*, distilling it to its fairy story roots.[62] His aim is not really to retell *Beowulf* at all, but to explore the story at the heart of the Old English poem through the act of creative reconstruction.

Tolkien's approach can be contrasted with earlier adaptations such as the 1908 versions by H.E. Marshall (*Stories of Beowulf*) and Thomas Cartwright (*Brave Beowulf*). Both of these presentations for children, while simplifying the story to some degree, tend to follow the structure of *Beowulf* more closely and in greater detail than later adaptations. Of the two, Marshall's adaptation is more liberal in its elimination of details and juxtaposed stories that might detract from the main, three-monster narrative. Still, she retains some episodes abandoned by looser adaptations, such as Beowulf's retelling of his exploits to Hygelac and Hrothgar's sermon. Cartwright preserves these scenes as well, along with the Finnsburg episode, the passage contrasting good queen Hygd with wicked queen Throtho, and the story of the Last Survivor (when describing the dragon hoard). Both adaptations place value on reproducing the narrative as faithfully as possible; they limit themselves to trimming unneeded material when necessary and avoid adding any material not present in the original poem. Tolkien's *Sellic Spell*, with its complete elimination of the historical past, could not be more remote.

Likewise contrasting with *Beowulf* renderings familiar at the time he was working was Tolkien's approach to stylization of his tale. The tendency towards the pseudo-archaic found in translations like William Morris and A.J. Wyatt's notoriously arcane 1895 *Tale of Beowulf Done out of the Old English Tongue* and children's versions such as A.J. Church's 1898 "Story of Beowulf," which Lise Jalliant describes as appealing to a "Victorian taste for archaisms,"[63] is more or less missing in *Sellic Spell*, whose archaisms do not come anywhere close to being as numerous as those in even in the milder adaptations by Marshall and Cartwright. One does find the occasional dated adjective such as "carven" and "gilded,"[64] and syntactic constructions such as Beewolf's exasperated "'Heavy is this hag!'"[65] which do not quite fit the modern age. But these occasional archaisms can be accounted for by Tolkien's essay "On Translating *Beowulf*," which draws attention to the *Beowulf* poet's own usage of old-fashioned, traditional poetic diction, and warns would-be translators that "you will misrepresent the first and most salient characteristic of the style and flavour of the author, if in translating *Beowulf*, you deliberately eschew the traditional literary and poetic diction which we now possess in favour of the current and trivial."[66] At the same time, Tolkien warns against using words simply because they are old, and specifically names Morris's translation as one that needlessly obscures meaning in a vain attempt to breathe new life into English words long dead (such as Morris's misguided use of *leeds*, or "people," as a rendering of OE *leode*).[67] The Old English version of *Sellic Spell*, which Tolkien claims flavours his story in its Modern English form, thus gives the text an air of frankness and simplicity rather than of ornate antiquity of the imagined past.[68] He practices restraint in his inclusion of old-fashioned terms and makes a point of not sacrificing clarity to style.

Tolkien's Old English translation method has the additional (perhaps unintended) effect of producing a story that would be fairly easy for a young child to follow and understand. It should be noted that Tolkien's simplified style also appears to follow changing tastes in children's literature; Strafford Riggs's 1933 *Story of Beowulf* likewise abandons the trappings of the pseudo-archaic common in earlier adaptations. Take Riggs's version of Unferth's taunt:

> Who is this boy, beardless and white of skin, that he should come over the sea-fields in a boat with his fourteen thanes? Where are his vaunted courage and strength, I ask?
>
> For let me tell you: Once upon a time this same Beowulf swam a race with one Breca, another young lord of the Geats, called the Bronding, and the story of that race is a shameful thing for honest men to hear. For in

this race with Breca the Bronding, Beowulf failed almost before he had started, and the Bronding beat him sorely, so that my lord Beowulf was the laughing-stock of his uncle's court, and ever since he was a boy he has been known for his sluggard nature and his avoidance of battle and his sloth in hunting.[69]

Compare to it the corresponding passage in Tolkien's *Sellic Spell*:

"Did I hear aright that your name was Beewolf?" said he. "There cannot be many with such a name. Surely it was you that Breaker challenged to a swimming-match, and left you far behind, and swam away home to his own country. Let us hope that you have become more of a man since then, for Grinder will treat you less gently than Breaker did." (366)[70]

Neither of these passages could exactly be called casual; there is still a semblance of grand rhetorical style preserved in them (appropriate given that the speaker, Unferth, is famous for his skill in words if not in deeds). Phrases such as Riggs's "one Breca" and Tolkien's "did I hear aright" give the passages a ceremonial flavour. They avoid, however, more archaic relics of earlier translations, such as the second-person singular pronoun "thou" and second-person plural "ye," which tend to be utilized by those adaptors who labour to cultivate an antique flavour.

Tolkien's original plans to publish *Sellic Spell* in the *Welsh Review*, a plan foiled when the magazine closed in 1948 before the story could appear,[71] are consistent with his by now established views that adults are (or ought to be) the target audience of the fairy story. However, just two years earlier in 1946, Tolkien wrote to Stanly Unwin's son, David Unwin (Severn), suggesting *Sellic Spell*, along with other short pieces, as works which might be published alongside a story that had originally been considered as a follow-up to *The Hobbit*'s success: *Farmer Giles of Ham*.[72] While *Farmer Giles*'s own genre classification and appeal for children has been the subject of discussion and criticism – Tolkien himself, while promoting *Farmer Giles* as having been amusing to "H.S. Bennet's children," admits that Allen & Unwin production manager C.A. Furth considered it to have "no obvious public"[73] – this establishes at least a tenuous link between *Sellic Spell* and a young audience. In any case, I think it fair enough for a reader of *Sellic Spell* and other fairy stories by Tolkien to question whether one ought to take Tolkien's ideas about the suitability of folklore for adults as reason enough to reject *Sellic Spell* as a children's story. Thus far, the evidence I have presented *against* assuming a young audience for *Sellic Spell* has relied upon additional texts: letters, scholarly essays, foiled publication plans, and the like. But is there anything *within the story itself* which suggests that *Sellic Spell* does not fit what was and is commonly considered to be a children's *Beowulf*? In what follows, I will suggest that the answer to this question is "no." I will base this reading upon examination of Tolkien's Bildungsroman approach to the *Beowulf* story in *Sellic Spell*, an approach which is shared by his near contemporary, Riggs.

In his depiction and renaming of *Sellic Spell*'s Beowulf, Tolkien embeds his own favoured interpretation of the hero's name. "Beowulf" becomes "Beewolf," this altered form of the name reflecting the kenning Tolkien believed it to be.[74] And because a bee-wolf is a bear, Beewolf must behave like a bear. As Dimitra Fimi points out, Tolkien is not the first scholar to posit a connection between *Beowulf* and an earlier bear-man folktale; Friedrich Panzer's 1910 *Studien zur germanischen Sagengeschichte, I: Beowulf* compares numerous folktales in order to argue that *Beowulf* derives from the "Bear's Son" folklore pattern. Fimi summarizes the "Bear's Son" pattern thus:

> The "Bear's Son" tale usually begins with a boy born to, or raised by, bears, who has bear-like characteristics, including super-human strength. The young hero sets out on adventures with various companions, fights a supernatural being which has already defeated his companions, and descends under the earth or under water to finish off the monster and/or fight its mother, often by means of a magical weapon. The hero is left in the lurch by companions who were supposed to wait for him and draw him up, but – of course – all ends well with the hero returning safe and being rewarded.[75]

This outline describes the basic narrative of *Sellic Spell* to a tee. As we have seen, the *Beowulf* / bear-man motif also features in *The Hobbit*'s Beorn and in *The Lay of Beowulf* and is characteristic of Tolkien's approach to Beowulf analogues in adaptation. In *Sellic Spell*, however, Tolkien is able to adopt not just the animal characterization, but also the "coming of age" aspect of the Bear's Son pattern in full.

In *Sellic Spell*, Beewolf is initially represented as a callow, brooding boy, calling to mind the original poem's brief mention of Beowulf's unpromising youth.[76] Young Beewolf is introduced as an adopted boy, first discovered in the cave of a bear slain by huntsman, who is resistant to the demands of civilization and grows into a super-powered bear-man hybrid with the strength of first seven and later thirty men.[77] He neglects to develop a human taste for tools, including weapons. He loves honey and resorts to crushing his enemies in his arms when he fights. *Sellic Spell* lingers on Beewolf's adolescence; if Tolkien saw *Beowulf* as a story about the tragedy of mortality,[78] he treats *Sellic Spell* as a kind of prehistoric Bildungsroman. In it, Beewolf grows from a disconnected, under-socialized bear-man into a weapon-bearing warrior and leader of men through his two monster fights.

Similarly, Riggs also makes a point of describing young Beowulf's promising yet shadowed young adulthood: "His movements were clumsy. He tripped over his sword. He broke whatever he touched. The other youths laughed at him for his awkwardness, but in secret they envied the immense spread of his shoulders and the terrible swiftness of his stride when he hunted in the forests" (6). While Riggs does not adopt the same animalistic characterization as Tolkien, his and Tolkien's approaches to adaptation are similar in two key ways. First, unlike many nineteenth- and early twentieth-century adaptors, they are both willing to embellish the events of the source material, resulting in complex protagonists to whom young readers might relate. Second, both Riggs and Tolkien centre their adaptations on the character Beowulf structurally; rather than echoing the poem by opening with a description of Heorot and the Grendel attack, they choose to frame the entire narrative around Beowulf's growth from a boy into a man (and, in Riggs's version, from a young man into an old one). We hear about Grendel at the same time that Beowulf does, and we are privy to the reasoning behind his acceptance of the hero's quest in both adaptations. Riggs gives us Beowulf's inner dialogue: "True, he thought, I have fought small dragons and hunted wild boars, but such hazards are mere games for boys, and I am now a man. My uncle Hygelac is at peace with his neighbours, and there is no war in which I can take part" (11). Beewolf in *Sellic Spell* likewise interprets the Grinder story as an opportunity to win fame and glory for himself. Comparing Tolkien's *Sellic Spell* to Riggs's *Story of Beowulf* demonstrates that regardless of whether it was originally meant for children, *Sellic Spell* successfully reproduces features of a contemporary approach to adaptation for young readers.

One major way in which Tolkien departs from other children's adaptations of the *Beowulf* narrative, however, is through the reimagining of Æschere and Hondscio as Beewolf's two lesser competitors, Ashwood and Handshoe. Tolkien's transformation of the two men into rivals is explained in terms of his mission to "de-historicize" the story and distil it down to a basic folkloric narrative.[79] The elimination of historical elements is also named as motivation for renaming Unferth "Unfriend" (originally "Unpeace").[80] Unferth's renaming and relocation in a "Bear's Son" tale answers the problem of an apparently folkloric rather than historical name existing in *Beowulf*.[81] In a similar way, Breca is transformed as swimming rival "Breaker."

Beewolf's interactions with all four characters simultaneously allows Tolkien to continue his characterization of the story's hero as a young man with potential, but whose immaturity and prankster tendencies manifest in a mildly hostile, competitive spirit (through which Beewolf chiefly seeks to amuse and gratify himself, not to win honour or approval from a lord). Whereas Beowulf, for example, meets Unferth's jeering with boasts and a blistering personal attack, Beewolf answers Unfriend's jabs in a comparatively laid-back manner: "My good Unfriend ... the mead has muddled your wit and you do not tell the tale aright. For it was I that won the match and not poor Breaker, though I was only a lad then. And indeed I have become more of a man since. But come, let us be friends!" (366). The crushing bear hug that follows this speech is, of course, as much a punishment and warning as it is a sign of friendship, but it also sets a much different tone from its source. The contrast between Beewolf's youth – "I was only a lad then" – and his growing sense of manhood is also noteworthy. He is aware that he has matured, but he does not claim that he is a grown man; rather, he is "more of a man." His trials yet stand between Beewolf and full realization of his potential.

Beewolf's initial characterization as a lacklustre would-be hero is further developed through his two rivals' scorn; Ashwood and Handshoe decline to cooperate in their goal of ridding the Golden Hall (Tolkien's folklorization of "Heorot") of the ogre Grinder, each deciding that he does not need the other's help, "and still less the help of Beewolf" (366). This setup divides the Grinder portion of the narrative into three fights: two failed attempts (ending in Ashwood's and then Handshoe's deaths) followed by Beewolf's victory over Grinder in the third encounter. The two rivals' deaths echo their analogues' fates in *Beowulf*; Ashwood has his head torn off, while Handshoe ends his life torn to pieces and stuffed into a pouch on Grinder's belt. Beewolf's character suffers one more indignity before his impressive victory when the King of the Golden Hall bids him farewell before the fight, "hoping but not expecting to see him again in the morning" (369). The morning, of course, brings with it the beginning of Beewolf's turn from ignoble bear-child to celebrated warrior.

From here, the *Beowulf* tale's reflection in *Sellic Spell* continues more or less as one would expect, with a few revisions made necessary by the folklorization of the source material. Because the Æschere analogue has already been slain, Beewolf decides to track the wounded Grinder to his lair in order to prevent later retaliation after Unfriend, resentful of his rival's success, predicts an unhappy aftermath to the fight. Tolkien also chooses to have Unfriend accompany and later abandon Beewolf once the water at the surface of the mere becomes bloody following Beewolf's struggle with Grinder's dam. In fact, Unfriend loosens the rope by which Beewolf had descended into the mere in order to ensure that the hero cannot return to the Golden Hall even if he does survive his struggle with the monsters.[82]

Upon Beewolf's return to the hall (merely delayed by the loss of the rope) to the astonishment of its king and inhabitants, who had already been informed of the bloody pool by Unfriend, Beewolf disciplines his traitorous companion with a beating. This violent act is marked by Unfriend's fear of death and Beewolf's reasoning for his apparent restraint: "No, I will not kill you ... for you are the King's man. But if I were the King I would not have you crawling in my house" (382). Beewolf's demeanour and behaviour upon returning to the hall gives the audience the first hint that the hero is no longer a mere warrior, but is also capable of understanding how society works and how he ought to behave within it. Furthermore, his judgment and punishment of Unfriend, in addition to his destruction of the hall's two monstrous enemies, contributes to a peaceful society: "and there was more friendship and less strife there ever after. For Unfriend was humbled, and from thenceforth was a man of fewer words" (382). Beewolf's rise is thus marked by his wielding of authority, meting out a punishment that proves to benefit both the king's hall and Unfriend himself, who later becomes Beewolf's ally.

As a reward for vanquishing the monsters, Beewolf is awarded a troop of twelve armed men, solidifying his development into a leader rather than a solitary, undisciplined, and essentially leaderless warrior. By the end of the tale, Beewolf has returned to his home and ascended to kingship of his own land. It is worth noting that although Beewolf does not involve his king in the decision to leave home, he follows the tradition represented in *Beowulf* of sharing his treasure with the king upon returning home, remarking to his foster father that "You thought little of the foundling that was brought from the bear's den; yet you have earned some thanks for your fostering, such as it was" (384). Once more, the journey to the Golden Hall becomes a formative experience that draws Beewolf out of self-involved adolescence so that he can understand and accept his place in society and his relationships with others.

As discussed earlier, Tolkien makes much of the fact that the adolescent Beewolf does not use weapons; his thirty-fold strength enables him to fight like a bear, grappling with and crushing his adversaries (recalling, as Beorn does, Beowulf's fight with Dæghrefn). The Grinder fight is not an aberration, but a representative example of Beewolf's battle tactics. His weaponlessness is one of the main qualities that not only separates Beewolf from adulthood, but from humanity itself. However, after the chastened Unfriend forges an intricate sword as a peace offering for his new friend, Beewolf "took it gladly and forgave him; and he called the sword Gildenhilt and wore it ever after, and despised weapons no longer" (383). The social bond brings about a new set of human characteristics. The formerly nameless and silent cub-child is now a giver of names and a wielder of tools. While Tolkien assures the audience that Beewolf does still occasionally put aside his weapons and fight like a bear in battle (his animalistic urges are suppressed, but not eliminated), Beewolf now has a choice. Pure strength is matched with a mastery of weapons, an important skill for a leader of armed men.

Narrative developments like these give *Sellic Spell* a theme of "growing up" comparable to the one in Riggs's *Story of Beowulf*, which might appeal to younger reader, who is already assumed by many adults (although not necessarily by Tolkien) to be the natural audience of the folktale. Compared to nineteenth-century *Beowulf*s, Tolkien's story is marked not only by its augmentation and celebration of the fairy story elements the author perceived in the original poem, but also by its rather more down-to-earth message: brute strength is all well and good, but even heroes need to grow up and learn how to behave before they can truly come into their own.

Furthermore, Tolkien's decision not to end the story in Beewolf's death is an intriguing move that points back, once more, to his theory of the fairy story, while simultaneously producing an ending for his tale rather more palatable to a young audience than the grim, apocalyptic conclusion to the Old English poem. The fairy story ought to console the reader with a happy ending.[83] It is true that *Beowulf* gives Tolkien little material with which to work in order to achieve his trademark eucatastrophe; Tom Shippey suggests that the only hint of the eucatastrophic in the Old English poem can be found "when the demoralized survivors of Beowulf's nation, the Geats, trapped in Raven's Wood by Ongentheow, the terrible old king of the Swedes ... hear *samod ærdæge*, 'with the dawn,' the horns and trumpets of the army of Beowulf's uncle Hygelac coming to their rescue."[84] This episode is eliminated from *Sellic Spell* altogether, along with the catastrophic ending of its source, the dragon fight. Having become a "mighty man in the land," Beewolf instead settles into his new status. He fights for the king, marries the king's only daughter, and becomes king in his turn. We leave Beewolf assured that he "lived long in glory" and that "As long as he lived he loved honey dearly, and the mead in his hall was ever of the best" (385). This is an ending typical of Tolkien's fairy story, which "does not deceive anyone" in its apparent conclusiveness and serves more as a frame, "no more to be thought of as the real end of any particular fragment of the seamless Web of Story than the frame is of the visionary scene, or the casement of the Outer World."[85] Certainly Beewolf had many adventures not included in *Sellic Spell*. Perhaps his last show of strength brought about his death as well, and perhaps it had something to do with a dragon; but if it did, Tolkien chooses not to end on that note. The reader's last impression is of peace and happiness: a bear with slightly more human and sophisticated tastes enjoying his honey in the form of mead. We must do without the eucatastropic turn typical of Tolkien's original fantasy narratives, but not without the consolation of the happy ending Tolkien considered inherent to the fairy story.[86]

In the introduction to her edition of Tolkien's *Story of Kullervo*, Verlyn Flieger remarks that this adaptation of the Finnish *Kalevala* is "emphatically not for children, neither playful nor satiric, not allegorical, and with little of the faërie quality Tolkien found essential for fairy stories."[87] Flieger's connection between the lack of fairy story quality in Tolkien's *Kullervo* and its lack of suitability for children is telling. For Tolkien, fairy stories are not *only* suitable for children, but they are also not *unsuitable* for children. In any case, Tolkien's adaptational decisions in *Sellic Spell* have the double effect, at nearly every turn, of not only restoring *Beowulf* to Tolkien's ideal fairy story pseudo-predecessor, but also producing an excellent story with a practical moral for young readers. Complex historical details have been cut, complex diction shorn (nearly) away. Even the grim conclusion is replaced with a "happily ever after." Furthermore, the Bear's Son characterization of Beewolf creates continuity between *Sellic Spell* and Tolkien's earlier *Beowulf*s for young audiences, *The Hobbit* and *The Lay of Beowulf*. Its similarities to Riggs's *Story of Beowulf* also situates *Sellic Spell* comfortably in the genre of 1930s children's literature. If we are to read *Sellic Spell* as a tale for a primary audience of adults rather than children, we must do so by means of Tolkien's extratextual commentary on the genre and audience of fairy stories; the text itself provides the reader with little reason to do so.

Of course, the main authority on a work's audience is the individual who reads it. One need only look to the diverse readership of contemporary young adult fiction to remind oneself that guides and preferences regarding audiences have limited power to shape readership in reality. In any case, it is unlikely that Tolkien would be distressed to find children reading his "adult" *Beowulf*s, or to find adults reading his "children's" *Beowulf*s. Waggeries aside, he himself might allow, based on his own lifelong appreciation for fairy stories, that *Sellic Spell* (as well as *The Lay of Beowulf* and *The Hobbit*) ought to be picked up at the age of six and revisited many times before the age of sixty, and many times afterward. This, I think, would be an agreeable compromise.

NOTES

1 J.R.R. Tolkien, *The Letters of J.R.R. Tolkien*, ed. Humphrey Carpenter (New York: Houghton Mifflin, 1981), 297.
2 Tolkien, *Letters*, 297.
3 *The Lay of Beowulf* and *Sellic Spell* were recently published for the first time in J.R.R. Tolkien, *Beowulf: A Translation and Commentary, together with Sellic Spell*, ed. Christopher Tolkien (New York: Houghton Mifflin, 2014): *The Lay of Beowulf* in two versions on pp. 415–25 (*Beowulf and Grendel*, pp. 417–19, and *Beowulf and the Monsters*, pp. 420–5), and *Sellic Spell* in two Modern English versions ("The Final Text," pp. 360–86, and an earlier version described and selectively presented by C. Tolkien on pp. 387–403) and an Old English version (pp. 404–14). Another *Beowulf*-related early work of Tolkien's will not be part of this study: "Iúmonna Gold Galdre Bewunden," first published in 1923 and later revised and published under the title "The Hoard" in *The Adventures of Tom Bombadil* (1962), takes its inspiration from line 3052 of *Beowulf*, as Douglas A. Anderson notes (J.R.R. Tolkien, *The Annotated Hobbit: Revised and Expanded Edition*, ed. Douglas A. Anderson [New York: Houghton Mifflin, 2002], 337). Because of its relatively loose and essentially thematic ties to *Beowulf* (namely, its sinister implications about the dragon hoard), I do not read it as a *Beowulf* adaptation per se.
4 J.R.R. Tolkien, *The Monsters and the Critics and Other Essays*, ed. Christopher Tolkien (London: HarperCollins, 2006), 128.
5 Tolkien, *Monsters and the Critics*, 129.
6 Tolkien, *Monsters and the Critics*, 129–30.
7 Tolkien, *Monsters and the Critics*, 138.
8 Tolkien, *Monsters and the Critics*, 153.
9 Verlyn Flieger, "'There Would Always Be a Fairy-Tale': J.R.R. Tolkien and the Folklore Controversy," in *Tolkien the Medievalist*, ed. Jane Chance (London: Routledge, 2003), 35.
10 In his essay *"Sir Gawain and the Green Knight,"* Tolkien approaches the poem as the product of an "elder myth," arguing that the *Gawain*-poet's work is "not *about* those old things, but it receives part of its life, its vividness, its tension from them. That is the way with the greater fairy-stories – of which this is one" (Tolkien, *Monsters and the Critics*, 73).
11 These notes are published under the title "Commentary" in Tolkien, *Beowulf: A Translation* and will be referred to as such in this chapter. As

Dimitra Fimi notes, Tolkien uses "fairy story" and "folktale," among other terms, interchangeably in his commentary, and appears to make little distinction between the terms elsewhere ("Tolkien and Folklore: *Sellic Spell* and *The Lay of Beowulf*," *Mallorn* 55 [2014]: 27). I will follow Tolkien's lead in my use of the terms within this chapter.

12 Tolkien, *Beowulf: A Translation*, 147.

13 Tolkien, *Beowulf: A Translation*, 207.

14 Tolkien, *Beowulf: A Translation*, 198–200.

15 Tolkien, *Beowulf: A Translation*, 208.

16 Tolkien, *Monsters and the Critics*, 114.

17 Tolkien, *Monsters and the Critics*, 116.

18 Tolkien, *Monsters and the Critics*, 115–18.

19 Tolkien, *Beowulf: A Translation*, 416.

20 Fimi, "Tolkien and Folklore," 28.

21 Tolkien, *Beowulf: A Translation*, 415–16.

22 *Beowulf and Grendel*, ll. 21–2 (cf. *Beowulf and the Monsters*, ll. 29–30), in Tolkien, *Beowulf: A Translation*, as cited in n. 3 above. Subsequent references to *The Lay of Beowulf* will be to the version *Beowulf and Grendel* and will be given parenthetically by line number.

23 Tolkien describes the juxtaposition thus: "[*Beowulf*] is essentially a balance, an opposition of ends and beginnings. In its simplest terms it is a contrasted description of two moments in a great life, rising and setting; an elaboration of the ancient and intensely moving contrast between youth and age, first achievement and final death" (Tolkien, *Monsters and the Critics*, 28).

24 Tolkien, *Monsters and the Critics*, 26.

25 "I would suggest, then, that the monsters are not an inexplicable blunder of taste; they are essential, fundamentally allied to the underlying ideas of the poem, which give it its lofty tone and high seriousness" (Tolkien, *Monsters and the Critics*, 19).

26 Tolkien, *Monsters and the Critics*, 20.

27 Tolkien, *Monsters and the Critics*, 23.

28 Tolkien, *Monsters and the Critics*, 28.

29 Tolkien, *Letters*, 310.

30 Tolkien, *Monsters and the Critics*, 137.

31 See Carl Edlund Anderson's essay in this volume for discussion of profoundly creative deployments of *Beowulf* elements, on the order of those in *The Hobbit*, as "reuses" of the Old English poem.

32 Tolkien, *Letters*, 31.

33 The dragon antagonist Smaug also showcases Tolkien's skill in the folklorization of *Beowulf* elements in *The Hobbit*, and much could be said about the way in which Tolkien constructs an immersive dragon lore within

the novel in order to correct one of the main failings he perceived in the *Beowulf* dragon (that the *Beowulf* dragon "approaches *draconitas* rather than *draco*" [Tolkien, *Monsters and the Critics*, 17]). However, because the *Beowulf* dragon does not provide a very strong through line connecting the three *Beowulf*s discussed in this chapter (it is adapted fully only in *The Hobbit*, and appears obliquely in *The Lay of Beowulf* and not at all in *Sellic Spell*), I have chosen to limit the discussion to Beorn, as all three works feature strikingly similar analogues of the Beowulf character.

34 Humphrey Carpenter, *J.R.R. Tolkien: A Biography* (New York: Houghton Mifflin, 2000), 184.

35 Tolkien, *Letters*, 297. Tolkien's 1955 letter to W.H. Auden also expresses the notion that *The Hobbit* was infected with a "silliness of manner" objectionable to "intelligent children" (*Letters*, 215).

36 Tolkien, *Letters*, 191.

37 Wayne G. Hammond and Christina Scull, *The Lord of the Rings: A Reader's Companion* (New York: Houghton Mifflin, 2005), 52.

38 Tolkien, *Letters*, 298.

39 Tolkien, *Letters*, 298. For the reference in the letter to Neave, see *Letters*, 310.

40 John D. Rateliff, *The History of "The Hobbit," Part One: Mr. Baggins* (London: HarperCollins, 2007), 253–6.

41 For a discussion of the dating of the earliest *Hobbit* drafts, see Anderson's Introduction (esp. pp. 7–12) to Tolkien, *Annotated "Hobbit,"* as cited in n. 3 above. For a detailed treatment, see Rateliff, *History of "The Hobbit," Part One*, and Rateliff, *The History of "The Hobbit," Part Two: Return to Bag-End* (London: HarperCollins, 2007), an edition of the original manuscripts and revisions of *The Hobbit* with excellent commentary.

42 *OED Online* (www.oed.com, accessed 11 September 2016), s.v. *berne*, n.

43 Tom Shippey, *The Road to Middle-Earth: Revised and Expanded Edition* (New York: Houghton Mifflin, 2003), 80.

44 Douglas A. Anderson, "R.W. Chambers and *The Hobbit*," *Tolkien Studies* 3 (2006): 143. See also the section titled "Medwed" (pp. 228–92) of Rateliff, *History of "The Hobbit," Part One*.

45 Shippey, *Road to Middle-Earth*, 80.

46 Tolkien, *Annotated "Hobbit,"* 165.

47 See, for instance, Anderson's note on Tolkien, *Annotated "Hobbit,"* 349.

48 Multiple sketches of Beorn's Hall by Tolkien that illustrate its debt to medieval Germanic architecture can be found in Wayne G. Hammond and Christina Scull, eds., *The Art of "The Hobbit" by J.R.R. Tolkien* (Boston: Houghton Mifflin Harcourt, 2012), 66–70.

49 Marjorie Burns, *Perilous Realms: Celtic and Norse in Tolkien's Middle-Earth* (Toronto: University of Toronto Press, 2005), 34.

50 Indeed, in a letter to his son Christopher, Tolkien says of *The Hobbit* that he recognized it as a "story of worth" when, upon rereading it, "I had suddenly in a fairly strong measure the 'eucatastrophic' emotion at Bilbo's exclamation: 'The Eagles! The Eagles are coming!'" (Tolkien, *Letters*, 101). Beorn, of course, is not an Eagle, but the winged allies' arrival coincides with the bear-man's own last-minute appearance and the turn of the battle.

51 Tolkien, *The Hobbit*, 244.

52 Tolkien, *Beowulf: A Translation*, 359.

53 Tolkien, *Beowulf: A Translation*, 355.

54 Paul Acker, "Tolkien's *Sellic Spell*: A Beowulfian Fairy Story," *Tolkien Studies* 13 (2016): 31–44.

55 Verlyn Flieger and Douglas A. Anderson, *Tolkien "On Fairy-Stories": Expanded Edition, with Commentary and Notes* (London: HarperCollins, 2014), 100.

56 Tolkien, *Beowulf: A Translation*, 358.

57 Tolkien, *Beowulf: A Translation*, 355.

58 Henry Sweet, *First Steps in Anglo-Saxon* (Oxford: Clarendon Press, 1897), 39–67.

59 Gwyn Jones, founder and editor of the *Welsh Review*, also saw the pedagogical application of *Sellic Spell*, and considered that it should be "prescribed reading for all university students of *Beowulf*" (Christina Scull and Wayne G. Hammond, *The J.R.R. Tolkien Companion and Guide: Reader's Guide* [Boston: Houghton Mifflin, 2006], 86, 439).

60 Tolkien, *Beowulf: A Translation*, 233.

61 See Anna Smol, "Heroic Ideology and the Children's *Beowulf*," *Children's Literature* 22 (1994): 94, for discussion of late nineteenth- and early twentieth-century *Beowulf* adaptations and their simplification of the poem's content in order to focus on Beowulf's three major fights against Grendel, Grendel's mother, and the dragon.

62 See also Acker, "Tolkien's *Sellic Spell*," which performs a thorough analysis of *Sellic Spell* as a fairy story adaptation of *Beowulf* and also discusses how its departures from its source may be explained in terms of R.W. Chambers's critical analysis of *Beowulf*, which was influential on Tolkien's own views.

63 Lise Jaillant, "'A Fine Old Tale of Adventure': *Beowulf* Told to the Children of the English Race, 1898–1908," *Children's Literature Association Quarterly* 38 (2013): 403.

64 Tolkien, *Beowulf: A Translation*, 362.

65 Tolkien, *Beowulf: A Translation*, 377.

66 Tolkien, *Monsters and the Critics*, 55.

67 Tolkien, *Monsters and the Critics*, 56.

68 See Tolkien, *Beowulf: A Translation*, 404–14. It should be noted that Christopher Tolkien believes that the Old English text must have been

based upon an earlier Modern English form of *Sellic Spell*, but perhaps predates the later manuscripts on which the published version is based. He acknowledges that this ordering appears to contradict his father's claim that the flavour of the Modern English form is derived from the Old English text (Tolkien, *Beowulf: A Translation*, 404–6).

69 Strafford Riggs, *The Story of Beowulf* (New York: D. Appleton-Century Company, 1933), 35. Subsequent references will be given parenthetically by page number.

70 *Sellic Spell* is cited from "The Final Text" as edited in Tolkien, *Beowulf: A Translation*, with references given parenthetically by page number.

71 Anderson, "R.W. Chambers and *The Hobbit*," 142.

72 Scull and Hammond, *Tolkien Companion and Guide: Reader's Guide*, 291–2.

73 Scull and Hammond, *Tolkien Companion and Guide: Reader's Guide*, 291, 293–4.

74 Tolkien, *Beowulf: A Translation*, 358.

75 Fimi, "Tolkien and Folklore,"27.

76 *Beowulf*, ll. 2183b–89.

77 Fimi touches on the "problem" of Beowulf's superhuman strength in her article: by making reference to the numbers seven and thirty in his description of Beewolf's strength (both magic numbers in folklore), Tolkien more firmly grounds the "historical" *Beowulf* in its folkloric past ("Tolkien and Folklore," 27).

78 Tolkien, *Monsters and the Critics*, 18.

79 See *Beowulf: A Translation*, 343–4, for more on Tolkien's reading of Hondscio as a "fairy-tale element."

80 Tolkien, *Beowulf: A Translation*, 356.

81 Fimi, "Tolkien and Folklore," 27.

82 Tolkien was well aware of the striking correspondence between the monsters' mere episode in *Beowulf* and the very similar waterfall fight in the *Grettis Saga*. In the commentary on *Beowulf*, he notes the apparent connection between the *Beowulf hæftméce* and *Grettis Saga heptisax*, words which refer to the weapons associated with the monster fight in each story. Further, he theorizes that Unferth must correspond with the priest who abandons Grettir (Tolkien, *Beowulf: A Translation*, 210). Unferth plays no such role in *Beowulf*, but this "original" role is restored in his folklorized *Sellic Spell* analogue, with a malicious twist.

83 Tolkien, *Monsters and the Critics*, 153.

84 Tom Shippey, *J.R.R. Tolkien: Author of the Century* (New York: Houghton Mifflin, 2000), 215.

85 Tolkien, *Monsters and the Critics*, 161.

86 In her discussion of fairy-story elements in Tolkien's *Beowulf* translations and adaptations, including *Sellic Spell*, Jane Chance also notes the

importance of eliminating the dragon – and Beewolf's death – so that
the hero can live "happily ever after" (*Tolkien, Self, and Other: "This Queer
Creature"* [New York: Palgrave Macmillan, 2016], 92). Jane Beal likewise
explores the connection between the conclusion to *Sellic Spell* and eucatastrophe, with a focus on Beewolf's marriage at the end of *Sellic Spell*
("Tolkien, Eucatastrophe, and the Re-Creation of Medieval Legend,"
Journal of Tolkien Research 4, no. 1 [2017]: 1–18).

87 J.R.R. Tolkien, *The Story of Kullervo*, ed. Verlyn Flieger (New York:
Houghton Mifflin Harcourt, 2016), xv.

4 Treatments of *Beowulf* as a Source in Mid-Twentieth-Century Children's Literature

CARL EDLUND ANDERSON

The mid-twentieth century, defined here as approximately 1930 to 1970, was a transitional period in both children's literature and academic *Beowulf* studies. Its starting point slightly anticipates the so-called Second Golden Age of English-language children's literature (c. 1940–70), and also the marked shift in *Beowulf* studies from viewing the poem as a source for ancient history and cultural origins to an artful work of literature.[1] In English-language adaptations of *Beowulf* for children, this period also brought a shift in focus from the didactic and moralizing tones that typify those produced before the First World War to freer, more personal artistic treatments of the narrative that have been more the norm ever since, although as we shall see, there is neither a clear dividing line between nor a smooth path of development from earlier "didactic" and later "literary" approaches to adapting *Beowulf* for younger readers.

Children's literature is sometimes remarked to be the only type of writing defined by its audience,[2] and indeed the Library of Congress of the United States classifies it as "material written and produced for the information or entertainment of children and young adults."[3] Some may balk at a definition of literature that includes (as the Library of Congress's definition goes on to do) not only "literary and artistic genres" but "all non-fiction,"[4] but as Frederick Joseph Harvey Darton noted long ago, literature for children has frequently been "the scene of a battle between instruction and amusement."[5] Adaptations of works considered classical or canonical, and therefore suitable for introducing young readers to desirable aspects of cultural heritage and values – but not appropriate in their raw forms (for whatever reason) – have often tended towards the instructional side of that struggle.[6]

Mid-twentieth-century adaptors of *Beowulf* for younger audiences had themselves grown up as readers of children's literature from the

Victorian and Edwardian periods, a time that incorporated what is still understood as the "First Golden Age" of children's literature.[7] They naturally enough reacted and responded to this background in different ways, coloured by their experiences and interests as well as the requirements of their publishers. The all-inclusive but audience-focused nature of children's literature may help its evolution stand somewhat apart from trends observed in other literature during the twentieth century,[8] yet the same shifting social, political, and cultural currents played their part in encouraging mid-twentieth-century writers approaching the adaptation of *Beowulf* for younger readers to move away from the exemplifying summaries of their predecessors and towards increasingly creative reworkings and reuses of the story.

This essay examines the emergent distinction between what I will call *retellings* and *reuses* of *Beowulf* as the latter type came into being and became well established. *Retellings* are here understood as adaptations that chiefly follow the plot of the Old English poem. Retellings in the form of compressed paraphrase had been the dominant mode of representing the poem for younger readers in the Victorian and Edwardian period, when the main goal of such adaptations was to familiarize this audience with an important cultural monument that presented them with exemplary life lessons. The goals of retellings themselves broaden during the mid-twentieth century, accommodating sometimes quite elliptical and inventive ways of following *Beowulf*'s basic story; but an even greater contrast with earlier approaches is found in mid-twentieth-century *reuses*, a type which had not previously existed: works in which an author draws on elements of *Beowulf* but repurposes them in ways that link them much less rigidly to the poem's plot. My discussion will touch on a number of works to illustrate developments in this period but will take as its analytical centerpiece the writings of a single prominent author, Rosemary Sutcliff, who produced adaptations or derivations of both kinds. Her 1961 retelling of *Beowulf* for children, *Dragonslayer* (the title adopted to identify it in this paper),[9] is widely known; rather less well known is Sutcliff's innovative reuse of elements from *Beowulf* in her 1956 youth novel *The Shield Ring*.[10] The comparison of two books by a successful children's writer exemplifies the range of approaches becoming available as *Beowulf* was increasingly regarded as a backdrop for modern authors' own creative expression.

The Expanding Range of Retelling and the Emergence of Reuse

By the time the period under consideration here began, *Beowulf* already had a long history of adaptation for young readers. Although children's literature from what is termed the "First Golden Age" is often characterized as moving away from overt didacticism and towards entertainment,[11] much of it was, at least implicitly, designed to prepare children for future roles in the expansion and maintenance of empire (perhaps as much for America's frontier as for Britain's overseas dominions).[12] To these interests *Beowulf*'s heroic action, aimed at subduing savage creatures that threaten civilization, was congenial. *Beowulf* also had cachet as a monument of antiquity, a factor that became increasingly important in an era of burgeoning nationalism as societies both discovered the past, with advances in scholarship and public education, and sought legitimacy and validation within it.[13] For the English-speaking world of the nineteenth century, this implied a veneration of all things "Anglo-Saxon";[14] that *Beowulf* was written in their tribal language while its story appeared to delve back into the mists of an even earlier Teutonic world made it so much the better. At the same time, peoples of the past were viewed almost as children themselves – as having somehow enjoyed a purer, more idyllic innocence – and folktales, too, even if collected only recently, were seen as windows on the past.[15] The content of *Beowulf*, though in need of streamlining to fit the task, was thus eminently suitable for both entertaining and instructing children, particularly boys.

Accordingly, even though *Beowulf* enjoyed little formal respect as literature during the nineteenth and early twentieth centuries, it should not surprise us that English adaptations prepared with children in mind (as opposed to those for general audiences that children might have read) began to appear at least as early as 1873.[16] By the end of 1910 about twenty English adaptations of *Beowulf* for younger readers had been published;[17] some appeared in popular magazines, others in books and collections intended for school use. Anna Smol has emphasized that most children's adaptations of *Beowulf* up to the early twentieth century presented the tale with a decidedly traditional moral and didactic slant: the hero is strong, brave, and self-sacrificing, a defender of civilization, a supporter of kings and eventually a king himself, ostensibly demonstrating the innate superiority of the "Anglo-Saxon race" from its earliest times.[18]

In terms of genuinely creative adaptation, however, the mid-twentieth century and the "Second Golden Age" of children's literature would tend to make much more of *Beowulf* than what had come before. After a slackening of their production during the First World War and the 1920s, the mid-twentieth century saw a great revival in the publication of *Beowulf* adaptations for youth. Many of these resume the Victorian and Edwardian approaches of their predecessors, offering relatively direct child-friendly simplifications of the Old English poem's plot, or portions of it. For example, Dorothy Hosford's prose *Beowulf* adaptation, seemingly intended for use in schools, largely avoids the moralizing common in earlier such efforts but eschews any creative elaboration.[19] C.F. Bricknell Smith's prose adaptation likewise presents a streamlined version of the original poem's story.[20] In slight contrast, Gladys Schmitt's prose adaptation of *Beowulf* ends with the hero being made king.[21] This truncated conclusion, in an adaptation aimed at younger children than most, avoids presentation of the hero's death in keeping with the reduced violence in the scenes with Grendel and Grendel's mother. With the exception of Schmitt's abbreviated plot, which is also laid over a background to the story that is particularly hers (again, perhaps intended to appeal more to young readers), these retellings all simplify the narratives by omitting the original's "digressions" but otherwise stick reasonably closely to *Beowulf*'s monster-slaying storyline.

Strafford Riggs's book *The Story of Beowulf*, strikingly illustrated with bold two-colour illustrations by Henry C. Pitz, is perhaps the first children's adaptation that indicates a real change of approach.[22] The difference may not be evident in the medievalizing title-page design, of the sort that Lise Jaillant argues is "tied to history, archeology, and the search for origins."[23] Nor is it signalled in Charles J. Finger's foreword, where observations such as "what we would see introduced into the life of a nation must be first introduced into the schools, or in other ways carried into the world of youth" (vi) suggest a moral and didactic approach that is alive and well. Nevertheless, Riggs's adaption itself – while simplified as all such children's versions tend to be – treats the story with marked freedom in comparison to its predecessors. The content of *Beowulf* is here genuinely remade (if not dramatically so) into a work of fiction intended to engage and entertain children at least as much as instruct them, rather than presenting a barer paraphrase. Riggs's approach to retelling *Beowulf* is the more remarkable considering that it predates Tolkien's watershed lecture "The Monsters and the Critics."

Riggs's adaption of *Beowulf* is divided into three roughly equal parts. The final two narrate the fights with Grendel and his mother and then the dragon; but the first is focused on Beowulf's own childhood, a strategy that is employed by many adaptors in an effort to make the story more appealing to younger readers.[24] Riggs makes the most extensive early use of this approach. His young Beowulf is strong, but clumsy and sluggardly, earning him a bad reputation among his peers. Even his victory over Breca in the swimming contest, though it would become "a famous legend" (7), seems to have earned him little immediate respect, as Hygelac's court rumbles with a "murmur of wonder" (15) when Beowulf vows to sail to Denmark and defeat Grendel. They might better have listened to the one old warrior of their number who, "with white flowing locks and a gentle sweet voice," had proclaimed that Beowulf's fame as a hero was "written in the stars" (10). Riggs's protagonist goes forward from that point to a celebrated heroic career with little further ado. His tale ends, after the conflict with the dragon, with his "noble earls" mourning at his pyre and concludes almost abruptly: "Thus passed to his own gods Beowulf, King of Geatsland, in the North" (84). The Beowulf that Riggs gives us is more expressive than previously and equipped with a fuller backstory, but he remains circumscribed to his own tale and context in the misty antique North.

A further innovation in retellings of *Beowulf* was made by Ian Serraillier, who later became well known for his children's books, particularly *The Silver Sword*. Besides original fiction, Serraillier tackled the adaptation of a number of myths and legends from both the classical world and medieval Europe; one of these, *The Ivory Horn*, was nominated for a Carnegie Medal.[25] Serraillier's *Beowulf*, featuring bold black-and-white illustrations by Mark Severin, was one of his earliest such adaptations of canonical narratives, and it is notable not so much for its inventions with plot – it is a very straight, simplified account in that respect – but for providing a poetic retelling in stately but powerful blank verse.[26] In this formal choice, Serraillier took care to capture something of the alliterative style of the Old English original, yet without overly complicated language or phrasing. It can give a younger (or any) reader some sense of the strength and movement of Old English poetry, especially when read aloud. Although Serraillier's presentation of the narrative is highly condensed, the more experienced reader will sometimes encounter a phrase that closely recalls the wording of the original: for example, Serraillier describes Grendel as "that fiend from hell, foul enemy of God" (12), recalling Old English phrases from *Beowulf* such as "feond on helle" (l. 101b) and "Godes andsaca" (l. 1682b).[27] Earlier retellings of the paraphrase type had mimicked some of the word patterning of the original, but Serraillier's project is aesthetic: he remakes *Beowulf* into a poem all over again, for children, and uses some of its poetic resources in the service of his own creative vision.

Few mid-twentieth-century adaptors made *Beowulf* as truly their own as did Robert Nye, whose retelling appeared right at the end of the period considered here.[28] Two versions of Nye's adaptation were published in 1968 under different titles: *Beowulf: A New Telling* in the US, and *Bee Hunter: Adventures of Beowulf* in the UK. Although they have sometimes been treated bibliographically as the same book merely packaged differently for British and American markets,[29] in fact they have completely different illustration programs, with *A New Telling* illustrated by Alan E. Cober and *Bee Hunter* illustrated by Nye's wife, Aileen Campbell. The texts also differ slightly in ways that suggest alterations made to *Bee Hunter* to enhance its suitability for younger readers.[30]

Nye's adaptation of *Beowulf* is lengthier than many, and he includes some material from the original that others strip out, such as a brief passage on the Swedish-Geatish wars. Yet no other mid-twentieth-century adaptor of *Beowulf* for children departs as greatly from earlier approaches to the poem, especially the standard idealizations of the protagonist as warrior and ruler, as does Nye. Nye's Beowulf is short of stature and nearsighted, with teeth that Unferth derides as "riddled with rot" (37). He remains formidable: he slays Grendel by embracing him with the force of his own goodness, and he seems to extinguish Grendel's mother through the power of his own self-knowledge that he, too, has darkness within himself; his heroism consists of recognizing it and holding it in check.[31] By identifying Beowulf as "the bee-hunter," Nye picks up and runs with the widely repeated etymology of Beowulf's name as "bee-wolf":[32] Nye's Beowulf keeps bees and actually slays the dragon by sending swarms from his hives flying down its throat. Other characters in the narrative also receive idiosyncratic spins from Nye, who adds whole new scenes and details. Hrothgar, for example, fights a bear, a curious reflection of Saxo Grammaticus's Biarco (a version of the hero known in Old Norse sources as Bǫðvarr Bjarki).[33] It is the character of Unferth who is most notably expanded by Nye, who turns him into the villain you love to hate. Unferth needles relentlessly at Beowulf and the Danish court before eventually going mad with the belief that Grendel, the outcast, had been coming to rescue him from Heorot as a fellow outcast. Grendel's mother apparently kills him.

Nye's stature as a literary author and poet attracted to his retelling more critical attention than many others received, though it was not always positive. Rebecca Barnhouse describes it as an "unimpressive prose 'interpretation'" that "includes many scenes from Nye's imagination,"[34] and Joyce Elizabeth Potter comments disapprovingly that Nye has turned the story "from a tragedy into a comedy, extrapolating its noble ethics and leaving behind its evocative nature imagery."[35] John Stephens and Robyn McCallum see his approach as representative of a view "prevalent in children's literature ... that evil will ultimately be self-destructive" and find misogynistic sexual overtones in the scene where Beowulf strangles Grendel's weakened mother, with "patriarchal assumptions" that are "symptomatic of heroic metanarratives."[36] But regardless of reception, Nye's retelling shows that mid-twentieth-century adaptors of *Beowulf* had become interested in far more than funneling didactic and moralistic messages through an abbreviated piece of canon – if they were interested in this at all. Even for those committed to reproducing the major story elements, *Beowulf* had become eligible to serve as a canvas upon which the mid-twentieth-century adaptor's own pictures could be painted.

From adapting *Beowulf* by reimagining the familiar plot and characters of the poem, it is a short step to seeing *Beowulf* as a source of ideas and inspiration that may inform and colour the author's own more individual creations. Charles A. Brady's youth novel *The King's Thane* repurposes aspects of the original poem's plot in a way that parts from *retelling* and takes us into the category of *reuse*.[37] Brady presents his story as having been written by an elderly English monk, Beorn, about his experiences as a lamed teenage boy who accompanied a Norse hero, Bjarki (identified as a descendent of the "original" Beowulf!), from Geatland to early seventh-century Northumbria and the court of King Edwin. Bjarki's mission to fight Grendel is juxtaposed with that of Christian missionaries seeking to convert the English. Brady's creative reuse of elements of *Beowulf* results in a complicated plot and large cast of characters; the relatively heavy reading for a younger audience may have contributed to this work being less well known than, for example, Nye's fast-moving retelling.

A different kind of reuse of *Beowulf* was made by both John O. Beaty and Jill Paton Walsh, who, at opposite ends of the period considered here, took *Beowulf*'s Finnsburg episode (and the separate Old English poem known as *The Battle of Finnsburh*) out of the poem's background to give it centre stage in their own fiction.[38] Beaty's *Swords in the Dawn* appears on the eve of the Second World War, and its subtitle, *A Story of the First Englishmen*, recalls the focus on nationalistic origins prominent in pre-Tolkien approaches to *Beowulf*. Yet despite the fame of Tolkien's call to approach *Beowulf* as literary art, Tolkien himself was more than willing to see it as a source for history, and his own historical conception of the Finnsburg episode is closely paralleled in Paton Walsh's *Hengest's Tale*.[39] Indeed, her fictionalized interpretation of Hengest as leader at Finnsburg and subsequent invader of Kent is so close to Tolkien's own analysis that, although the available chronologies suggest that Tolkien did not lecture on this subject during Paton Walsh's undergraduate career at Oxford,[40] one wonders if she somehow encountered his ideas.

Sutcliff's *Dragonslayer* and *The Shield Ring*

Perhaps no mid-century author of youth literature other than J.R.R. Tolkien was as deeply immersed in *Beowulf* as Rosemary Sutcliff.[41] Sutcliff herself emphasized the significance *Beowulf* had for her as a childhood story, singling out the early twentieth-century paraphrase included in M.I. Ebbutt's *Hero Myths and Legends of the British Race* as the story she "demanded most often and loved better than all beside."[42] Few *Beowulf* adaptors, too, can claim anything like her level of success. Sutcliff's acclaimed 1961 *Dragonslayer* has been printed dozens of times, under various titles, down to the present day.[43]

In structure, Sutcliff's retelling is like many other mid-twentieth-century adaptations of *Beowulf* for children. It expands on the circumstances by which Beowulf comes to hear of the monster plaguing the Danes, but otherwise follows the hero's monster-fighting closely, while dispensing with the original poem's lengthy speeches and digressions from the main storyline. Sutcliff made broad and open use of numerous sources throughout her own work, and the influence of Ebbutt's *Beowulf* adaptation on Sutcliff's is readily detectable. Nevertheless, in *Dragonslayer* (as generally with Sutcliff's works) she has reforged her influences into a finely wrought personal vision. Sutcliff is well known for evocative use of the language of landscape in her fiction,[44] for example, and Potter has analysed the "geographical grammar" that underlies Sutcliff's *Beowulf* adaptation, noting how she "has linked victorious, joyous, and especially anticipatory times to spacial heights; times of lonely and dire struggle to lower areas near sea level; and times of transient encounters or of annihilation to the sea itself."[45] This method of tracing the plot's movement through different spaces, Potter argues, helps younger readers grasp the story's emotional import. It also seems a central part of Sutcliff's means of personalizing her vision of the hero for her reader. Her treatment of the plot is hardly beyond moral didacticism, but the reader's focus is far more on the shared journey through high and low, victory and danger, with both hero and author.

Even as the story ends with Beowulf's funeral and the departure of his mourning chieftains, it concludes in one of its "high places" where the environment itself has the last elegiac words: "And when the song was all sung, all men went away, and left Beowulf's barrow alone with the sea wind and the wheeling gulls and the distant ships that passed on the Sail-Road" (93). We know this is fitting for a hero who has both scaled the heights and plumbed the depths as none other in his world. Beowulf's death, sometimes avoided by adaptations of the story for children, and the fight with the dragon that leads to it seem to have together created a strong impression on Sutcliff. She does not dwell on the original poem's implication that the Geats without Beowulf are at risk of invasion and conquest – although it receives a fleeting observation from Wiglaf – but the image of Beowulf's howe, alone with the wind and gulls, leaves the reader with the impression that with Beowulf a more heroic and epic age has passed away.

A similar theme emerges strongly in her novel *The Shield Ring*, which reuses elements of Beowulf's dragon fight and death in both obvious and more subtle ways. Set in England's Lake District during the early twelfth century, *The Shield Ring* has received less attention than Sutcliff's novels set in Roman Britain, though it was the publication that immediately followed her better-known book *The Eagle of the Ninth* (set some nine centuries earlier)[46] and forms the chronological end point of the group of loosely connected novels that Sutcliff would go on to set between the time frames of those two books. The element connecting the several books in this constellation (it was not conceived as, nor really forms, a "series") is a particular ring with a dolphin insignia that is borne by various characters in the different stories set in different times. These books perhaps more than most of Sutcliff's are also linked by a concern with the "making of Britain"[47] through the interactions of various invaders and migrants, or inhabitants of differing backgrounds and cultures, all set against a richly evocative depiction of Britain's landscape that serves almost as a unifying character in itself. The deep influence of Kipling on Sutcliff has often been noted, including by Sutcliff herself,[48] and she arguably takes up some of Kipling's approach to the British Empire – and Britain itself – as a colourful mélange of peoples, casting early Britain in a role like that of Kipling's India while Rome or the Continent shadows the role of Imperial Britain.[49]

The Shield Ring was inspired by Nicholas Size's novella *The Secret Valley*, a curious work of semi-narrative popular history itself developed from Size's earlier self-published, pseudo-historical pamphlet *The Epic of Buttermere*.[50] Both *The Secret Valley* and *The Epic of Buttermere* were produced in part to help promote Size's hotel business in Buttermere, capitalizing on early twentieth-century Britain's ongoing fascination with "Old Northernism," which had already spawned other works of imaginative Norse-inspired fiction set in the Lake District.[51] Size, who died three years prior to Sutcliff's publication of *The Shield Ring*, had himself rewritten C.A. Parker's historical novella *The Story of Shelagh* as *Shelagh of Eskdale*,[52] so he could not have justly objected to Sutcliff taking a similar approach to his own work. From Size's *Secret Valley* Sutcliff freely lifts background, concepts, and whole characters, though one might say she handles them all rather better than did their originator.

The Shield Ring, like *The Secret Valley*, presents a kind of an Anglo-Norse paradise centred in early twelfth-century Buttermere, where "Saxon" refugees join with the descendants of Norse settlers (along with a leavening of Welsh) to resist Norman encroachment on the region.

In this portrayal of resistance, Sutcliff continues a theme that Fred Inglis argues appears in her Roman-period stories in which "her heroes and heroines ... stubbornly resist the cruelties of empires and ideologies."[53] This theme would never develop into a blanket condemnation of empire in Sutcliff's hands, but as Kipling was to a lesser extent, Sutcliff is aware of the contradictions that an empire's life cycle may involve. Inglis also identifies as a message of Sutcliff's fiction set in the aftermath of Roman Britain "that the individual spirit will survive the loss of nation, family, tribe, or regiment."[54] *The Shield Ring*, set much later, similarly suggests that individual spirits that survived the fall to the Normans come together for one last stand in the Lake District. In Sutcliff's novels, incoming Romans, Saxons, and Vikings all tend to "go native" in Britain, the rough edges of their interactions with each other and with whichever groups are then native being eventually smoothed away by a shared, geographically mandated spiritual destiny. In *The Shield Ring*, however, it seems questionable whether Normans may be granted membership this communion; as Sutcliff herself said, "after the late Norman times, I just don't understand the people."[55] Following *The Shield Ring*'s climax in a great battle that sees the Normans defeated and, in theory, the Lakelanders' independence preserved, there is nevertheless the implication that Britain's heroic age is finally at an end, even if the individual spirit may once again have the hope of survival.

To an extent, this is all as might seem right and natural to a Victorian admirer of "Old Northernism," a Victorian of the sort who wrote the books with which Sutcliff and others of her generation had grown up. Sutcliff has been criticized for repeating Imperial Victorian values in patterns of plots and characters that focus on young men (often ones of the officer class, accompanied by a kind of lower-status "batman") who embark on lonely, noble quests into the wild, suffering great hardships in the name of family or country; by this view, the scarcity of female protagonists in Sutcliff's works results likewise from her own "late Imperial" upbringing, including its familiar literary patterns that discouraged her from placing female characters in leading roles.[56] Be that as it may, *The Shield Ring* does offer a female protagonist in the character of Frytha,[57] even though her role is often in danger of being subsumed into that of "viewpoint companion" alongside that of the other main protagonist, Bjorn, on whom much of the plot hinges – and whose name hints at the submerged role of *Beowulf* in the novel.

The Shield Ring follows the childhood of two orphans: Frytha, a Saxon girl, and Bjorn, a Norse boy of partially British ancestry. Frytha's semi-aristocratic Saxon family is slain somewhat unjustly in retaliation for the killing of a Norman knight, but a trusted family servant keeps her safe and brings her to the Lakeland's mainly Anglo-Norse community, which is presented as having accepted many refugees from the Normans. The first part of the novel then takes Frytha and Bjorn through childhood, while following the ongoing conflict between the Anglo-Norse Lakelanders and Normans. The location of and way to the Lakelanders' refuge at Butharsmere (as Sutcliff, following Size, identifies Buttermere) is not known to the Normans, but the Lakelanders, knowing they are hard pressed, send one of their senior warriors, Ari Knudsen (a character from Size), to negotiate terms of peace with the Normans. They torture him, hoping to learn the location of the Anglo-Norse stronghold in the fells, and eventually slay him and his companions. This becomes a motivation for revenge for Ari's foster-son Aiken "the Beloved" (another character lifted from Size), but also a point of concern for young Bjorn, who worries whether, if captured, he would be able to resist torture and keep the Lakelanders' secret safe as Ari had. As we are told from Frytha's viewpoint, "That was Bjorn's trouble. Other people did not wonder those sort of things ... But Bjorn could picture it with hideous clearness, and so he wondered; which was a bad thing to do" (64). The next part of the novel continues to follow Bjorn's and Frytha's lives in the Lakeland, in which Bjorn becomes a skilled harper, and during this time Frytha's awareness of his preoccupation with the threat of torture by the Normans comes between them. The Lakelanders continue to hold off the Normans, but the pressure grows.

Little discernible influence from *Beowulf* is present in these earlier parts of *The Shield Ring*, which are mostly given over to establishing the narrative environment, based on Size's books, and the characters of Frytha and Bjorn. The only echo of *Beowulf* in this portion of the novel may be the centrality for the book's Anglo-Norse community of the chiefly hall at Butharsmere, which is complete with a harpist (Bjorn's foster-father and teacher of the harp). Hrothgar's Danes would have found it homey, all the more so as no monsters haunt it; Norman soldiers stalking the lowlands are enemy enough.

But *Beowulf* does appear explicitly in the novel's final sections. Knowing that the Normans plan a grand assault on the Lakelands, the Anglo-Norse of Butharsmere decide to send a spy to the Norman camp to learn their plans in advance of what must clearly be a final do-or-die battle (pp. 133–9). In a scene presenting the attendant deliberations, set within the hall, the harpist performs a song of Beowulf, describing the hero as he prepares for his "last fight" with the dragon (133). There are even two brief passages of verse adaptation (predating the publication of Sutcliff's prose adaptation, where these lines are not so emphasized), corresponding roughly to lines 2518–37 and 2538–44 of the Old English poem. The idea of Beowulf as a hero and *Beowulf* as a narrative is introduced in this scene without preamble or explanation; Sutcliff's readers are expected to have the same general familiarity with *Beowulf* as are the fictional twelfth-century Anglo-Norse Lakelanders.

Bjorn successfully argues that he should be the one chosen to spy on the Normans, stressing that his skill with the harp might allow him to pass among them as a minstrel. Yet Bjorn is also deliberately placing himself in harm's way to at last test his courage in the face of the enemies who tortured and slew Ari Knudsen many years before. Frytha, in a dream, spells out Sutcliff's main reuse of *Beowulf* here, although, again, the reader would have to know the story being referred to:

> [In Frytha's dream] Bjorn got confused with Ari Knudson, and both of them with Beowulf. Beowulf and the Firedrake; Bjorn and the Firedrake – but that was just what it was: Bjorn going out alone to face his own particular Firedrake. "He has come to his adventure ..." For a moment, she saw him [...] going down into the valley of the Firedrake, alone. "But Ari Knudsen did not go alone," she thought, "and in the end Beowulf's shield bearer ran to be with him." (141)

Thus Frytha decides to accompany Bjorn, the distance between them in recent years notwithstanding. Both go together to the Norman camp, and there in a chapter titled "The Fire-drake" the parallelism between Bjorn and Beowulf is heightened when, after Frytha and Beorn are discovered by the Normans, Bjorn is tortured by fire (pp. 163–75). The alert reader may now even be thinking that Bjorn's name – he is also the son of a man named Bjorn and was referred to in his childhood as "the Bear-cub" – was not idly chosen. Although it is questionable whether Beowulf's name should be genuinely etymologized so as to connect it with bears,[58] the widespread idea seems to have been known to Sutcliff, and she makes more subtle use of it than would Nye a dozen years later. Yet Bjorn does not die in confronting his firedrake, and he arguably defeats it by refusing to give up any secrets to the Normans, despite being tortured.

At this point Bjorn's association with the original Beowulf is fulfilled, but it will soon be taken up by another character. Philip Burton has noted how characteristics of particular historical, legendary, or mythical figures are sometimes spread across multiple characters in *The Eagle of the Ninth*: in reference to "Sutcliff's treatment of the [mythological] figure of Herne the Hunter – in part to be identified with [Sutcliff's character] Guern the Hunter and in part with the [her representation in the story of] Horned God, and fully with neither," Burton remarks that

> These dislocations in time and place are ... important for our reading of The Eagle as a whole. Guenevere the wife of Arthur is, in some sense, [Sutcliff's character] the regal, mysterious wife [Guinhumara] of Cradoc. Cradoc the resistance leader [in Sutcliff's story] is the Caratacus who fought against Rome nearly a century before – and also the Sir Christopher Cradock with whom Sutcliff's father served [in the Imperial-era British navy].[59]

Similarly in *The Shield Ring*, as some aspects of Beowulf are reflected in Bjorn, they also appear in the character of Aikin "the Beloved." The death by torture of Ari and its lingering psychological impact on the characters and community serve through the book as an object lesson on what can be expected from the Normans. Ari's self-sacrifice provides inspiration for group loyalty and heroic resistance in the face of terrible odds, though it also forces individual characters, especially Bjorn, to contemplate the limits of their capacities for such resistance and loyalty. After Bjorn, accompanied by Frytha, faces and passes this test, escaping with his life, the role of sacrificing oneself to protect the community (as did Beowulf in his combat with his dragon) becomes Aiken's. It is Aiken who effectively leads the Anglo-Norse army in the final battle with the Normans, which is given overtones of Ragnarǫk through stormy weather imagery and the explicit sense that even victory cannot stave off the end of the world that the Lakeland Anglo-Norse have known.

Victory is gained, though Aikin like Beowulf falls in securing it, and he is given a Beowulfian funeral: without cremation, but with interment in a burial mound on a high place above Keskadale – identified with the actual rocky outcrop now known principally as Aikin Knott, but sometimes in the past as Aikin's How.[60] Prior to a denouement in which it is acknowledged that despite victory, the Anglo-Norse community will disperse ("It will be the end of the only life we know," observes Bjorn [149]),[61] Sutcliff's words describing Aikin's funeral anticipate those that would close her *Beowulf* retelling (quoted above) five years later:

> So Aikin Jarlson was how-laid after the manner of his forefathers, as the Chieftains of the Viking kind had been how-laid on high place and sea

> headland wherever the wandering Northmen ran their keels ashore. And
> his Sword-brothers piled the stones high, and left him to the wind and the
> rain and the curlews calling. (211)

"Chieftains of the Viking kind" were only exceptionally buried in mounds on sea headlands;[62] Aikin Knott is not on one of those, but Sutcliff had introduced a metaphorical conception of it as being so at an earlier point in the book. Thus, her association between the funeral of Aikin and that of Beowulf seems quite conscious. Similarly, Sutcliff's emphasis on Beowulf's dragon-slaying role, as well as on his role as self-sacrificing protector of his people and on Wiglaf's role as the one friend who does not abandon him, all suggests that these aspects of *Beowulf* resonated powerfully with her, and we see that she was already exploring them through *The Shield Ring* some years before *Dragonslayer* was published.

Conclusion

Mid-twentieth-century adaptations of *Beowulf* for children show unprecedented diversity. Some remain basically simplifications of the Old English poem's plot, often with moral-didactic purposes in mind, and like their Victorian and Edwardian precursors were intended to introduce young readers to an instructive monument from the English-speaking world's literary canon. However, this period also sees authors begin exercising great freedom in recasting the old story, or even just selected elements of it, to reflect their own interests, ideas, and creative visions. *Beowulf* is no longer only retold to children, but increasingly reimagined for them, and even reused as a source of dissociable motifs or episodes in works that are quite new and unique to the individual modern author.

This broad range of treatments of a cultural monument may align with larger trends in the period between the First World and Vietnam Wars. But it also seems that thanks to the Victorian- and Edwardian-era *Beowulf* retellings that strove so hard to establish *Beowulf* as an ideally heroic tale in the literary canon, the story had indeed become a familiar part of young readers' literary landscapes, including those of mid-twentieth-century adaptors as they had grown up. This later wave of *Beowulf* adaptors may have felt that they had something more to prove, or may have felt authorized by what had gone before to re-adapt the inherited material at a further remove. They applied their creativity in various ways; for example, Nye's more subversive, tragicomic retelling, with its unconventional hero, differs greatly from Sutcliff's more traditional, but deeply insightful and emotionally resonant reuses. Sutcliff's *Shield Ring*, especially, reveals an author who, like Tolkien, has fully absorbed narratives and themes from *Beowulf* into a new creative matrix and can make both explicit and far more subtle uses of it in original fiction.

Looking back, adult readers of our day may be surprised by the variety of sophisticated themes and language found in mid-twentieth-century children's adaptations of *Beowulf*. Yet young readers of those generations rose to meet such challenges, and some have gone on to become new creators of one sort or another themselves. Regardless of how we approach the use of myths and legends in children's literature as we move towards the mid-twenty-first century, we should not forget that the intended audience is, if young, nevertheless intelligent and sophisticated. In *The Shield Ring*, one of Sutcliff's Anglo-Norse characters surveys the rugged Lakeland landscape and avers: "That is our Shield Ring, our last stronghold; not the barrier fells and the totter-moss between, but something in the hearts of men." The varied, challenging, and often beautiful approaches found in mid-twentieth-century adaptations of *Beowulf* for children can remind us that it is always the hearts of children that safeguard our futures.

NOTES

1 The shift in academic focus on *Beowulf* is often associated with J.R.R. Tolkien, "*Beowulf*: The Monsters and the Critics," *Proceedings of the British Academy* 22 (1936): 245–95. The role played by Tolkien's lecture in this shift is easily overestimated, though it was certainly influential.

2 Peter Hunt, "Children's Literature," in *Keywords for Children's Literature*, ed. Philip Nel and Lissa Paul (New York: New York University Press, 2011), 42–7.

3 Library of Congress, "Children's Literature," *Library of Congress Collections Policy Statements* (Washington, DC: Library of Congress, 2008), 1.

4 Library of Congress, "Children's Literature," 1.

5 Frederick Joseph Harvey Darton, *Children's Books in England: Five Centuries of Social Life* (Cambridge: Cambridge University Press, 1932), vii. Darton also emphasizes that "by children's books" *he* means "printed works produced ostensibly to give children spontaneous pleasure, and not primarily to teach them, nor solely to make them good, nor to keep them profitably quiet" (1), though that he felt the need to emphasize this in the first sentence of his first chapter highlights the often didactic nature of children's literature.

6   See Łukasz Neubauer, "Adapting an Old English Epic: The Case of
    Rosemary Sutcliff's *Beowulf: Dragonslayer*," in *Adapting Canonical Texts
    in Children's Literature*, ed. Anja Müller (London: Bloomsbury Academic,
    2013), 113–26.

7   Angela Sorby, "Golden Age," in *Keywords for Children's Literature*, ed.
    Philip Nel and Lissa Paul (New York: New York University Press, 2011),
    96–9.

8   Though see Deborah Thacker and Jean Webb, *Introducing Children's
    Literature: From Romanticism to Postmodernism* (London: Routledge,
    2002).

9   Rosemary Sutcliff, *Beowulf*, illus. Charles Keeping (London Bodley Head,
    1961); Sutcliff's book has since been reprinted by several publishers under
    variant titles, with *Dragon Slayer* or *Dragonslayer* frequently appearing as
    either subtitle or primary title. For convenience in distinguishing Sutcliff's
    retelling from others (and from the original poem), this paper refers to
    hers generically as *Dragonslayer*; all citations are to this edition and appear
    parenthetically in the text.

10 Rosemary Sutcliff, *The Shield Ring* (Oxford: Oxford University Press, 1956);
    later citations appear parenthetically in the text.

11 The "First Golden Age" of children's literature is often considered to have
    begun with Lewis Carroll, *Alice's Adventures in Wonderland* (London, UK:
    Macmillan, 1865). Its end is associated with the First World War or the fol-
    lowing decade (Sorby, "Golden Age").

12 Fiona McCulloch, *Children's Literature in Context* (London: Continuum,
    2011), 13–19.

13 See Lise Jaillant, "'A Fine Old Tale of Adventure': *Beowulf* Told to the
    Children of the English Race, 1898–1908," *Children's Literature Association
    Quarterly* 38 (2013): 399–419; Rosemary Mitchell, *Picturing the Past: English
    History in Text and Image, 1830–1870* (Oxford: Clarendon Press, 2000); Peter
    Mandler, *History and National Life* (London: Profile, 2002).

14 Anna Smol, "Heroic Ideology and the Children's *Beowulf*"; R. Horsman,
    Race and Manifest Destiny: The Origins of American Racial Anglo-Saxonism
    (Cambridge, MA: Harvard University Press, 1981); John D. Niles, *The Idea
    of Anglo-Saxon England 1066–1901: Remembering, Forgetting, Deciphering, and
    Renewing the Past* (Malden: Wiley, 2015).

15 Smol, "Heroic Ideology."

16 In E.L. Hervey's *Children of the Pear-Garden*, first identified as a *Beowulf*
    adaptation in Renée Ward's essay in this volume.

17 See Bruce Gilchrist's bibliography in this volume; also, Dominic
    Cheetham, "Dragons in English: The Great Change of the Late Nineteenth
    Century," *Children's Literature in Education* 45 (2014): 17–32.

18 Smol, "Heroic Ideology"; McCulloch, *Children's Literature in Context*, 41.

19 Dorothy Hosford, *By His Own Might: The Battles of Beowulf*, illus. Laszlo Matulay (New York: Henry Holt, 1947).

20 C.F. Bricknell Smith, *Beowulf*, illus. L.H. Bennett-Collins (Exeter: A. Wheaton & Company, 1951).

21 Gladys Schmitt, *The Heroic Deeds of Beowulf*, illus. Walter Ferro (New York: Random House, 1962).

22 Strafford Riggs, *The Story of Beowulf*, illus. Henry C. Pitz, with a foreword by Charles J. Finger (New York: D. Appleton-Century, 1933). Henceforth cited parenthetically in the text.

23 Jaillant, "'Fine Old Tale of Adventure.'"

24 See Kirsti Ann Bobo, "Representations of Anglo-Saxon England in Children's Literature" (unpublished MA thesis, Brigham Young University, 2004).

25 Ian Serraillier, *The Ivory Horn* (London: Oxford University Press, 1960); Ian Serraillier, *The Silver Sword* (London: Cape, 1956).

26 Ian Serraillier, *Beowulf the Warrior*, illus. [Mark] Severin (London: Oxford University Press, 1954). Henceforth cited parenthetically in the text.

27 References to the Old English *Beowulf* are from R.D. Fulk, Robert E. Bjork, and John D. Niles, eds., *Klaeber's Beowulf and the Fight at Finnsburg*, 4th ed. (Toronto: University of Toronto Press, 2008).

28 Robert Nye, *Beowulf: A New Telling*, illus. Alan Cober (New York: Hill and Wang, 1968); Robert Nye, *Bee Hunter: Adventures of Beowulf*, illus. Aileen Campbell (London: Faber & Faber, 1968). I cite from *Bee Hunter* parenthetically in the text.

29 E.g., Marijane Osborn, "The Translations of *Beowulf* (and 'The Fight at Finnsburg')," in *The Translations of "Beowulf": A Critical Bibliography*, by Chauncey B. Tinker, rev. ed. (Hamden, CT: Archon Books, 1974), 151–80, at 170; Stanley B. Greenfield and Fred C. Robinson, *A Bibliography of Publications on Old English Literature to the End of 1972* (Toronto: University of Toronto Press, 1980), entry 1765.

30 A collation by Britt Mize and Ruby Perry-Mize found twenty-nine points of textual divergence. For example, besides occasional minor simplifications to wording or syntax, *Bee Hunter* deletes several references to Grendel's mother's breasts. Britt Mize, personal communication, 22 May 2016.

31 Other authors of the post–world wars period have sought aspects of the monstrous in the character Beowulf as well as aspects of the downtrodden victim within Grendel. The classic example, closely following Nye's chronologically, remains John Gardner, *Grendel* (New York: Alfred A. Knopf, 1971).

32 Originally proposed by Jacob Grimm, the etymology is found in many handbooks, such as Raymond Wilson Chambers and C.L. Wrenn,

Beowulf: An Introduction to the Study of the Poem, 3rd ed. (Cambridge: Cambridge University Press, 1959). The traditional etymology has been called into question: see discussions by Robert D. Fulk, "The Etymology and Significance of Beowulf's Name," *Anglo-Saxon* 1 (2007): 109–36; and Christopher Abram, "Bee-Wolf and the Hand of Victory: Identifying the Heroes of *Beowulf* and *Vǫlsunga saga*," *JEGP* 116 (2017): 387–414, at 390–5.

33 J. Olrik and H. Raeder, eds., *Saxonis Gesta Danorum: Primum a C. Knabe & P. Herrmann Recensita*, vol. 1 (Copenhagen: Levin & Munksgaard, 1931), 51; Hilda Ellis Davidson, ed., *Saxo Grammaticus: The History of the Danes, Books I–IX, Volume 1: English Text*, trans. Peter Fisher (Cambridge: D.S. Brewer, 1979), 55.

34 Rebecca Barnhouse, *The Middle Ages in Literature for Youth: A Guide and Resource Book* (Lanham, MD: Scarecrow Press, 2004), 68.

35 Joyce Elizabeth Potter, "Eternal Relic: A Study of Setting in Rosemary Sutcliff's *Dragon Slayer*," *Children's Literature Association Quarterly* 10 (1985): 108–10, at 108.

36 John Stephens and Robyn McCallum, *Retelling Stories, Framing Culture: Traditional Story and Metanarratives in Children's Literature* (New York: Garland, 1998), 113, 115–16.

37 Charles A. Brady, *The King's Thane*, illus. Henry C. Pitz (New York: Doubleday & Company, 1961).

38 John O. Beaty, *Swords in the Dawn: A Story of the First Englishmen*, illus. Henry C. Pitz (New York: Longmans, Green, & Co., 1937); Jill Paton Walsh, *Hengest's Tale*, illus. Janet Margrie (London: Macmillan, 1966).

39 See J.R.R. Tolkien, *Finn and Hengest: The Fragment and the Episode*, ed. Alan Bliss (London: Allen & Unwin, 1982).

40 Tolkien's lectures on Finnsburg, notes for which form the basis of the 1982 *Finn and Hengest* publication, date principally to the period 1928–37, though they were delivered again in 1963, shortly before the appearance of Paton Walsh's novel. She had already graduated, but possibly she received notes from someone who attended or did so herself. See Thomas A. Shippey, "Names in *Beowulf* and Anglo-Saxon England," in *The Dating of Beowulf: A Reassessment*, ed. Leonard Neidorf (Woodbridge, Suffolk: Boydell & Brewer, 2014), 78; and a little more detail is given in a paper not formally published but made available online: Thomas A. Shippey, "Tolkien's Two Views of *Beowulf*: One Hailed, One Ignored. But Did We Get This Right?" (2010), 10 pp., at p. 6, as posted at Academia.edu and accessed 28 June 2019 (https://www.academia.edu/17608835/Tolkiens _two_views_of_beowulf).

41 On Tolkien's reuses of *Beowulf*, see Amber Dunai's essay in this volume and, for example, Bonniejean McGuire Christensen, "*Beowulf* and *The Hobbit*: Elegy into Fantasy in J.R.R. Tolkien's Creative Technique"

(unpublished PhD dissertation., University of Southern California, 1969); Tom Shippey, *The Road to Middle-Earth*, 2nd rev. and expanded ed. (Boston: Houghton Mifflin, 2003); Tom Shippey, *J.R.R. Tolkien: Author of the Century* (London: HarperCollins, 2000).

42 Maud Isabel Ebbutt, "Beowulf," in *Hero Myths and Legends of the British Race* (London: George G. Harrap, 1910), 11–41; quotation from Rosemary Sutcliff, "Beginning with *Beowulf*," *Horn Book Magazine* 29 (1953): 36–8, at 36.

43 See n. 9 above.

44 Carolyn Horovitz, "Dimensions in Time: A Critical View of Historical Fiction for Children," in *Horn Book Reflections: On Children's Books and Readings, Selected from 18 Years of The Horn Book Magazine, 1949–1966*, ed. E.W. Field (Boston: Horn Book, 1969), 137–50, at 142 (reprinted from an article first published in 1962); Janet Fisher, "Historical Fiction," in *International Companion Encyclopedia of Children's Literature*, ed. Peter Hunt, 2nd ed. (London: Routledge, 2004), 490–8, at 490.

45 Potter, "Eternal Relic," 109.

46 Rosemary Sutcliff, *The Eagle of the Ninth* (Oxford: Oxford University Press, 1954).

47 John Rowe Townsend, "British Children's Literature: A Historical Overview," in *International Companion Encyclopedia of Children's Literature*, ed. Peter Hunt (London: Routledge, 1996), 668–79.

48 Fisher, "Historical Fiction," 491–2.

49 See Hilary Wright, "Shadows on the Downs: Some Influences of Rudyard Kipling on Rosemary Sutcliff," *Children's Literature in Education* 12 (1981): 90–102; Deborah H. Roberts, "Reconstructed Pasts: Rome and Britain, Child and Adult in Kipling's *Puck of Pook's Hill* and Rosemary Sutcliff's Historical Fiction," in *Remaking the Classics: Literature, Genre and Media in Britain 1800–2000*, ed. Christopher Stray (London: Gerald Duckworth, 2007), 107–23; Philip Burton, "Rosemary Sutcliff's *The Eagle of the Ninth*: A Festival of Britain?" *Greece and Rome* 58 (2011): 82–103.

50 Nicholas Size, *The Secret Valley: The Real Romance of Unconquered Lakeland* (London: Warne, 1929); Nicholas Size, *The Epic of Buttermere: Historical Picture of the Great Events in Lakeland during Norman Times* (Buttermere: Nicholas Size, 1928). Drawing and elaborating on "different perspectives on history from earlier writers" has been a frequent approach taken by authors of children's historical fiction, including Gillian Avery, Hester Burton, Cynthia Harnett, Kathleen Peyton, and Barbara Willard (Dennis Butts, "Shaping Boyhood: British Empire Builders and Adventurers," in *International Companion Encyclopedia of Children's Literature*, ed. Hunt, 2nd ed., 340–51, at 349).

51 See Andrew Wawn, *The Vikings and the Victorians: Inventing the Old North in Nineteenth-Century Britain* (Woodbridge, Suffolk: D.S. Brewer, 2000);

Matthew Townend, "In Search of the Lakeland Saga: Antiquarian Fiction and the Norse Settlement in Cumbria," in *Old Norse Made New: Essays on the Post-Medieval Reception of Old Norse Literature and Culture*, ed. David Clark and Carl Phelpstead (London: Viking Society for Northern Research, 2000), 63–82.

52 Nicholas Size, *Shelagh of Eskdale, or: The Stone of Shame* (London: Warne, 1932); Charles Arundel Parker, *The Story of Shelagh, Olaf Cuaran's Daughter: A Saga of the Northmen in Cumberland in the Tenth Century* (Kendal: Wilson, 1909).

53 Fred Inglis, *The Promise of Happiness: Value and Meaning in Children's Fiction* (Cambridge: Cambridge University Press, 1981), 220.

54 Inglis, *Promise of Happiness*, 220.

55 Quoted from J. Wintle and E. Fisher, *The Pied Pipers: Interviews with the Influential Creators of Children's Literature* (London: Paddington, 1974), 186.

56 Fiona M. Collins and Judith Graham, "The Twentieth Century: Giving Everybody a History," in *Historical Fiction for Children: Capturing the Past*, ed. Fiona M. Collins and Judith Graham (London: Fulton, 2013), 17–18.

57 Another of her rare female heroines would be Boudicca, the protagonist in Rosemary Sutcliff, *Song for a Dark Queen* (London: Pelham, 1978).

58 See n. 32 above.

59 Burton, "Rosemary Sutcliff's *The Eagle of the Ninth*," quotations from pp. 91 and 93.

60 This is another detail lifted from Size. Though the real Aikin's Knott is a natural feature, not a burial mound, Size had romanticized it as the latter, moreover folk-etymologizing "Ackin" (Size's spelling) as a form of the Norse name *Hákon* (Size, *Secret Valley*, 23–5, 76–7).

61 But Bjorn and Frytha, now grown and with their rift healed by the shared experience of "the Fire-drake," will go together to reclaim Bjorn's father's abandoned lands above Eskdale and together start "a song of new beginnings"; Sutcliff, *Shield Ring*, 214–15. Once again in Sutcliff's work, though the wider community passes away, the individual spirit forges on.

62 One example is the burial on the Île de Groix in Brittany. See Neil S. Price, *The Vikings in Brittany* (London: Viking Society for Northern Research, 1989); Michael Müller-Will, Ole Crumlin-Pedersen, and Maria Dekówna, *Das Bootkammergrab von Haithabu* (Neumünster: Wachholtz, 1976).

5 Visualizing Femininity in Children's and Illustrated Versions of *Beowulf*

BRUCE GILCHRIST

Ðær wæs hæleþa hleahtor,   hlyn swynsode,
word wæron wynsume.   Eode Wealhþeow forð,
cwen Hroðgares,   cynna gemyndig,
grette goldhroden   guman on healle.   (ll. 610–13)[1]

[There was the laughter of warriors, a clamour resounded, / and the words
were pleasing. Wealhþeow went forth, / Hroðgar's queen, mindful of
courtesy; / decked in gold, she greeted the men in the hall.]

When Wealhþeow first appears in *Beowulf*, she makes her entrance
amid a joyous sonority, with three consecutive phrases marking the
sound of men in communal pleasure preceding her. Then, as she comes
forth, resplendent with gold, the ceremony turns from one of auditory
delight to one of visual grace, to a demonstration of ritual as this most
important female human figure in the poem honours her husband and
receives the foreign noblemen in turn by bearing them the cup. The
alliteration binds her to her role, for she, as *cwen*, is "cynna gemyndig,"
mindful of courtesy; yet, as we will soon enough learn, Wealhþeow is
also mindful of *cyn*, of her nation, and, more carefully, of the fate of her
sons, when her own words will change from winsome talk to calculated
entreaties.

This spectacle of regality, of queenly presence, marks the high point
of female human power in *Beowulf*, and its earliest portrayal, in an illustrated version of 1898,[2] sets a type-standard against which later adaptations, especially those produced for younger readers, can be measured
in their representation of femininity. By tracing this signal image and
other key depictions of women and Grendel's mother in illustrated adaptations of the poem, this chapter works diachronically to mark the
visual presentation of gender as a critical axis for the reception and the

continuation of the poem's cultural work. In particular, the portrayal of gender roles manifests and instils the poem's ethical and social codes, doubly so for child readers, whose versions are narratively abridged and visually condensed into typifying imagery. At the same time, each new adaptation also tends to perform an idealization of femininity reflective of its own era and context of production. Last, as this chapter reads *Beowulf* through its one-hundred-plus illustrated versions, it regards a history of children's publishing via a single lens.

In a previous examination of this corpus,[3] I traced the depiction of masculinity and emotion by studying two key sequences: Hroðgar's tears at Beowulf's parting and Wiglaf's embrace of the dying Beowulf. My discovery was that while the "Death of Beowulf" was an exemplary image from 1881 onwards,[4] even serving as a frontispiece[5] and front cover image,[6] no illustration of "Hroðgar's Tears" came until 1954.[7] This showed that grief at death is a noble if restrained and stylized emotion, but that interior weakness is to be withheld, turned away from our gaze, or elided entirely – a man must not be seen to weep. A corollary was that the more hyper-masculine and violent the illustrations for the poem were, the more likely that Wiglaf was separated from his dying king and Hroðgar turned away from his subjects.[8] These were clear strategies of aversion and displacement: male embrace and inner emotions are *dyrne*, secret and obscure, not to be foregrounded.[9]

I continue here to study the gendered reception of the poem by regarding the depiction of four female figures in this corpus: Wealhþeow, Hygd, the *Geatisc meowle* (Geatish woman), and Grendel's mother. For convenience, I have delineated four broad eras of book production whose characteristic styles I hope will explain the names: Edwardian Regality (1885–1920), Modernist Sweep (1920–45), Mid-Century Inking (1945–80), and the Postmodern Graphic Phase (1980–present).[10] Within each illustration, the key signifiers of gender and status are position within the frame and posture (especially relative to male figures), hair (bound up, loose, or wild), robes and ornamented dress, and accoutrements such as belts, rings, headgear, necklaces, and the *seax*, the knife Grendel's mother wields. Collectively, they form a set of visual strategies for child and adult readers to navigate an understanding of the female presence within the setting of *Beowulf*; these markers are also highly conserved across time, as illustrators often repeat in close detail the work of previous editions.

My conclusions are dispiriting, suggesting overall a loss of human female presence and authority in the illustration history of the poem, and a concomitant unpleasant gain in the aberrant monstrosity of Grendel's mother. Almost all the women of the poem are diminished in their visual portrayal, or absented altogether, across the 140 years of illustrated adaptations, with Hygd as a curious exception, one explicable by another shift away from female power towards male fantasy. A great deal of this loss, sharply accentuated in children's versions, is due to the abridgement of the text for length and complexity, as the digressions telling of Hildeburh, Freawearu, and Þryðo[11] are excised, along with Wealhþeow's two speeches. Nevertheless, the ongoing diminution of the female human presence in illustrated versions is worrying, for it suggests simplification of gender types and a loss of potential identification, especially for girl readers, with the female figures of the poem, be they a restive queen, a failed peace-weaving princess, or a grieving, vengeful mother. It is also greatly at odds with the recent breadth of free reworkings of the *Beowulf* legend that recentre the narrative from the perspective of the poem's female characters,[12] and likewise with recent historical fiction set in early medieval England that features teenage female protagonists.[13] Such a disparity marks fault lines not only between child and older audiences, and male and female readers in young adult audiences,[14] but also between strictly textual storytelling and the hybrid of textual and graphic narration in children's and illustrated versions of the poem.

Wealhþeow

When Wealhþeow enters the hall and first presents the cup to Hroðgar, then to the Geatish troops, and finally to Beowulf himself, the narrator stages the scene as a sequence of ritual mirror images. When she gives the cup to her husband, Wealhþeow is a "freolic wif" (l. 614a), a noble and glad or comely woman, gold-decked and mindful of courtesy, who bids him to be easy, to be glad at the beer-drinking ("bæd hine bliðne æt þære beorþege," l. 616).[15] Then, when she turns to the Geats, she is the "ides Helminga" (l. 619b), the Lady of the Helmings, marked like the Geats are as foreign to the Danish court. Last, when she comes to Beowulf himself, the parallel of her earlier description at ll. 611b–14 is completed as she is now the "beaghroden cwen" (l. 622b), the ring-laden queen, "mode geþungen," (l. 623a), of excellent or virtuous spirit, who greets the Geatish prince "wisfæst wordum" (l. 625a), in sure, wise speech. The use of the verb *biddan* to instruct or cajole Hroðgar implies a negotiation of terms for the reception as a whole, with Wealhþeow as gracious intermediary between the potential violence the guests bring to the Danish hall, and the threat of death they must take up in place of her king; it also prefaces her political manoeuvring when she bestows the torque on Beowulf after he has defeated Grendel, and gives two speeches in the imperative mood with her aim to keep the Scylding dynasty intact. These are the two key sequences whose portrayal I trace through the illustrated adaptations.

The Edwardian-era depiction of Wealhþeow honours her cup-bearing regality: she is at once daughter to the Victorian Empire and emblem of the Nordic goddesses, a valkyrie. She typically stands in a dominant position, in profile right or left, dressed in a flowing, ornate robe, with long, braided hair.[16] In the exemplary image by George T. Tobin (1898) already cited, Wealhþeow is at her most queenly: wearing a small crown, sash, and ermine cape, she is poised and waiting for Beowulf to come to her; moreover, she is at centre and young, with a far older Hroðgar in the rear right of the image (see fig. 5.1). Successive illustrations of this type-scene, such as Brinsley Le Fanu's,[17] portray Wealhþeow with jewelled belt and breast emphasizing her femininity in Pre-Raphaelite terms, and even orientalize her. The ink drawing from Andrew Lang's *Red Book of Animal Stories* (1899) by noted illustrator H.J. Ford[18] both orientalizes her through an abstract-panelled surcoat, headscarf, and pointed slippers, and makes her an Arts and Crafts valkyrie by giving her a dragon headdress and ornately interlaced gown. In the illustration, she is fully at left, but strongly vertical above a kneeling Beowulf, whose helmet bears wings worthy of a Wagner production, and whose armour and shoes are likewise ornately tooled.

In contrast, the unknown illustrator of C.L. Thomson's *The Adventures of Beowulf* (1904)[19] softens the portrayal of Wealhþeow by giving her a freer single braid with a more modest headband, and a loosely belted dress with large jewels at the breast and loins. The illustration also suggests a sexual subtext given its imagery of Wealhþeow tipping ale from a wide bowl into Beowulf's upright-curving drinking horn; as Thomson's version of the poem is "Adapted to the Use of Schools," this pictorial subtext is either unintentional or sly. J.R. Skelton (1908) returns to a more decorous portrayal while maintaining Wealhþeow's softness, rendering her in a deep-blue gown with a broad, jewelled belt and full crown as she holds the cup; her hair is a lustrous copper red, again in two long braids (see fig. 5.2). Her positioning within the scene is important, for while she has a milder, more deferential posture, as she leans forward with her hands angled downwards, she is still very much at front versus Hroðgar, who looks resigned in his seat at centre-rear.

Interestingly, the exemplary portrayal of Wealhþeow as regal cup-bearer in these five depictions matches the predominance of female adaptors of the poem in this era: of twenty-two notable English adaptations from 1881 to 1914, thirteen of them are by women; this ratio is not repeated in later eras. Moreover, it speaks to the role of children's

Figure 5.1. *Queen Wealhtheow Pledges Beowulf*, by George T. Tobin, from Ragozin and Tobin, *Tales of the Heroic Ages*, facing p. 242.

stories in the promotion of literacy for girls, and to the Edwardian Regality era as the apex of aesthetic production of the book as physical artefact with lush colour illustrations and gold-embossed art nouveau covers.[20] A late abridgement in the Edwardian Regality era, from Olive Beaupré Miller and Donn P. Crane's anthology of medieval tales for the *My Bookhouse* series (1921), emulates Kate Greenaway's Victorian manner of illustration with sharp black lines against pallid watercolour; however, in Crane's one large illustration of Heorot, Wealhþeow has been pushed left, and stands passively holding a platter of drinking horns and small torques, with little to identify her as queen, let alone Hroðgar's equal in the ceremony.[21]

Following the First World War, there is a significant lull in deluxe adaptations of *Beowulf* for a children's audience as the Edwardian vogue for prestige editions falls away. This continues through the Second World War, where the illustrated versions of the poem are more sober affairs, seemingly geared for an adult, high-art audience. These include Rockwell Kent's prestigious and highly collectible limited series of eight lithographs (1931),[22] the Heritage Press reprint of William Ellery Leonard's long-line verse translation with fabulously sweeping trichromatic pictures by Lynd Ward (1939),[23] and E.V. Sandys's abridgement with fine lithographs by Rolf Klep (1941).[24] In each of these Modernist versions, however, the seemly and queenly Wealhþeow bearing

Figure 5.2. "Giving to each warrior, young and old, wine from the golden cup," by J.R. Skelton, from Marshall and Skelton, *Stories of Beowulf*, facing p. 28.

the cup is elided, as she is simply absent in scenes depicting Heorot. Moreover, in Ward's illustration, it is as if she has been displaced by the cup itself when Beowulf hoists it high before his admiring troop.[25] A single exception is perhaps the most richly designed and beautiful adaptation of *Beowulf* of any era, Strafford Riggs's 1933 edition "decorated" by Henry C. Pitz.[26] Yet, even in this book with ornament and drawings throughout, Wealhþeow is reduced to a small figure at the bottom of the page; her bearing is regal, and her gown is a throwback to the Edwardian taste for oriental splendour, but she is still only two inches high in a picture book otherwise flush with full-page, two-colour woodcut illustrations.[27]

The reduction of Wealhþeow's role continues into Mid-Century Inkings as she is absent entirely in Rosemary Sutcliff and Charles Keeping's widely reprinted children's novel, *Beowulf* (1961).[28] Heorot itself has been displaced in the illustrations, as the book opens with an invented figure, a "Sea Captain," telling the story of the Danish miseries to Hygelac, who sits on the facing page, with blank space across the fold, listening carefully on his throne while his hand rests on the hand of a boy kneeling beside him.[29] Then, in a second across-the-fold drawing, this time at Heorot, Keeping has depicted several young boys and girls on the left, and two women at work on the right, one carding, and one at the loom.[30] The depiction of children and weavers at Heorot is highly unusual, but rather than representing a positive inclusiveness, it appears that Keeping has displaced the poem's most political woman with figures of low economic status. The girls have unkempt, wild hair, while the two women at work have loose braids; one of the girls is even without a tunic. Meanwhile, in Jane Leighton and Gerhard Steffen's saddle-stitched adaptation designed for second-language acquisition (1962), Heorot is inked in a boisterous drinking scene with some fifteen men and horses jammed together; it is at first hard to see Wealhþeow, but she is there at the rear, crowned and holding the cup, yet her gaze is turned aside from everyone else, and she is curiously taller than even the horses. The effect is simultaneously one of being hidden in plain sight, and yet standing apart.[31]

There are three notable exceptions in the Mid-Century Inkings, two depicted in drawings for Ian Serraillier's long-line verse retelling, and all three throwbacks in design. The original hardcover edition of Serraillier with engravings by Severin (1954) restores Wealhþeow as a fierce queen bearing the cup in an archly stylized and well-attended ceremonial procession; though her hair is unusually free under her crown, her central position in a dramatically symmetrical scene and the long train of her cape fully dominate the picture (see fig. 5.3).[32] Then, in a later American edition with heavy woodcut illustrations by Bill Pesce, a crowned Wealhþeow is flanked by two maidens and small stars in a triptych suggestive of stained glass; the effect is pleasing in this otherwise coarsely pictured version.[33] Third is Kevin Crossley-Holland and Virgil Burnett's Folio Society edition (1973), where a full-page Wealhþeow stands alone at a curtain in heavy robes and a magnificent neck ring of five smaller brooches, but has one arm hidden in the hitched-up folds of her robes while the other clasps a small goblet as if it were hers alone to drink from. She bears a Beardsley-esque expression of ennui,

Figure 5.3. "She glided forth to greet her guests," by Mark Severin, from Serraillier and Severin, *Beowulf the Warrior*, p. 11.

perhaps fitting for a book sold to an adult audience, but strange for a queen officiating at a joyous drinking ceremony.[34]

A tempered regality does persist in some recent illustrations of Wealhþeow, as in Penelope Hicks and James McLean's illustrated chapter book (2007), where she is drawn facing forwards, presenting the gold cup to the reader, as it were, in shapely robes and lightly braided hair that almost sparkles,[35] and in John Green's colouring book version (2007), where the queen, now middle aged, wears a plain headdress with a small circlet and chaste robes with no jewels, yet holds forth the cup elegantly at Beowulf's parting and thanks him for his honourable deeds.[36] This second, more sober portrayal of Wealhþeow is aligned with an alternate type-standard, one which starts mid-century with Dorothy Hosford and Laszlo Matulay (1947), and continues through the Post-Modern Graphic Phase: Wealhþeow maintains her crown, but is now older, wimpled, severe of aspect, an unhappy wife relegated to the rear of the scene. Matulay's only woodcut to depict Heorot is set the evening before Beowulf's parting, after he has dispatched Grendel's mother. Wealhþeow is not only encased in shapeless black headscarf and robe, she is positioned beside and slightly behind a glum, elderly Hroðgar, and holds forth an empty hand; moreover, in her role as courtly stage manager, she has been displaced by an emaciated-looking scop (see fig. 5.4). Such an aged and diminished Wealhþeow appears again in the greeting feast in Eric L. Kimmel and Leonard Everett Fisher's garish large picture book (2005), where she wears a white wimple with a touch of white hair visible that matches the aged Hroðgar beside her; her countenance is one of concern as she leans forward anxiously.[37] Wealhþeow is older still in James Rumford's splendid picture book (2007), when she is drawn at the feast celebrating Beowulf's victory over Grendel; yet, while she is wearing not only a white wimple, but a billowing, unbelted white gown with neither pattern nor jewels, her demonstrative, upraised arm and positioning in front of a dark-robed Hroðgar restore a sense of consequence to her, even though the text does not have her refer to her children.[38]

The generalized diminution of Wealhþeow's role as queen carries forward in the most recent adapations, where she is frequently given the weakest position in the visual field; even when young and beautiful, she tends to rest at Hroðgar's side with a sober, impassive mien, her role to distribute the cup taken up by younger, cheerier females. In Gareth Hinds's widely appreciated graphic novel (2007), Wealhþeow appears in five panels on a single page, but is drawn with head down and eyes closed in each one, completely deferential to both Hroðgar and Beowulf (see fig. 5.5). She is similarly passive and even ghostly or elven

Figure 5.4. "Again the banquet was renewed for the earls and warriors in the hall," by Laszlo Matulay, from Hosford and Matulay, *By His Own Might: The Battles of Beowulf*, 35.

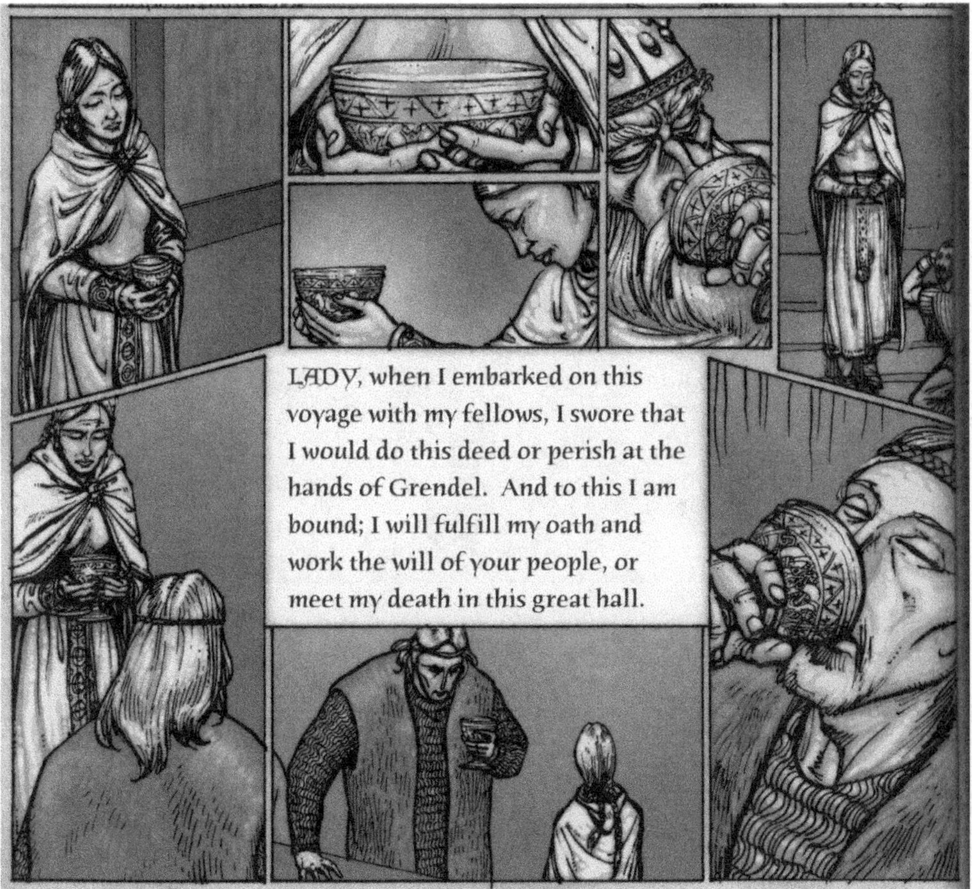

Figure 5.5. Wealhþeow bears the cup to Beowulf, who pledges his oath to the lady, from Hinds, *Beowulf*, p. [24].

in Michelle L. Szobody and Justin Gerard's Tolkien-esque large picture book (2007), where she is first seen positioned well behind a grieving Hroðgar, her hands cradling her face, as sadness and shock at the aftermath of Grendel's first attack forestall cup-bearing at Heorot.[39] Next, at the greeting feast, Gerard again depicts her as a beautiful fairy or elf, with an elegant, tall, but thin beaker matching her form; however, she is offset and isolated at the bottom left, again with eyes closed and her face passive in monochrome sepia, while across the fold Hroðgar and the Geatish warriors carouse, bathed in golden light. Wealhþeow is also in this full-page illustration, but she stands wraithlike in front of the

Figure 5.6. "The huge hall shook with singing and laughter," by Victor Tavares, from Jones and Tavares, *Beowulf*, 8–9.

drinking men, with exactly the same posture and expression as before; her femininity could almost be said to haunt them.[40]

In the same vein, Rob Lloyd Jones and Victor Tavares (2009; see fig. 5.6) and Mick Gowar and Paul McCaffrey (2010)[41] present almost perfectly mirrored depictions of the feasting scenes: in both, Wealhþeow sits solemnly at Hroðgar's side in one corner of an across-the-fold illustration, while the mead tables are in revelry and Danish women bear the cup to the Geatish warriors in her place; the only differences are that the first is in colour, the second black and white, and that the joyless Wealhþeow is drawn at far right in the first, and at far left in the second. Such a weak portrayal reaches an almost comical peak in Jacqueline Morley and Li Sidong's short graphic novel (2010): in the first panel, Hroðgar wields the cup instead of Wealhþeow; then, in the second, she is literally left holding the cup alone, displaced and shrunk to the side, where she may as well be red silk wallpaper projected behind Hroðgar and a hyper-masculinized Beowulf who have grasped each others hands as they pledge mutal oaths (see fig. 5.7).

The second of the poem's Wealhþeow type-scenes, from line 1161 forward, after Beowulf has dispatched Grendel and cleansed Heorot,

Figure 5.7. "Drink, my lord, and may your heart be lightened," by Li Sidong, from Morley and Li, *Beowulf*, 13.

presents an even more complex ceremony of Wealhþeow moving about the hall, giving gifts, and speech-making. She again comes "forð" (l. 1161b), and is again associated with gold, as she walks "under gyld-num beage" (l. 1162), under her crown or a golden collar. She then comes to the king's table, where he and Hroþulf are seated; the narrator also points out Unferð the kin-murderer, so providing proleptic commentary on the trouble to come between Wealhþeow's two sons and their cousin. Negotiating the possible futures of blood-strife, Wealhþeow presents the cup to Hroðgar and speaks to him with authority, using the imperative mood time after time, reminding him of his duty to distribute wealth and speak graciously to his guests, and, more pointedly, not to hold Beowulf dear before his own two sons; even further, she openly imagines a future where Hroðgar has died, and where Hroþulf must remain *glæd* (l. 1183a), must protect those same sons in good spirit. In a signal gesture, she then turns (l. 1190a) to the bench where Beowulf sits with Hreðric and Hroðmund and gives him the cup and numerous gifts, with a marvellous *healsbeag* (l. 1197b), a torque or neck ring, greatest of all, as fine – the narrator reminds us – as the legendary necklace of the Brosnings. In her corresponding entreaty to Beowulf, again in the imperative mood, she binds him to being responsible for the two boys he sits between, to hold them in joy and to act on their behalf: "Beo þu suna minum / dædum gedefe, dreamhealdende!" (ll. 1228b–29). Finally, she returns to her seat, her *setl* (l. 1234a). A rendering of this episode proportionate to the emphases of the original should thus depict the cup, the *healsbeag*, her turn, and her two long speeches, which comprise thirty-five lines in total, over 1 per cent of the poem as a whole.

But where we should expect to see Wealhþeow in her greatest agency, as a queen skilled in ritual and a mother keenly aware of dynasty and edge-hate, we see her the least, for I have found only six depictions of this scene. Each is recent, except for Ruth Knorr's illustration for Hüttner's novella version (1975), where Wealhþeow gifts two torques and a mailshirt to a kneeling Beowulf as Hrothgar sits at rear gazing on.[42] While Knorr's freehand ink drawing is simpler in design than Tobin's 1898 type image, it is nonetheless a strong callback to it for posture and placement. In Rumford (2007) she is an aged but demonstrative queen.[43] Michael Foreman (2006) depicts the bestowal of the neck ring in a fine double-page watercolour, but as the scale of the picture leaves Wealhþeow and Beowulf at centre-rear, each less than an inch high inside a cavernous Heorot, so the lustre of the ceremony is reduced.[44] In Li's version of the scene (2010), a hulking Beowulf looms over Wealhþeow in a depiction suggesting a marriage of Harlequin romance and professional wrestling.[45] And McLean (2007) draws Wealhþeow from behind, with long, straight hair, a simple circlet, and shapeless robes as she holds forth the neck ring; in this instance, she is not even afforded a face, nor the textual space to speak for the safety of her children, saying merely, "Beloved Beowulf, enjoy this ancient treasure that I now give to you with my thanks."[46] None of these four portrayals of the *healsbeag* scene positively asserts Wealhþeow's role. Only once is she depicted advocating for her children. That this inclusion occurs in Stefan Petrucha and Kody Chamberlain (2007), a fantasy-oriented graphic novel, is remarkable, but just as she is bold earlier with the cup in the first type-scene in this book,[47] and so an outlier from the contemporary reduction of her role, so she is now bold here with the neck ring (see

Figure 5.8. "The Queen presented their new hero with her own special gift," from Petrucha and Chamberlain, *Beowulf*, p. [38].

fig. 5.8). In the left panel, Wealhþeow stands with arms outstretched above a worshipful Beowulf kneeling before her, her speech cascading in word bubbles beside him, binding him to a subjunctive future of mutual concern, guardianship, and joy: "that [he] be as *generous* with ... the noble Geats, as we have been with *you*"; the right panel then reverses the focalization, as we now see her hands in closeup in front of his respectfully downcast face.

Notwithstanding a few surprises like those in Petrucha and Chamberlain, one could say that on the whole, it is more important to illustrators of *Beowulf* for Wealhþeow to be an instrument, to be seen holding the cup or the torque, than it is for her to talk, to bring narrative into being. With few exceptions,[48] she becomes a visual digression.

Hygd

The Geatish queen Hygd appears in four separate passages in the poem. She is first described as Hygelac's counterpart in the splendid hall in anticipation of Beowulf's homecoming after he and his men have been ushered on by the home coast guard. The epithets empha-size not her looks and bearing, as with Wealhþeow, but her youth and wisdom: "Hygd swiðe geong, / wis welþungen, þeah ðe wintra lyt / gebiden hæbbe" (ll. 1929b–30) [Hygd was indeed young, / wise and advanced, though she had passed few winters]; and they stress also that she is unsparing in giving gifts and treasures, is neither *hnah* nor too *gneað* (ll. 1932b, 1933a), neither lowly nor miserly. Her virtues, un-common for her age, are advanced by juxtaposition with the vicious behaviour of Þryðo, who had men killed for looking at her, but was in turn tamed by the legendary ruler Offa. After Beowulf has been re-ceived and seated by Hygelac, Hygd takes on the role of cup-bearer and passes the vessel to the men of lesser rank, for she "lufode ða leode" (l. 1985a), loved the people. Then, after Beowulf reveals the forebodings he has about the Danes, and Freawaru's destiny in particular, the narrator tells the listener in an aside that he gave to Hygd the torque given him: "Hyrde ic þæt he ðone healsbeah Hygde gesealde, / wrætlicne wun-durmaððum, ðone þe him Wealhðeo geaf" (ll. 2175–6) [Then I heard that [Beowulf] gave the neck ring to Hygd, / the ornate wonder-treasure, which Wealhþeow gave him]. Though the poem does not dwell on this bestowal, the gift crucially links the two queens, even as it also initiates a story of tragedy, for this is the same torque that Hygelac will wear when he falls in the raid on the Frisians. The repeated passing of this treasure from hand to hand and nation to nation thus cements the role of the woman as intermediary, as instrument, in the poem. Finally, at the end of its account of the doomed raid, the poem relates that Hygd beseeched Beowulf to take up the kingdom, because she did not trust her own son ("bearne ne truwode," l. 2370b) to withstand the attacks of the Swedes, which indeed come after Beowulf refuses the *bregostol* (l. 2371a), the throne. As Wealhþeow sought to protect her sons by bind-ing Beowulf through speech, so Hygd attempts to have Beowulf shield her princeling, Heardred; this is the burden of queenship.

Adaptors and illustrators of the poem have several options in por-traying Hygd, including making deliberate echoes of their portrayal of Wealhþeow with the cup, the torque, and securing the protection of issue. However, Hygd is completely absent from all children's and illustrated versions of the poem until she – or sometimes a figure suggesting her – suddenly appears multiple times around 2007, the *annus mirabilis* of ten *Beowulf* adaptations for children. She may be first drawn, but unidentified, in Morpurgo and Foreman (2006), where two women are depicted at centre, but behind a decorated sword Hygelac presents horizontally across them to Beowulf; the woman on the right could be Hygd, as she wears a cape with large round clasps at the shoulders and possibly a small crown in her blonde hair, but the positioning of the scene reduces her noticeably versus Hygelac, so leaving her role ambiguous.[49] Curiously, the same layout in a reversed horizontal appears in Green's colouring book (2007); the woman at left is given more regal attire, though no crown, and is much closer to Hygelac, with her arm at his shoulder, and has a more distinctly drawn face and young, almost gamine figure, so suggesting Hygd more clearly, though the accompanying text does not mention her.[50] As a distinctly identified figure, Hygd first appears in Hinds's graphic novel (2007) and Hicks and McLean's illustrated chapter book (2007), and then in Morley and Li's short graphic novel (2010). Hinds portrays Hygd above a kneeling Beowulf in a full-height vertical strip that is roughly one-fourth of the page width (see fig. 5.9). The portrait is sumptuous in giving her dark chartreuse robes circled by a garnet-studded belt, a tawny cape, and amber hair, and is complex in its depiction of posture, suggesting an emotion of muted wonder at the silver neck-ring by combination of her hands upraised and her face cast down with eyes closed. The image is a throwback in its ornateness and its subtly evocative quality; it is also a far more lustrous, and tall, image than Hinds affords Wealhþeow, so manifesting yet another displacement of the Danish queen.

Hygd is portrayed twice in the coarse pen drawings of McLean: first, she is drawn beside and somewhat lower than Hygelac in his throne at the homecoming, and with no ornament whatsoever;[51] second, she is depicted facing the reader (as Wealhþeow had been earlier in the book), but with downcast expression, as she worries intensely about her young son, Heardred, who looks up at her as if for help and guidance while his hand at his side holds the butt of a sheathed blade. As this is a full-length chapter book, Hicks has space to flesh out this scene, and she goes beyond the poem to present it in direct dialogue: "Beloved Beowulf, we are all grieving the death of our king ... but we must think about the future. My son, Heardred, is too young to carry the burdens of a king."[52] Hygd's verbal appeal is therefore doubled by the illustration, which serves as a direct plea to the reader's conscience.

The last portrait of Hygd, in Morley and Li (2010), is more uncommon still, for it depicts an invented scene with a crowned Hygd in fine linen shift and royal blue robes standing over a petulant, young-adult Heardred slumped under his crown on the Geatish throne.[53] Her posture with arms outstretched ably conveys her worry, while in turn, he thrusts an arm out from his red robes, dismissing her without so much as looking at her. The accompanying text box offers a blunt appraisal in short sentences fitting the graphic novel medium: "Hygelac's young

Figure 5.9. "To Hygda he gave a jeweled necklace wondrously wrought," from Hinds, *Beowulf*, p. [78].

son was a weakling. Even his mother thought him unfit to rule. Before long, he too was killed." Good metafictional detail is also built into the scene, as a pallid copper dragon sails on the rose-tinged tapestry behind the symbolically uncarved throne.

Hygd's sudden appearance in these recent children's and illustrated versions may seem inexplicable, but it corresponds to the anticipation and release of Robert Zemeckis's motion-capture feature film *Beowulf* (2007).[54] Indeed, in the film's loose adaptation of the poem, the older king Beowulf has not zero but two women in his circle, as he has remained in the Danish lands with Wealhþeow, and has acquired a blonde princess, Ursula, who begs him feverishly not to fight the dragon. A trend we see in the Postmodern Graphic Phase, then, is to add female figures to retellings of the legend, or to recoup the women already present in the poem, but the tendency does not seem unconnected to the growing familiarity of portrayals indicative of male fantasy like those in the Zemeckis film, portrayals that have their own genealogy in the media of film and comics.[55] One could also say that in the recent illustrations of her with Heardred, Hygd comes not only to supplement, but to replace Wealhþeow's dynastic angst, which is absent from these same versions.

The Geatish *Meowle*

In all these hundred-plus children's and illustrated versions of *Beowulf*, there is but a single depiction of the female mourner at Beowulf's funeral who projects ruin to come now that her nation has lost its king. Her status in the poem has always been one of scholarly contention, given that the manuscript is heavily damaged at the top of folio 198v and must be emended to make a coherent reading;[56] nevertheless, the narrative at this point is devastating and deeply aligned with the performative mourning of Hildeburh in the Finnsburh episode. The poem presents the *meowle* as a solitary female figure who is emotionally distraught and laments publicly: "Swylce giomorgyd Geatisc anmeowle / næs bliðheorte, bundenheorde, / sang sorgcearig sælðe geneahhe" (ll. 3152–4) [And likewise, the Geatish woman sang a mournful lament, / by herself, bereft at heart, with hair bound up, / keened again and again of fortunes turned to dreadful misery].[57] She appears in Burnett's severe two-colour woodcut for Crossley-Holland's full translation (1977), foregrounded in profile with her hair bound up, while Beowulf's body and treasure burn on the tall pyre far behind her, across a river chasm (see fig. 5.10). A rope circles her robes just below the breast, and her posture of kneeling forward on the ground,

Figure 5.10. "A maiden of the Geats intoned a dirge for Beowulf time after time," by Virgil Burnett, from Crossley-Holland and Burnett, *Beowulf*, p. 117.

gripping the rocky earth before her, clearly foreshadows the "hyðo 7 hæftnyd" (l. 3157a), the "slavery and abasement" to come, as Seamus Heaney chillingly words it.[58] Last, her mouth is open just enough to keen. This is a presentation for adult readers, one which breaks the upright, assertive elegance of Wealhþeow from the Edwardian age and grounds it in stylized agony.

As with Hildeburh, the *meowle* is otherwise absent from illustrated presentations of the poem; on top of the fact that a great many children's versions elide the dragon episode entirely, they would not be able to fit a sybilline prophecy of catastrophe into the visual framework of an already tragic outcome for the hero.

Grendel's Mother

The illustrations of the second major antagonist in the poem betray the problem of representing a figure who is at once human in form, yet a monstrous deformation of a person; there is also the challenge of having to base her likeness on that of her son for visual and familial continuity, yet transform his male likeness into a female body conveying motherhood. The resulting tensions between human and other, male and female, and mother and revenging demon spill over into a destabilizing range of depictions that eventually and exaggeratedly become post-human as the Postmodern Graphic Phase advances. Grendel's mother's form is always as oppositional to men and Heorot as the cave she inhabits at the bottom of the serpent-ridden mere, but in the most recent illustrations her monstrosity accelerates to cross species boundaries of disturbing and fantastical nature.

Hroðgar's account of Grendel's mother, spoken the morning after she has raided Heorot in vengeance, directly exposes these polarities. Grief-stricken, the king tells Beowulf that his shoulder-companion Æschere is dead and reveals that his hall-counsellors have long known there was not just Grendel, but a matched female creature too:

> hie gesawon   swylce twegen
> micle mearcstapan   moras healdan,
> ellorgæstas.   Ðæra oðer wæs,
> þæs þe hie gewislicost   gewitan meahton,
> idese onlicnæs.   Oðer earmsceapen
> on weres wæstmum   wræclastas træd,
> næfne he wæs mara   þonne ænig man oðer.   (ll. 1349–55)

[they saw two / great border-steppers holding the moors, / alien spirits. The second of the pair was, / as far as they were able to make out most

carefully, / of a woman's likeness. The first wretched one / trod steps of
exile in the shape of a common man, / except that he was of more size than
any other man.]

This description emphasizes that they are a pair, that they hold the
moors together as exiles, as alien-spirits, *ellorgastas*. They have the like-
nesses of human beings too, with Grendel's mother having the shape
of a woman, an *ides*, a poetic term for a noblewoman, a figure of history or power,[59] although the counsellors have an upsetting trouble in
discerning this. For his part, Grendel has a man's *wæstm* – a term with
theological import, used in the sense of the created angelic or human
form in the poem *Genesis B*[60] – yet exceedes the limits of a man's form,
as he is "mara," simply "greater." However, the narrator has played
on her description in advance, earlier calling her "ides aglæcwif" (l.
1261a), an epithet which genders her twice while marking her power
and opposition status as *aglæca*, a warrior-foe, and slyly overturning
expectations concerning her strength when she raids Heorot: "Wæs se
gryre læssa / efne swa micle, swa bið mægþa cræft / wiggryre wifes,
bewæpned men" (ll. 1284b–86) [The horror was lesser / by as much as
a maiden's strength, / a woman's battle-terror, is than that of an armed
man]. Grendel may be *mara* and Grendel's mother *læssa*, but read as
litotes, this comparison reveals her capacity for battle-horror exceeds
his, that she is a more considerable foe than her son, a dismaying truth
that Beowulf soon discovers.

If the above descriptors suggest a range of type-scenes – mother
and son together as the two moor-walkers, enraged mother strid-
ing towards Heorot intending violence, female troll dragging the
bloody corpse of Æschere away – it is in the fight in her underwater lair that Grendel's mother enacts her signal image for illustrators: "Ofsæt þa þone selegyst, 7 hyre seax geteah, / brad, brunecg.
Wolde hire bearn wrecan / angan eaferan" (ll. 1547–9a) [Then she
sat upon her hall-guest, and drew her knife, / broad and browned at
its edge. She intended to avenge her boy, / her sole offspring]. This
scene of the *merewif mihtig*, the powerful female of the mere, straddling a pinned-down Beowulf, knife in hand and ready to avenge her
son's killer, unsettles the audience in every fashion.[61] He is the guest
in her hall, and so out of place; his fearsome skill at grappling has
been overmatched by hers; his sword, the gifted Hrunting, is useless,
and her *seax* is ready to strike; and she is justified in intending to kill
him. All this constructs the most threatening image of the poem and
the most potent one in its reversal of gender roles. How illustrators
handle this scene is therefore key to their conceptions of femininity,

Figure 5.11. *Beowulf and the Old Wife of the Mere*, by George Tobin, from Ragozin and Tobin, *Tales of the Heroic Ages*, facing p. 268.

of peril, and of the inversion of humanity and social codes her monstrosity represents.

In the earliest drawings of her in children's books, Grendel's mother is depicted as a large humanoid, a recognizable woman rather than a beast. The first drawing, Tobin's breathtaking lithograph of diving into the mere (1898), presents a goblin-faced Grendel's mother holding a young Beowulf at arm's length beside her as the pair rush through a sweep of underwater streaks that violates the picture's boundaries; it is as if their faces are caught in freeze-frame while the rest of the image blurs under a watery lens, melding the two figures to the elements (see fig. 5.11). The portrayal in Lang and Ford (1899) tilts the image ninety degrees to a tremendous plunge, where Grendel's mother, now drawn with an elf's face, hurtles to the bottom of the page, her huge arm and clawed hand pinning Beowulf to her bosom.[62] Echoing the watery sweep of Tobin's picture, a gargantuan mass of her unbound dark hair billows upwards to the surface; the heap of alien fronds surrounds the diving warrior and embraces him as does a placenta an unborn child. The effect is strikingly feminine, yet unreliant on any other characteristics or signals; the drawing is thus menacing, otherworldly, and graceful all at once. Brinsley Le Fanu (1900) changes Grendel's mother from an elf or goblin to a tall death-crone, an anti-Wealhþeow with hair bound in long twin braids, a close-fitting, ankle-length gown, and a jewelled belt; her skeletal, angular arms grasp Beowulf's waist and pull his armoured body down into the mere in a pronounced vertical image that matches her stretched, fleshless form.[63] Patten Wilson (1908) continues this emphasis on surrounding the male figure while painting Grendel's mother as a spectral crone whose unbound grey-white hair swirls and fills the page above her and matches in colour and shape the sweeping fabric of her dress, one so large that as Beowulf stands between her legs, he is enveloped by it (see fig. 5.12). The sense of Beowulf being overmatched and lost within an enormous feminine waterborne body obtains again here, just as it did in Ford's image, but is now flipped on the vertical axis and richly coloured with blue and purple hues. This Grendel's mother is the most regal and towering of any depiction, again pointing to the Edwardian association of the feminine with ruling power and imposing dress, even in a ghastly antagonist.

Two other Edwardian Regality adaptations present the second type-scene, where Grendel's mother pins down Beowulf, holding her *seax* above him, and do so with distinct sexualization, suddenly giving her breasts. Skelton (1908) renders perhaps the most goblin-like of all depictions of Grendel's mother, as her skin is tinged green, yet her body is properly woman-like in size and composition, unlike that of her hulking, fanged son;[64] as she holds Beowulf down with a muscled arm and side-straddles him, her torso is exposed by her sheer, pale-blue dress, her breasts marked by tawny shadow lines. Her hair is unkempt, though not wild or overly long, and she has gained a small skull-necklace as accoutrement, a feature later amplified by other illustrators. Beowulf's completely prone posture here is noteworthy; offering no resistance whatsoever, he lies helplessly awaiting the killing strike, with only the round-breasted corselet to save him, itself a kind of mirror image. Skovgaard's ink drawing in Konstantin-Hansen's Danish version (1914) demonically exaggerates her female features in the freedom of her lair, giving her a wild troll's aspect of bared teeth and a half-bald head of flaming hair (see fig. 5.13). She is naked here, fur-covered and heavyset with full breasts, and wields a larger, more phallic blade, again dominating a young, blond Beowulf, though he is partially off the floor. This is perhaps the most obviously feminized illustration of Grendel's mother, but done by signalling motherhood through grotesque, threatening features.[65]

Figure 5.12. *Beowulf's Fight with Grendel's Mother* by Patten Wilson, from Cartwright and Wilson, *Brave Beowulf*, facing p. 40.

Figure 5.13. "Kampen i Troldekæret" [The battle in the troll-pond], by Niels Skovgaard, from Konstantin-Hansen and Skovgaard, *Bjovulf: Et Angelsaksisk Heltedigt*, p. 53.

In the older-audience depictions of the Modernist era, Grendel's mother is given rigid, statuesque proportions and heavy dress. Kent's high-art lithograph (1931) draws her as physically impressive and goblin faced, though bent backwards by Beowulf as he pulls her head down by its long, gathered hair.[66] His body is again enveloped within hers visually as the fabric of his clothing matches her long dress, but the postures show him in a position of strength; they are thus an evenly matched pair against the expansive, void background. In contrast, Ward's two-colour illustration (1939) is particularly sweeping, again presenting a tall, crone-like Grendel's mother, but with long white hair and yellowed hem blown rightwards across the page into clouds and purplish-blue moors.[67] Though she is similarly drawn as a Modernist Sweep statue, her posture and expression are chilling: she is heading to Heorot, but her face is turned back to the viewer, communicating strong pathos mixed with terrible agency. Her sense of being an alien to the hall as well a mother bereft is fully captured; she will be an implacable enemy. The struggle in the mere is not depicted by Ward, by Klep (1941), nor, surprisingly, in the ornate artwork of Pitz (1933), where Grendel's mother has seemingly been displaced in her mere by a giant squid-like creature in a vivid two-page illustration.[68]

Several of the Mid-Century Inkings and Postmodern Graphic Phase representations continue to depict Grendel's mother as a goblin or crone, often emphasizing her reach and grasp, as with Walter Ferro's wonderful across-the-fold woodcut (1962), where her arm extends from bottom left to top right in order to snare a diving Beowulf,[69] but they also increasingly use her hair as a marker of her savage nature. Gone is the elegant or pathos-filled sweeping mass of the earlier illustrations in favour of a wilder, freakish aspect. Her hair is roughly cropped and loose in Ferro's depiction, but in two illustrations by Keeping – for Sutcliff's widely read novella (1961) and Crossley-Holland's stark picture book (1982) – her hair is far longer, its wildness reflecting her capacity for battle horror. In both inkings, Grendel's mother clasps Beowulf vertically to her bosom, holding the *seax* high above him. While in an earlier chapter heading from Sutcliff's novella, "The Sea-Hag," her coarse hair frames her face,[70] in the struggle in the full-page picture her reedy hair swarms high behind her, halfway to a beehive, and its thin aspect matches her body, which seems composed of only muscles and tendons.[71] Her face here is only hair, all directed to a lupine snout that merges into her torso. Keeping's later drawing for Crossley-Holland is profoundly disturbing, rendering a peak of the type-standard: she is a spectre of fear, her electrified hair reaching out in curvilinear strands to the blank edges of the page, while her face is sunk into a black massy void, its eye sockets empty.[72] She is otherwise naked, thinly delineated, and positioned in an open, masculinizing stance, haunches exposed. Moreover, she imprisons Beowulf in an all-consuming embrace, sucking his life force so thoroughly that we see only his helmet, sexualized as a glans,[73] and his body bent limply under him. If this is a mother's grasp, it is a Freudian nightmare image of mother as Thanatos.

Raven and Howe's lustrous picture book (2007) presents the opposing pole in this type-standard. In a double-page, saturated-colour depiction of her lair, Grendel's mother is seen head-on, focalized for us from over Beowulf's shoulder, himself pushed far left (see fig. 5.14).[74] She stares not at him, but directly at the reader, from the centre of the painting and the centre of the cave, with goblin head thrust forward, pale-blue tattooed skin, lurid red eyes and maw, and a massive wolf's jawbone for a necklace, an accoutrement of death. Her long, flat hair radiates out darkly, giving the full picture the look of a demonic, exploded

Figure 5.14. "The bones and carcasses of her kills decked the floor; the hag grinned fiercely to herself," by John Howe, from Raven and Howe, *Beowulf*, pp. 42–3.

corona, with just a single braid tethering her to civilization. As her left hand holds an enormous cross-like *seax* up, as if to thrust it into the reader, the right, hideously jet black, subtly reaches forward below. And all around her, piling up over her shoulders, is a mass of human skulls, a morbid collection of jewels to match the dragon's gold. The whole is designed to terrify an older child as much as possible, to be a detailed, literal portrait of ravening death, one violating the boundary between book and reader.

If the first type-standard depicts Grendel's mother as a tall, frightening goblin or crone, the second renders her as usurping the boundaries of species and human evolution. Starting mid-century, depictions come to fantasize and fetishize her as a beast, a lizard, a primordial human, or as an aquatic creature outright. The earliest animalized depiction of Grendel's mother appears in Serraillier and Severin (1954), where she is a gigantic, fur-covered troll pinning down a tiny, helpless Beowulf; her *seax* is poised fearsomely, her hair hangs freely, her breasts are outlined (though not grotesquely), her thick hip bears enormous power, and her shape is completed by a long, spear-tipped tail and reverse-talons at the ankles.[75] She is still humanoid, but bears feline features in place of the goblin or crone features of earlier drawings.

Another method illustrators use is to hybridize Grendel's mother as a proto-human, one combining primordial features with a reptilian cast. This is the case with Brenda Ralph Lewis and Rob McCaig's hardcover anthology of monsters and heroes (1980), where the viewer sees her from behind, over her shoulder, which is a highly unusual focalization. Her pale, purple-tinged body is palaeo-human, but covered with lizard-like lumps that concentrate in the skin of her face, which in turn reveals a giant, slitted-iris eye and well-spaced, shark-like teeth; even stranger, above this horrible face protrudes a rough-cut shock of blonde hair, almost wig-like. She is clothed in an animal skin, complete with small skull accoutrement, and, confusingly, holds a wire-handled cauldron, suggesting Iron Age development even though the scene otherwise presents a hunter-gatherer locale. Katz and Gal's vivid picture book (1999) softens its depiction of Grendel's mother, as her green-grey skin is smooth here and her long hair straight, yet she now bears a heavy, ridged lizard's tail, one starting from mid-back, like that of a theropod.[76] As she carries Æschere away, her face is mask-like. A second picture, where Grendel's mother plunges feet first down the mere is less ambiguous; here, her jaw protrudes, her irises are slits, and her free hair trails upwards wildly; she still has distinct fingers though, terminating in triangular nails.[77]

In the teenage-oriented comic books and graphic novels, Grendel's mother's reptilian hybridity accelerates in order to give her a more frightening and violent cast. In a series of panels in Hinds (2007), her head is a mix of lizard and ape, with small, pointed teeth running the length of her distended jaw, small-slitted eyes, and short, snaky hair.[78] Her body is again larger than Beowulf's, with bony, elongated arms encompassing him, broad hips, and a hanging belly, a pannus signalling motherhood. The most obvious feature, however, is her breasts, so pendulous it is as if one were suckling Beowulf's helmet as she grapples him from behind. If this embrace in Hinds represents a kind of symbolically misplaced maternity, implicit oral fixation and rage are given a hyperbolic presentation in Petrucha and Chamberlain's graphic novel (2007), where Grendel's mother becomes a cinematic demon. Here, she is humanoid in upright stature only, with dark green skin, and is barely distinguished from her son; there is only a thick jet of hair arcing behind her to mark her as female, resembling nothing so much as the elongated cranium

Figure 5.15. "Grendel had not been alone: the new monster had claimed her prize," by Kody Chamberlain, from Petrucha and Chamberlain, *Beowulf*, p. [42].

of the Queen from the *Alien* films. This visual allusion is heightened by a double set of jaws; the second, interior set do not jump-protrude, however, but are arrayed circularly, like those of a giant lamprey. In one nightmarish image of her revenge on Heorot she is all jaws, a faceless mouth upon mouth splurting black blood at the reader (see fig. 5.15).

Such a grotesque, interspecies transformation of Grendel's mother away from a female humanoid to a reptilian or aquatic hybrid is made complete in Jones and Tavares (2009) and Morley and Li (2010). In the former, a small picture book in chapters aimed for the British school market, she bears no resemblance to her club-wielding troll-like son; she is instead outrageously chimerical as a white-skinned, bipedal octopus, with eight tentacles in place of two arms, but still with a goblin's face and long, stringy hair to mark her as female (see fig. 5.16). While a bizarre take on the poem's kenning of Grendel's mother as *brimwylf* (l. 1601a), water-wolf,[79] it is at least fantastical and age appropriate. But in the latter graphic novel the metamorphosis is finalized in a post-Jolie acceleration of the hypersexualized, aquatic hybrid mother

Figure 5.16. "Grendel's mother slithered closer. Beams of blackness shot from her eyes," by Victor Tavares, from Jones and Tavares, *Beowulf*, p. [42].

Figure 5.17. "As his mother wept over him, Grendel died," by Rob McCaig, from Lewis and McCaig, "Beowulf," in *Myths and Legends*, 32–41, at p. 37.

of Zemeckis's motion-capture film. While Grendel's mother is virtually faceless here, all jaws on top as with her illustration in Petrucha and Chamberlain, and oddly flat-chested, her lower body is exaggerated with slick, giant thighs and a sinuous tail emanating from muscular haunches and rounded buttocks.[80] One alarming drawing of disorienting perspective is a variation on the up-skirt photograph;[81] it seems that science fiction and sexual fantasy merge here in a passive-aggressive allurement of the teenage reader.

This doubleness, this hybridity, has perhaps been there all along, for in the blur of the earliest depiction of Grendel's mother in Tobin's lithograph (1898, see fig. 5.11 above), one can see that Grendel's mother may be an aquatic creature from the waist down, with two claw-like appendages where a horse's or a terrapin's forelegs are, and a large, undefined black body behind her torso. Given that there is no clear linkage between the upper and lower halves, however, this putative hybrid is created by shadow and implied effect rather than by careful delineation. All the same, the parabolic sweep of the image is destabilizing in its watery depth suggestive of birth and death.

But what is invisible in almost all these depictions, despite the presence or absence of long hair, breasts, distended hips, and *seax*, is that she is a mother who has lost her son, for only one adaptation shows her in an emotional posture with her dead offspring. This comes unexpectedly in the outlier version of Lewis and McCaig (1980; see fig. 5.17), where Grendel's mother is depicted as a cave-dwelling palaeo-human. It is here we see her, pink skinned and grass skirted, kneeling over her prone, green-skinned son, about to cradle him with her right arm under his thigh, and her left arm under his lifeless head, lifting his reptilian face towards us.[82] In the otherwise menacing illustrations of this adaptation, here is a moment of tenderness, of unmistakable maternal affection and loss; this is an exactly human posture and portrayal that transcends their hybrid, lizard-like nature.[83] Its uniqueness in the illustration history of the poem reminds us that just as Wealhþeow's maternal imperatives are sacrificed to empty ceremony or absent altogether, so too is Grendel's mother's female nature transposed into her pinning embrace of Beowulf and her justified vengeance hyper-characterized as oral rage. Neither female figure fares well as the illustration history advances in the Postmodern Graphic Phase.

Conclusions

The accumulated evidence of these depictions suggests two major, if apparently silent, strategies. The first is the diminution, elision, and displacement of Wealhþeow's role. She, who is an active speaker and regal mother in the poem, becomes a passive, childless observer; further, she is reduced by synecdoche to the instruments she bears; then, even the instruments are taken from her. The second is the dehumanization of Grendel's mother, who, so rich in the context of sexual inversion and maternal homicidal rage, has now become instead an unfathomable zoomorph.

Any attempt to situate these images within broader constructions of gender in the poem and its adaptations must eventually confront the looping problem of stereotype: the tendency of artists and readers to take the visual cues demarcating gender as gender itself, when these

Figure 5.18. "Stories Told to the Children: sister reads to brother," by J.R. Skelton, from Marshall and Skelton, *Stories of Beowulf*, frontispiece.

markers on a spectrum of masculine-feminine roles cannot exist without a performative iteration of unquestioned codes. The shift in portrayals over the last 130 years shows the degree to which visualized femininity is always in negotiation. Furthermore, as the plethora of adaptations of the poem for children is now in view, I encourage scholars of feminism and gender to critique and extend upon my findings with the primary sources.

As a final consideration, I wish to ask what is there for girls reading *Beowulf* picture books and graphic novels today? As illustrated, the aesthetic and ethical appeal for a young female audience seems less now than it did in the iconic frontispiece of the Stories Told to the Children series that gave us Henrietta Marshall's 1908 *Beowulf*, where a well-dressed girl reads to her younger brother (see fig. 5.18). Still, there

Figure 5.19. "He asked for his sword, which had never once let him down in a fight," from Rumford, *Beowulf: A Hero's Tale Retold*, pp. [34]–[35].

is some occasion for discovery of unexpected female figures in visual adaptations of the poem for child readers. I think in particular of the drawing in Rumford's picture book where a young woman with a long blonde braid and a ginger-haired boy in a loose overcoat are helping the aged, thin, white-bearded Beowulf dress for his final battle (see fig. 5.19).[84] Though it is the boy holding the sword Nægling before him, and the young woman (or teenage girl) helping him into his mail coat, she is closer to Beowulf in position and size. In making her the *eaxlgestealla*, the shoulder-companion, the picture renders a balanced triptych, perhaps a vision of the family Beowulf never has. Moreover, his robes, now draped over his large shield, are the same blue colour with red trim as her own, again suggesting family unity, or even a future transference of rule. Through the king's appropriate weakness, and her youthful aid in the illustration, Rumford is able to capture a tenderness and a sense of generations otherwise missing from adaptations of the poem that fail to understand the elegiac heart of the epic. This necessary sadness, leavened with help from the young in this adaptation, measures a thoughtful interpretive fulcrum for the reader, young or old.

NOTES

1 References to the Old English *Beowulf* are to Kevin Kiernan, ed., *The Electronic Beowulf*, programmed by Emil Iacob, 4th ed. (University of Kentucky, 2015), available at http://ebeowulf.uky.edu/ebeo4.0/CD /main.html. Translations throughout, in brackets following quotations or more informally in running text, are my own unless otherwise attributed.

2 Zenaïde A. Ragozin, *Tales of the Heroic Ages: Siegfried and Beowulf*, illus. George T. Tobin (New York and London: G.P. Putnam's Sons, 1898), 211–330, facing p. 242. Shown as figure 1 below.

3 Bruce Gilchrist, "Emotion and Masculinity in Children's and Illustrated Versions of *Beowulf*," conference presentation at the 44th International Congress on Medieval Studies, 2009.

4 John Gibb, *Gudrun and Other Stories from the Epics of the Middle Ages*, illus. unknown (New York: Scribner and Welford, 1881), 164.

5 Ragozin and Tobin, *Tales of the Heroic Ages*. See also A[lfred] J[ohn] Church, "The Story of Beowulf," in *Heroes of Chivalry and Romance*, illus. George Morrow (London: Seeley, Service & Co., 1898), 1–63. This anthology opens with an ornate, orientalized frontispiece, subtitled "How They Called Scyld to the Ship," in which Scyld rests on a lavish bier while two kneeling retainers lean toward him in respect but do not touch him. This displacement of Beowulf by Scyld is notable as a metafictional device, one mirroring the poem's own use of the Scyld story and funeral as prologue.

6 H[enrietta] E[lizabeth] Marshall, *Stories of Beowulf: Told to the Children*, illus. J[oseph] R[atcliffe] Skelton (London: T.C. & E.C. Jack; New York: E.P. Dutton & Co., 1908).

7 Ian Serraillier, *Beowulf the Warrior*, illus. [Mark] Severin (Oxford: Oxford University Press, 1954), 33.

8 This is true especially of graphic novel versions: see, for example, Gareth Hinds, *Beowulf* (Cambridge, MA: Candlewick Press, 2007); and Stefan Petrucha, *Beowulf*, illus. Kody Chamberlain (New York: HarperTrophy, 2007).

9 An exception is James Rumford, *Beowulf: A Hero's Tale Retold* (Boston: Houghton Mifflin, 2007), [42]–[43], where not only does Wiglaf cradle a prone and failing Beowulf, but the two look directly into each other's eyes in awareness of the grief to come (this illustration can be seen in the cover

art for the present book). See also Kevin Crossley-Holland, *Beowulf*, illus. Charles Keeping (Oxford: Oxford University Press, 1982), for its intensely distressing ink depiction of Wiglaf holding a battle-spattered Beowulf.

10 These terms are meant only to represent the major trends of the eras in book production and should not be regarded as exclusive within each era or as claims to authority concerning art history.

11 The name of this princess, and even whether she is a separate figure from Hygd, is one of the signal cruxes in *Beowulf*. I follow Kiernan's reading of her name. She is conventionally named Modþryð or Þryð by other scholars, and regarded as a distinct female character.

12 E.g., Ashley Crownover, *Wealtheow: Her Retelling of Beowulf* (Nashville: Iroquois Press, 2008); Susan Signe Morrison, *Grendel's Mother: The Saga of the Wyrd-Wife* (n.p.: Top Hat, 2015); and Maria Dahvana Headley, *The Mere Wife: A Novel* (New York: MCD, 2018).

13 Such as Rebecca Tingle, *The Edge on the Sword* (New York: G.P. Putnam's Sons, 2001) and its sequel, *Far Traveler* (New York: G.P. Putnam's Sons, 2005); Rebecca Barnhouse, *Peaceweaver* (New York: Random House, 2012); and Nicola Griffith, *Hild: A Novel* (New York: Farrar, Strauss, & Giroux, 2013).

14 That all seven of these recent re-envisionings and historical fictions are novels by female authors argues as much for a feminist reappropriation of the poem as it does a focussed strategy to engage young women in historical fiction and fantasy, and to penetrate the considerable high school assigned reading market. See also A.E. Kaplan, *Grendel's Guide to Love and War* (New York: Knopf Books for Younger Readers, 2017), a whip-smart modernization set in high school.

15 It is also worth noting that the term *freolic* counters the second element in her compund name, *þeow*, which means servant or slave. Her name as a whole richly suggests her role as peace-weaver.

16 A depiction evoking the poetic term *wundenlocc* for a noblewoman's splended hair, not actually found in *Beowulf* but present in *Judith* in the same manuscript.

17 Le Fanu first draws Wealhþeow after she has given Beowulf the cup, but she still stands above him, with an elegant full-length dress, necklace, . and jewelled belt; atypically, however, her hair is short (anticipating the bob cut of the 1910s), she wears only a thin circlet in place of a crown, and her expression seems disengaged, porcelain-like. W[illiam] T[homas] Stead, ed., *Tales of Long Ago. 1. Childe Horn 2. Beowulf and the Dragon*, illus. Brinsley Le Fanu, Books for the Bairns 51 (London: Stead's Publishing House, [1900]), 40.

18 Andrew Lang, ed., *The Red Book of Animal Stories*, illus. H.J. Ford (London: Longmans, Green & Co., 1899), 35.

19 C[lara] L[inklater] Thomson, *The Adventures of Beowulf: Translated from the Old English and Adapted to the Use of Schools*, illus. unknown (London: Horace Marshall and Son, 1899), 53. (The 1904 2nd ed. has no illustrations.)

20 The *Stories … Told to the Children* series published by T.C. & E.C. Jack is especially noteworthy for these deluxe – and now highly collectible – features. The series is also remarkable in its fondness for medieval tales: alongside Marshall and Skelton's *Beowulf* [1908] are versions of *Robin Hood, King Arthur's Knights, Celtic Tales, Chaucer, Dante, Three Saints, Roland, Siegfried*, and even *Guy of Warwick*.

21 Olive Beaupré Miller, "How Beowulf Delivered Heorot," in *From the Tower Window of My Bookhouse* (Chicago: The Bookhouse for Children, 1921), 419.

22 Rockwell Kent, *Beowulf*, eight lithographs (New York: George Miller Printing, 1931). Series issued in a signed limited edition prior to their 1932 use in a deluxe limited edition of William Ellery Leonard's translation (*Beowulf*, illus. Rockwell Kent [New York: Random House, 1932]); the Leonard translation had originally been published in an inexpensive edition explicitly intended for family and school use (*Beowulf: A New Verse Translation for Fireside and Classroom* [New York: Century Co., 1923]).

23 William Ellery Leonard, *Beowulf*, illus. Lynd Ward (New York: Heritage Press, 1939).

24 E.V. Sandys, *Beowulf*, illus. Rolf Klep (New York: Thomas Y. Crowell, 1941).

25 Leonard and Ward, *Beowulf*, 37.

26 Strafford Riggs, *The Story of Beowulf Retold from the Ancient Epic*, illus. Henry C. Pitz (New York and London: D. Appleton Century Company, 1933).

27 Riggs and Pitz, *Story of Beowulf*, 39.

28 Rosemary Sutcliff, *Beowulf*, illus. Charles Keeping (London: Bodley Head, 1961).

29 Sutcliff and Keeping, *Beowulf*, 10–11.

30 Sutcliff and Keeping, *Beowulf*, 20–1.

31 Jane Leighton, *The Story of Beowulf*, illus. Gerhard Steffen (Frankfurt am Main: Verlag Moritz Diesterweg, 1959), 11.

32 See also the illustration on p. 15, where Wealhþeow is drawn in profile at centre, with her cortège trailing her, while Beowulf stands apart respectfully, helmet in his hands, and a fellow Geat at his side kneels. She holds her large right hand forward in dominant position, and her facial expression is also powerful. Overall, the engraving is a fine match for Ragozin and Tobin (1898).

33 Ian Serraillier, *Beowulf the Warrior: A Tale of Monsters*, illus. Bill Pesce (New York: Scholastic Book Services, 1968), 21.

34 Kevin Crossley-Holland, *Beowulf*, illus. Virgil Burnett (London: The Folio Society, 1973), facing p. 52. The drawing's location in the book is

also unintentionally curious, for the list of illustrations gives the title "To Beowulf she carried the cup" (4), even though the illustration itself faces the scop's retelling of the Finnsburh episode, with the mourning Hildeburh. Given that the female figure is alone and abject of expression, the drawing could work just as well to represent the isolated, fateful position of Hildeburh.

35 Penelope Hicks, *Beowulf*, illus. James McLean (New York: Kingfisher, 2007), 54.

36 John Green, *Beowulf* (Minneola, NY: Dover, 2007), 20. See also Welwyn Wilton Katz, *Beowulf*, illus. Laszlo Gal (Toronto: Groundwood, 1999), 34. The illustration from this large picture book has a noble, older-looking Wealhþeow pouring the mead after Beowulf's defeat of Grendel's mother; she wears a golden crown and shoulder clasps, and is in dominant centre position, but is otherwise coloured a sombre brown in pencil crayon, and has an almost expressionless face.

37 Eric L. Kimmel, *The Hero Beowulf*, illus. Leonard Everett Fisher (New York: FSG Kids, 2005), 11.

38 James Rumford, *Beowulf: A Hero's Tale Retold* (Boston: Houghton Mifflin, 2007), [16]–[17]. Wealhþeow looks older in Rumford's illustration than in any other picture: a match for the elderly, almost frail Beowulf Rumford renders in the dragon episode, and another example of the thoughtful nature of his picture book. In Anita Ganeri, *Beowulf*, illus. James Ives (London: Collins [Big Cat], 2013), a feast honouring the building of Heorot is depicted to start this small picture book for primary school readers; in the tableau on p. 3, a smiling, crone-like woman wearing a crown and holding a cup dominates the scene. As the book does not depict Heorot further, the reader cannot identify if she is Wealhþeow or not, but the image effectively displaces her role all the same, and follows in the logic of portraying her as aged.

39 Michelle L. Szobody, *Beowulf: Grendel the Ghastly*, illus. Justin Gerard (Greenville, SC: Portland Studios, 2007), 13. For more on the Tolkien-inspired quality of this book, see Yvette Kisor's chapter in this collection.

40 Szobody and Gerard, *Beowulf: Grendel the Ghastly*, 18–19.

41 Mick Gowar, *Treetop Myths and Legends: Beowulf, Grendel and the Dragon*, illus. Paul McCaffrey (Oxford: Oxford University Press, 2010), 24–5.

42 Hannes Hüttner, *Beowulf*, illus. Ruth Knorr (Berlin, Kinderbuchverlag, 1975), 35. Knorr makes a bold decision to alternate between simple black line drawings for the Danes and Geats and gigantesque, psychedelic colour imagery for the monsters.

43 Rumford, *Beowulf: A Hero's Tale Retold*, [16].

44 Michael Morpurgo, *Beowulf*, illus. Michael Foreman (New York: Candlewick, 2006), 38–9.

45 Morley and Li, *Beowulf*, 17.

46 Hicks and McLean, *Beowulf*, 68.

47 Petrucha and Chamberlain, *Beowulf*, [23].

48 One worth noting is Georgía Galanopoúlou, Μπέογουλφ [Béögoulf], illus. Panagiótis Beldékos (Athens: Ekdoseis Delfini, 1996), which is unusual in portraying Wealhþeow as equal of stature, dress, and crown in two images that bookend the story, essentially making king and queen a perfect match (7/37 and 34/37, ebook). However, in a mid-story illustration depicting the drinking oaths before the Grendel fight, Wealhþeow is drawn in the typical recessed position, well behind Hrothgar and the men assembled at the bench, so continuing that Mid-Century diminution of her role at her key moment (28/37).

49 Morpurgo and Foreman, *Beowulf*, 66. The watercolour technique, in addition to the small size of the figures, makes it hard to read small details such as a golden crown in blonde hair.

50 Green, *Beowulf*, 22. Similarly, McCaffrey (2010) portrays an unidentified queen at a table of food and riches enjoyed in the glory age of the Lay of the Last Survivor episode, before the ruin came and the people fell. She too wears a modest headdress, but contrary to the recent chastened portraits of Wealhþeow, this younger-looking queen smiles and is seated in equal pairing with her king beside her. Gowar and McCaffrey, *Beowulf, Grendel and the Dragon*, 36.

51 Hicks and McLean, *Beowulf*, 99.

52 Hicks and McLean, *Beowulf*, 112.

53 Morley and Li, *Beowulf*, 30.

54 Robert Zemeckis, dir., *Beowulf* (Paramount Pictures, 2007).

55 The addition of sexual fantasy women to versions of the *Beowulf* story goes back at least as far as Michael Uslan and Ricardo Villamonte, *Beowulf: Dragon Slayer*, 6 issues (New York: DC Comics, 1975–6), with its scantily clad sidekick Nan-Zee, a character type imported from the Robert E. Howard universe of *Conan the Barbarian*. Other examples among comics or graphic novels include Grendel's mother in David Hutchison, *Beowulf*, three issues (San Antonio, TX: Antarctic Press, 2006), and in Tony Bedard and Jesus Saiz, "Beowulf," *Sword of Sorcery* 0–3 (New York: DC Comics, 2012–13). In its hypersexualized portrayal of Grendel's mother, the 2007 Zemeckis film was preceded by Graham Baker, dir., *Beowulf* (Dimension Films, 1999), which advertised that it cast a *Playboy* Playmate in the role.

56 See R.D. Fulk, Robert E. Bjork, and John D. Niles, eds., *Klaeber's Beowulf and the Fight at Finnsburg*, 4th ed. (Toronto: University of Toronto Press), 107 and 270; and Kiernan's critical edition, ll. 3152b ff.

57 Kiernan attaches the superscript correction *an* to *meowle* in line 3152, translating, "solitary Geatish woman"; no other major editor of the poem has done so.

58 Seamus Heaney, *Beowulf: A New Verse Translation* (New York: Norton, 2000), l. 3155.

59 Joseph Bosworth and T. Northcote Toller, *An Anglo-Saxon Dictionary* (Oxford: Clarendon, 1879), s.v. *ides.*

60 See *Genesis B,* l. 255, where *wæstm* is the term for Lucifer's beautiful form, l. 520, where Satan entices Eve with a more beautiful form, *wæstm þy wlitegra,* and again at l. 613; cited from A.N. Doane, ed., *The Saxon Genesis: An Edition of the West Saxon Genesis B and the Old Saxon Vatican Genesis* (Madison: University of Wisconsin Press, 1991). See also Bosworth and Toller, *Anglo-Saxon Dictionary,* s.v. *wæstm,* definition III.

61 The translation "sat upon" for *ofsæt* is philologically doubtful, as Fred C. Robinson has shown ("Did Grendel's Mother Sit on Beowulf?" in *From Anglo-Saxon to Early Middle English,* ed. Malcolm Godden, Douglas Gray, and Terry Hoad [Oxford: Clarendon, 1994], 1–7). In keeping with my use of Kiernan's *Electronic Beowulf,* however, I have followed its translation and glossary, each rendering the word as "sat on." Sensation may well have trumped philological accuracy in the traditional and dominating iconicity of this image, which my comments reflect.

62 Lang and Ford, *Red Book of Animal Stories,* 39.

63 Stead and Le Fanu, *Tales of Long Ago,* 49.

64 Marshall and Skelton, *Stories of Beowulf,* facing p. 59. See in comparison the picture facing p. 4 for its famous depiction of Grendel as a large, rounded troll, with goblin face and his shoulder-belted *glof,* the sack for his victims.

65 See also Knorr's colour illustration in Hüttner (1975) of Grendel's mother as a round-breasted, blue-skinned giantess five times the size of Beowulf, pinning him down by straddling his groin with her six-fingered hand (45). Nevertheless, while she is naked, the effect is more like an oversize Blue Meanie from the Beatles' *Yellow Submarine* than anything overtly sexual.

66 Kent, *Beowulf* lithograph series, 1931. Reprinted in Leonard, *Beowulf,* facing p. 70.

67 Leonard and Ward, *Beowulf,* facing p. 49.

68 Riggs and Pitz, *Story of Beowulf,* 56–7.

69 Gladys Schmitt, *The Heroic Deeds of Beowulf,* illus. Walter Ferro (New York: Random House, 1962), 36–7.

70 Sutcliff and Keeping, *Beowulf,* 55.

71 Sutcliff and Keeping, *Beowulf,* 58.

72 Crossley-Holland and Keeping, *Beowulf,* 31.

73 See John Stephens, "Distinction, Individuality, Sociality: Patterns for a Heroic Life," in *Retelling Stories, Framing Culture: Traditional Story and Metanarratives in Children's Literature,* ed. John Stephens and Robyn McCallum (New York: Routledge, 1998), 91–125, at 116–17.

74 See also Janet Schrunk Ericksen's essay in this book for discussion of this scene's use of focalization.

75 Serraillier and Severin, *Beowulf the Warrior*, 28.

76 Katz and Gal, *Beowulf*, 24.

77 Katz and Gal, *Beowulf*, 26.

78 Hinds, *Beowulf*, [59].

79 This term is most foolishly literalized in an image of Grendel's mother with a dog's snout, goat horns, and parted hair, plus bubbles to remind us she is underwater: Julia Green, *Beowulf*, illus. Tom Percival (London: A&C Black, 2008), 26.

80 Morley and Li, *Beowulf*, 5.

81 Morley and Li, *Beowulf*, 18.

82 Grendel's appearance is suggestive of the lizard-humanoid Gorn, which Captain Kirk battles to the death in a rocky desert in the famous *Star Trek* episode "Arena" (season 1, episode 18; Desilu Productions, 1967).

83 In the Zemeckis film, an intriguing and well-carried scene of Grendel's mother weeping over her slain son and cradling him enacts and possibly draws on the visual staging of this illustration.

84 Beowulf is dressed in a simple white undergarment, Christ-like. There is also strong proleptic content in the image, as over the ledge a raven caws its foreboding of death in battle, and a burning viking ship, another funeral marker, sends a plume diagonally across the green-gray skies, the red dragon small and distant, but above all.

6 What We See in the Grendel Cave: Manipulations of Perspective in *Beowulf* for Children

JANET SCHRUNK ERICKSEN

The scariest scene in the Old English *Beowulf* takes place in the Grendel cave. Acknowledgment of the difficulties in adapting this scene for younger readers might be assumed from the fact that some versions, such as Eric A. Kimmel's *The Hero Beowulf*,[1] leave out or severely curtail the scene, leaving Beowulf defined only by the neatness of his heroic defeat of Grendel. Fear is not, however, consistently set aside, even among picture books that are accessible to younger readers; James Rumford's vibrantly illustrated *Beowulf: A Hero's Tale Retold* includes a more than full-page image of a threatening Grendel's mother, long knife drawn, bending over a horrified Beowulf, who is falling backward, trying to catch himself on a bed of serpents.[2] Each adaptor has to decide how much of the threat to Beowulf to convey and how far to acknowledge or reframe the horror in the Old English scene of the struggle between Beowulf and Grendel's mother. One of the most useful tools adaptors have for managing the degree of terror lies in the restriction of narrative information and perspective, or what narrative theory labels *focalization*. The nature of both the story and the storytelling in the Old English Grendel-cave scene not only makes possible but encourages variety in the young-reader adaptations.

The distinctive possibilities in adapting the Grendel-cave scene rest on instabilities in the Old English. The factors arrayed against Beowulf as he attempts to defeat Grendel's mother in her home are beyond any he has previously faced: not only does the already-proven hero have to fight in isolation in alien surroundings – ones that required him to expend energy even to reach – but his foe, initially driven by an intense desire for vengeance, is now defending her home. The Old English narrative associates both Grendel and his mother, "micle mearcstapan" (l. 1348) ["great march-stalkers"], with terror, but in consequence of Beowulf's arrival at Heorot, Grendel is moved from being the bringer of *gryre*, terror or horror, to the one who suffers it: "gryreleoð galan godes andsacan" (l. 786) ["God's enemy shrieked a grisly song"].[3] Like her son, Grendel's mother is associated with horror when she attacks the hall: Hroðgar describes her, in words that echo what has been said of her son, as a "wælgæst" (l. 1331a) ["death spirit"], "æse wlanc ... / fylle gefrecnod" (ll. 1332–3a) ["gloating with its carcass, / rejoicing in its feast"]. Yet initially, the association between Grendel's mother and horror seems destabilizing rather than just overwhelming, as Grendel's attacks were "nydwracu niþgrim, nihtbealwa mæst" (l. 193) ["violent, grim, cruel, greatest of night-evils"]. I say "seems" in part because of a passage that remains difficult for us to understand fully, in which the narrator explains:

> Wæs se gryre læssa
> efne swa micle   swa bið mægþa cræft,
> wiggryre wifes   be wæpnedmen,
> þonne heoru bunden,   hamere geþruen,
> sweord swate fah   swin ofer helme
> ecgum dyhttig   andweard scireð.   (ll. 1282b–87)

[The terror [i.e., engendered by Grendel's mother], the war-terror of a
woman, was less even by as much as is the might of maidens against men
and their weapons, when the bound blade – the blood-stained sword –
forged by hammers, enduring in edge, shears the opposing boar-image
above the helmet.][4]

Despite difficulties with the phrasing, the terror of the attack by Grendel's mother is clear enough that she at least momentarily unmans the warriors in the hall: "helm ne gemunde, / byrnan side, þa hine se broga angeat" (ll. 1290b–91) ["none remembered his helmet / or broad mail-shirt when that terror seized them"]. This enemy is, in multiple ways, not what the warriors were expecting.

The horror associated with Grendel's mother is heightened when Beowulf subsequently seeks her out in her home: she is impervious to Beowulf's sword, no matter how strong his stroke, and this is something that he apparently did not expect given how well armoured and well weaponed he is when he arrives to face this foe (ll. 1522b–25). His barehanded strength is this time well met by her own "grimman grapum" (l. 1542a) ["grim grasp"]. Unlike in the Beowulf-Grendel encounter, this enemy is not described as wanting to flee from Beowulf, and Beowulf's own agency is insufficient for victory: this female foe gains, literally, the upper hand, and if not for Beowulf's mail shirt, the narrative plainly states, the hero would have died in that underground cave (ll. 1550–6). Renée Trilling usefully extends the explanation of why Grendel's mother is significantly more threatening than is Grendel himself, focusing on not just how she acts but what she represents within the cultural framework of the poem, "visible, tangible proof that the heroic world has a hidden inverse":

> It is possible, then, that instead of being simply a reprise of the horrifying Grendel, Grendel's mother is intended to be something even more terrifying. Grendel himself is a fearsome threat to the life and well-being of Heorot's inhabitants, but his mother represents something far worse. Grendel, at least, is a clear adversary. His mother, on the other hand, is ambiguity incarnate; her indeterminate nature wreaks havoc with representation, and her attack threatens not the life and well-being of the Danes and Geats – she only kills one of them before she makes her exit – but the very structure of the society Heorot is founded on: she calls into question the legitimacy of the heroic order, of a feud-oriented and exchange-based culture that excludes certain people (namely women and outsiders) from meaningful action.[5]

The distancing of Beowulf as he swims away from his companions and the familiar structures of the heroic world builds suspense and relocates him to a space where his point of view, both figuratively and literally, is challenged. The separation from so much that is familiar heightens the terror of the Grendel-cave scene and offers distinctive challenges and, simultaneously, opportunities to writers and illustrators trying to adapt the story for younger readers.

Manipulations of perspective allow adapters of *Beowulf* to manage the degree of horror in this scene while also providing a means by which to define key aspects of heroic character at a moment of great risk and potential vulnerability – and a moment of distinctive perspectival issues. When Beowulf fights Grendel, the hall is filled with observers, turning the struggle into something of a community event with Beowulf as a central performer for a supportive audience. The narrative can, and does in the Old English, position the narrator as an observer among the thanes, first at a somewhat safe distance, among Hrothgar's thanes listening to the action unfold: "Denum eallum wearð / ... / ... ealuscerwen" (ll. 767b–69a) ["to the Danes it seemed / ... / like a wild ale-sharing"]. The narrator steps closer for the final struggle between Beowulf and Grendel, seeing just before Grendel's "burston banlocan" (l. 818a) ["joints burst asunder"] that Beowulf's followers want to provide active support, although their work remains more preparatory than actual: "Þær genehost brægd / eorl Beowulfes ealde lafe, / wolde freadrihtnes feorh ealgian" (ll. 794b–96) ["Many an earl / in Beowulf's troop drew his old blade, / longed to protect the life of his liege-lord"]. No such option occurs within the framework of the fight between Grendel's mother and Beowulf, and the isolation of the action encourages reconsideration of the narrative perspective: we can witness the scene as if an invisible observer in the cave or from a more involved perspective, one that positions the narrator with one or the other of the participants in the struggle. In the Old English poem, the Grendel-cave scene is delivered with familiar third-person narration but with narrative perspective primarily, although not exclusively, tied to Beowulf. The narrator still tells the story, but the audience views the scene largely in terms of what Beowulf saw and, to some extent, felt, including information on the force with which he swung the swords and on his attitude of both resolve and anger. For young readers, adaptations of the scene often echo that choice but restrict or redirect the horror evident in the Old English poem and utilize Beowulf's perspective to offer a distinctive comment on or definition of heroism.

Interest in clarifying the distinction between who tells and who sees a story – as opposed to the blurring of such distinctions in the term *point of view* – prompted narrative theorist Gérard Genette to map the relationships that a narrator could have to a narrative, particularly in relation to perspective and concerning the ways in which knowledge and information were restricted in a narrative. A narrator can, for instance, tell a story from within it (as if a character in the story, a homodiegetic narrator) or outside it (as an omniscient narrator usually does, a heterodiegetic narrator), or partly both within and outside, without necessarily also or always being the eyes through which the story is seen. Genette employed the term *focalization* to help explain the distinction: "by focalization I certainly mean a restriction of 'field' – actually, that is, a selection of narrative information with respect to what was traditionally called *omniscience*."[6] In other words, "focalization is connected with a limitation of the amount of information that the reader obtains through the text about the fictional world."[7] Refinements of Genette's framework are ongoing, often also building on the work of Mieke Bal, who describes the "subject of focalization," or focalizer, as "the point from which the elements are viewed. That point can lie with a character (i.e. an element of the fabula [story]), or outside it."[8]

Focalization in modern narrative tends to amplify a reader's sympathies with a character. Bal notes that if the "reader watches with the character's eyes," then the reader "will, in principle, be inclined to accept the vision presented by that character."[9] The fundamental power of "who sees" can perhaps most strikingly be confirmed in reference to virtual reality. In litigation, virtual reality offers both possibility and risk in conveying events as if through the eyes of a victim, an attacker, or a nearby witness. While clarifying what might have happened in a case under review, such perception also carries "an unintended effect," as Damian Schofield, director of Human Computer Interaction at SUNY Oswego, explains: "'Think of a murder scene: whether you view it from the point of view of the murderer, the victim or a third person will totally change your perception of what's happening.'"[10] Correspondingly, what a reader thinks of the characters involved in a narrative scene – how they are defined and understood – can be a function of that same perception. Sarah Stanbury, for instance, in her study of the Middle English *Pearl*, explains focalization as referring to "the relationship between an object and an act of sight that locates a viewer in the text": "The description, in *Pearl*, carefully focalized by the dreamer, becomes not simply a precisely realized scene but also a perceptual frame that marks and signifies the fictional viewer's epistemological horizon: what is seen is what is known."[11] In the Old English *Beowulf*, Peter Richardson similarly showed that the narrative is at times focalized on Beowulf's thanes, perhaps as a way to encourage audiences to identify with these thanes and to understand them as a model of "the conduct, attitudes, and loyalties appropriate to this emergent class of royal servants."[12] When the narrator of *Beowulf* tells what the Geatish troop is thinking – that they "longed to protect" Beowulf – the information does not reflect an external, observed point of view but one specifically tied to the nearby loyal companions watching this first public battle. The third-person external narrator speaks, but the thanes see, and their seeing (the focalization) provides the visual window onto events, along with some of the emotional sympathies of their perspective. Understanding focalization can, as well, help explain the underwater cave scene in *Beowulf*, particularly the ways in which twentieth-century and early twenty-first-century adaptations of that narrative recast or restrict the scene's horror.

The Old English *Beowulf*, notably but not exclusively in the Grendel-cave scene, employs narrative perspective with less privileging of the protagonist than readers of modern fiction might expect. Indeed, as Britt Mize has demonstrated, "the usual practice of Anglo-Saxon poets is to let the third-person narration circulate its focalization through multiple loci of subjectivity, granting readers access to a variety of perceptual and cognitive orientations toward events."[13] Early readers might, then, have found nothing unusual in focalization that positions us, for instance, with Grendel's mother in the mere when Beowulf arrives to do battle with her. We know that she "þæt þær gumena sum / ælwihta eard ufan cunnode" (ll. 1499b–1500) ["perceived that some man / was exploring from above that alien land"]. The perspective is muddied, though; presumably we are seeing what Grendel's mother sees, a man descending from above, but the term "ælwihta eard" ["alien land"] seems not to reflect her view, unless to heighten the understanding that Beowulf does not belong in this place. Especially because most of the scene in Old English is focalized on or alongside Beowulf, however, even a brief shift in perspective initiates this encounter between Beowulf and Grendel's mother on somewhat unstable ground, forcing readers to consider at least one perspective other than the heroic warrior's. Seeing with Grendel's mother hints at the complexities more fully articulated by such things as the story of Hildeburh; narration of Hildeburh's much less active female perspective strikingly comes just before Grendel's mother attacks Heorot, as if in prefatory explanation of what might happen if a mother participates in vengeance.[14] The momentary shift makes clear that Grendel's mother, markedly without aggression here, sees things distinctly differently than does Beowulf.

Writers of modern, generally briefer, adaptations of *Beowulf* for younger readers often restrict the focalization more than does the Old English and use it in order to develop sympathies, but the perspectival shifts in the Old English poem might also encourage some adaptors to experiment, particularly if writers are interested in heightening the sense of threat in the story. As a group and in the Grendel-cave scene in particular, the adaptations suggest that the more the writer feels confident that readers will be willing to be afraid, the more dramatically the focalization shifts, providing access to Beowulf's perspective and also to the alien and hostile, or sympathetic, perspective of Grendel's mother. When he fights Grendel, Beowulf is surrounded by friends and on his home turf, and adaptations often develop Beowulf's thinking or imagine the views of those men in Heorot. Against Grendel's mother, alone and far from any aid, Beowulf might again be the focalizer, or, more frighteningly, focalization might be developed with a shift to Grendel's mother. When restricted to Beowulf, the focalization in the Grendel-cave scene often fosters sympathy with a hesitant or thoughtful aspect of his heroic character, particularly in versions written after about the middle of the twentieth century, although no neat chronological pattern emerges across the adaptations.

Mara Pratt, in her 1895 *Stories from Old Germany*, explains her approach to retelling *Beowulf* and the other tales in her collection as guided by her desire to include "only such parts of [each story] as appeal to the poetic imagination of the child reader, and to hold before him such pictures of the hero ... as are safe to influence the boy's conception of what a hero should be."[15] Pratt proceeds to whittle down *Beowulf* to present a highly secure and confident hero, and the narrative, correspondingly, shows little sign of real risk to him, with one small exception. The fight with Grendel is narrated with external focalization, that is, as if the narrator watched from one of corners of the hall, although the narrative does not so precisely locate a point of view or connect readers to the action. Readers learn that Beowulf is "exhausted" after the struggle, but the narrator stands by without really drawing the audience into the action. The fight with Grendel's mother, however, expands upon the Old English in focalizing more distinctly on Beowulf. In Pratt's version, as Beowulf swims down to face Grendel's mother, we see the cave light below the water just as Beowulf does, and the narrative even supplies a comment by Beowulf to himself: "'There, there is the monster's home,' he thought" (151). The narrative focalization then remains restricted to Beowulf and heightens the presentation of the hero's power. Instead of shifting to Grendel's mother's perception in the Old English of "gumena sum" who "ufan cunnode" ["some man ... [who] was exploring from above"] (ll. 1499b–1500), in Pratt's version, as Beowulf descends to the cave, the narrative reveals what he sees and feels: "Suddenly he felt himself seized and drawn rapidly through the water with such speed that he could hardly breathe" (152). By not directly identifying who is seizing Beowulf, Pratt's narrative restricts readers' information to what Beowulf knows and sees, which is limited indeed in the dark, monster-infested waters; he cannot see who has seized him, and the water itself threatens to overwhelm him. The lapse, though, is very brief. The next sentence returns a more knowing, more in-control Beowulf: "In another moment, he *found himself* in a great, green cavern" (152, my emphasis; the Old English simply asserts at ll. 1512b and 1518a that Beowulf "ongeat" ["perceived," "saw"] his location). The momentary shift effectively if fleetingly conveys a sense of real peril that, in turn, heightens the power of Beowulf's quick recovery of heroic control. Beowulf subsequently deals swiftly and decisively with the "giantess"; the rest of the fight between Beowulf and Grendel's mother is given just four sentences before Beowulf triumphantly "came forth once more from out the waters" (153).

The heroic distance of Pratt's dominant focalization both conveys and tightly limits the risk that Beowulf encounters, and in that aspect her approach to the underwater cave scene is echoed by later adaptors, perhaps in part to avoid becoming too unsettling in a story directed at children. Maurice Saxby, in his account of "Beowulf the Dragon Slayer" in the tellingly titled collection *The Great Deeds of Superheroes* (1989), actually takes even fewer risks with perspective than does Pratt, presenting a firmly confident and utterly steady hero. The only shift in focalization in Saxby's adaptation of the scene comes near the end of the "almost superhuman contest," as Saxby describes it, when the narrative positions us alongside Beowulf, as he "caught sight of the famous sword of the giants" and then, after using the sword to dispatch his female foe, "caught sight of Grendel himself."[16] The swift and superficial – and rather casually phrased – perspectival information allows nothing to Grendel's mother and little even to Beowulf himself. The narrative keeps its audience safely detached; Beowulf, once he sees the giant sword, uses it to cut off Grendel's head, then quickly swims up to present his trophies to Hrothgar before "sail[ing] in glory back to his homeland."[17] Brian Patten's *Beowulf and the Monster* (1999) adds a more dynamic riddling sequence to the encounter between Beowulf and Grendel's mother, but like Saxby, Patten maintains a narrative distance that never allows any suggestion that the female opponent's challenge might be more than Beowulf can handle.[18]

Even the more poetic language of Kevin Crossley-Holland's *Beowulf* (1982) remains external, never restricting the view to either Beowulf's or Grendel's mother's and reinforcing distance by referring to Beowulf as simply "the Geat": "The Geat wrestled free of Grendel's mother; she was coated with her own filth, red-eyed and roaring. He whirled the sword Hrunting, and played terrible war-music on the monster's skull."[19] Charles Keeping's illustrations of Crossley-Holland's version do effectively heighten the menacing effect, although they too present the perspective of a third-person observer. The narrator begins to describe, in a sentence that appears at the bottom of a right-hand page, Beowulf's descent into the mere: "Then Grendel's mother saw him heading for her lair; the sea-wolf rose to meet ..." The sentence is interrupted with a turn of the page and two full-page illustrations, black-and-white line drawings that convey entanglement and motion as Beowulf is swallowed in his opponent's embrace. The sentence then ends on the following page, and across the bottom half of that page and its facing page appear large drawings of the two severed heads of Beowulf's defeated foes, vividly no longer a threat.[20] The effect is certainly horrifying, but still without much sense of risk to Beowulf or complication of his heroic status.

More inventive adaptations of the Beowulf story from the second half of the twentieth century include those by Robert Nye, *Beowulf: A New Telling* (1968), in which the narrator remarks that Grendel's mother "looked at Unferth and She smiled" (the pronoun capitalization is Nye's), and by Welwyn Wilton Katz, *Beowulf* (1999), in which the narrative is told by Wiglaf's grandfather to Wiglaf, and the Grendel-cave fight was actually observed by him.[21] Among the adaptations that hew at least a little more closely to the Old English narrative – but not so closely as do versions such as Dorothy Hosford's near translation, *By His Own Might: The Battles of Beowulf* (1947)[22] – are those that present the Grendel-cave scene in one or both of two ways: by developing the extent to which the narrative is focalized by Beowulf and by including and even amplifying the perspective of Grendel's mother. In these two variations, the focalization encourages narrative sympathies and provides a fairly clear, if not entirely consistent, definition of what it means to be a hero.

A hero is a warrior who seizes opportunity in order to triumph over enemies, or at least that is how Rosemary Sutcliff presents her account of Beowulf in the dragon cave, in *Beowulf: Dragon Slayer*, illustrated in its 1961 edition, as Crossley-Holland's adaptation later would be, by Charles Keeping.[23] Sutcliff's narrative focalizes externally in the underwater cave, keeping readers largely away from both the actors and the action. The narrative does, though, slip occasionally closer, focalizing on Beowulf. After several sentences of seeing from some undefined point in the cave the struggle between Beowulf and "the sea-hag," as Sutcliff identifies the foe here, we suddenly see just what Beowulf sees, up close: "He saw her fangs sharp behind her snarling lips, and her eyes shone with balefire amid the tangle of her hair" (57). Almost immediately after this moment of perceived terror, however, the narrative view steps far back, effectively containing any sense of threat and suspending the action in a moment of landscape observation that presents the struggling pair nearly as equals: "There on the silver sand, with the roar of the sea echoing about them hollow like the echo in a vast shell, he with one arm locked about her and the other straining at her dagger wrist, she striving always with fang and claw to come at his heart" (57–9). The narrative remains quite restrained, as if too much frenzy or worry would be less than heroic, in explaining Beowulf's perceptions and actions as he sees and uses the giant sword, first on Grendel's mother and then on Grendel. The sword brings him "fresh hope" that fuels "all his strength and cunning" so that he can, "with a triumphant battle-shout," nearly decapitate Grendel's mother. The act itself follows the Old English – Beowulf "yrringa sloh / þæt hire wið halse heard grapode, / banhringas bræc" (ll. 1565b–67a) ["struck in fury / so that it caught her hard in the neck, / broke her bone-rings"] – but Sutcliff then utilizes the internal focalization, seeing through Beowulf, to transform the Old English "yrre ond anræd" (l. 1575a) ["angry and resolute"] warrior into a hero whose understanding of the moment is conveyed more fully, with a sense of relief that justice as he sees it can be done: "Here at last, it seemed, he had a blade that could pierce the flesh of Grendel and his kin," and he uses it with "mighty effort" to cut "loathsome head and loathsome body asunder" (59–60).

Far more pronounced in its sympathies for Beowulf and clearer still in both its definition of a hero and its restriction of horror is Tony Bradman's and Tony Ross's short chapter book, *Beowulf the Hero* (2010).[24] The narrative here, aimed at readers significantly less practiced than those implied for Sutcliff's version, never actually ventures inside the Grendel cave. So safe is its account of the underwater action that it comes at multiple removes, prioritizing distance over directness: narrated after the fact, with externally focalized narration, and presented as narration within narration, as a song sung in the hall. Beowulf's preparation to fight, however, is internally focalized – restricted to what Beowulf perceives – and it reveals to readers Beowulf's worries about being up to the fight, about being heroic enough, and his motivation in going ahead to face Grendel's mother. Beowulf asks "Rothgar," as Bradman spells it, "'And what if there is another monster, after I kill this one?'" To which Rothgar replies, "'Beowulf, there is always another monster' … And that's when Beowulf realised," the narrator explains, "there was a lot more to this business of being a hero than he had thought" (42). The point is further developed as Beowulf "scanned the ring of faces before him, saw the hope and trust in their eyes" (43). What he sees drives his choice and at the same time almost entirely removes the possibility of actually including narration of the fight with Grendel's mother. The "hope and trust" of those around him affect Beowulf's self-perception and action: "Suddenly all the fear inside him fell away. He knew he couldn't let these people down, even if it meant losing his life. 'So be it,' he said, standing tall and proud. 'I choose … to fight!'" (43). Sustaining that attitude in isolation, in the grip of a very strong monster, seems difficult territory to attempt in a story aimed at fairly new readers, and leaving out the fight itself allows the narrative to leap forward and follow up Beowulf's new-found understanding and corresponding choice with absolute triumph. This hero faces his fears and overcomes them, not for himself so much as for others. In such a narrative, a hero fights less for personal glory than for sustaining a community and becomes a figure with whom a younger audience is encouraged to identify.

When focalization varies more dramatically, the conflict in the cave becomes both more complicated in its ethical implications and more frightening. Rich, alliteration-laced language distinguishes Ian Serraillier's *Beowulf the Warrior* (1954), as does the use of internal focalization in the Grendel-cave scene.[25] With the focalization shifting from Beowulf to his female foe and to some undefined external observer, moves that in themselves echo the shifting perspectives in the Old English narrative, Serraillier provides a scene with some horror and, correspondingly, a hero who very clearly is not entirely in control. As Beowulf descends into the mere's depths, Grendel's mother's perspective is minimally touched on, but alignment with Beowulf is well established before it is challenged. The narrative view is initially external; we watch as Beowulf is dragged down to the depths, and only then do we see what he sees, and sense what he senses: "He beheld a paved floor unrolling at his feet" (26), the narrative tells us, before we sink more fully into Beowulf's unstable perception:

> And dreamily, O dreamily in his ear sounded
> The far-off oozy murmur of the flood. Before him
> Huge flames were leaping, and horrid shadows
> Dancing in the firelight, whence issued a shape
> More massy than the rest, dark-shouldered,
> Towering high, like a mountain hiding the sun.   (26)

When Grendel's mother and Beowulf fight, the narrative remains mostly restricted to Beowulf's perception; he is

> Then, like a dizzy sailor trapped in the shrouds
> When sea and heaven swing sickening past
> As a sudden wave, topheavy, grinds him down
> Into the whirl clinging madly, yet struggling
> All the while to fight free.   (26–8)

At Beowulf's most vulnerable moment, however, when he is pinned to the ground by Grendel's mother, the focalization suddenly shifts to her.

Her moment of control becomes as a result a moment of sympathy, which interrupts and momentarily deflects the horror: "she, softly keening, brooded upon Grendel / Her son – her only son – whom long ago / By the lapping water tenderly herself had suckled" (28). The memory brings another memory, of protection, and then another of anger as she remembers that Beowulf killed Grendel. The rising tension culminates in action externally narrated and sympathizing with both her and her would-be victim: "boiling for revenge," Grendel's mother draws her knife, which glitters in the firelight, as if Beowulf sees it so, and with a description of her eyes as "gloating," sympathy and perspective fall back to Beowulf just as the knife "str[ikes] home" (28). Serraillier's adaptation retreats to more conventional territory in telling of Beowulf's triumph, made more remarkable by his very near brush with death but also carefully defined as a triumph over Grendel rather than Grendel's mother. After Beowulf kills Grendel's mother "stone-dead" (29), Grendel's body presents a "grim reminder of old griefs" (29), which internal focalization briefly revives as motivation for the decapitation of the dead Grendel. This is a hero who seeks and acts with clearer purpose than just glory, and one who is vulnerable when such a sense of justice or purpose is obscured to some degree.

The most complex representations of Beowulf's heroism in adaptations for younger readers are those that most develop views other than his, in particular although not exclusively those that push readers into seeing what Grendel's mother sees. Welwyn Wilton Katz's *Beowulf*, with illustrations by Laszlo Gal (1999), and Nicky Raven's *Beowulf: A Tale of Blood, Heat, and Ashes*, vividly illustrated by John Howe (2007), both develop the character of Wiglaf as the story's narrator.[26] Both also directly address the question of who sees the fight in the Grendel cave, although only Raven extensively utilizes Grendel's mother as focalizer, and his version is distinctly the more disturbing. Emphasizing the absence of a neat chronology in the treatments of Grendel's mother, Katz's *Beowulf* invites less sympathy for Grendel's mother than does Serraillier's some forty-five years earlier, and it stays away from focalization on her at all. The hero who emerges from Katz's narrative, however, still seems less neatly triumphant than Serraillier's. Katz uses the figure of Wiglaf to frame the heroic story with another tale of heroism, or of developing heroism at least. Both Wiglaf and his grandfather Aelfhere are defined as having the power to see events at which they were not present, whether in the past, the present, or the future, and both serve Beowulf. Aelfhere went with Beowulf to Heorot, and he tells the story of events there to his grandson, explaining that while Beowulf went down to the cave alone, "in a way I did go with him, for as I sat on the rock my Gift came to life, and I saw what Beowulf had to endure in the underwater hell he had now entered" (28). But while Aelfhere narrates by means of his "Gift," what the narrative allows readers to see are views that are distinctly Beowulf's rather than observed from alongside events. Either perspective could reveal that Beowulf "saw a firepit, but the flames in it seemed small for the eerie balefire that lit the cave," but Beowulf alone is "nauseated by the terrible sights and smells of the cave" (28, 29); only he takes "great panting breaths of air that filled his mouth with the metallic taste of blood and his nose with the stench of foul droppings and rotten meat," and for him, "Shadows flitted through the cave like creatures of darkness" (28). While the focalization never shifts to Grendel's mother, the narrative does include in the midst of the assault on Beowulf's body and senses her words in her final attack on Beowulf: "*'You're the one who killed my son,'* she howled" (29, italics in original). While the remark might not be sufficient to generate sympathy for "the hag," as Katz refers to Grendel's mother, it adds to the humanizing aspects of the scene and, in turn, contributes to the narrative's rendering of the hero as more familiar and less invincible. This Beowulf nearly drowns on his way down to the cave; this Beowulf is "weary from all his battling and sickened by the smell of her breath," and he recognizes "that he was overmatched" in the fight with Grendel's mother (29). Once he defeats this foe, this Beowulf tries to take two trophies back to the surface, but "he couldn't manage the weight of the hag's head as well as Grendel's" (32). Aelfhere the seer even moderates Beowulf's accomplishment by comparing him, in his moment of triumph, to other men rather than elevating him above all others: "A man who has almost died rejoices when the enemy takes his place, and so Beowulf did then" (30).

Even after the company's return to Heorot, this hero's vulnerability remains a central feature of Katz's adaptation, in language that is likely to seem startlingly at odds to anyone familiar with Beowulf's boasting in the Old English version but distinctly more in line with a culture that values self-aware honesty: "He told the raw truth about his own weakness, his need for Fate's help, and his inability to bring both bodies with him. But there was no dishonor given him for it, only the more love for his modest honesty" (35). In revising the story for younger readers, Katz provides two models of more accessible heroism: Beowulf's and young Wiglaf's, and the latter's actions echo the former's, as if to clarify an invitation to the reader to aim for what these warriors achieve, including persistence, acknowledgment of weakness, and gratitude. In fighting against the dragon, Wiglaf, like Beowulf in the Grendel cave, struggles to do what he thinks he ought to do: "Quick, Wiglaf told himself, do it before the air inside turns to fire! One boy and one sword and one thrust only to stop the terrible thing that was about to happen" (54). Like Beowulf, he succeeds in killing the foe, but again the triumph is not absolute. Wiglaf "almost panicked" in grabbing treasure for the dying Beowulf to see, and Beowulf once again admits his own weakness in relying on the wrong men to come to his aid: "People cannot be made to love their lords. The fault here must be as much mine as theirs" (59). The heroes in Katz's adaptation do accomplish great things and are heroes and then kings, but at the same time they have and acknowledge their limits and so function not just as more familiarly human figures but as more accessible behavioural models. Katz effectively does what Pratt in her retelling of the tales of Germanic heroes did: Katz's *Beowulf* presents the story in such form as to "influence the boy's conception of what a hero should be." Her narrative, however, is less concerned with providing the imagined superhuman ideal than with something more reachable to emulate, regardless, perhaps, of gender – still heroic, just with a less exclusive definition of what that means.

More dramatic use of focalization occurs in Raven and Howe's *Beowulf: A Tale of Blood, Heat, and Ashes*, which, like Katz's version, tells the whole tale with first-person narration by Wiglaf, although with far more relish for fear and much less attachment to prioritizing Beowulf as hero. The narrative again directly remarks on narrative perspective in relation to the fight between Beowulf and Grendel's mother: "No one bore witness to the mighty struggle that took place in that cave; the indestructible monster against the irresistible courage of a hero" (41). Yet without a device comparable to Katz's Aelfhere the seer, Raven gives a more intimate account of the underwater fight that comes between Beowulf's departure from the mere-side group and their reaction first to the blood in the water and then to Beowulf's return, which here includes Wiglaf as a reasonably plausible extension.[27] Standing mere-side as Beowulf prepares to descend, Wiglaf also prepares readers for a shift in narrative perspective: "We saw the last heave of his shoulders as he drew a deep breath into those gargantuan lungs, and then he fell" (39).

The shift that comes builds on the Old English narrative's brief sight through the eyes of Grendel's mother (ll. 1499b–1500, quoted above). But whereas the poem moves, eleven and a half lines later, to what "se eorl ongeat" (l. 1512b) ["the earl perceived"], Raven excises Beowulf's perspective from the scene. Instead of Beowulf's account of events as they unfold, readers have only Grendel's mother's. After Beowulf "drop[s] into the freezing waters" (39), the narrative distance of the mere-side watchers immediately gives way to more participatory focalization defined by Grendel's mother, which slides between external focalization, in which a third-person narrator is aligned with but still external to her, and fully internal focalization, so that we see what she sees as Beowulf descends. Not only could "*she ... see his face now, strong and proud, even with the strain of holding his breath,*" but her advantage is defined in terms of sight: "*She saw him enter the water; her eyes accustomed to the murky blue-black depths*" (40, italics in original). Inset and distinguished by typeface from the text's dominant narrative voice and perspective, this narrative perspective, across four full paragraphs, explains and encourages readers to consider the motivations, suffering, and goals of Grendel's mother: "*She would make this slow – he would suffer, just as Grendel had ... Before she could bring teeth and claws into play, she felt herself seized in a bear hug, the breath whooshing from her. He had spirit – this would be a fine kill!*" (41, italics in original). And for the moment, the narrative leaves the fight there. Instead of Beowulf's or Grendel's mother's or a third-person narrator's account of the remainder of the battle – and Beowulf's triumph – the narrative moves abruptly, much as does the Old English version, from Grendel's mother's expectations up to the surface, to the less confident expectations of the two groups of watchers, Hrothgar's and Beowulf's men.

The perspectival manipulations in Raven and Howe's adaptation utilize more than words, and the shift between Grendel's mother and the waiting thanes at the edge of the mere is deftly amplified by a visual jump worthy of a horror film; Howe worked on Peter Jackson's *Lord of the Rings* films a few years earlier, and his *Beowulf* illustrations suggest a cinematographer's eye for the relationship between viewer and subject.[28] Grendel's mother's view begins on pages without illustration other than the marginal strips of Old English script that occur throughout the book. Two pages before the shift to her as focalizer is a full-page illustration of Beowulf descending upright, a sword aloft in each hand, among the sea serpents, and while the perspective is from below, the view could be understood as either Grendel's mother's or a third-person narrator's. Until the shift in narrative focalization, readers would have no real reason to expect to see things as the waiting foe does. The account from Grendel's mother's view and then back to that of the waiting thanes, up to the moment that they see "dark swirls of rusty water appearing," occupies two full facing pages, the last line of which is a remark from one of the thanes: "'That is blood,' he said" (41). A turn of the page puts the reader suddenly alongside Beowulf and facing with him the terrible foe as she fills the space with energy and threat in a centrefold illustration: no words, just a chance to fear. The illustration heightens the threat by placing Beowulf off to one side and slightly higher than the viewer, so that Grendel's mother seems to look less at him than at the centrally and more vulnerably positioned reader. The effect is heightened by the lingering knowledge that this horrific foe has understanding as well as battle skill and revenge motivation.

Even after turning away from the image, the narrative delays acknowledgment of Beowulf's success in this fight, amplifying the sense of threat from this monster. The first words after the illustration return to the previously unspoken question about the blood on the water, voiced now by one of Beowulf's close companions: "'Aye,' replied Scaife, 'but whose?'" (44). With the resumption of Wiglaf's narration and what is largely external focalization (more like that of an omniscient narrator than consistently restricted to what Wiglaf alone would see), a gasping Beowulf resurfaces, but the threat remains vivid and powerful. As if in acknowledgment of what the narrative has previously given of her point of view, the power of Grendel's mother is maintained in Beowulf's account of their fight, where the focalization can fall more closely on him and where, for the first time, readers learn what happened after Grendel's mother tried to accomplish her "fine kill." Beowulf's version of events comes as a memory, filtered through time and his own expectations, after he is "back at Heorot, when food and warmth had brought color back in the hero's cheeks," and when the threat has been survived. Still, Beowulf admits that this foe was "strong beyond anything" he had before experienced and that he had "wrestled with her for an age" (45). Raven's narrative sympathies with Grendel's mother are sustained even in her death: the narrative explains that Beowulf, pinned down by his female foe, anticipated defeat rather than victory:[29] "He gritted his teeth and waited for the final blow" after he hears what he takes for "her gurgling cries of triumph." He manages, nevertheless, to stab through "her seemingly invulnerable armor" and kill her, only discovering then a flaw in his perception: what he had heard was not a cry of triumph but "the monster's death rattle" (45).

A hero with flawed and incomplete perception of his enemy – we gain Grendel's mother's perspective in the cave, but Beowulf does not – becomes, in Raven's version, not less remarkable but less reducible and, in turn, perhaps less necessary. Raven and Howe complicate the story and suggest, as does the Old English narrative itself, that the past was never as neat in its good versus evil as other versions can make it seem, and the hero is not as singular and superior as in adaptations such as Pratt's, Saxby's, or even Crossley-Holland's. In Raven's telling, the heroism derived from defeating Grendel's mother is constructed not by a laudatory external narrator but by Beowulf himself. The narrative remarkably does not allow readers to watch events in the Grendel cave directly, from any point of view, and readers receive the narration only with an opposing perspective already encountered. When Beowulf then gives his account of what happened in the cave, readers already know from experience – from seeing with other eyes – that his view of events is not the only view. Grendel's mother thinks and feels, and she relishes a good fight just as much as a hero might. The substitution of the female foe's perspective for any other written account of their encounter, even in juxtaposition to the illustrated perspective, leaves readers unavoidably more aware of and, because of its content, more sympathetic to Grendel's mother than they would likely be if given only or primarily Beowulf's version or even a more distanced narrator's version. Even when Beowulf tells his story of the encounter, it is a memory, and as such, as Bal puts it, "is an act of 'vision' of the past but, as an act, [is] situated in the present."[30] The illustration and the power of Grendel's mother's view and words intensify the underwater scene itself and make it more frightening. At the same time, distancing both Beowulf and readers from the actual fight makes any heroism involved harder to distinguish. Raven and Howe's adaptation concludes that the "time for warrior-heroes has passed," and the focalization in and about the underwater cave scene show it passing, blurring lines between hero and monster and giving way to less confident, less uniform, less easy definitions of the heroic.

No continuous trajectory from simple to complex or the reverse in manipulations of narrative perspective emerges across these tellings of the *Beowulf* story. Indeed, variation across and within time periods is striking, and some of the twentieth- and twenty-first-century adaptations more rigidly construct heroic perspective in the Grendel-cave scene than does the Old English narrative, which delivers genuine risk to Beowulf from the power of Grendel's mother even though her perspective is only momentarily given. Two general trajectories do, however, emerge in this group of adaptations, one tied to chronology and one tied to expectations of readers' experience. Unsurprisingly, the more advanced the reader expected by the adaptor, the stronger the element of horror tends to be and, in turn, the greater the complexity in characterization of both Beowulf and Grendel's mother. Counter- or complicating examples are, however, not difficult to find, as Rumford's vividly illustrated picture-book version of the fight with Grendel's mother makes clear. Similarly, the chronological trajectory can only be loosely defined. It moves from the distanced and celebratory view of the heroic, with relatively minimal if any internal focalization, to more complex and sympathetic connections of perspective to characterization. Few of the adaptations for younger readers are, however, simplistic in either narration or characterization, despite fairly typical reductive views of the basic Old English story, such as that in *Booklist*'s favourable review of Rumford's version: "Beowulf's action-heavy and single-minded take on heroism makes it an appealing choice for younger readers, while posing the challenge of tempering the intensity of the violent, limb-rending bloodbaths that make up much of the story."[31] What the varied and skilful adaptations as a group better reveal is that the degree to which horror and hero are entangled in any version of the Grendel-cave scene provides one guide to how the writer has managed both the violence and the construction of Old English heroism, and they demonstrate that the role of perspective is fundamental to that management.

NOTES

1 Eric A. Kimmel, *The Hero Beowulf*, illus. Leonard Everett Fisher (New York: Farrar, Straus and Giroux, 2005).
2 James Rumford, *Beowulf: A Hero's Tale Retold* (Boston: Houghton Mifflin, 2007).
3 Quotations of *Beowulf* in Old English are from R.D. Fulk, Robert E. Bjork, and John D. Niles, ed., *Klaeber's Beowulf*, 4th ed. (Toronto: University of Toronto Press, 2008), with references given parenthetically. Translations are given from R.M. Liuzza, trans., *Beowulf*, 2nd ed. (Peterborough, ON: Broadview Press, 2013), unless otherwise indicated.
4 Here I depart from Liuzza's translation. Daniel P. O'Donnell argues effectively for his translation, given here ("The Collective Sense of Concrete Singular Nouns in *Beowulf*: Emendations of Sense," *Neuphilologische Mitteilungen* 92 [1991]: 433–40, at 434).
5 Renée R. Trilling, "Beyond Abjection: The Problem with Grendel's Mother Again," *Parergon* 24 (2007): 1–20, at 19.
6 Gérard Genette, *Narrative Discourse Revisited*, trans. Jane E. Lewin (Ithaca, NY: Cornell University Press, 1988), 74.
7 Tomáš Kubíček, "Focalization, the Subject and Act of Shaping Perspective," in *Narratologia: Point of View, Perspective, and Focalization: Modeling Mediation in Narrative*, ed. Peter Hühn, Wolf Schmid, and Jörg Schönert (Berlin: De Gruyter, 2009), 184.
8 Mieke Bal, *Narratology: Introduction to the Theory of Narrative*, 3rd ed. (Toronto: University of Toronto Press, 2009), 118.
9 Bal, *Narratology*, 149–50. See also Goran Nieragden, "Focalization and Narration: Theoretical and Terminological Refinements," *Poetics Today* 23 (2002): 685–97.
10 Jessica Hamzelou, "Forensic Holodeck to Transport Jury to the Crime Scene," *New Scientist* (9 January 2015), at https://www.newscientist.com/article/dn26764-forensic-holodeck-to-transport-jury-to-the-crime-scene.
11 Sarah Stanbury, *Seeing the Gawain-Poet: Description and the Act of Perception* (Philadelphia: University of Pennsylvania Press, 1991), 4.
12 Peter Richardson, "Point of View and Identification in *Beowulf*," *Neophilologus* 81 (1997): 289–98, at 296.
13 Britt Mize, *Traditional Subjectivities: The Old English Poetics of Mentality* (Toronto: University of Toronto Press, 2013), 16.
14 In the Old English account of Grendel's attack on Heorot, after the famously cinematic approach of Grendel to the hall sets up his perspective, focalization in the actual fight inside the hall also begins with a brief shift to Grendel, when "Geseah he in recede rinca manige, / swefan sibbegedriht samod ætgædere, / magorinca heap. Þa his mod ahlog" (ll. 728–30) ["He saw in

the hall many a soldier, / a peaceful troop sleeping all together, / a large company of thanes – and he laughed inside"].

15 Mara L. Pratt, *Stories from Old Germany*, vol. 1 (Boston: Educational Publishing Company, 1895). Citations will be given parenthetically.

16 Maurice Saxby, *The Great Deeds of Superheroes*, illus. Robert Ingpen (Newtown, New South Wales: Millennium Books, 1989), 128.

17 Saxby, *Great Deeds of Superheroes*, 128.

18 Brian Patten, *Beowulf and the Monster*, illus. Chris Riddell (London: Scholastic Children's Books, 1999); see 52–9.

19 Kevin Crossley-Holland, *Beowulf*, illus. Charles Keeping (Oxford: Oxford University Press, 1982), 32.

20 Crossley-Holland, *Beowulf*, 29–32.

21 Robert Nye, *Beowulf: A New Telling*, illus. Alan E. Cober (New York: Hill and Wang, 1968); Welwyn Wilton Katz, *Beowulf*, illus. Laszlo Gal (Toronto: Groundwood Books, 1999).

22 Dorothy Hosford, *By His Own Might: The Battles of Beowulf*, illus. Laszlo Matulay (New York: Henry Holt, 1947).

23 Rosemary Sutcliff, *Beowulf: Dragon Slayer*, illus. Charles Keeping (London: Bodley Head, 1961). Citations will be given parenthetically.

24 Tony Bradman and Tony Ross, *Beowulf the Hero* (London: Orchard Books, 2010). Citations will be given parenthetically.

25 Ian Serraillier, *Beowulf: The Warrior*, illus. Severin (Oxford: Oxford University Press, 1954; first American edition, New York: Henry Z. Walck, 1961). Citations will be given parenthetically.

26 Katz, *Beowulf*; Nicky Raven, *Beowulf: A Tale of Blood, Heat, and Ashes*, illus. John Howe (Cambridge, MA: Candlewick Press, 2007). Citations of both of these books will be given parenthetically.

27 Beowulf's companions in the Old English version remain unnamed, so placing Wiglaf among them does not create an explicit contradiction.

28 For analysis of Raven and Howe's book as embodying aesthetic trends related to the Jackson *Lord of the Rings* films and designed to appeal to a "new Tolkien generation," see Yvette Kisor's essay in this volume.

29 The comment is presumably built on the line in Old English that tells us that Beowulf was "aldres orwena" ["despairing of his life"] (l. 1565a) when he uses the giant sword.

30 Bal, *Narratology*, 150.

31 Ian Chipman in *Booklist* 103 (2007): 67.

7 *Beowulf*, *Bèi'àowǔfǔ*, and the Social Hero

BRITT MIZE

The international presence of *Beowulf* as literature for younger audiences increased with the 2011 appearance of the Mandarin 《贝奥武甫》 (hereafter *Bèi'àowǔfǔ*),[1] an illustrated middle-grades retelling in twelve chapters which the book's creator, the Tóngqù Publishing Company, states is the first version of the story for Chinese children.[2] The explicitly educational project is framed in terms of a cultural alterity that education allows one to negotiate. As the Publisher's Preface explains, *Bèi'àowǔfǔ* belongs to Tóngqù's series of ten classic Western texts adapted for youth in order to provide a foundation for understanding modern Western literature and culture: because pre-modern works from Europe and America are not commonly studied in China, "many students have trouble understanding contemporary [Western] stories and do not know why" (v [M v]). After the 108-page narrative, an eight-page essay pitched to the book's primary audience of young people describes some aspects of early English history and culture and the origins of *Beowulf*.

Bèi'àowǔfǔ shows familiarity with the content of *Beowulf* down to the scale of the sentence, indicating some access by the Tóngqù team to either the Old English text or a full representation of it, such as one of the several complete translations into Chinese.[3] For the most part *Bèi'àowǔfǔ* follows the poem's story closely, while adding the kinds of elaboration to imagery, psychology, and dialogue typical of such novelizations, but it does make a number of local changes to the storyline. Some of these simplify complexities of the narrative or rationalize elements of the original deemed to need explanation;[4] other alterations seem purely creative. Given that the Tóngqù version shows detailed acquaintance with *Beowulf*, deviations must be purposeful, but I also take at face value the book's educational goals as stated, which would not be served by reconceiving *Beowulf* so thoroughly as to naturalize it to what Chinese youth readers expect of their own literature. My working assumption, then, is that although the creators of *Bèi'àowǔfǔ* are making profound transformations (language, genre, audience) and exercise some freedom with the story, they are not imposing messages on their source that they would see as uncongenial to it.

This essay has two goals. The first is to introduce readers of English to a children's adaptation of *Beowulf* that appears not to have been documented before now in this language. I will characterize its treatment of the story, foregrounding themes that are distinctive in comparison to Western children's versions. This survey will lay groundwork for my second, more challenging goal: to consider how *Bèi'àowǔfǔ* might prompt us to look differently at *Beowulf*. The Tóngqù adaptors of course develop the material according to their ideas about what young readers should encounter, but they do so by selecting from, adjusting, and building upon elements they believe the original provides. In examining the adaptational character of their work – that is, in regarding it as an active reading of *Beowulf* that mediates between what the poem offers and what the adaptors wish to convey – we may gain a new sense of the poem by watching it give rise to features of this book that are not part of Western retellings. I am not interested in using *Bèi'àowǔfǔ* to make claims about Chinese culture, or in drawing conclusions about the broader agendas of the Tóngqù project. I want to think freshly about *Beowulf* through a study of what these writers found there to work with.

The discussion below will start and end with two moments in *Bèi'àowǔfǔ* that are surprising when viewed through the norms of children's versions in English: the monster Gélúndé'ěr's (Grendel's) devouring of one of Bèi'àowǔfǔ's companions early in the story, and the mass suicide of the faithless retainers at the end. These two events are unexpected in a children's *Beowulf* for opposite reasons: the first for its fidelity to the poem, and the second for its bold departure from it. Yet both contribute to a thematic whole that has much to offer as a vantage point back onto *Beowulf*.

~

In the scene culminating in the hero's fight with Gélúndé'ěr, Bèi'àowǔfǔ watches one of his men get eaten in order to understand how the monster masters his victims. As the unfortunate Geatish warrior is consumed – not quickly, it seems – we are told that

> Bèi'àowǔfǔ saw this clearly, but he did not immediately rise to attack
> Gélúndé'ěr. He suppressed his emotions ... He was patient, observing

Gélúndé'ĕr's movements to try and find his weakness, and waited for the
right moment to attack.

Bèi'àowǔfǔ was a very strategic warrior, so he did not attack immediately ... He was not about to let his warrior die in vain, but he needed to be
careful so he could attack his enemy at the right time, with the most fatal
blow possible! (28–9 [M 25])

An entire short paragraph next describes Gélúndé'ĕr's appearance
from Bèi'àowǔfǔ's perspective, giving a further impression of the passage of time while Bèi'àowǔfǔ sizes up his adversary, before the narration returns to the hero's attempt to form a plan: "'This monster must
have a weakness!' Bèi'àowǔfǔ thought. He continued to observe the
monster, trying to think of a counter-attack" (29 [M 25]).

Readers of *Beowulf* will recognize the origin of this scene in the Old
English poem's statement that as Grendel attacks and eats the Geatish
warrior Hondscio, "þryðswyð beheold / mæg Higelaces hu se man-
scaða / under færgripum gefaran wolde" (ll. 736b–38) [the powerful
kinsman of Hygelac watched how the evildoer liked to proceed in sudden assaults].[5] But it is extremely rare that a post-1930 book for this age
group should retain from the poem Beowulf's interested spectation as
Hondscio dies.[6] Creators of children's adaptations in English have come
up with several ways to sidestep this detail of the received story. Some
of them change the order of events such that Hondscio gets killed in the
course of Beowulf's struggle with Grendel.[7] Other writers state that the
attack on Hondscio happens too quickly for Beowulf to prevent,[8] or de-
vise scenarios in which Beowulf is stunned, enchanted, or otherwise in-
capacitated while Grendel eats his companion.[9] Even when the account
of the events themselves in *Beowulf* is not tweaked, adaptors delete the
Old English poem's explanation that Beowulf had a strategic reason
for not intervening.[10] The near imperative to reshape Hondscio's death
scene by eliding the protagonist's choice of momentary inaction indicates that this story element has been widely perceived as incompatible
with the adaptational goals of children's versions. Yet the Tóngqù adaptors not only reproduce the poem's explanation of Beowulf's ruse but
embrace it so fully as to allude to it again at a point where the original
does not prompt such a reminder.[11]

Bèi'àowǔfǔ's treatment of the Hondscio episode fits a pattern of
continual emphasis on strategic acumen. The hero's observation of
that attack leads him to calculate that he can gain an advantage over
Gélúndé'ĕr if he is able to seize him by the arms and hold him securely
(29 [M 25–6]); once he gets his grip and locks Gélúndé'ĕr's wrists together, he adjusts his hold downward and breaks the monster's fingers,

then cries out to bring his warriors into the fight (30 [M 26]). When he fights Gélúndé'ěr's mother, after his initial plan to use the sword does not succeed because of her evasiveness, Bèi'àowǔfǔ baits her by deliberately exposing his neck, hoping to grab her arms like he did her son's when she tries to strangle him. Although this ploy does not work as he intends, it does cause her to grapple with him, which eventually gains him an opportunity to strike her with the sword after all (61 [M 53–4]). Before his fight with the dragon, Bèi'àowǔfǔ explains to his men that he will use agility as his main tactic in order to prevent his foe from ever facing him directly to blast him with fire (92 [M 74]). Bèi'àowǔfǔ's strategizing is foregrounded each time in extended scenes that show him as thoughtful and intelligent in his approach to combat. No English version for children matches the Tóngqù *Bèi'àowǔfǔ* in simultaneously elaborating on tactical reasoning while staying close to the poem's narration of the fights' nature and progress. Those writers of English versions who do emphasize strategic thinking on Beowulf's part – Robert Nye, John Harris, Thomas O. Jones – work almost from scratch in these scenes, thoroughly reconceptualizing the fights rather than developing a strategic dimension of the events that are narrated in the poem.[12]

This interest in strategy fits the book's conception of fighting skill as a holistic techne to be practised and mastered, rather than something that will follow naturally from the possession of superior bodily strength. We are told at the beginning of the story that young Xī'ěrdé (Scyld) "wanted to enhance his body and mind" and "practiced Kung Fu a lot" (1 [M 1]). Bèi'àowǔfǔ has difficulty with Gélúndé'ěr's mother despite being "known for having nearly perfect combat skills" (60 [M 53]), and when Huòsījiā (Hrothgar) praises the hero for defeating her, saying that "all warriors should learn from you," Bèi'àowǔfǔ replies, "Thank you ... I will continue to discipline myself every day" (67 [M 57]). But the emphasis on strategic reasoning ties into other interests of the book as well. By moving key elements of physical confrontation inward to the mind, *Bèi'àowǔfǔ* brings not just intelligence but also personality and attitude to bear on success. Virtuous or vicious character qualities affect tactical choices and hence the outcome of the fight.

We see the connection clearly in the monsters, whose arrogance and rage cause them to make errors of strategy. During the fight in the mere, when Gélúndé'ěr's mother becomes confident of an easy victory, she "couldn't help but chuckle at her enemy ... [She] thought to herself that this was not enough of a challenge" before relaxing her hold on Bèi'àowǔfǔ (61 [M 53]), which allows him to surprise her by striking with the sword he had earlier stopped using because of her elusiveness. Similarly, Gélúndé'ěr is described as "the demon that always laughed at the weakness of mankind" until being bested by a human whose strength surprised him (33 [M 29]). Whereas Gélúndé'ĕr and his mother fatally underestimate their adversary, the dragon's thoughts are dominated by frustration and confusion at the difficulty of defeating Bèi'àowŭfŭ. The dragon begins the fight "irritated" and "arrogant," thinking that it will be "such an easy task ... To tear this small man apart" (95 [M 76]). As Bèi'àowŭfŭ avoids its fire blasts, "the evil dragon saw that Bèi'àowŭfŭ successfully escaped its attacks and became angrier. Other people were so easy to kill, but this one was so flexible and cunning. Again and again it missed its attacks and became more and more angry" (96 [M 77]). The heat and flame do take their toll on the man as the rocks become "like ice cream melting on a hot summer day" (95 [M 77]): "Bèi'àowŭfŭ was surrounded by fire ... He did not have the power, or strength, to fight back" (96–7 [M 77–8]). However, failing to recognize the damage it has done, shortly after Wéigélāfū (Wiglaf) joins Bèi'àowŭfŭ the dragon abandons tactics that were in fact working: it "saw that neither of these two humans were burnt to death, and became more and more anxious with each passing moment. The dragon decided to try a different attack, and stopped spitting flames" (99 [M 80]). It is the choice to stop breathing fire that creates the opening for Bèi'àowŭfŭ and Wéigélāfū to rush forward and kill the dragon, although the strategy of biting to which it resorts will mortally wound the hero.

Bèi'àowŭfŭ's strategic decisions, by contrast to those of the monsters, exhibit patient, clear reasoning amid the stress of combat, as in each fight he assesses strengths and weaknesses and waits for his best opportunity to gain an advantage. This pattern in *Bèi'àowŭfŭ* forms the context within which we must understand his allowing the Hondscio analogue to die, and later, as he recounts his adventures in Daneland to King Hǎigàilākè (Hygelac), he connects that death and Yīsīqiè'ĕr's (Æschere's) to his decision to go into the mere alone after Gélúndé'ĕr's mother (75–7 [M 62–3]); he limits the risk to which he will subject others when he has time to plan. Bèi'àowŭfŭ's calculating approach to combat does not mean that he is dispassionate. He is said to feel anger and other strong emotions, but these motivate him and strengthen his determination at critical moments rather than impeding his judgment. Other personal qualities contribute to Bèi'àowŭfŭ's effectiveness as a warrior as well. His bravery is extolled throughout the book, unsurprisingly, but nearly as often remarked is his humility. He answers Wǎnsìyào's (Wealhtheow's) praise by demurring, "I was just doing what I was meant to do" (45 [M 40]), and Huòsījiā's by saying that he "was only fulfilling my mission" (71 [M 59]). The Tóngqù version of Hrothgar's "sermon" transmutes the exemplum of the tyrant Heremod from a caution not to succumb to pride into a lengthy compliment on Bèi'àowǔfǔ's lack of it (66–7 [M 57]).

One manifestation of Bèi'àowǔfǔ's humility is his readiness to share credit with his men for his accomplishments. Although their weapon attacks are just as ineffectual against Gélúndé'ěr as they are against Grendel in the Old English poem, Bèi'àowǔfǔ twice credits them for helping defeat the monster (41 [M 36], 74 [M 62]). This is not mere politeness or face-saving on their behalf, however: details are added in the account of the fight that support Bèi'àowǔfǔ's attribution to them of meaningful aid. Even though the other Geatish warriors cannot harm Gélúndé'ěr, their efforts affect their leader, fortifying his courage and boosting his strength (33 [M 29]). As Gélúndé'ěr flees, the book states in summary fashion that "he had been beaten by Bèi'àowǔfǔ and his warriors" (34 [M 29]). Bèi'àowǔfǔ's humility, these details imply, makes him a superior collaborator: just as his physical strength and his acumen make him the natural leader of the Geatish warriors, in his oversight of his men he shows the ability to use their group spirit to achieve victory.[13]

In addition to being validated on its own as a personal quality compatible with heroism, then, an ideal of humility functions in *Bèi'àowǔfǔ* to create rhetorical space for assertions of collaborative effectiveness, and details of the story are adjusted by the Tóngqù adaptors to align with such assertions. This is most conspicuous in a series of alterations having to do with the sword Bèi'àowǔfǔ uses to kill Gélúndé'ěr's mother. In *Beowulf,* Unferth lends his own sword to Beowulf to take into the mere, apparently in a gesture of reconciliation. *Bèi'àowǔfǔ* includes this scene and makes the conciliatory intent plainer. But then in one of the bolder changes to the Old English story, rather than finding Ānfúsī's (Unferth's) sword ineffective against Gélúndé'ěr's mother and improvising with a giant sword found on the spot, in the Tóngqù version Bèi'àowǔfǔ is eventually able to use Ānfúsī's successfully. There are not two swords in the scene at all: it is Ānfúsī's sword that was forged by giants and bears images of the Deluge, and it is Ānfúsī's sword whose blade melts away as Bèi'àowǔfǔ begins to return to the surface. This change simplifies a complexity that might have seemed unnecessary to the adaptors, but given its integration into larger themes of teamwork, I suspect that it also purposefully mitigates the original poem's absolute isolation of Beowulf in the mere. Collaboration is a strategy, and in *Bèi'àowǔfǔ,* it usually works – though not infallibly. Both Gélúndé'ěr (10 [M 9]) and his mother (48–50 [M 42–4]) are able to defeat Danish guarding schemes that are presented as carefully planned and intensely collaborative (men stationed in certain places, whistled signals), and in context this seems to be part of their monstrosity: "in the land of a crazed demon, such preparedness is futile" (10 [M 9]).

The theme of collaboration in fighting is part of a larger emphasis on collective identity and feeling. The link between combat tactics and a broad conceptualization of the individual's role in the larger group is clear in the Tóngqù illustration program of the fight with Gélúndé'ěr. Having had no pictures since the title page, on pages 31–5 [M 27–31] *Bèi'àowǔfǔ* explodes into a series of full-colour images demonstrating Bèi'àowǔfǔ's pre-eminence within a group that fully includes him, in pointed contrast with Gélúndé'ěr's isolation. In Western children's versions of the story I have seen nothing comparable to the visual rhetoric of this sequence. Most often, artists depict Beowulf alone as he grapples with Grendel.[14] When other Geats are portrayed in images of the fight, they are either frightened and confused non-participants,[15] or else they are sharply separated from the hero in the picture's composition, indicating their ineffectuality.[16] Some of these representations are stunningly conceived – John Howe simultaneously offers and retracts a hint of companionship for Beowulf by placing the fight against a backdrop of dozens of human skulls, and in Justin Gerard's unexpected overhead view, as if from a camera on a boom, Grendel's massive arm, caught in Beowulf's lock, is itself a physical barrier between the hero and the panicked Geats[17] – but all have the effect of isolating Beowulf visually.[18]

In the Tóngqù illustrations, by contrast, Bèi'àowǔfǔ's men are his partners in combat. The hero's singular strength is established visually as he leaps at the slightly larger Gélúndé'ěr and pushes him off balance in an image on page 31 [M 27]. Although only Bèi'àowǔfǔ is capable of wrestling with the monster, a spread on pages 32–3 [M 28–9] shows the other warriors fully engaged with the struggle, surrounding their leader in ready fighting stances with weapons raised. One of the Geats is foregrounded and turned away from the viewer, so that the artist's choice of perspective situates the reader at the periphery of an action space defined by a coordinated team of men who have Gélúndé'ěr hemmed in. This image is followed by a diptych on pages 34–5 [M 30–1] that juxtaposes the wounded Gélúndé'ěr, staggering down a desolate road looking back into emptiness behind him, with Bèi'àowǔfǔ, hoisting the dismembered arm high above his head, amid a press of cheering Geats, whose hands upraised in triumph mirror Bèi'àowǔfǔ's own gesture. The connection of prowess in combat with teamwork, and of teamwork in combat with a greater sense of group identity, is made visible. The hero of this story always has unique abilities, but his role vis-à-vis those around him differs. Whereas Western children's versions of *Beowulf* heavily privilege the individual hero's difference from others, holding him suspended, as it were, above the group, *Bèi'àowǔfǔ* privileges his membership in the group whose interests his accomplishments advance.

The message that the gifted individual is embedded in a group permeates *Bèi'àowǔfǔ*, as does the expectation that groups will cooperate and perhaps coalesce. After Xī'ěrdé (Scyld) rises to leadership he is said to assert dominance over surrounding villages and frighten them into sending tribute (3 [M 2–3]), in a reflex of the poem's statement that Scyld attacked "sceaþena þreatum" (l. 4b) [packs of enemies] until "him æghwylc þara ymbsittendra / ofer hronrade hyran scolde, / gomban gyldan" (ll. 9–11a) [each of the surrounding peoples over the whale-road had to obey him, yield tribute]. But the later intertribal conflicts of Huòsījiā, Bèi'àowǔfǔ, and even Hǎigàilākè are stated or implied to be for the protection of their lands and people rather than campaigns to conquer, raid, or subordinate foreign powers. A significant element of Bèi'àowǔfǔ's rhetoric of leadership is his promotion of cooperation on both large and small scales. He resolves to "help our Danish friends," as he says to Hǎigàilākè (12 [M 11]). He explains both to the Danish coast guard and to Huòsījiā that the Geats intend to fight Gélúndé'ěr alongside the Danes (14 [M 13], 18 [M 15]) rather than in their place. Bèi'àowǔfǔ later assures Huòsījiā that he and his warriors, not he alone, will track down Gélúndé'ěr's mother (52 [M 46]). None of these details is unique to the Tóngqù retelling, but together they and many others produce a consistent valorization of collective effort and goals that is unusual among children's adaptations of *Beowulf*.

Other manifestations of this commitment are both more distinctive, when compared to other versions, and more significant in the storytelling. A striking example of social coalescence is found in the scene at the mere. Whereas *Beowulf* and Western children's retellings distinguish between Geats and Danes throughout this episode, in which the Danes return to Heorot assuming the worst while the Geats remain at the shore hoping for Beowulf's reappearance, the Tóngqù version describes an undifferentiated group that acts together: "the king and his warriors sadly packed up Bèi'àowǔfǔ's weapon and began to retreat from the lake" but "still kept their eyes on the lake, for the small chance that their hero would emerge" (62 [M 55]). When he does, the unified cohort "stopped, and their joyful cheers echoed throughout the trees around them ... They all began dancing, ecstatic ... Pulling Bèi'àowǔfǔ into a group embrace" (63 [M 55]). Despite the *Bèi'àowǔfǔ* creators' reluctance to excise whole episodes from the original poem, they can make no room in this version for the Finnsburh account of insuppressible feuding.[19] And an enormous amount of attention is given in *Bèi'àowǔfǔ* to the hero's leave-taking in Daneland and homecoming in Geatland; no analogous Western version of the story comes close to matching this emphasis, which transcends portrayals of diplomacy and welcoming to become an assertion of Bèi'àowǔfǔ's essential integration in each of the communities between which he moves.

Even speaking is often collaborative in *Bèi'àowǔfǔ*. There is a noticeable lack of unbroken speechmaking by comparison to the original, and it is not a result merely of the compression that is common in children's versions. Discourse that is presented continuously in the poem is constantly broken up in the Tóngqù version by listeners who offer affirmation and encouragment. Bèi'àowǔfǔ's account of his adventure among the Danes is interrupted several times by Hǎigàilākè's interjections: "Is that so? I was worried about you"; "That sounds amazing!"; "My dear nephew, you are so powerful!" (74–5 [M 62]). Even the analogue to Hrothgar's sermon, following Beowulf's defeat of Grendel's mother, is a sequence of interactions. Huòsījiā holds the floor and controls the dialogue, in which he is given more space than Bèi'àowǔfǔ; the speech remains Huòsījiā's, with Bèi'àowǔfǔ responding to his words, not vice versa. But a principle of turn taking is evident, and Bèi'àowǔfǔ's contributions involve more than polite acknowledgment of praise or generosity. They dramatize Bèi'àowǔfǔ's support of the principal speaker and invite Huòsījiā to say more. Like the congregational cries of approval that punctuate preaching in some churches, these continual reaffirmations propel the discourse forward. The interruptions establish and build camaraderie.

Occasional mentions of humour or laughter work similarly in the Tóngqù retelling. In the encounter with the coast guard, for instance, tension dissolves into ribbing:

> "We have come to help your country defeat the demon Gélúndé'ěr ..."
>
> "Oh my! Why did you not mention this before?" The officer breathed a sigh of relief and his tone immediately softened.
>
> "Haha, you were so fierce, we did not have a chance to say anything!" Bèi'àowǔfǔ said with a laugh. (14–15 [M 13])

Even the Ānfúsī episode, where hostility is explicit,[20] ends with Bèi'àowǔfǔ's laughter, as he chooses to interpret a sour parting shot by Ānfúsī ("Well, it seems that you are the new savior of the Danish people!") as a joke ("Haha, Ānfúsī," 23 [M 20]). The scop is said to insert humour when he celebrates Beowulf's defeat of Gélúndé'ěr and tells about Xīgéméngdé (Sigemund, 38–9 [M 33–4]), implying group participation through laughter and the creation of opportunities for his listeners to express appreciation. Although the book has quirks in its concluding educational essay that could seem farcical in a different context,[21] this is not a comical or light treatment of *Beowulf*; there is no sign that readers of *Bèi'àowǔfū* are expected to find it humorous. Rather, we are observing the characters finding humour in each other's words, as a display of their esprit de corps.

The give and take of speaking and laughter in *Bèi'àowǔfū* corresponds to a broadly dialogic sense of social relations in the book. People and groups pay attention to and form opinions about each other, and these acts of noticing and evaluation are reported. There is a public in *Bèi'àowǔfū*, and significantly, it is not limited to war band or court but cuts across social hierarchy. The ambient presence of non-aristocratic people that we find in the Tóngqù narration is dissimilar to any Western children's version of *Beowulf* that I have seen. References to a public of commoners are occasionally found in English versions,[22] but these are isolated instances, infrequent and never programmatic. Many children's retellings of *Beowulf* foreground the hope of fame, reproducing the original poem's expectation that a community of people who watch, know, and remember will recount great or notorious deeds, but this public appears by default to consist of persons with access to kings or chieftains and their retinues. The elite class of the hall community is the observing and speaking class; it is among rulers and warriors that stories circulate and reputations matter.

In *Bèi'àowǔfū*, by contrast, kings and their intimates notice common people. What is more, commoners look back at them. The treatment of Xī'ěrdé epitomizes this feature of the Tóngqù retelling. Whereas the opening of the Old English poem presents Scyld's arrival among the Danes as mysterious and providential, using mythologizing rhetoric to propel a dynastic foundation narrative, in *Bèi'àowǔfū* there is no uncanny or miraculous advent of Xī'ěrdé, who is simply an orphaned child already present in a rural village as the story begins. His unknown parentage is not made strange or implied to have special meaning. He is cared for by those around him and tries to make himself helpful to them, in turn, as he grows and develops his skills. That Xī'ěrdé has unusual ability becomes apparent when he kills an attacking bear in defence of an old man; this event gives him new prominence among the local people, who recognize a budding leader with good qualities and support the young man as he rises to beneficent rule of the surrounding region. Xī'ěrdé "loved all of his people as if they were his own children," and they loved him as well, finding that "under his sanctuary, the people of Denmark were able to live peaceful working lives" (3 [M 3]).

Such statements of rulers' awareness of commoners, and especially acknowledgments that non-aristocratic people have a reciprocal perspective on their rulers too, are rare in Western versions of *Beowulf* for young people. A comment like Nye's that Scyld's "people loved him," or C.F. Bricknell Smith's that Hrothgar was "respected and loved by his subjects," stands out as exceptional, even within Nye's and Smith's own books.[23] However, lines of sight that cross layers of social hierarchy in both directions are continually mentioned in *Bèi'àowǔfǔ*. Xī'ěrdé's son Bèi'ào (Beow) "did not live up to the people's expectations" formed in the reign of his father, although he does provide for and protect the populace (4 [M 4]). Huòsījiā is inspired to build Heorot by his observation, while walking around his army's encampments, that the soldiers' tents are in poor condition; his vision reaches beyond a corps of elite warriors or officers to the "thousands of people" he intends to accommodate in his new hall in order to "make the quality of life better for all" (6 [M 6]). Wǎnsìyào affirms for Huòsījiā that his people love him very much (24 [M 21]), and the Tóngqù adaptors put the famous elegy that concludes *Beowulf* into the mouths of "people" who "often visit Bèi'àowǔfǔ's tomb" and who "always say" that Bèi'àowǔfǔ was, among other things, "the king with the most loving subjects" (111–12 [M 89]). Such statements are often put in familial terms of love, protection, and provision.

In sum, *Bèi'àowǔfǔ*'s vision of heroism shows us exceptional talent emerging in unexpected places, and then developed to optimize the effect of natural gifts. Extraordinary ability is revealed situationally, as opportunities for its manifestation are created by admirable qualities of character such as strategic intelligence and the desire to collaborate with others. Achievement earns individuals prominence and leadership in groups within which they remain firmly embedded, and those groups grow and thrive as the leader's personal virtues find increasingly public expression. Good leaders see and are seen by the common people, the gaze from both directions crossing lines of social hierarchy, and rule is paternalistic, organized rhetorically by familial paradigms of love and protection.

That is not the *Beowulf* we offer to English-speaking children. Every part of the Tóngqù version's themes as summarized here diverges from the norms of Western presentations of *Beowulf* for younger audiences. Now I want to hold *Beowulf* back up to its less familiar reflection for re-examination. How do the more distinctive aspects of the Tóngqù adaptation respond to identifiable elements of the Old English poem, and what can those responses encourage us to see there that we may not have seen in quite the same way before? In not giving back to us the *Beowulf* we expect, *Bèi'àowǔfǔ* can shake us loose from too-easy views of the original and provoke fresh thought about the rise of heroic figures and their relationship to community.

An idea of emergent leadership and talent similar to that which *Bèi'àowǔfǔ* promotes can be found in *Beowulf* as a cue for this representation, but as a whole the poem equivocates on the question of whether successful leaders are born or made. On the one hand, Beowulf is exceptional in ways that are implied to be innate. The Danish coast guard instantly identifies him as superior to his companions and indicates that the signs of that superiority are not such as have been bestowed by men: "nis þæt seldguma, / wæpnum geweorðad, næfne him his wlite leoge, / ænlic ansyn" (ll. 249b–51a) [that is not some hall-man honoured with weapons, unless his countenance belies him, (his) peerless look]. On the other hand, Beowulf is said – belatedly and in passing – to have had an undistinguished youth (ll. 2183b–88a), a statement that *Bèi'àowǔfǔ* replicates (78 [M 64]).

The implication of this retrospective remark in *Beowulf*, that a seemingly ordinary child might develop into an extraordinary adult, appears to influence other parts of *Bèi'àowǔfǔ* in a kind of adaptational reduplication, particularly the very beginning of the story when Xī'ěrdé's childhood is narrated with little prompting by the source. The Old English poem says only that even though Scyld "ærest wearð / feasceaft funden" (ll. 6b–7a) [was first found destitute], later "he þæs frofre gebad, / weox under wolcnum, weorðmyndum þah" (ll. 7b–8) [he experienced comfort for that: grew under the skies, thrived in honourable opinions (of him)]. Our usual readings of these lines are dominated by the sense of destiny or providence with which the poet suffuses this sketch of the beginning of the Danish royal line. Besides the mysteriousness of Scyld's arrival (sent "ænne ofer yðe umborwesende" [l. 46] [alone upon the wave, an infant], mirrored by the equally mysterious fate of his body and treasure in ll. 50b–52) and the implication that his consolation for those beginnings is seen to by a higher power, his heir Beow is sent by God "folce to frofre" (14a) [as a comfort to the people], a formulaic phrase that signals providential action.[24] This success and succession are explained by God's recognition of the Danes'

> fyrenðearf ...
> þæt hie ær drugon   aldorlease
> lange hwile.   Him þæs liffrea,
> wuldres wealdend   woroldare forgeaf.   (ll. 14b–17)

[terrible need: that they had previously suffered, lordless for a long time.
For that the life-lord, ruler of glory, gave them worldly benefit.]

Yet even *Beowulf*'s account of Scyld has its "unpromising" aspect, in
Scyld's destitution – he will have needed help – and it does acknowledge a trajectory of development and maturation as he "weox" and
"þah."

Elsewhere the poem similarly recognizes that young people must find
their way into the adult world, learning and coming into their own, and
that they receive help in this process from their elders. Beow is said to
have behaved wisely as a youth, planning for the future by cultivating
loyalties while still in his father's mentorship (ll. 20–5). Wealhtheow calls
attention to her and Hrothgar's caretaking of their nephew Hrothulf
from his childhood and indirectly reminds Hrothulf of his obligation in turn to their juvenile sons (ll. 1180b–87). Beowulf promises
protective Geatish reception of Hrothgar's heir Hrethric if he wishes
to leave Daneland (ll. 1836–9, taking a cue from another speech of
Wealhtheow's, ll. 1226b–27); mentors the minor Heardred into readiness
for kingship rather than accepting the Geatish crown as Hygd hoped
he would do (ll. 2367–79a); and later, as king, supports the Swedish
prince Eadgils, who, together with his brother Eanmund, had previously been sheltered by Heardred as a refugee (ll. 2379b–96).

Many of these figures – Eadgils and Eanmund, Hrothulf, Hrethric,
and Beowulf – are spoken of as actually or potentially benefitting from
care and help in lands not their own before reaching full autonomy.
Thus *Beowulf*'s elision of social connections for Scyld in the community that must have cared for him from infancy can be seen as a rhetorical choice, one that works in the dynastic introduction to emphasize
his status as *fons et origo* but goes against the grain of other parts of
the poem. The Tóngqù adaptors fill in *Beowulf*'s unnarrated rise of
Scyld by imagining how an orphan might thrive as he is said to have
done. Their answer, that Xī'ěrdé was supported and given time to develop until his talent bloomed, much to everyone's surprise, imports
to the prefatory genealogy of the Danish kings something comparable to the poem's glimpses of Beowulf as a little boy present with his
father at Hrothgar's court (ll. 372–6), then fostered by Hrethel from
age seven (ll. 2428–34), then trying his strength against another boy in
a swimming competition on whose results opinions differ, and for a
time not thought very meritorious among the Geats. *Beowulf*'s emphasis on Scyld's uncanny, providential advent tends to overpower its
brief acknowledgment that he was also a child who grew and learned,
but *Bèi'àowǔfǔ*'s resolution of this account in an unexpected direction

makes more visible its mixed nature. The Old English poet pushes the community that made Scyld's success possible out of sight at the margins of his accomplishments, a distinctive choice at this point in the text because *Beowulf* actually does call attention to mentorship and maturation when there are not special reasons, as there seem to be in the Scyld story, to elide them.

Another adaptational reduplication, and a more forceful one, is the humility for which Bèi'àowǔfǔ is praised. In *Beowulf* some aspects of the hero's thought and action are compatible with this quality, but on the whole, any behaviour of Beowulf's that can be so described is determined by social place – within systems in which he will eventually ascend – and would be difficult to analyse in context as signs of a humble disposition. For the most part the poem allows the boasts of Beowulf as part and parcel of heroic rhetoric. However, at one point humility is prominently idealized: in Hrothgar's speech to the hero after his slaying of Grendel's mother, reminding the young warrior that decline and death come to all and counselling him against pride in his accomplishments. The Tóngqù team, finding humility topicalized as a virtue in that scene, chooses to topicalize it more powerfully, propagating the concept to other parts of the story as an appropriate lesson for young readers. This requires crediting the hero in *Bèi'àowǔfǔ* with possessing a quality he is only advised to have in *Beowulf*. Transforming the virtue to which Beowulf is exhorted into an achieved trait perhaps rationalizes Hrothgar's speech as appropriate to an occasion of celebration, but it also affects Bèi'àowǔfǔ's character as a whole, and even prompts revision of the elegy at the end, where the descriptor *lofgeornost*, or "most eager for praise," is replaced with "the king most eager for victory, and the king with the most loving subjects" (112 [M 89]), surgically separating the eagerness from the praise.

Some readers have perceived Hrothgar's sermon as unlike other parts of *Beowulf*, finding in it a moral frame of reference different from that validated elsewhere. But it is the conceptual pivot point on which young Beowulf, advised by a wise old king, turns into old King Beowulf, whose success in actualizing Hrothgar's advice the poem's diptych structure thus invites us to consider. The sermon is part of the poem's wisdom dimension, and it is possible to join the Tóngqù adaptors in assigning this speech central importance to an interpretation of Beowulf the character. Although *Bèi'àowǔfǔ* does this by having its hero exhibit the quality throughout, its impulse to reconcile possibly dissonant elements of the poem by generalizing the virtue of humility may invite a view back onto *Beowulf* that questions his eventual moral success.

Another personal quality that *Bèi'àowǔfǔ* highlights, as we have seen, is strategic awareness, which is connected both to virtue and to a sense that there is a techne of fighting, a broader practice of being a warrior. In *Beowulf*, there is far less reference to strategy than in the Tóngqù book,[25] and such as there is does not bespeak a special interest in fighting tactics. Descriptions of action are mainly exterior rather than explaining purpose, and descriptions of thought focus more on emotions and expectations than on strategic reasoning. For the most part, the Old English text implies that physical strength equals fighting prowess; it is Beowulf's bodily power more than his know-how that enables him to prevail. Even in the dragon fight, where he never grapples with his adversary, attention is called to his overwhelming handgrip by the explanation that he tends to break swords (ll. 2680b–87).

Instead, *Beowulf* repeatedly stresses what we might informally think of as luck, and what the poem conceptualizes as providence. Several times, things just work out for the hero, with the implication, occasionally stated, that God has his back. When Beowulf chooses to face Grendel without weaponry, his reasons suggest no knowledge that swords cannot hurt the monster (ll. 677–83a), so when that invulnerability becomes known, his choice to wrestle with him appears fortunate. Grendel's mother's cave happens to contain the giant sword that will harm her as Unferth's could not. Wiglaf's sword blow that stops the dragon from breathing fire enables Beowulf to slash its midsection (ll. 2700b–5), but Wiglaf strikes that place in the body only because his hand has already been burned, causing him to avoid the creature's head (ll. 2697b–99). Beowulf's voice, like the poet's own, expresses trust in a providential order, sometimes in terms that are compatible with the Christian version of this concept (e.g., ll. 685b–87) and other times with reference to a more impersonal *wyrd*, conceived of as the course of events that are in store. That course of events is not immutable or fully predictable, but it will take care of itself – "gæð a wyrd swa hio scel" (l. 455b) [fate always goes as it should] – and it tends to operate in favour of the deserving: "wyrd oft nereð / unfægne eorl þonne his ellen deah" (ll. 572b–73) [fate often saves an undoomed man if his courage lasts]. Insofar as the poem offers a sense that a warrior needs to be holistically prepared in some way, that preparation centres on a philosophical commitment to courage and to a belief that things will go right rather than on any kind of physical or technical discipline.

This philosophical bent, a different form of thoughtfulness about violent conflict, may be a stimulus for the Tóngqù book's attention to strategy and its link to qualities of character. Emphasis on Beowulf's quality of thought is not normally carried over into Western children's versions, but the Tóngqù adaptors notice and respond to it, shifting the focus to tactical thinking and the influence upon it of the virtues they are inclined to privilege. *Bèi'àowǔfǔ*'s message that personal qualities influence a warrior's success raises the question of whether the same link exists at all in *Beowulf*. Hrothgar twice pairs within the space of a single line (1706a, 1844) Beowulf's physical gifts with the wisdom on which Hrothgar is focusing his praise, yet the connection between the two is vaguer in *Beowulf* than in *Bèi'àowǔfǔ*. Beowulf's physical power advances the story, enabling him to do things no one else can do, and his speeches advance the poem's concepts, including attitudes about *wyrd* or the providential workings of a higher power, but the hero's philosophical perspective seems to affect events only by leading him to join the fray. Once he is in it, his strength takes over, in an environment of opportunity created by chance or fate.

The looseness of this connection may be intelligible as another way of accessing the tragic or elegiac tone of *Beowulf*. In *Bèi'àowǔfǔ*, there is a clear relationship between what the hero is like and what happens. In tandem with his skill as a fighter, Bèi'àowǔfǔ's character – brave, humble, tactically intelligent, protective – leads to success in battle, yielding the message that virtuous agency is rewarded with success. *Beowulf* presents a much more fatalistic vision, one in which the hero must respond to uncontrollable circumstances. The character qualities that are most important in the poem – courage, eagerness for reputation, wisdom – create not victory, but engagement and effort. From a position within the violent coil of competing forces and interests, governed mysteriously by a divine power, the primary form of agency available to the hero is to think clearly and face with resolved equanimity whatever may come.

Beowulf is at least as much about speaking as it is about action, and here again the Tóngqù adaptors make choices of presentation that can call our attention to features of the poem we tend to pay little attention to. The supportive interruptions of extended speeches that are so noticeable in *Bèi'àowǔfǔ* make conspicuous something that is true everywhere: a speech act always has multiple parties, speaker and addressee at minimum, and often other listeners as well. All contribute in some way to the total discourse situation. That *Beowulf* favours an oratorical over a dialogic model does not mean that the discourse is truly one-sided, even when no response is narrated. The Tóngqù version's presentation of continual assent by listeners helps us see that in *Beowulf*, assent goes without saying: it is assumed as the unmarked, default case. This plays out complexly in *Beowulf*, because a speaker's assumption of assent is sometimes false. Several times, for example, disagreement with Hrothgar is spoken, but either not directly to him or not framed clearly as a contradiction,[26] and this tendency to indirectness, as well as the existence elsewhere of narrative elisions of dissenting opinion,[27] reveals the strength of the poem's communication paradigm in which words spoken are expected to stand.

From the narrative or rhetorical habit of assuming assent, it also follows that since affirmation is not usually explicit, statements of positive response, when they do occur, may be no less salient than statements of dissent. It turns out that the relationship between Hrothgar and Beowulf is marked by both reported dissent and reported affirmation: Beowulf openly corrects Hrothgar's attitude about the death of Æschere, and we are told that Hrothgar thanks God for this reply (ll. 1384–98). Although Hrothgar does not speak after Beowulf's response to Unferth, the poet says that he is pleased by it (ll. 607–10). Hrothgar's effusive praise of Beowulf's wisdom (ll. 1841–45a) powerfully affirms Beowulf's speech promising continued friendship and alliance between the Geats and the Danes (ll. 1818–39). Hrothgar's sermon qualifies Beowulf's announcement of his success against Grendel's mother, and Beowulf is said to be pleased after hearing it (ll. 1785–6). This pattern suggests a dimension of wisdom in the interactions of these two men, who teach and learn from each other.

Wisdom, strategy, and collaboration all come together in the interface of individual with group in Beowulf's fights. On the topic of collaboration in fighting, the poem again gives mixed signals: in different ways Beowulf both does and does not insist on fighting unaided. Prior to all three confrontations Beowulf expresses his intent to fight alone, framing the anticipated event as single combat with an adversary whom he believes himself uniquely able to defeat.[28] He speaks of his confrontations with the monsters less as battles than as contests or competitions, albeit mortal ones. In a battle, the goal of victory overrides most other considerations, and it is assumed that either party would exploit an advantage of numbers or weaponry if possible. The rhetoric around Beowulf's fights indicates a different objective, namely, demonstration of his superiority for observers whose knowledge of the result will have social outcomes for him as victor, like elevated status.[29] Yet Beowulf does also have an extra-rhetorical goal of solving a problem of aggression, and despite his words and some actions framing the fights as solo feats to perform, he welcomes assistance in all three cases, twice by direct participation of his men and once in the acceptance of Unferth's lent sword. The poem's accounts of the first and second fights emphasize the hero's isolation, as the help he receives proves ineffectual, and this is consistent with other episodes.[30] Isolation is topicalized in the third fight, too, but the message seems to reverse: this time help does make a difference when it comes, a detail to which I will return.

The effectiveness of collaboration relates to the hero's integral membership in the group, to which *Bèi'àowǔfǔ* is very committed. There are some signs of strong group identity in *Beowulf*, at various scales ranging from poetic formulas of collectivity or kinship (*fiftyna sum* "one of fifteen," l. 207b; *bearn Ecgþeowes* "son of Ecgtheow"; etc.) to the tribally organized landscape in which the entire story takes place, or even the adversariality between humankind and an intermittently racialized monstrous other. Beowulf is linked to others through kinship and alliance. However, many other features of the text separate him from the warriors around him, and these seem to govern the ethos of the poem as a whole, in which the hero's greatness is an end in itself and his pursuit of glory is valorized. Beowulf's choice to approach the dragon's barrow as "one of twelve," but then instruct the other eleven to wait for him as he faces the creature alone, epitomizes the tension in the poem between individual and group identity. The same tension is evident many other times, as when Beowulf asks Hrothgar "þæt ic ana mote, minra eorla gedryht / ond þes hearda heap, Heorot fælsian" (ll. 431–2) [that I alone be permitted – the troop of my earls and this strong company – to cleanse Heorot], appearing to take an instrumental view of his men. They are the means by which he will succeed, but the success is his.

The hero's enmeshment with the group, much more total in *Bèi'àowǔfǔ* than in the Old English poem, has bearing on the position and shape of an evaluating public in both works. The Tóngqù version strongly reflects *Beowulf*'s preoccupation with opinion and reputation, but lines of sight onto members of the ruling class cross boundaries of social status as those in the poem do not, and in this respect Western children's versions usually follow *Beowulf* closely, as already noted. In *Bèi'àowǔfǔ*, the distancing that is needed to escape the reach of personal relationships is created by both scale and social strata: it is the comprehensiveness of the judging and speaking public that creates space in which opinion can form and circulate. In *Beowulf*, by contrast, the community of opinion about heroic actions includes only social elites. Beowulf's uniqueness helps to create within that stratum the distance needed for others to hold him separate as an object of judgment; it renders unnecessary any view from other social positions.

But the most important distancing factor in *Beowulf*, and one that similarly obviates any presence of common observers and speakers, is the insularity of each local hall society. In *Beowulf* and other Old English poems, story seems to leap from one hall to the next, scarcely touching the ground between, as lordly doings are reported to lordly ears. One conduit of such information is the singer of tales, as Widsith explains in the Exeter Book text known by his name.[31] Although any real counterpart to the impossibly mobile Widsith would presumably have shared stories and news in exchange for help at all stops in his journeys, in literary contexts one gets the impression that distant halls are social islands in a blank and silent sea. Ælfwine in *The Battle of Maldon* imagines this kind of aristocratic, warrior-class public when he announces his descent from a Mercian ealdorman and declares that "ne sceolon me on þære þeode *þegenas* ætwitan" (l. 220, my emphasis) [*thanes* shall not reproach me among that people]. Unferth and Beowulf themselves represent this rarefied public. They, companions of kings, have heard about one another, and Beowulf learns of Hrothgar's troubles from travellers who have appeared at Hygelac's court. No voice is given to non-aristocratic vantage points on aristocrats, a fact thrown into relief by the regularity with which *Bèi'àowǔfǔ* does have ordinary people doing and thinking and feeling things.

Ordinary people may not be acknowledged to have their own point of view in *Beowulf*, but the narrative does occasionally notice them, as when Hrothgar plans to share out in Heorot everything except the common lands and men's lives (ll. 71–3), or when he recalls that *landbuend* and *foldbuend* "land-dwellers" (as well as *seleræded* "hall counsellors") have reported seeing two monsters (ll. 1345–57a). The poet observes that the dragon's attack harmed all the people of the region (ll. 2316–22a). These neutral or benevolent mentions are offset by the fact that that same dragon was provoked by the only non-aristocratic actor in *Beowulf*, the slave whose voice enters the story-events when he must explain his theft and is then forced to show the king and his men the barrow's location. The coerced inclusiveness of the group that approaches the dragon's lair, I suggest, is compatible with a reading of the conclusion in which the seemingly happy help of Wiglaf, even in breaking the poem's usual pattern of isolating Beowulf in combat, produces a much darker emphasis on failure and dissolution.

The creators of *Bèi'àowǔfǔ* are at pains to rationalize the hero's solitary entry into the dragon fight. They make it a strategic choice: Bèi'àowǔfǔ intends never to get directly in front of the dragon, which will be unfeasible with a larger group of warriors. This plan does not weaken his retainers' obligation to the shared goal, so Wéigélāfū's assistance when it is needed is a matter of duty, and the eventual deserters – although they remain near the fight longer in *Bèi'àowǔfǔ* than in *Beowulf* – are deeply dishonoured, as in the poem. The reason for their dishonour differs subtly: Bèi'àowǔfǔ's needing their help means the tactics that motivated single combat did not work, so naturally the other men should join the battle at that point. The Old English poem, as we have seen, equivocates throughout on whether Beowulf should be fighting alone and on what his inclination to fight alone means. Were the retainers expected to intervene despite being instructed to observe, or was Beowulf performing a feat that they were present to witness and declaim? Panicked flight is unseemly, to be sure, and in Wiglaf's and the poet's opinion the other men should have acted as Wiglaf did, but they each would have been stepping up heroically as individuals, not fulfilling a contract as unambiguous as it is later made to sound.

Wiglaf does try to persuade them that this is the time to make good on their boasts of loyalty and support in battle, and when they come slinking back he will finalize his construction of their cowardice as the one that governs their future as Geats. But I would like to consider how within the moment, according to other things we are told, the situation may have been less clear, particularly if we organize it around Wiglaf's emergence as a leader. The poem's treatment of his decision to intervene emphasizes his personal reflections in a way that supports understanding this as a scene of dynamic development, a coming of age,[32] not unlike Beowulf's own passage into heroic maturity at Hrothgar's court decades before. The lengthy explanation of Wiglaf's motivations hints at a fuller story as he recalls his induction into manhood both by his father, who preserved heirloom war gear for him until he was old enough to use it, and by Beowulf, who ensconced him in the family homestead (ll. 2606–25a). Wiglaf's young age is stressed (ll. 2626a, 2674a, 2675a, 2756b, 2811a, 2821b), as is his inexperience in battle (ll. 2625b–27), and Beowulf speaks to him as a surrogate son (ll. 2729–32a), his position as the last of their shared Wægmunding clan substituting for direct descent (ll. 2813–14a). All these details in *Beowulf* suggest the kind of development and mentorship that *Bèi'àowŭfŭ* highlights as a theme when it opens with the Xī'ĕrdé story, diverging from *Beowulf* in that place but fabricating a tale harmonious with other aspects of the poem. We may see the man rushing forward to help Beowulf fight the dragon not as a warrior who statically remains faithful, but as a youth who makes a terrifying choice, in a moment of crisis, that identifies him as a uniquely courageous retainer and heir apparent. Perhaps his actions are extraordinary rather than expected; perhaps the effect of the contrast is less to show that the other warriors are exceptional in their failure of resolve than to identify Wiglaf as exceptional in his own heroic potential.

Young Wiglaf's undoubted virtue complicates the ethical position of old Beowulf, whose decisions some details of the poem call into question, especially if we take seriously the Tóngqù version's perspective on humility, which does find one firm foothold in the original in Hrothgar's sermon. It is possible that Beowulf's spirit of self-sacrifice, while admirable, is misguided. Hrothgar, repeatedly praised for his wisdom, did not fight Grendel in his old age, and he advises Beowulf not to consider himself invulnerable to failure on the basis of his accomplishments; yet Beowulf confronts the dragon alone explicitly because of his previous successes, knowing he may die but confident in his ability to defeat this last in a long line of adversaries (ll. 2425–537). The markedness in the poem's rhetoric, as observed above, of indications of assent and dissent means we must give some notice to the narrative elision of a disagreement that is revealed when we learn only after Beowulf's death – and not during the lengthy account of his thoughts and speech leading up to his last fight – that his men had tried to dissuade him from attacking the dragon: in Wiglaf's words, "ne meahton we gelæran leofne þeoden / ... ræd ænigne / þæt he ne grette goldweard þone" (ll. 3079–81a) [we could not convince the dear prince of any advice that he should not meet that gold-guardian]. His analysis of Beowulf's stubbornness on this point resonates powerfully: "Oft sceall eorl monig anes willan / wræc adreogan, swa us geworden is" (ll. 3077–8) [often many a man must suffer misery for the will of one, as has now happened to us].

Beowulf allows his retainers' desertion to pass without comment, but Wiglaf does not. In the Old English poem he audits starkly the waste of the war gear they wear and carry before he dispossesses and exiles them. Here we find the most remarkable of the Tóngqù version's departures from the original:

> People stood at the bottom of the cliff and saw the old king lying in the sand, motionless, with his eyes closed ... The exhausted Wéigélāfū cried as he knelt in front of his king.
>
> "Wéigélāfū, how did this happen?" people asked, confused, angered, and full of sorrow.
>
> Wéigélāfū stood up from the sand and pointed his fingers toward the cowards in the distance, angrily shouting: "Ask them! These guards jumped away quicker than rabbits!"
>
> People angrily stared at the warriors who all blamed themselves and were ashamed of what they had done. Every pair of eyes was like a little knife, cutting away bits of their skin, into their muscles, then deep in their chest, slicing open their internal organs, and throwing their innards to wild dogs to eat, and reaching inside to throw their bladders to the sharks. (107 [M 85–6])

"Come, now commit suicide!" one person shouted ... and they all used
their swords to kill themselves ... People silently stood on the side and
watched as the men ended their lives. (109–10 [M 87])

That a deviation from the poem occurs here is not surprising; like the
death of Hondscio, the condemnation of the companions who fled
creates challenges for children's adaptors. Although several do have
Wiglaf confront and punish the deserters as in *Beowulf*,[33] others omit
the warriors' faithlessness from the story altogether,[34] or recount their
flight but not their return,[35] or have Wiglaf shame but not exile them.[36]
A number of children's writers allow them to be forgiven, or to suffer only from their own sense of guilt with no apparent social conse-
quences.[37] But no Western version, however free its hand or however
willing it is to treat the ten retainers harshly, has anything like the imagery of evisceration (metaphorical) or the group suicide (quite literal)
that we find in *Bèi'àowǔfǔ*.

Yet as radical as this change of story is, it is not unprompted by the
original: the Tóngqù adaptors have chosen to realize what is in *Beowulf*
only a hypothetical alternative, suggested in Wiglaf's statement that
death would be better than the shame that the cowardly warriors must
suffer (ll. 2890b–91). The choice highlights the difference between re-
sponsibility and accountability. Wiglaf holds the deserters responsible
for their action, but their accountability to the community of Geats will
end when they exit that community. They may live or die, suffer or
thrive, and although Wiglaf forecasts their permanent disgrace and
misery, the facts of the poem indicate a less certain prospect: other out-
casts or criminals, including Beowulf's father Ecgtheow and Unferth,
have managed to rebound into places of acceptance. The warriors' failure to support Beowulf was a single, discrete event, with the specific
consequence of severing their ties to the tribe, and what happens to
them later is of no concern. *Bèi'àowǔfǔ*, on the other hand, insists on a
profound, present accountability. Rather than being denied membership in the community of Geats, the retainers must continue to accept
that membership, and with it, the end that is required of them by public
outcry. In the logic of *Bèi'àowǔfǔ*, they cannot be simply removed from
sight; their action must be resolved within the community they have
failed. The faithless retainers die precisely because there is a public and
its existence will continue.

From this perspective *Beowulf* might be seen as devaluing community through its rejection of accountability to an ongoing social body.
Indeed, in the poem we know that the community itself will not survive. Both Wiglaf and Beowulf have something to do with this. Wiglaf

holds the Geatish warriors to the standard of his own behaviour, and the unacceptability to him of their failure to rise to that standard must be catastrophically destabilizing. Because not everyone can or will be heroic – something the poem has not in fact required until this episode – the conditions in which Wiglaf emerges as a leader undermine the community he was to lead. In a manner of speaking, his expulsion of the retainers, presumably those who had been seen as the best or most promising, already anticipates the absence of a political body that requires a conclusion to their story.

But it seems that Beowulf's death has already made inevitable the demise of the Geats as an identity group. The messenger is frank in forecasting the tribe's suffering and dispersal (ll. 2900–3027), and the poet affirms his prediction (ll. 3028–30a). While in the poem's elegiac rhetoric this motif of loss signals the absolute superiority of Beowulf, it also figures that superiority as finally contributing to the destruction of his people. Apart from Wiglaf's loyalty, the poem's indexes of social cohesion are entirely negative even amid the Geats' collective grief over the death of their king. Beowulf ends his life with no descendants and only one retainer capable of heroic action among those he thought most worthy. He recounts his own reign for those men, a self-memorializing impulse already suggestive, I think, of a discontinuity of story or memory: beneath the superficial purpose of his long battle boast, this may be one of the saddest moments in *Beowulf*. The great king exchanges his life for the dragon's gold, but the gold is not rendered useful to the Geats by his sacrifice – as the poet points out (ll. 3163–8) – so in the final analysis his death looks like a simple loss, not the costly yet beneficial trade for his people's safety that Beowulf conceives it to be. The action with which the poem concludes is lamentation at a grave by a doomed remnant.

Beowulf's death is the death of the Geats because their attenuation, long hidden under his protection, is exposed by his absence; the group's strength lacks an ongoing foundation. It is striking in *Beowulf* that although the king prides himself on having stopped the Swedish-Geatish wars, the lingering memory of that conflict and the lack of sustained alliances will make the Geats vulnerable to neighbours who are expected to turn opportunistic and predatory. *Bèi'àowǔfǔ* does not dismiss the poem's predictions of war and hardship, but it softens them by foregrounding personal sadness rather than national catastrophe, as well as by suggesting continuing connections with surrounding peoples: Bèi'àowǔfǔ instructs Wéigélāfū that the treasure is to be shared not just among the Geats but with neighbouring countries too (103–4 [M 81–2]), and builders for the tomb "came from hundreds of miles away" (111 [M 88]).

Wiglaf's remark about many suffering for the will of one (ll. 3077–8, quoted above) gains interpretive weight in a reading of *Beowulf* guided by the poem's ambivalence about the hero's enmeshment with the group, an ambivalence to which *Bèi'àowǔfǔ* calls our attention by its very determination to produce univocality though selection and enhancement of certain features. From this perspective on *Beowulf,* the poem's equivocation on individual versus group primacy suggests tragedy in Beowulf's uniqueness: the tribe matters, but Beowulf cannot save it because he cannot be integral to it without reducing it to little more than himself. In *Bèi'àowǔfǔ,* the hero is a normal person, with unusual skills and qualities of character, whose greatness is a community resource. In *Beowulf,* the hero at times seems to be a different kind of person, one whose singularity isolates him. Beowulf's strength is equal to that of thirty men, but on the flip side of this formulation, the metonymic thirty men therefore also have only the strength of one, however magnificent. By refusing to image back to us the *Beowulf* to which we are accustomed, the Tóngqù *Bèi'àowǔfǔ* shows us a hero in the Old English poem whose effects on his own community make it unsustainable after his passing. Beowulf's might is so overwhelming that the Geats themselves cannot survive it.

NOTES

1 Tóngqù Publishing Company, «贝奥武甫» [*Bèi'àowǔfǔ*] (Beijing: The People's Posts and Telecommunications Press, 2011). I lack knowledge of the Chinese language and rely on a commissioned, unpublished translation by Kilie McCain, from which all English quotations are drawn; my analysis is carefully restricted to the content and images of *Bèi'àowǔfǔ* and makes no claims that rest on nuances of word choice. Citations will be given parenthetically by page number of the Chinese text, followed in square brackets by the page number in McCain's translation (abbreviated "M"). Like the work's title, the names of characters will be given in the Latin alphabet using the Pinyin transcription system adopted by the People's Republic of China and the United Nations, according to which I silently make small changes to McCain's romanization of names. I am grateful to Texas A&M University's Department of English for funding McCain's work and to her for permission to use it in my teaching and research.

2 *Bèi'àowǔfǔ,* vi [M v]. It may be the first monolingual children's version in Chinese. There is an earlier bilingual English and Chinese children's version: Henriette Barkow, «贝奥伍尔夫» / *Beowulf,* illus. Alan Down, trans. Sylvia Denham (London: Mantra Lingua, 2004).

3 See Stella Wang, "Chinese Translations of *Beowulf*," in *Recording English, Researching English, Transforming English*, ed. Hans Sauer and Gaby Waxenberger (Frankfurt: Peter Lang, 2013), 299–328. Zhao Dong is credited in *Bèi'àowǔfú*'s prefatory material as an expert on medieval English literature (vi [M v]), so dependence on a translation is not certain.

4 Like making Hǎigàilākè's (Hygelac's) death occur in a raid on the Swedes, thus helping to motivate the Swedish-Geatish wars (80 [M 66]); or having Bèi'àowǔfú bring back Gélúndé'ěr's (Grendel's) mother's head rather than Gélúndé'ěr's from the mere (62 [M 54], 65 [M 56]); or causally attributing the dragon episode to the curse on the treasure, which is put on it by the Last Survivor and whose fulfilment the dragon is (83 [M 68]).

5 Quotations from *Beowulf* are from R.D. Fulk, Robert E. Bjork, and John D. Niles, eds., *Klaeber's Beowulf and The Fight at Finnsburg*, 4th ed. (Toronto: University of Toronto Press, 2008), omitting editorial diacritics. All translations from Old English are my own. My use of this episode as a starting point is indebted to Mallorie Williams's identification of Hondscio's death as a point of intense difficulty for children's adaptors of *Beowulf* ("Handling Hondscio: Personal Bonds in Children's Adaptations of *Beowulf*," unpublished paper presented at the conference of the Texas Medieval Association, 24 September 2016). Williams's analysis focused on Strafford Riggs, *The Story of Beowulf*, illus. Henry C. Pitz (New York: D. Appleton-Century, 1933); and Nicky Raven, *Beowulf: A Tale of Blood, Heat, and Ashes*, illus. John Howe (Cambridge, MA: Candlewick Press, 2007).

6 The one notable exception to the pattern of avoidance among English-language versions is found in Dorothy Hosford, *By His Own Might: The Battles of Beowulf*, illus. Lazslo Matulay (New York: Henry Holt and Co., 1949), 15–16. Hosford's commitment to exact reproduction of *Beowulf*'s content is more extreme throughout than was typical by the mid-twentieth century: cf. Carl Edlund Anderson's essay on mid-century trends in this volume.

7 Raven, *Beowulf*, 20; John Harris, *The Geat: The Story of Beowulf and Grendel*, illus. Tom Morgan-Jones (Chelmsford, Essex: Notreallybooks, 2007), 56 (where Hondscio is renamed Ghorat).

8 Robert Nye, *Beowulf: A New Telling*, illus. Alan E. Cober (New York: Hill and Wang, 1968), 44; Penelope Hicks, *Beowulf*, illus. James McLean (Boston: Kingfisher, 2007), 58; Julia Green, *Beowulf the Brave*, illus. Tom Percival (London: A & C Black, 2008), 17.

9 Riggs, *Story of Beowulf*, 43; Gladys Schmitt, *The Heroic Deeds of Beowulf*, illus. Walter Ferro (New York: Random House, 1962), 22; Thomas O. Jones, *Lord of the Geats* (Unionville, NY: Royal Fireworks Press, 1995), 37 (in this version Hondscio turns out not to have been killed after all, and reappears

on p. 91 to help Beowulf fight Grendel's mother); Welwyn Wilton Katz, *Beowulf,* illus. Lazlo Gal (Toronto: Groundwood Books, 1999), 18–20.

10 Jane Leighton, *The Story of Beowulf,* illus. Gerhard Steffen (Frankfurt am Main: Verlag Moritz Diesterweg, 1959), 8–9; Rosemary Sutcliff, *Beowulf: Dragon Slayer,* illus. Charles Keeping (Oxford: Bodley Head, 1961), 36; Kevin Crossley-Holland, *Beowulf,* illus. Charles Keeping (Oxford: Oxford University Press, 1982), 17 (where Hondscio is renamed Leofric); Michael Morpurgo, *Beowulf,* illus. Michael Foreman (Cambridge, MA: Candlewick Press, 2006), 28.

11 When Bèi'àowǔfǔ returns to Geatland and tells Hǎigàilākè about his fight with Gélúndé'ěr, he reports that "The demon tried to grab me *while I pretended to sleep,* and at that moment I grabbed his arms" (75 [M 62, italics mine]); in *Beowulf,* ll. 2076ff., there is no reference to his strategem.

12 Nye, *Bee Hunter*; Harris, *The Geat*; Jones, *Lord of the Geats.*

13 The one English children's version that has a notably humble Beowulf makes his humility of a different kind: Nye, *Bee Hunter,* shows us a hero who has personal weaknesses of which he is aware.

14 E.g., Matulay in Hosford, *By His Own Might,* 17; Ferro in Schmitt, *Heroic Deeds,* 23; Keeping in Crossley-Holland, *Beowulf,* 19; Gal in Katz, *Beowulf,* 19; Foreman in Morpurgo, *Beowulf,* 31; Ross in Tony Bradman, "Terror in the Night: The Story of Beowulf the Hero," illus. Tony Ross, in *The Orchard Book of Heroes and Villains* (London: Orchard Books, 2008), 39; and Ross in Tony Bradman, *Beowulf the Hero,* illus. Tony Ross (London: Orchard Books, 2010), 24–31.

15 J.L. Herrera, *Beowulfo,* illus. Julio Castro (Madrid: Aguilar, 1965), 26–7; Clare Scott-Mitchell, "Beowulf," illus. Bryan Pollard, in *Beowulf: A Traditional Collection,* rev. US ed. (Auckland: Shortland Publications, 1989), 14; Eric A. Kimmel, *The Hero Beowulf,* illus. Leonard Everett Fisher (New York: Farrar, Straus, and Giroux, 2005), [20]–[21] and [24]–[25]; John Green, *Beowulf* (Mineola, NY: Dover Publications, 2007), 11.

16 [Uncredited], "Beowulf and Grendel," illus. Brian Froud, *Childcraft Annual* (1975): 80–1; María Fernanda Cano, *Beowulf: La leyenda de las dos criaturas,* illus. Oscar Rojas (Buenos Aires: Ediciones del Eclipse, 2005), 28–9.

17 Howe in Raven, *Beowulf,* 42–3; Gerard in Michelle L. Szobody, *Beowulf, Book One: Grendel the Ghastly,* illus. Justin Gerard (Greenville, SC: Portland Studios, 2008), 25.

18 Only as drawn by James Rumford do other warriors look truly involved in the fight, and even there, the art heavily emphasizes Beowulf, grappling with Grendel, while his sword-wielding companions' straining faces form a background, distanced by muted coloration. Rumford, *A Hero's Tale Retold* (Boston: Houghton Mifflin, 2007), [14]–[15].

19 They appear to have found the tale intractable, replacing it with statements that "beautiful music was played, followed by laughter and tears,"

and that the scop sang "heroic tunes of Bèi'àowǔfǔ's victory" (43 [M 38]).
The Swedish-Geatish war is represented as a feud but Bèi'àowǔfǔ explicitly regards it as tragic; he says that his Geatish predecessors and the
Swedes "vented ... hatred upon one another, and neither wanted peace,"
and that Xīqīn (Hæthcyn) "paid for his hatred with his life" (91 [M 72–3]).

20 "It was apparent that [Ānfúsī] had a strong feeling of jealousy toward
Bèi'àowǔfǔ" (21 [M 18]); "Bèi'àowǔfǔ became more and more angry" (23
[M 20]).

21 Beowulf's adventure is likened to that of the Beatles in *Yellow Submarine*
(116–17 [M 93]), a comparison that appears to derive from the back cover
copy of the American release of the *Yellow Submarine* LP record (quoted
in full by *The Beatles Bible*, "U. S. Album Release: *Yellow Submarine*, Mon-
day 13 January 1969," at https://www.beatlesbible.com/1969/01/13/
us-lp-yellow-submarine [accessed 24 August 2018]). Just prior to this reference, a picture by Ryota Murayama of a dog dressed as a seventeenth-
century courtier and playing a lute is used as an illustration of the kind
of travelling poet that would have performed *Beowulf* (115 [M 92]; artist
uncredited in the text but identified with the help of Google Images on 21
September 2017).

22 For instance, in *The Geat* (11), Harris stresses that Hrothgar invites all of
his subjects, not only those of high status, to Heorot's inaugural feast; and
in Jones's *Lord of the Geats* (158), commoners gather on the beach – though
below the funeral site, separated from it – to observe.

23 Nye, *Bee Hunter*, 12; Smith, *The Story of Beowulf*, illus. L.H. Bennett-Collins
(Exeter: A. Wheaton and Co., 1951), 9.

24 Similarly referencing a divinely ordained birth in *Genesis A* 1108a, *Genesis
A* 2219a (desired), *Exodus* 88a, and *Christ III* 1421a; for other providential
applications cf. *Andreas* 606a, *Elene* 502a, and *Elene* 1142a. Citations of Old
English poems other than *Beowulf* are from *ASPR*.

25 Beowulf's feigning sleep and watching Hondscio's death to learn how
Grendel attacks is a clear example, and he apparently uses that knowledge
in choosing how to grasp the monster's arm as he reaches for him: he "on-
feng hraþe / ... Ond wið earm gesæt" (ll. 748b–49) [grabbed quickly and sat
up against the arm]. As he plans for the dragon fight ("wræce leornode,"
l. 2336b [studied on revenge]), he orders an iron shield made, knowing that
a normal wooden shield will not protect him from flame (ll. 2336–41a).

26 One of these dissenting views is expressed much later: Beowulf holds
his doubts about Hrothgar's match of Freawaru with Ingeld until he is
back home, where he speaks of them to Hygelac (ll. 2020–69a). Unferth's
challenge of Beowulf's ability to defeat Grendel is an indirect dissenting
reply to Hrothgar's acceptance of Beowulf's help; and Wealhtheow twice
responds tactfully but negatively to Hrothgar's endowment of Beowulf

with filial status (ll. 946b–49a), once addressing Hrothgar (ll. 1175–80a) and again in her simultaneously grateful, congratulatory, and cautionary speech to Beowulf (ll. 1216–31).

27 When Beowulf recounts to Hrothgar his decision to go to Daneland, he claims that the best and wisest of Hygelac's court encouraged him to go (ll. 415–18), yet in Hygelac's own account to Beowulf he says that fearing for his nephew's safety, he pleaded with Beowulf not to seek out Grendel but let the Danes solve their own problem (ll. 1994b–98a). Another narrative elision of disagreement will be discussed below.

28 Ll. 415–26a, 677–87, 1474–91, 2529–37, 2642b–46a.

29 As the comparisons to Unferth's courage or achievements make clear; the poet states that Unferth lost honour by not being the one to follow Grendel's mother into the mere (ll. 1468b–71a). Both Hrothgar and Wealhtheow confirm that Beowulf's glory will spread (ll. 1221–24a, 1703b–5a), and Wiglaf later indicates that this has been so throughout Beowulf's life (ll. 2642b–46a).

30 As when he slays Dæghrafn (ll. 2499–502) or battles sea monsters alone after being separated from Breca (ll. 541b–75a).

31 Several children's adaptations (e.g., Riggs, *Story of Beowulf*; Sutcliff, *Beowulf*; and Crossley-Holland, *Beowulf*) develop such a character as the bearer of news about Hrothgar's predicament.

32 A possibility that some Western children's versions have developed, notably Katz, *Beowulf*, and Rebecca Barnhouse, *The Coming of the Dragon* (New York: Random House Children's Books, 2010).

33 E.g., Crossley-Holland, *Beowulf*, 43; Hosford, *By His Own Might*, 57–8; Leighton, *Story of Beowulf*, 24–5; Morpurgo, *Beowulf*, 86–7; E.V. Sandys, *Beowulf*, illus. Rolf Klep (New York: Thomas Y. Crowell Co., 1941), 87; Ian Serraillier, *Beowulf the Warrior*, illus. Severin (New York: Henry Z. Walck, 1961), 46.

34 Julia Green, *Beowulf the Brave*, 38–45; Nye, *Bee Hunter*, 102–7.

35 Joshua Gray, *Beowulf: A Verse Adaptation with Young Readers in Mind*, illus. Sean Yates ([n.p.]: Zouch Six Shilling Press, 2012); Tessa Potter, *Beowulf and the Dragon*, illus. Simon Noyes (Crystal Lake, IL: Rigby Interactive Library, 1996).

36 Katz, *Beowulf*, 60; Rumford, *Beowulf*, [44]; Ralph Mason, *Beowulf* ([Diamond Creek, Victoria, Australia]: Books for Learning, 2007), 17; Barbara Leonie Picard, "Beowulf," illus. Eric Fraser, in *Tales of the British People* (New York: Criterion Books), 71.

37 Jones, *Lord of the Geats*, 156; Barnhouse, *Coming of the Dragon*, 216–17; Raven, *Beowulf*, 68; Riggs, *Story of Beowulf*, 79; Smith, *Story of Beowulf*, 51; Sutcliff, *Beowulf*, 89–90.

8 The Monsters and the Animals: Theriocentric *Beowulfs*

ROBERT STANTON

Adapting an orally performed poem of uncertain date, transmitted in a fragile, fire-damaged thousand-year-old manuscript, to the needs and interests of children and general readers from the Victorian era onward seems a dizzying high-wire act, bridging a temporal abyss while juggling multiple themes, literary forms, and audience ethos. But as the chapters in this volume amply show, the cultural afterlife of *Beowulf* has proven the poem to be unusually nimble, flexible, and highly responsive to movements and trends in morals, ideologies, and aesthetics. In part, this relative ease of adaptation springs from the fact that *Beowulf* was unknown to all but a small number of scholars until the middle of the nineteenth century, incorporating the ideologies of the Middle Ages, the Early Modern period, and the Enlightenment along the way.[1] The chronological hiatus of textual reception, as well as the antiquity of the epic poetic form, allowed an unusual degree of playful freedom when the poem was finally adapted for broader audiences in the later nineteenth century.

Linda Hutcheon considers the pleasure of "adaptations *as adaptations*" to be among their essential characteristics: "Part of this pleasure," she writes, "comes simply from repetition with variation, from the comfort of ritual combined with the piquancy of surprise. Recognition and remembrance are part of the pleasure (and risk) of experiencing an adaptation; so too is change ... For the reader, spectator, or listener, adaptation *as adaptation* is unavoidably a kind of intertextuality *if the receiver is acquainted with the adapted text*."[2] In the case of *Beowulf*, nineteenth- and twentieth-century readers' acquaintance with the Old English poem varied according to their age, class, and educational background, and the extent to which the poem was taught in secondary and higher educational environments. *Beowulf*'s reputation as a very old (perhaps even the oldest) English poem, its rapid recruitment as a national epic, and its increasingly canonical status inside and out-side the educational system all make it a remarkably useful transmitter of national, ethnic, class, and gender values, especially when adapted for younger audiences in the first decades of the twentieth century. As Anna Smol notes, "The Anglo-Saxons, those simple, remote, and un-learned peoples, were viewed in relation to sophisticated, modern, and learned English-speaking peoples as children are to adults. From here it is easy to slide into the belief that the literature of these cultural primitives is appropriate to those usually taken to be the simple and unlearned always in our midst – children."[3] This mutual mapping of a developmental process onto children and civilizations functioned in multiple, related ways: the child and the primitive needed to be tran-scended by adults and advanced civilizations, but also lived and felt closer to nature, in a way that more developed beings could learn from and emulate. In the world of children's literature, animals too were heavily deployed in this atavistic patterning: as we shall see, the equa-tion of animals, children, and noble primitives enabled a didactic struc-ture that both benefited and interrogated established notions of family, culture, and human uniqueness.[4]

Other writers in this volume address the ideological uses of *Beowulf* as a foundational text in projects of gender, race, and nation. In this chapter, I want to explore a specific structural strategy on the adapta-tion spectrum: the animalizing of one or more characters in the story. If casting early medieval English people as neotenous cultural actors facilitates the didactic deployment of the epic for young audiences, in-troducing animals into the narrative mix pushes the search for funda-mental cultural values one step further. In biological terms, neoteny is defined as the retention of juvenile characteristics in adult organisms, but Steve Baker and others have analysed an analogous cultural process whereby animations and illustrations of animals emphasize youthful traits in order to produce an emotional identification with the animal character.[5] In my reading of animalized *Beowulf* versions, I will suggest that the cultural, educational, and ideological work performed by each of these adaptations is enabled by an overlay of childlike identification and animal behaviour onto the pervasive idea of *Beowulf* as a prim-itive epic that embodies class, gender, and national ideals. Crucially, the deployment of animal characteristics in cultural projects is neither inherently progressive nor inherently reactionary: putting non-human characters into a familiar story can reinforce oppressive power struc-tures, but it can just as easily modify or interrogate those structures, generating identification and sympathy with both vulnerable humans and animals in unexpected ways. As we shall see, the versions that go most deeply into the fundamental animal natures of the characters offer much more in the way of progressive sympathy than those that rearrange human and animal natures in a purely ludic way.[6]

Investigating the functions and effects of animalization in *Beowulf* versions is both facilitated and complicated by the blurred categories of human, animal, and monster in the original poem. The descriptor "monster" – for which there is no close equivalent in the Old English – is, as Jeffrey Jerome Cohen argues, not so much a category as a "harbinger of category crisis," "embodying a relentless hybridity that resists assimilation into secure epistemologies."[7] Grendel's genealogy within the race of Cain excludes him from human society and civilization, but it also abjects the fratricidal impulse *within* humanity that the Cain and Abel story allegorizes. Numerous studies have examined the indeterminate boundary between Grendel the monster and Beowulf the human being; Andy Orchard has noted, in fact, that there is "something deeply human" about all three of the monsters in the poem.[8] The most frequent word used to describe Grendel, *aglæca*, is defined by the *Dictionary of Old English* as "awesome opponent, ferocious fighter," and is also used of the hero Siegfried in the poem, and crucially of Beowulf and the dragon as a plural pair (*ða aglæcean*, l. 2591).[9] Furthermore, several moments in the poem describe Grendel's state of mind, in ways that align easily with the concerns of human communities based on kin groups, mutual protection, and a strongly place-based identity. The most evocative of these is our introduction to Grendel via his pain at hearing the noise in Heorot, a building "[p]erhaps carved from land he once wandered":[10]

> Ða se ellengæst   earfoðlice
> þrage geþolode,   ...
> þæt he dogora gehwam   dream gehyrde
> hludne in healle.   (ll. 86–89a)

[Then the powerful spirit painfully endured the time when he heard every day the loud mirth in the hall.][11]

Our second glimpse into Grendel's perspective connects Grendel's pain and terror when he realizes the deadly strength of Beowulf's grasp.

We should be very wary of using the many heavily interiorized, even emotionalized scenes in Old English poetry to construct an implied subjectivity: such poetic patterning draws on an interplay between traditional material and poetic (re)working that is best apprehended through a detailed awareness of source material and generic expectation.[12] It would seem odd to imagine these early glimpses of Grendel evoking immediate, emotionally direct sympathy in the hearer, since they clearly refer to a deadly enemy who threatens not only every human in the immediate setting, but the material basis and metaphorical expression of the kinship society at the poem's heart. Thus it is all the more striking that Grendel's exile and his terrified desire to be at home (along with his mother's later grief at his death and desire for revenge) are expressed in language that draws immediately on the experience of a Germanic society with regional interests, regular experience of pain and fear, and highly developed mechanisms for punishing the taking of life.[13] The pain of Grendel's mother after his bloody death, her desire for revenge, and her tragic inability to pursue a proper feud further generate sympathy for a monster in straightforward human terms. The poem itself thus opens up significant areas of interrogation around the categories of human, animal, and monster, and with them, lines of potential identification and sympathy with the not fully human characters.

Somewhat surprisingly, then, few animalized versions of *Beowulf* do much to alter Grendel's fundamental, if hybrid, monstrous nature; for the most part, he and his mother remain quite close to the race-of-Cain monsters that they are in the poem. There are, however, a couple of notable exceptions. In 1994, Henry Beard published a delightful collection of poetic parodies called *Poetry for Cats*, featuring the settings or characters of canonical English poems reconfigured to include cats. The first poem in the volume, entitled "Grendel's Dog, from *Beocat*" and said to be authored by "the Old English Epic's Unknown Author's Cat," is a highly skilled imitation of Old English alliterative verse, complete with stressed alliterating syllables, mid-line caesuras, extensive apposition, and many clever kennings. The basic situation is that Beocat, greatest of the pussy-Geats and Hrothgar's pet, can hear Grendel's dog grunting outside on the other side of a latched door, and vents his heroic rage that they cannot do battle:

> Then boasted Beocat,   noble battle-kitten,
> Bane of barrow-bunnies,   bold seeker of nest-booty:
> "If hand of man unhasped   the heavy hall-door
> And freed me to frolic forth   to fight the fang-bearing fiend,
> I would lay the whelpling low   with lethal claw-blows."   (ll. 14–18)[14]

The humour of the parody arises from a number of formal and structural elements. First, the two pets serve as proxies for Hrothgar and Grendel, who are offstage throughout the poem; the resulting change of scale turns epic grandeur into domestic humour, as the stakes of the fight are seemingly lowered by human standards. (The fact that Grendel's dog is a Great Dane seems to collapse the cultural difference between Grendel and his antagonists, but the species-based cat/dog antagonism upholds it.) But deeper consideration of the narrative point of view shows just the opposite: the proverbial enmity between cats and dogs replaces the hostility between humans and monsters, but the domestication of the conflict minimizes its seriousness only if we regard the household as less important than a tribe or nation such as the Danes.

In reality, the fundamental unit of a kinship economy such as the one portrayed with nostalgia in *Beowulf* is in fact a household, and many of the struggles for land, power, political primacy, honour, and vengeance are played out on a familial level. Family connections, in fact, are emphasized in the opening two lines, which introduce the hero:

> Brave Beocat,   brood-kit of Ecgthmeow,
> Hearth-pet of Hrothgar   in whose high halls
> He mauled without mercy   many fat mice,
> Night did not find napping   nor snack-feasting.   (ll. 1–4)

The first poetic compound, "brood-kit," begins with an Old English word that is applied only to animals, but the appositive compound for the cat, "hearth-pet," opens with a very familiar word frequently used to describe retainers in a lord's household. The traditional image of a cat on a hearth provides gentle humour, but the primacy of the hearth, the cat's main function as a rodent killer, and the reliance of mutually dependent humans on heat and shelter, embodied by the hearth, put the cat very near the centre of the social system. Once the reader makes the comic leap into the cat's point of view, the struggle is deadly serious and the stakes are high. Grendel's dog, described in formulas that closely echo descriptions of Grendel in the poem, is a "hell-hound" (l. 11), "Deadly doom-mutt, dread demon-dog" (l. 13), "fang-bearing fiend" (l. 17), "grim ghoul-pooch" (l. 24); to the cat, the dog is demonically dangerous.

The cat's situation is made even more serious by the negligent absence of humans from the poem: the door remains latched because the humans are snoring soundly after heavy drinking ("Nose-music of men snoring mead-hammered in the wine-hall," l. 21). Like the sleeping Danes in *Beowulf*, whom the Geatish hero hints are lax in their guardianship of the hall, these people are failing to deal with an imminent menace, and the animal world becomes the entire world of the poem.

Stories for young readers frequently feature an emergency situation in which children must act in the face of negligence or obliviousness on the part of adults, a scene replicated here by domestic pets and unavailable humans; once again, the child/primitive/animal is closer to the urgent, elemental heart of the situation than the more developed beings who are supposedly in charge.

The end of the poem shifts its genre from epic to elegy, as the cat laments his inability to act, concluding with a formula reminiscent of *The Wanderer*: "Thus spoke the mouse-shredder ..." (l. 25). A key element links this short piece with many of the other animal adaptations discussed here, namely, animal ethology. The actual behaviour of a hunting cat ("hunter of hall-pests," l. 25) shares crucial features with the warrior ethos of *Beowulf*, such as bravery, lack of mercy, nocturnal alertness, and wariness. These fundamental points of connection, humorously depicted in the feline and canine world, implicitly reflect back the animalization inherent in the warrior ethos (consider the kenning of the hero's name, "Bee-Wolf" or "bear," according to a traditional scholarly view, and the totemic boar helmets referred to in the poem). By playfully transposing a story about humans and monsters into the world of domestic pets, "Grendel's Dog" invites the reader to attend to the functions of species, age, and ethnic differences in a narrative that explores the working of conflict, triumph, and loss within and among kinship groups.

One other animalized adaptation of *Beowulf* centers its species rearrangement in the domestic sphere, creating a brilliant mashup with a canonical children's book that uses a family setting to dramatize the conflicts of youth, death, independence, and heroism. The American artist James Rumford, after rewriting and illustrating *Beowulf* for young readers in 2007,[15] decided to use the story to rehabilitate a tale that had frightened him very much as a child: Beatrix Potter's *The Tale of Peter Rabbit*. In an Afterword to the resulting book, *Beo-Bunny*, Rumford explains that both narratives have two fundamental things in common: they are "very, very English" and "very, very scary": as a child, he identified closely with Peter Rabbit and cast Mr. McGregor in the image of a mean neighbor.[16] He goes on to locate an even more fundamental thematic connection:

> Both tales deal with facing fear. Beowulf, a real hero, of course, never backs down, and, in the end, he perishes. Peter Rabbit starts off fearless, and is ready to face ole Mr. McGregor, but in the end, being just a bunny, he runs back to the safety of his mother's arms. I guess I wrote this book to give Peter Rabbit a bit more Beowulf gumption.

The reader is thus alerted to the fact that the rabbits in this book are not going to depend on stereotypical bunny behaviour such as shyness or fearfulness (when Potter wrote her book around the turn of the twentieth century, the slang meaning of *rabbit*, "a person likened to a rabbit, typically in being timid or ineffectual," was current).[17] Rumford's brave Peter, drawing on the strain of individualism and family subversion in children's literature, disobeys the strict rules of family behaviour and is rewarded for his heroic misbehaviour.

The merger of *Beowulf* and *The Tale of Peter Rabbit* invites detailed comparison at every point of text and image. At the audience level, *Beo-Bunny* is explicitly labelled twice (once on a flyleaf and once on the back cover) as "not for children," a humorously disingenuous claim given the author's rehabilitative purpose as stated in the afterword, and the familiar device of a label like "not for children" being tailor-made to draw in a readership of children and their parents. Furthermore, the close resemblance of Rumford's illustrations to Potter's invites comparisons of the degree of anthropomorphism in the tale. Potter's rabbits are variously clad: in the first coloured illustration, the entire Rabbit family is unclothed, but Peter's mother subsequently wears a blue dress and an apron, while his siblings Flopsy, Mopsy, and Cotton-tail are naked throughout, except for some short red capes that they wear on their permitted excursions (although they shed them when they get down to the work of gathering blackberries). Peter himself wears his signature blue jacket and two shoes, in which he walks bipedally; after he loses the shoes on his adventure, he runs on four feet and makes better time, but loses his jacket while wriggling out from under Mr. McGregor's sieve. While he is trapped au naturel inside Mr. McGregor's garden wall, two illustrations contrast sharply: in one, he is a very naturalistic rabbit in a wary attitude, sitting up on his hind legs with his forelegs in front of him, and in the other, "unable to get out of the door of Mr. McGregor's garden, [he is] an anatomically correct, unclothed rabbit in a human posture of grief," one paw pushing on the door, one held to his mouth in anguish, and a single tear running down his furry cheek.[18] Rumford standardizes the rabbits' attire so that they are always clothed: the mother wears her blue dress and apron, the siblings their red capes, and Peter his blue jacket, later supplemented by a paper helmet and a wooden sword. None of the rabbits in *Beo-Bunny* is ever unclothed: the opening establishing portrait of the family contrasts explicitly with the pre-clothing bunnies at the beginning of *The Tale of Peter Rabbit*. Furthermore, the fact that Peter never loses either his jacket or his warm helmet reinforces the contrast between Potter's fearful, vulnerable adventurer and Rumford's focused, vengeful warrior.

True to his declared intent, Rumford presents the Rabbits not as a semi-anthropomorphized family with timid, stereotypically rabbity habits, but as a clothed clan victimized by a murderous race of enemies. In Potter's original, the mother warns her children not to go into Mr. McGregor's garden because "your Father had an accident there; he was put in a pie by Mrs. McGregor." In Rumford's version, rendered in brilliant neo-Old English followed by typographically subordinated translations, the McGregors are immediately identified as an alien race bent on killing rabbits:

> McGregor wæs an orcen. Orcen McGregor and his wif wæron æfer hungrig for haran-cistam. Dæg æfter dæge, Orcen McGregor betræpte haran, and his wif boc haran-cistan.

> McGregor was an ogre. Ogre McGregor and his wife were ever hungry for rabbit pie. Day after day, Ogre McGregor trapped rabbits, and his wife baked rabbit pies.[19]

A vivid illustration dramatizes the effect of the carnage, showing rabbit women and children mourning the loss of a family member. Peter, inspired by the tale of *Beowulf*, dons his helmet and sword and vows revenge, although his mother forbids this out of fear. Peter kills Mr. McGregor with his teeth, Mrs. McGregor traps him by his throat, and he claws her eyes out, not only avenging his family members but preventing future ravages. Bloodstained and still in his blue jacket, he shouts a victory chant:

> "Ho-ho-o-o-o-o! Orcen McGregor and his wif earon dead, and Ic **eom** Beowulf, strong and beald!"

> "Ho-ho-o-o-o! Ogre McGregor and his wife are dead, and I **am** Beowulf, strong and bold."

Finally, he is then lauded by the other rabbits in a song celebrating his achievement and dubbing him "Beo Bana," "Beo the Slayer." The illustrations depicting Peter's killing of the McGregors and his ensuing celebration are unapologetically bloody, evoking the graphic language of Beowulf's fights with the Grendelkin and departing notably from most children's books, especially those for very young readers (see fig. 8.1).

The shifts in species orientation and anthropomorphic orientation in this mashup are dizzying. The McGregors, who are pictorially human but narratively ogres, kill the rabbits, who are pictorially and

Figure 8.1. Peter attacking, from James Rumford, *Beo-Bunny*.

narratively rabbits, but – thanks to their situation at the centre of the narrative and the conventions of children's literature – strongly human-identified. When Peter vanquishes the ogres, he and his clan celebrate in ritual song that evokes human tribes in general, and Old English heroic formulas in particular. Significantly, the tale distorts the central motif of civilization and incursion in both *Beowulf* and *The Tale of Peter Rabbit*. A thoroughly humanistic rewriting of Beatrix Potter might cast the McGregors as Danes trying to live their human lives and the Rabbits as the Grendelkin enraged by their exclusion from the fruits of human society; instead, the locus of clan-based civilization is the Rabbits' arboreal home, and the McGregors are the alien outsiders. They seem like wild animals in that they kill merely to satisfy their bodily appetites, but they are othered as ogres in that they are (by rabbit standards) huge, unnaturally strong, and exceedingly ugly.

Furthermore, Rumford's version thoroughly revises and rehabilitates the somewhat occluded psychological element in Potter's story, namely, the trauma of Peter's father's death at the hands of the McGregors and his mother's terror that he will fall victim to the same fate. Potter's original illustration depicting the mother's warning shows Flopsy, Mopsy, and Cotton-tail paying due attention while Peter turns defiantly away, clearly determined to break the rules. Wynn William Yarbrough has noted the Freudian element in Peter's defiance: "[T]he escape must take place, in the mythical sense, where domesticity can't intrude ... where the father was lost."[20] True to his stated purpose in the afterword, Rumford casts Peter as a brave avenger from early in the story. No living or dead father is mentioned, though it can be assumed that the absent Mr. Rabbit was among the McGregors' victims. Peter mourns with the others, dons his war gear (and is mocked by the other rabbits for doing so), and goes straight for the kill. Like a Germanic warrior-hero or exile, he reserves his speech, saving his agency for strong and decisive action.

Like Potter, Rumford removes his hero from domestic space as he copes with loss, but by removing the Freudian trauma of the lost father he elevates Peter's achievement above an individual's revenge of a kinsman to make him the saviour of his entire clan. He acts both unselfishly (to save his kinfolk) and selfishly (to achieve glory for himself), aligning him through and through with his literary inspiration and giving him "a bit more Beowulf gumption." Of all the versions discussed here, *Beo-Bunny* most pointedly demonstrates the relativism of civilization: the McGregors' socio-economic arrangements, based on consuming the flesh of their neighbours, constitute a continual tragedy for the rabbit family with whom, by narrative and illustrative convention, the reader identifies. Taking its cue perhaps from the uncertain, semi-human status of *Beowulf*'s monsters, *Beo-Bunny* extracts the fundamental structure and meaning of the heroic ethos but rearranges its species-based assumptions: by parodying two genres, the book vividly dramatizes the fundamental process of defending one's kin, across blurred species lines.

Another animalized version of *Beowulf* follows the story quite closely and retains a Grendel very like the Old English poem's monster, but like *Beo-Bunny*, realigns species boundaries in ways that fundamentally question the human-centred configuration of the heroic genre. Brad Strickland's *Be a Wolf!* (1997) novelizes an unfilmed episode from the television show *Wishbone*, which ran on PBS Kids from 1995 to 1998.[21] The show features a family of a single mother, two young children, and a very well-read Jack Russell terrier, the eponymous Wishbone. Each week, a crisis in his human family's life reminds our hero of a theme or plot from one of his favourite literary classics; the domestic drama, featuring Wishbone as observer and/or helper, then unfolds in alternating sequences with a dramatization of the work in question, featuring Wishbone as a character (occasionally the hero, but more often in a co-starring role such as the hero's best friend). Filmed adaptations with medieval material include "Bone of Arc," "Sniffing the Gauntlet" (*Ivanhoe*), "The Hunch-Dog of Notre Dame," "Paw Prints of Thieves" (*Robin Hood*), and "War of the Noses" (*The Black Arrow*).

The frame story of *Be a Wolf!* involves Wishbone's human companion, Joe, losing his backpack, probably at the hands of a neighbour, Mrs. Grindle, who has a reputation as a terrifying old lady, and who also has a fearsome bulldog. Joe is very nervous about trying to get it back because "she's a real monster" (17). The situation reminds Wishbone of the story of *Beowulf*, and after some basic historical information, we learn that "it's a heroic tale. It shows you that sometimes you have to face terrible odds with great courage. Sometimes it's just not enough to be a tame dog. You have to listen to the call of the wild! You have to be like your remote ancestors! Sometimes you have to be a wolf!" (18). The theme of courage plays out in Joe's story when he finally faces Mrs. Grindle, who turns out to be a lonely widow who is reclusive only because she is sad. Joe's family befriends her, and her bulldog turns out to be a total sweetheart who becomes pals with Wishbone. The blandness of the frame story only highlights the vivid rewriting of *Beowulf* that follows, featuring Wishbone as the Geatish hero with the same genealogy as the human version (son of "Ectheow") and the same mission to help the Danes, both to return a favour done by Hrothgar to his father and for fame and glory.

Of the animalized *Beowulf* versions, *Be a Wolf!* is, unsurprisingly, the most thoroughly didactic: PBS Kids and Scholastic Books both have a mission to entertain while imparting valuable life lessons. In this case, as Wishbone's introductory description indicates, showing courage is the main lesson to be learned,[22] but the dog's understanding of this theme and the subsequent narrative emphasis rest on an atavism that reveals just how thoroughly the canine rearrangement affects the ethical and historical setting of the story. Wishbone's mention of "the call of the wild" and being "like your remote ancestors" – in other words, "be a wolf!" – casts personal courage as a deep-rooted, species-based imperative, activated by a willed connection with primitive ancestors. Wishbone's invocation of his feral substructure slyly situates the adaptation alongside its obvious parallel story, Jack London's *Call of the*

Wild, in which a dog exhibits strength and loyalty both inside and outside the world of human civilization. In the end, the reference turns out to be an in-joke, which readers of Jack London at any age will get: although Wishbone/Beowulf does indeed draw on his wild-dog attributes to win fights and glory, he remains a helper in a human world. Whereas Buck from *Call of the Wild* finally merges with his feral nature outside the human world, the warrior Wishbone more closely resembles London's White Fang, helping people by being a dog.[23]

The didacticism of *Be a Wolf!* can be usefully compared with early English versions for children in which courage is a fundamentally English (and implicitly male) virtue, proposing *Beowulf* as an imitable model for young imperial subjects.[24] But recasting human virtue in a canine character has more complex implications for the moral world of heroism than this primitivist reading implies. The device of replacing a human hero with a dog holds an obvious appeal for children's books, films, or television shows, since children identify so readily with animals and their perceived qualities, especially through their shared identity as relatively innocent, vulnerable beings.[25] As we have seen with *Beo-Bunny*, however, vulnerability can quickly be transmuted into other personal, psychological, and cultural attributes through unexpected narrative strategies. Beneath the plot similarities of the Wishbone series lie more fundamental connections between the dog and the literary characters. Thanks to the highly skilled dog actor on television and the numerous illustrations in the novelization, Wishbone's identity as a small, scrappy Jack Russell terrier can never be elided or forgotten, prompting us to consider the qualities and characteristics he shares with the characters he portrays in the adaptations.

A prime example crops up in the very first fight in the story, with Grendel in Heorot. The human warrior forgoes the use of weapons in fairness to Grendel, who does not use them either; the canine hero does use a sword elsewhere in the story, but here he makes the same vow, and as a result he fights much more like a dog. Sinking his teeth into Grendel's arm, he clings on doggedly as the monster tries to shake him off with increasing violence, ultimately tearing his arm completely off. When he fights Grendel's mother in the mere-cave, he uses a sword like the human Beowulf, but to acquire the effective weapon with the ancient runes on it, he has to leap onto the mantel in a very canine fashion, grabbing hold with his two front paws, suspensefully scrabbling with his hind legs, finally obtaining purchase, and seizing the hilt in his jaw.

Wishbone also does dog things and has dog feelings that are not strictly necessary to the heroic plot structure, but which are well integrated into the story. He likes warm, dry places, loves his dinner, and craves treats: at the feast after Grendel is killed, "Beowulf was pre-sented with a great helping of venison, served to him in a dish with his name on it. He licked his chops and dug in" (53). The dog's heroic nature, in fact, is very much of a piece with his natural canine instincts and desires: after fighting Grendel, he falls into a well-earned sleep, "and his dreams were wonderful ones. Dreams of victory in battle, dreams of great postwar festivities, dreams of juicy bones and of dig-ging holes filled his head. He dreamed of chasing rabbits, of swimming in quiet pools, of running free and strong under a full moon, howling his wolfish joy" (56). In addition, specifically canine details are added to the story, most obviously, a good deal of sniffing: Beowulf identifies all three monsters by their scent, and in the final episode the dragon sniffs him out before their fatal battle. *Beowulf* is famously rich in visual detail and also in aural effects, especially during the fights, but lacking in ol-factory references; in this respect, the novelization uses the substitution of a canine hero to expand and enrich the sensory world of the poem.[26]

Our hero, then, undertakes the same deeds as his human counter-part by drawing on archetypal canine traits such as loyalty, bravery, perseverance, and skill at tracking. What relationship can we perceive between the human and canine versions of these qualities? Writing about the rhetoric of animal representation, Steve Baker proposes two closely related but distinct modes of animal behaviour: theriomor-phism (an image in which a person has the form of an animal) and the-rianthropism (an image combining animal and human forms): "Where animal imagery is used to make statements about human identity, *metonymic representations of selfhood will typically take theriomorphic form, whereas metaphoric representations of otherness will typically take therian-thropic form.*"[27] In the case of a dog protagonist substituting for a human hero, we could perhaps understand Wishbone as therianthropic, and his canine virtues as metaphors for the human virtues inherent in the warrior ethic. But the thorough integration of his deeds into his own dog nature argues much more strongly for a metonymic comparison, whereby specific characteristics are more or less fully shared by hu-mans and animals. The addition of sniffing notwithstanding, the dog Beowulf does the things that he does by drawing on functionally iden-tical traits such as loyalty and perseverance; in this respect, Strickland's simplifying atavism (be a wolf!) is not so much the regressive primitiv-ism of early jingoistic readings of *Beowulf*, but rather an invocation of characteristics seen as positive and useful across species boundaries.

Traits shared by human and non-human animals raise a challenge to those who would argue against anthropomorphism in representation as a fundamentally humanistic tendency that demeans non-humans and robs them of agency.[28] John Simons, citing the work of Jeffrey Moussaieff Masson, notes that "the non-human experience can be made accessible by an anthropomorphism that operates through the assumption that similar kinds of behaviour when exhibited in both humans and non-humans are the result of a shared set of emotional responses."[29] He notes the example of a dog who, after the death of a human companion, mopes, refuses to eat, and even sits on the human's grave: "it is not fantastically obtuse," says Simons, "to suggest that the dog has lost a loved one and is in mourning just as a human might be in the same circumstances."[30] The closing sequence of *Be a Wolf!* presents the hero's death as only superficially human: in his final minutes, the canine Beowulf tells (human) Wiglaf, "I hear my ancestors calling me now, from somewhere out on that dark sea of eternity" (129). Whether dogs have a concept of eternity or not, the introduction of the story has already established Beowulf's ancestors as wolves, from whom he has drawn his strength and valour; thus, in the story's terms, we are now in a world demarcated by the bounds of canine ethology.

Don Punchatz's final illustration in the *Be a Wolf!* Beowulf story makes this point even more strongly: the mortally wounded Beowulf lies immobile while Wiglaf grieves in the background. Early book illustrations of Beowulf's death scene canonized a visual pattern in which a visibly grieving Wiglaf is close to the hero, but not close enough to touch him; in pictures like these, the vital homosocial bonds between the king/ loyal thane pair, and within heroic groups more broadly, are striking in both their vivid immediacy and their "displacement and aversion."[31] By using this conventionalized iconography, the artist draws Wishbone/Beowulf even more fully into the human world, associating the character with familiar Beowulfs from previous illustrated versions. In this respect, any differences (humorous or not) that might exist between Wishbone and his human co-stars are drawn into the fully human, male pattern of difference between Beowulf and Wiglaf: they are emotionally linked and physically close, but do not touch. At the same time, the hero lies as an injured dog might lie, clearly in pain, his injured limbs clearly visible underneath him. His gaze, directed at the water and the cliffs beyond, returns to the atavistic theme, closely following the text passage in which he hears his ancestors calling him "from somewhere out on that dark sea of eternity." Representing the dying hero in his fully canine form, combined with Wiglaf's traditional posture of grief, again draws on a shared world of loyalty, bravery, and vulnerability across species lines. Both Wishbone and *Beo-Bunny* go to the heart of the humanimal paradox: fundamentally shared values, especially the very basic ones of survival (on an individual, family, and species level). Those that are metonymic to survival (bravery, perseverance, desire for fame) span seemingly obvious boundaries, and their evocation with animal actors calls into question the literary privileging of such qualities as exclusively human.

I want to conclude by examining two canonical works that are well known in their own right but rarely considered in relation to *Beowulf*. Both works preserve fundamental aspects of the poem, especially the deep structure of a locus of civilization being threatened by a jealous and excluded figure, who must be either killed or (comically) integrated into the social world. In both cases, the radical change of setting and the integration of additional elements not present in *Beowulf* end up highlighting the fertile, archaic power of the central problem of Grendel: his misery and rage at his outsider status and his violent resistance to the civilizing human centre represented by the Danes' Heorot. In both cases, as in the other adaptations at hand, the animalizing of certain characters asks, and partially answers, important questions about power differentials and institutional systems across species boundaries.

Dr. Seuss's 1957 book *How the Grinch Stole Christmas* playfully complicates the motif of the outsider monster; Robert Schichler is the only scholar, to my knowledge, who has examined the similarities between Grendel and the Grinch.[32] Schichler notes the resemblance of the initial *gr-* sound in each of their names, as well as the *Oxford English Dictionary*'s two definitions of *grinch* (a verb meaning "to make a harsh grating noise" and a past participle *grinched* meaning "tightly closed, clenched") and the range of possible meanings for *Grendel* (possibly derived from words related to "grind," "evil/injury," "bar/bolt," "bellow," or "sand/bottom of a body of water"). Piotr Sadowski has uncovered a range of Middle English words that could certainly relate to Grendel or the Grinch in various ways: 1. to feel with the hands (grasp, grope) 2. vegetation (growth, green) 3. holes, pits, or graves (grave, grotto) 4. crushing or grinding (grind, gravel, grist) 5. terror, fear, anger, hatred (grim, grisly, gruesome).[33] Further examples in popular culture might include Oscar the Grouch from Sesame Street and the Groke from the Swedish book and comic series *The Moomins*. (The Groke is an uncanny character with blank, staring eyes and a frosty atmosphere that freezes everything near her. She constantly seeks the company of others, but is generally rejected and has to dwell in an icy cave in the mountains like the Grinch's lair on Mt. Crumpit.) An even more pervasive example is the grue, a predatory monster that appeared originally in Jack Vance's *Dying Earth* series of fantasy novels, was popularized by the interactive fiction computer game *Zork*, and recurs frequently in subsequent games.[34]

The Grinch, a monstrous pink-eyed creature who lives atop Mt. Crumpit within earshot of Whoville, hates the smaller Whos and their Christmas celebrations for reasons that are purely speculative:

> It *could* be his head wasn't screwed on just right.
> It *could* be, perhaps, that his shoes were too tight.
> But I think that the most likely reason of all
> May have been that his heart was two sizes too small.

A further hint is given on the following page, when he frowns at "the warm lighted windows below in their town"; this separation from Who civilization is highlighted by the illustration of his cold, icy cave. He is especially maddened by the "noise, noise, noise, noise!" of the revelling Whos, recalling Grendel's pain at hearing the Danish festivities in Heorot. The poet hints strongly that Grendel is enraged not only by the general noise and glee, but specifically by the content of the song sung by a scop in the hall, a performance that celebrates God's creation of the world, and especially the favoured place of humans in it, figured by the warm, joyous hall from which Grendel is excluded as a member of the race of Cain. The question of species and identity, then, will be crucial to drawing any sort of parallels between Grendel among the Danes and the Grinch among the Whos. The Grinch's nature is uncertain: he somewhat resembles the Whos in his general shape, although he is shaggier and more unkempt. Ron Howard's 2000 movie version tells his backstory: he was adopted as a baby, but because of his unusual appearance he was ostracized and eventually had to retreat to his mountain cave.

The Grinch, as a monstrous figure, is initially animalized in that unlike the Whos, he wears no clothes, a clear marker of civilization. His plan to spoil Christmas for the Whos, however, begins with his brainwave of dressing up as Santa Claus. Even very young readers will notice the comic thinness of the disguise, which in the end, perhaps fortunately, is called on only to fool a sleepy two-year-old child. Throughout the story, and especially after he dons the Santa outfit, the Grinch is more of a hybrid than any of the other animals or semi-animals I have been discussing. As he is despoiling Whoville, his appearance is a grotesque combination of the familiar and the evil: Seuss's illustrations brilliantly juxtapose the iconic jauntiness of Santa's garb with the Grinch's malevolent grin. After he is born again and celebrates Christmas with the Whos, he resembles them much more closely, a connection emphasized in the final illustration by the red colouring of his Santa clothes, the bow in Cindy Lou Who's hair, and a bowl on the festive table. The same picture shows the final stage of his integration into Who society, as he carves the traditional Roast Beast. Significantly, in order to purloin the Whos' Christmas gifts and trimmings, the Grinch makes use of animal labour, namely, his abused and miserable-looking dog, Max, whose tied-on antler mimics his master's unconvincing Santa get-up. Throughout the story, the Grinch relies on the domination of other animals to achieve his ends and express his identity: before his conversion he uses Max to move his sleigh around, and afterwards he presides over the carving of the Roast Beast. Like the dog-headed Cynocephali of fabulous medieval travel lore, the beast is humanized by his mastery of other creatures.[35]

The last, and perhaps most elusive, analogue of the Grendel and Beowulf story reaches even more deeply into the human organization of race and power. Rudyard Kipling's *Rikki-Tikki-Tavi* originally appeared as a magazine piece in 1893 and formed part of *The Jungle Book* collection published the following year.[36] The main human characters are an English family living in a bungalow in India: a mother, father, and their young son Teddy. The Grendel-like antagonists are two snakes, the black cobra Nag and his wife Nagaina, who are explicitly threatened by the English family in their indigenous space. Nagaina puts the crisis starkly around the midpoint of the story:

> "When the house is emptied of people," said Nagaina to her husband, "he will have to go away, and then the garden will be our own again ... When there were no people in the bungalow, did we have any mongoose in the garden? So long as the bungalow is empty, we are king and queen of the garden; and remember that as soon as our eggs in the melon-bed hatch (as they may to-morrow), our children will need room and quiet."[37]

Nag and Nagaina clearly parallel Grendel and his mother here, and the mongoose Rikki-tikki-tavi, the Beowulf figure, kills them in the same order (male first, female second).

There is much ambiguity here: as in all Kipling's *Jungle Book* and *Just So Stories*, the self-interest of the enemy animals is front and centre, and whatever evil they possess resides purely in their opposition to the heroes of the stories, whether they are other animals, humans, or the animalized human Mowgli. The fact that Nag and Nagaina are serpents might encourage us to associate them with the race of Cain, and the garden setting might reinforce this, as might Nagaina's hubris in referring to Nag and herself as the king and queen. The mongoose, of course, is also an indigenous animal, and not without his own interests, but his hero status in the story arises from the fact that he protects the human family by not only killing the snakes but also crushing their eggs, which he is clever enough to know is necessary for permanent freedom from danger.

The colonial politics are clear: Rikki-tikki is a good Indian subject who is fully integrated into the British family and hence fights on their side, and the cobras are bad indigenous animals who want to retain their own patrimony, which they have held since before the English family arrived. Rikki-tikki's relationship to the English inhabitants of the bungalow is solidly established early in the story (see fig. 8.2) when the narrator provides a rationale for his ready integration into the family:

> Early in the morning Rikki-tikki came to early breakfast in the verandah riding on Teddy's shoulder, and they gave him banana and some boiled egg; and he sat on all their laps one after the other, because every well-brought-up mongoose always hopes to be a house-mongoose some day and have rooms to run about in, and Rikki-tikki's mother (she used to live in the General's house at Segowlee) had carefully told Rikki what to do if ever he came across white men.[38]

Kipling emphasizes the traditional enmity between snakes and mongooses, in a characteristically naturalizing move that occludes these colonial politics. There are two possible responses to this naturalizing impulse. First, in historical terms, it might remind us of the way colonial powers exploited national, tribal, and clan rivalries within the borders of their colonies to their own advantage. Second, it is conspicuous that Rikki-tikki, as an individual rather than a member of the mongoose class, never appears to have any personal animus against the cobras – he simply recognizes their threat to his new home, which has been furthered and fostered by his English masters.

Animal behaviour is thus deployed in a familial and colonial project: in a sense, Kipling's animal fable validates hegemonic culture in the same way that the *Beowulf* poet's animalization and monsterization of the race of Cain validates the inherent virtue of the Danish kingdom (which, despite its paganism, is paradigmatic via its Germanic kinship with the English producers and consumers of the poem). Here, the archetypal role of the snake returns to the forefront: if Nag and Nagaina are viewed through the tradition of serpents as biblical enemies, then their vanquishment reinforces, in a religious mode, the rightness of English rule in India. By bearing in mind the biblical stigmatization of the Grendelkin as the race of Cain, we can see Kipling's anglicizing project drawing deeply on the cultural and political work already done by an epic that validated Germanic racial glory in a Christian context.

Figure 8.2. Rikki-tikki on Teddy's shoulder, by W.H. Drake, from Kipling, "Rikki-tikki-tavi," p. 4.

A fundamental project of much Critical Animal Studies is to take up boundaries between humans and non-human animals and blur them, call them into question, deconstruct them, historicize them, and use them to expose a power structure that needs to remain hidden to work properly. But, like literature in general, and children's literature in particular, blurring boundaries has no inherent ethical valence; it can, in fact, simply help each text to pursue the project it wants to do anyway. *Beo-Bunny*'s success in calling attention to the non-inevitable arrangements of kin groups and modern families results partly from its deft integration of two genres across species lines, but even more from the author's stated goal of rehabilitating the system of rewards and punishments attending a familiar animal character. *Be a Wolf!*, specifically because it is the most didactic text in the group, has the clearest platform to manipulate the narrative to ask fundamental questions, especially to young readers accustomed to animal characters. What differences would it make if Beowulf were a dog? By introducing a species boundary into the story, and by exploring the shared heroic elements across that boundary, this canine adaptation shifts the traditionally anthropocentric alignment of epic poetry to reach humans across another divide: that of the child and the adult. Kipling, on the other hand, uses animal characters in a more obviously human structure, and relates their characteristics and behaviour to illuminate other significant relations in his fiction (especially British and Indians in a colonial situation). At its best, the animalizing of characters in a familiar, canonical human epic enables genuinely new kinds of cultural work that draw deeply on the world of the original text, as well as on the history of the various genres that came after it, and the audience and purpose of the new version. The resulting shift in identities and power relationships is made thoroughly possible by the traditionally heavy use of animals in all genres, whether as monstrous others, sympathetic surrogates, or many things in between.

NOTES

1 The first edition of the poem was by the Danish scholar Grímur Jónsson Thorkelin in 1815, and the first complete English translation was by John Kemble in 1837. The 1880s and 1890s saw a considerable surge in popular translations and adaptations for children. See Andrew Prescott, "The Electronic Beowulf and Digital Restoration," in *The Electronic Beowulf*, ed. Kevin Kiernan, 4th ed. (Louisville: University of Kentucky; London: British Library, 2016), at http://ebeowulf.uky.edu/; Marijane Osborne, "Annotated List of Beowulf Translations" (2003) originally published online by the Arizona Center for Medieval and Renaissance Studies but removed in 2019, and now being republished in *Medieval Perspectives* 35 (2021).
2 Linda Hutcheon, *A Theory of Adaptation*, 2nd ed. (New York: Routledge, 2013), 4, 21 (emphasis in original).
3 Anna Smol, "Heroic Ideology and the Children's *Beowulf*," *Children's Literature* 22 (1994): 93.
4 Tess Cosslett, *Talking Animals in British Fiction, 1786–1914* (Aldershot, UK: Ashgate, 2006), 126.
5 Steve Baker, *Picturing the Beast: Animals, Identity, and Representation* (Urbana: University of Illinois Press, 2001), 181–4; Stephen Jay Gould, "Mickey Mouse Meets Konrad Lorenz," *Natural History* 88 (1979): 30–6; Elizabeth Lawrence, "In the Mick of Time: Reflections on Disney's Ageless Mouse," *Journal of Popular Culture* 20 (1986): 65–72.

6 Two animalized versions that I do not discuss here are Bruce Edward Blackistone's alliterative poem *Beowabbit* (Takoma Park, MD: Centa Publishing, 1977 and 1983), whose parody involves human characters with animal characteristics; and "Brainwulf," in *Animaniacs Featuring Pinky and the Brain,* no. 49, written by Jeff Suess and drawn by Walter Carzon and Horacio Ottolini (New York: DC Comics, June 1999), a comic book tie-in with the television show *Animaniacs* that injects Pinky and the Brain as trickster characters into the *Beowulf* story.

7 Jeffrey Jerome Cohen, "Monster Culture: Seven Theses," in *Monster Theory: Reading Culture,* ed. Jeffrey Jerome Cohen (Minneapolis: University of Minnesota Press, 1996), 6–7; Jeffrey Jerome Cohen, "The Promise of Monsters," in *The Ashgate Research Companion to Monsters and the Monstrous,* ed. Asa Simon Mittman with Peter J. Dendle (Farnham, Surrey: Ashgate, 2013), 452.

8 Andy Orchard, *Pride and Prodigies: Studies in the Monsters of the Beowulf-Manuscript* (Cambridge: D.S. Brewer, 1995; reprint, Toronto: University of Toronto Press, 2003), 29.

9 Angus Cameron, Ashley Crandell Amos, Antonette diPaolo Healey, Haruko Momma, et al., eds., *Dictionary of Old English,* online edition (Toronto: Dictionary of Old English Project, 2007–), s.v. *aglæca.* Available at http://tapor.library.utoronto.ca/doe/.

10 Cohen, "Promise of Monsters," 456.

11 My translation. References to *Beowulf* are to R.D. Fulk, Robert E. Bjork, and John D. Niles, eds., *Klaeber's Beowulf,* 4th ed. (Toronto: University of Toronto Press, 2008).

12 See Britt Mize, *Traditional Subjectivities: The Old English Poetics of Mentality* (Toronto: University of Toronto Press, 2013), 3–22 and 237–9.

13 *Beowulf,* ll. 749–53, 761–3. Further on the blurred lines between humans and monsters in the poem, see Katherine O'Brien O'Keeffe, "*Beowulf,* Lines 702b–836: Transformations and the Limits of the Human," *Texas Studies in Literature and Language* 23 (1981): 484–94; Philip Cardew, "Grendel: Bordering the Human," in *The Shadow-Walkers: Jacob Grimm's Mythology of the Monstrous,* ed. T.A. Shippey (Tempe: Arizona Center for Medieval and Renaissance Studies, 2005), 189–205; Renée Trilling, "Beyond Abjection: The Problem with Grendel's Mother Again," *Parergon* 24 (2007): 1–20.

14 Henry Beard, "Grendel's Dog," in *Poetry for Cats* (New York: Villard Books, 1994), 2. References given parenthetically by line number.

15 James Rumford, *Beowulf: A Hero's Tale Retold* (Boston: Houghton Mifflin, 2007).

16 James Rumford, *Beo-Bunny* (Honolulu: Mānoa Press, 2012). The book is unpaginated, so no page references will be given in subsequent citations.

17 Beatrix Potter, *The Tale of Peter Rabbit* (London: Frederick Warne and Co., 1902), to which my comments on Potter's illustrations below refer. The

story was originally written in 1893. *Oxford English Dictionary*, online edition (Oxford: Oxford University Press, 2016), www.oed.com, s.v. *rabbit, n.1.*

18 Cosslett, *Talking Animals*, 154.

19 Rumford explains in the afterword that since the word *pie* is not Old English, he used the earliest term for a pie that he could find, the early fourteenth-century *coffin*, meaning "box." He then joined the Old English words *hara* "hare" and *cist* "chest, box" to make a word for rabbit pie. The accompanying illustration of the McGregors draws on Rumford's memory of the scary neighbour from his childhood.

20 Wynn William Yarbrough, *Masculinity in Children's Animal Stories, 1888–1928* (Jefferson, NC: McFarland, 2011), 38.

21 Brad Strickland, *Be a Wolf!*, illus. Don Punchatz (New York: Scholastic, 1997); *Wishbone* (PBS Kids, 1995–8). References are given parenthetically.

22 In the frame story, courage is the only strong parallel to *Beowulf*: the themes of loyalty to friends and family and the desire for fame are very lightly sketched in, if at all.

23 I am indebted to Bruce Gilchrist for this observation.

24 Smol, "Heroic Ideology," 90–3.

25 The metaphorical equation of children and animals has been criticized as part of a harmful anthropomorphizing project by Lisa Rowe Fraustino, "The Rights and Wrongs of Anthropomorphism in Picture Books," in *Ethics and Children's Literature*, ed. Claudia Mills (Farnham, UK: Ashgate, 2014), 153–5.

26 In the poem, there is only one disputed occurrence of smelling: in l. 2288, the dragon "stonc," from *stincan*: either "to smell out, sniff out" (as defined in Kiernan, *Electronic Beowulf*, where it is l. 2289), or "to spring, leap, move rapidly" (as defined in Joseph Bosworth and T. Northcote Toller, *An Anglo-Saxon Dictionary*, online ed., comp. Sean Crist and Ondřej Tichý [Prague: Faculty of Arts, Charles University, 2010, 2013], s.v. *stincan*, available at https://bosworthtoller.com/29004, accessed 30 November 2020).

27 Baker, *Picturing the Beast*, 108 (emphasis in original).

28 Fraustino, "Rights and Wrongs": "our metaphorical theory of mind can be both the cause of and the solution to human separation from nature, as it allows us to identify with other animals even as we try to hold ourselves as separate and somehow superior" (154).

29 John Simons, *Animal Rights and the Politics of Literary Representation* (London: Palgrave, 2002), 116–17. Simons broadly cites Masson's three books *When Elephants Weep, Dogs Never Lie about Love*, and *The Emperor's Embrace*.

30 Simons, *Animal Rights*, 117.

31 This pattern in *Beowulf* illustration programs is pointed out in Bruce Gilchrist's essay in this volume, from which the phrase "displacement and aversion" is taken.

32   Dr. Seuss, *How the Grinch Stole Christmas* (New York: Random House, 1957); the book is unpaginated so no page citations will be given. Robert Schichler, "Understanding the Outsider: Grendel, Geisel, and the Grinch," *Popular Culture Review* 11 (2000): 99–105.

33   Piotr Sadowski, "The Sound-Symbolic Quality of Word-Initial 'Gr-Cluster' in Middle English Alliterative Verse," *Neuphilologische Mitteilungen* 102 (2001): 41–2. See also Michael Lapidge, "'Beowulf,' Aldhelm, the 'Liber Monstrorum' and Wessex," *Studi Medievali* 23 (1982): 181–2.

34   The *Dying Earth* books appeared between 1950 and 1984 and were collected in *Tales of the Dying Earth* (New York: Macmillan, 2000). The word appears to mean a phantom or spirit in Robert Louis Stevenson's short story "The Waif Woman" (London: Chatto and Windus, 1916), available at http://www.gutenberg.org/files/19750/19750-h/19750-h.htm. See also "Know Your Meme: You are likely to be eaten by a grue," http:// knowyourmeme.com/memes/you-are-likely-to-be-eaten-by-a-grue.

35   Ratramnus of Corbie, *Letter on the Cynocephali*, ed. J.-P. Migne, in *Patrologia Latina* (Paris, 1852), 121:1153–6.

36   Rudyard Kipling, "Rikki-Tikki-Tavi," *St. Nicholas* 21, no. 1 (November 1893): 3–13; *The Jungle Book* (London: Macmillan, 1894). Page references are given from the magazine. Bard Cosman, in "Rikki-Tikki-Tavi as Beowulf," *Kipling Journal* 75 (2001): 16–27, noted the *Beowulf* parallels; Cosman's analysis is mostly on the structural level, and when he does consider the colonial setting, he avoids any ideological awareness of Kipling's situation and politics, seeing the story as "a meeting of East and West that involves co-operation rather than conflict, domestication rather than oppression" (Cosman, "Rikki-Tikki-Tavi," 24).

37   Kipling, "Rikki-Tikki-Tavi," 8.

38   Kipling, "Rikki-Tikki-Tavi," 4, and see accompanying illustration in fig. 8.2.

9 Children's *Beowulf*s for the New Tolkien Generation

BY YVETTE KISOR[1]

J.R.R. Tolkien is sometimes referred to as the Father of Modern Fantasy (or High Fantasy, or Epic Fantasy).[2] While some would not grant him such pre-eminence,[3] few doubt that *The Lord of the Rings* was an important driver of the twentieth-century development of fantasy literature, or that Tolkien's fiction boosted the genre's popularity a second time through the success of Peter Jackson's film trilogy (2001–3). That second wave of influence can be seen in the success of George R.R. Martin's *Song of Ice and Fire* series and the resultant HBO *Game of Thrones* adaptation, as well as a renewed interest in the medieval and the pseudo-medieval more generally. It extends to medieval texts like *Beowulf* and is evident as well in children's and young adult literature. These trends come together in some adaptations of the Old English poem for younger audiences that appeared around 2007, just a few years after the success of Jackson's films and concurrent with the release of the Robert Zemeckis *Beowulf* movie, itself arguably encouraged by the success of Jackson's *Lord of the Rings* series. These books appeal to what could be called the "new Tolkien generation": the generation of youth in the first decade of the millennium whose pop-culture and literary sensibilities are formed partly on high-tech, CGI-enhanced filmic versions of fantasy books, like the Harry Potter series and especially Jackson's movies of Tolkien's *Lord of the Rings*.

The renewed enthusiasm for fantasy, and especially Tolkien, both represented in and fuelled by Jackson's films seems to have newly defined a market demographic of young people ripe for the Zemeckis film and the many other *Beowulf* adaptations that accompanied it in and around 2007. This essay will look at those that I argue are most closely tied to Tolkienesque medievalism in the shape it took in the early 2000s: Nicky Raven and John Howe's *Beowulf: A Tale of Blood, Heat, and Ashes* (2007), Michael Morpurgo and Michael Foreman's *Beowulf* (2006), and

Michelle L. Szobody and Justin Gerard's *Beowulf, Book One: Grendel the Ghastly* (2008).[4] All these texts have one foot in the medieval – especially as refracted through Tolkien – and one foot in the straightforwardly contemporary as they utilize both story and image to satisfy an appetite for the medieval, the ancient, the distant, while at the same time appealing to modern sensibilities. The same aesthetics of medievalism is evident in the 2007 *Beowulf* film, but Paramount and Warner Brothers take it a step further by attempting, through the unsolicited distribution of "educational packets" to thousands of schoolteachers, to bring this film into junior high and high school classrooms not as an enticement to *Beowulf* or a tool for teaching about it, but as *Beowulf* itself.

Perhaps the most overt attempt to reach the audience created by the success of Jackson's films is *Beowulf: A Tale of Blood, Heat, and Ashes*, featuring as it does the artwork of John Howe, an artist strongly associated with Tolkien.[5] The book's cover emphasizes the well-known illustrator and his connections to Tolkien. Howe's name is in larger type than Raven's on the front cover and the gold-lettered type used for the title recalls that used in Jackson's film titles. The choice of artwork for the cover, an image of Beowulf battling the fire-breathing dragon, resembles Howe's illustrations of the balrog; the circle enclosing the image evokes the Ring. Further, the marketing emphasizes the illustrator's connection to Tolkien, describing the book as "an enthralling edition illustrated by a noted Tolkien artist."[6] Howe's artistic relationship with Tolkien's fiction is long-standing, and along with Alan Lee, Howe was a consultant on Jackson's *The Lord of the Rings* films. The illustrations are not original to this book. They grow directly out of the artwork Howe produced for the 2005 board game *Beowulf: The Legend*; in fact, most of the book's images reuse Howe's earlier art for the board game.[7] Howe is given the last word in the book, a final section entitled "The Artist: A Note from John Howe," in which he details his experience with the poem, speaking with admiration of "Beowulf's refusal to surrender, first to the rending darkness that reaches into Heorot, and then to creaking old age where the dragon waits" (82).[8] In his account he describes encountering *Beowulf* first through John Gardner's *Grendel*, or more specifically, through Emil Antonucci's cover illustration of the monster, and then through J.R.R. Tolkien's "*Beowulf*: The Monsters and the Critics," before finally reading a translation of the poem itself (82).[9] The choice of illustrator and his account of the poem make clear the target audience for *Beowulf: A Tale of Blood, Heat, and Ashes* – it is a *Beowulf* for the new Tolkien generation, a lavishly illustrated epic aimed at the young adult fantasy market, celebrating Tolkien's interpretation of the poem and giving us a hero who exemplifies his Northern theory of courage.

Yet the appearance of *Beowulf: A Tale of Blood, Heat, and Ashes* is often at odds with the story it contains, creating a tension that remains finally unresolved. It is a somewhat difficult book to categorize. On the one hand, it is a large, elaborately illustrated picture book featuring art on almost every page, sometimes spreading over adjacent pages. On the other hand, the accompanying text is dense, its prose set in a small font and divided into seven substantial chapters. In addition, the ninety-seven-page book includes facsimile images of the first two pages of *Beowulf* from its manuscript, an introduction, appendices, maps, and (as will be discussed below) the Old English text of the poem as an accompanying decoration on several pages, including the jacket cover. It is categorized as juvenile fiction,[10] yet the paratextual material would seem to suggest more scholarly translations or editions of the poem. Even the way the book was marketed speaks to its mixed identity, placed in at least one chain bookstore not in the children's section but in a separate display case next to the information desk along with John D. Niles' illustrated edition of Heaney's translation[11] and several movie tie-in books associated with the Zemeckis 2007 movie.[12] Strange company indeed, as this grouping by theme brings together books that would more likely be found in the poetry section (Heaney), the children's/YA section (Raven and Howe), and the new releases area (movie tie-ins). Both the association with the *Beowulf* film (and with Jackson's movies, too, through its physical appearance) and its use of some of the machinery of scholarship are part of the book's appeal to the new Tolkien generation and their desire for a flavour of the old, the medieval, by giving an impression of an authentic experience of the poem in formats familiar to present-day popular culture.[13]

One of the ways the book appeals to a desire for the medieval and suggests an authentic experience is through its use of the Old English text as part of the book's visual program. As one reviewer who emphasizes Howe's connection to Tolkien notes, "the entire book is handsomely adorned with flourishes of Old English lettering that heavily recall the now-familiar Elven script that covered mounds of Rings ephemera."[14] The note of condescension is perhaps understandable, as is the reviewer's frustration with *Lord of the Rings* "ephemera," but just as the use of Elvish script or Tengwar in Tolkien's works serves as much more than mere adornment, the "flourishes of Old English lettering" noted by the reviewer here are also more than simply decorative. All are excerpts from the Old English text of *Beowulf*, and all are not only beautifully reproduced but carefully selected and placed within the story. The book utilizes eight sections of Old English text, each between twelve and eighteen lines in length. With the exception of the opening lines of the poem, given in a cleaned-up version of the first manuscript page of *Beowulf*, the sections of poetry are lineated according to editorial convention, with a larger space between half-lines, and include modern punctuation. A specific block of text is associated with each of the seven chapters while the opening lines of the poem accompany much of the front and back matter. Besides the lines featured on the opening page of the manuscript, only two other sections are given in their entirety, preceding the first and following the last chapters. For the other five, only small sections of the text are visible, sometimes showing only a few letters of each word. This means that only a very small percentage of readers could be expected to recognize the section of the poem being referenced – yet the text is reproduced, and accurately (I noted two errors in the modern English retelling but found none in the reproduced Old English text).[15]

For the reader who can recognize them, the segments of Old English text are well chosen. Chapter 1, "Hrothgar's Hall," recounts the beginning of the attacks of the monster and ends with Hrothgar sending Wiglaf to ask the Geats for aid. It is prefaced by a brief italicized description in third person of the monster's experience from its point of view and a full-page image, in gold, of lines 120–37, appearing twice.[16] These lines recount Grendel's first two attacks on Heorot. Sections of this text appear again on the last two pages of the chapter, but the eighteen lines of text appear in two long thin strips showing only the first few letters of each line on the left and the last few letters of each line on the right. As each strip is only about four letters wide, almost no complete words appear and it is unlikely that readers would recognize the text as the same one reproduced fully in the pages preceding the chapter. Yet the text is entirely appropriate to the content of the chapter.

This fitness in choice of text continues in the succeeding chapters. Chapter 2, "Search for the Hero," is associated with lines 195–209, in which Beowulf is introduced in the poem for the first time, though not named, as he hears of Grendel's ravaging of Heorot and prepares to sail; in Raven's text this chapter tells of Wiglaf's trip to Geatland and Beowulf's accompanying him back to Denmark to face the monster. Chapter 3, "A Fight in the Dark," recounts the battle with Grendel, the following feast, and the attack of Grendel's mother; it is accompanied by lines 720–33 of the poem detailing Grendel's entrance into Heorot unaware that Beowulf waits. Chapter 4, "Into the Depths," takes us through the fight with Grendel's mother; it is adorned with lines 1518–32, which recount the first part of Beowulf's fight with the sea-hag. Chapter 5, "Honor and Peace," features lines 1845–58, narrating Hrothgar's prediction that Beowulf will become king; Raven's text

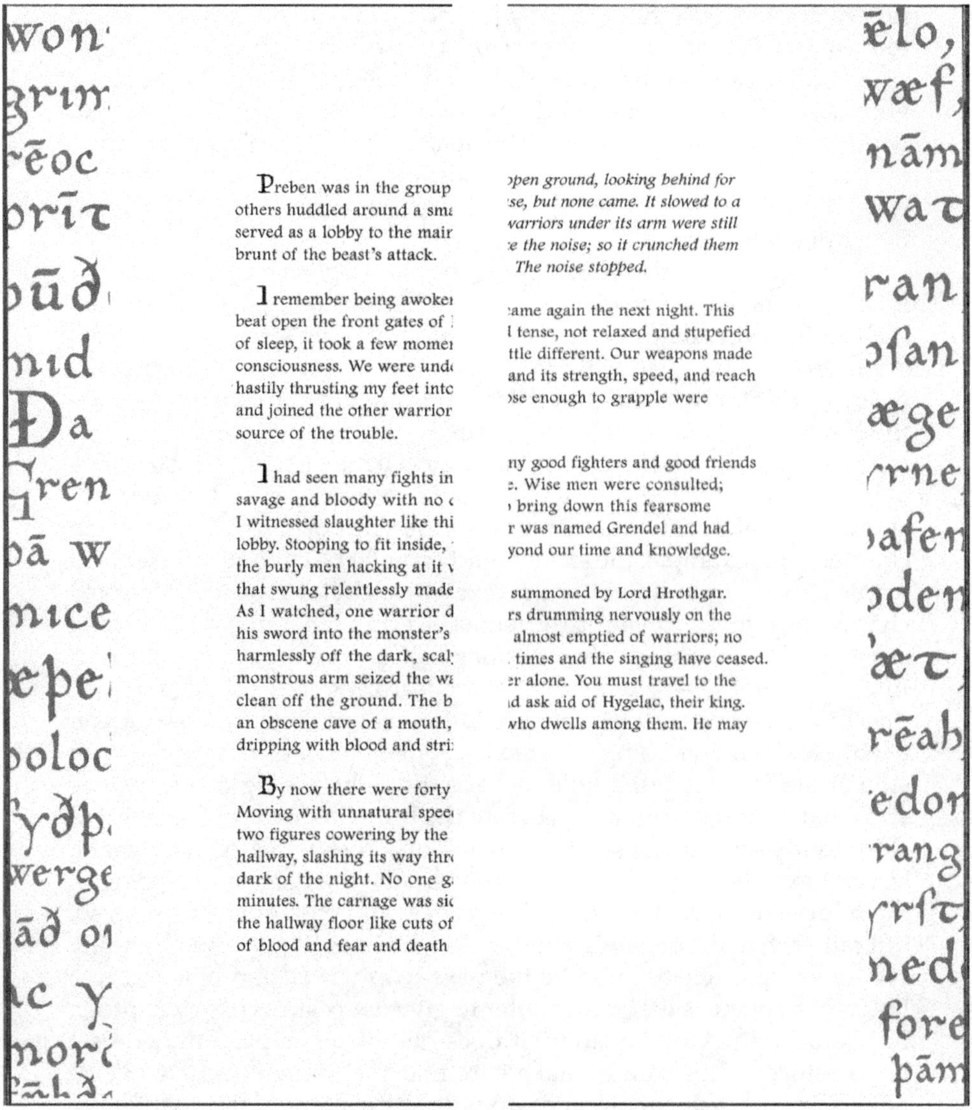

Preben was in the group [...] others huddled around a sma[ll...] served as a lobby to the mai[n...] brunt of the beast's attack.

I remember being awoke[n...] beat open the front gates of [...] of sleep, it took a few mome[nts...] consciousness. We were und[er...] hastily thrusting my feet int[o...] and joined the other warrior[s...] source of the trouble.

I had seen many fights in [...] savage and bloody with no [...] I witnessed slaughter like thi[s...] lobby. Stooping to fit inside, [...] the burly men hacking at it v[...] that swung relentlessly made [...] As I watched, one warrior d[...] his sword into the monster's [...] harmlessly off the dark, scal[y...] monstrous arm seized the w[...] clean off the ground. The b[...] an obscene cave of a mouth, [...] dripping with blood and stri[...]

By now there were forty [...] Moving with unnatural spee[d...] two figures cowering by the [...] hallway, slashing its way thr[ough...] dark of the night. No one g[...] minutes. The carnage was si[ck...] the hallway floor like cuts of [...] of blood and fear and death [...]

[...]pen ground, looking behind for [...]se, but none came. It slowed to a [...]warriors under its arm were still [...]e the noise; so it crunched them [...] The noise stopped.

[...]ame again the next night. This [...] tense, not relaxed and stupefied [...]ttle different. Our weapons made [...] and its strength, speed, and reach [...]se enough to grapple were

[...]ny good fighters and good friends [...]. Wise men were consulted; [...] bring down this fearsome [...]r was named Grendel and had [...] yond our time and knowledge.

[...] summoned by Lord Hrothgar. [...]rs drumming nervously on the [...] almost emptied of warriors; no [...] times and the singing have ceased. [...]er alone. You must travel to the [...]d ask aid of Hygelac, their king. [...]who dwells among them. He may

Figure 9.1. Decorative Old English text, from Raven and Howe, *Beowulf: A Tale of Blood, Heat, and Ashes*, pp. 10–11.

relates the victory feast, Wiglaf's journey to Geatland, and his return to Heorot five years later. Chapter 6, "A New Peril," gives us the incursion of the thief into the dragon's lair and the final mortal battle along with lines 2663–77 of the Old English text, detailing Wiglaf's speech to Beowulf as he comes to his aid. The final chapter, "The End of an Age," tells of the death of Beowulf, the choosing of Wiglaf as successor, and ends with Beowulf's funeral; lines 2724–36a recount the first part of Beowulf's final speech.

Yet the aptness of the placement of the Old English text would be difficult for a reader to perceive. For chapters 2 through 6, the accompanying text is never complete. It appears either in long strips of text down the sides of each page (see fig. 9.1) or as corners visible on the upper left or lower right. While the corner segments appear consistently to show the expected portion, as if the corner of the page were turned up revealing just a peep at a full page of Old English beneath, the edge strips are more varied. Often the left page shows the leftmost strip while the right shows the rightmost, but sometimes different portions are chosen. In chapter 3, for example, the strips could actually be cut out and laid next to one another to reveal the entire text – though not in order.[17] The next chapter also gives three sets of text strips and again there is seeming randomness in the strips chosen. Chapter 4 gives us a near match on its first set of three (34–5), with the left side featuring the beginning of each line and the strip on the right side continuing each line with only about a letter and a half missing. The next set (40–1) repeats most of the right side of the first set, but a little more to the right; the right side gives a strip that would be about two before the last. The final set (44–5) gives close to the second last strip on the left and the last strip on the right, but not exactly. There are gaps and overlaps, the biggest gap being in the middle of the line. Chapter 5 provides only one set of strips (48–9), but rather than the beginning and end of the lines it gives the beginning on the left and what would be the next strip with a gap of about two letters. Chapter 6 is the only chapter to give us six strips of text in order, but because the strips overlap, it does not even complete the first set of half-lines.[18] This care to make sure that the content of each section of Old English text chosen lines up with the content of the adaptation, while at the same time disguising that content by presenting such small portions, often out of order, suggests that however unlikely that readers will recognize the Old English, there is an unexpected pleasure waiting for those who do. After all, many avid Tolkien readers learn, or at least look up, the passages in Quenya and Sindarin that Tolkien includes in *The Lord of the Rings*, often untranslated,[19] and the inclusion of the Old English text of the poem creates a similar effect as the untranslated

Elvish does in Tolkien's text, and appeals to the same desire in readers to explore and decipher the esoteric.

In many ways, Howe's illustrations do the same work as the images of Old English text by emphasizing grandeur and antiquity. They depict an ancient world where the natural environment is vast and often dwarfs the man-made one. His illustrations use light and dark to good effect, again often contrasting the dark and threatening natural world with the small but light-radiating human one. The monsters are associated with that threatening natural world, and often seem of a piece with it. The dragon is especially noteworthy in this regard, and its association with shadow and flame again recalls Howe's illustrations of Tolkien's balrogs. Howe's illustrations rarely accompany the excerpts of Old English. His larger illustrations cover entire pages, often two adjacent pages. Occasionally an illustration will appear opposite a page with a corner of Old English visible or smaller illustrations will appear on pages that show corners where the Old English text can be seen, but they are never adorned with the long strips of Old English lettering. Instead it is the passages of text, without pictorial illustration, that are often framed on each side by the strips of Old English lettering, and whenever facing pages of plain text appear they are framed in this manner. In terms of the overall illustration scheme of the book, the Old English lettering works in concert with Howe's images, both providing in different ways the sense of the ancient that is desired by the new Tolkien generation.

The element that is out of sync with that grand sense of the ancient is Raven's retelling, in prose that takes on only a slight note of formality in public speeches as opposed to private exchanges, being very much of a modern and novelistic idiom.[20] The main text is told in first-person narration from the perspective of Wiglaf, who is here a Dane (though he does eventually succeed Beowulf on the Geatish throne). Interspersed in Wiglaf's first-person account of events are italicized passages in the third person narrating the experience and point of view of the monsters and, in the final third, the thief.[21] These italicized passages do differ somewhat in tone and, while not verse, contain elements of alliteration and rhythm not seen in the regular text, as for example in this account of Grendel: "Defeated and driven into hiding by heroes of other days, it had sought out this damp, dark, miserable place in which to fester and dream of revenge ... A fearful, furtive thing, it lived in the damp lands, feeding on fish, frogs, and unsuspecting birds that came there thinking to be predator not prey" (3). There is a penchant for relieving the tension of fight scenes with unsophisticated humour that seems to me to jar with the epic, grand scope suggested by the images.

It is not just the tone and idiom of the prose, however, that appear out of joint with the tenor achieved by the physical appearance of the volume. The narrative is simplified in some ways and developed in others, but with the latter type of adjustment usually being of a mundane, explanatory, rationalizing kind. There are none of the digressions familiar to those who know *Beowulf*, and thus the sense of expansion in time and space that they provide is largely absent. The only passage that comes close is Wiglaf's recitation at the feast, after Grendel is defeated, of the invented tale of Handscio's rescue from bandits by Beowulf. Unferth is here a drunk, and the fratricide is revealed only in his character biography in the appendix where it is characterized as accidental; he taunts Beowulf not with the account of the swimming race with Breca but with Beowulf's inability to prevent the death of Handscio in the battle with Grendel that has just taken place. Unferth becomes a more important character as he takes on some of the qualities of Heremod and undergoes a transformation of sorts; he ends up delivering to Beowulf the sermon on pride that in the original poem is presented by Hrothgar. Wealhtheow is not completely absent, as she and her women appear to bestow gifts at each of the feasts (in fact the connection between her entrance and that of Grendel's mother is here made explicit), but she is nameless, and the political and diplomatic aspects of her character are eliminated.

Other than the introduction's odd assertion that "Beowulf is one such early Christian hero" (xi), there is no Christianity in the poem – and no pagan religion either, the consultation of oracles being replaced with "wise men" who identify the monster as "Grendel," a creature who had "existed for generations of Man, beyond our time and knowledge" (11); his biblical lineage is excised. In general, the supernatural or mysterious aspects of the poem are removed and logical explanations provided. Beowulf is victorious in his fight with Grendel largely because he has a plan that is well executed; he had his men prepare sharpened stakes that Grendel tires himself combating. There is no "magical" giant sword that appears at just the right moment to help Beowulf in the fight with Grendel's mother; instead he uses Unferth's sword, the superiority of which is given a practical reason, as it is made of obsidian. The sword is then passed on to Wiglaf.

Whereas in the original only the person of the hero connects the two halves of the poem, in this retelling the most consistent presence is that of the narrator Wiglaf; he is even given an "I am Wiglaf" (4) in the opening paragraph to replace the famous "Beowulf is min nama" (l. 343) (and echoing the oft-repeated "I am Beowulf!" from the 2007 movie). Wiglaf is given an older brother, Preben,[22] who perishes at the hands of the monster Grendel while Wiglaf is away in Geatland fetching Beowulf; he and his brother come to Heorot as orphans. Wiglaf's character is more developed; he is a figure known, as he tells us, for "tact and courtesy" (12). Beowulf has several other named companions who are fleshed out and somewhat developed. Besides the unfortunate Handscio, Beowulf is accompanied by Waegmund (recalling the Wæg-mundings Beowulf and Wiglaf) and the one-eyed Scaife.

Scaife is an enigmatic presence described in the appendix's character biography as "the greatest warrior among the Geats" next to Beowulf, with "quick wits and unnatural speed" as well as "battle strategy and cunning." Both the character biography and the story itself remark on the mental synergy between Beowulf and Scaife and their ability to work as one in battle. He is not related to any figure in the poem, simply appearing one day among the Geats and disappearing again after Beowulf's death; "[n]o one knew where he came from" (77). Besides echoing in some ways the poem's Scyld Scefing, Scaife's identity as one-eyed wanderer and his association with battle and cunning relate him to Odin. He is given the final word of the story, as, after refusing the kingship from Beowulf and nominating the Dane Wiglaf instead, he sits with Wiglaf after Beowulf's funeral, here drawn as a fiery ship burial. To Wiglaf's "We shall never see the like again," he responds, "We have no need ... The dragon was the last of the beasts of legend ... The time for warrior-heroes has passed. Man now need fear only his own inhumanity" (69).

This statement from the mysterious Scaife delivers the moral message of the story and corresponds to the view Howe presents in his afterword. It is the only real expansion of perspective comparable to the ancient grandeur suggested by Howe's illustrations (and the original *Beowulf*) and a rare relief from Wiglaf's prosaic point of view. Wiglaf's character biography makes clear that the Geats dwindle after Beowulf's death, and, though there is no impending war with the Swedes, the despair of the original ending is replaced with sadness at the passing of the age of heroes and monsters. If Scaife stands in for an Odin figure he is the most innovative aspect of the retelling; nevertheless, most of it does not live up to the promise of Howe's illustrations. Or, perhaps the more contemporary idiom of the retelling functions like the hobbits in Middle-earth – familiar, but providing an entrée into the more legendary world of elves and men. Whatever its intended function, the text is generally at odds with the sense of the mythical, ancient world suggested through the appearance of Howe's illustrations and the other decorative elements of the book, and it fails also to create an aura of pre-modern authenticity; outside of the visual program, such impressions are the work of paratext, not the text proper.

While the beauty of the Raven and Howe book might appeal to children of any age (at least, those who will not be frightened by some dark imagery), a more than superficial engagement with its various visual elements requires acknowledgment of, and appreciation of the existence of, bodies of knowledge not immediately present and available. It is precisely this sense of the esoteric lurking within the apparent that feeds curiosity in readers of the new Tolkien generation. Published just the previous year by the same press, the 2006 *Beowulf* by Michael Morpurgo and Michael Foreman taps into similar desires but produces rather different aesthetic results; whereas *Beowulf: A Tale of Blood, Head, and Ashes* focuses its medievalizing energy on the visual and offers a mostly modern-feeling text, Morpurgo and Foreman shift the balance in the other direction.[23]

Like Raven and Howe's book, Morpurgo and Foreman's *Beowulf* looks like a picture book, yet the text is clearly written for a middle-school audience.[24] The illustrations do not achieve the sense of ancient grandeur of Howe's, having a more cartoonish appearance in the monsters and human figures, yet they are similarly prominent. Every single page, including those glued to the front and back boards, contains a large picture, a painting that extends over the two-page opening. Superimposed on the image is any text, and with the single exception of the title page, every block of text (including copyright information) is enclosed in a rectangular border featuring an interlace pattern typical of early insular art. In this suggestion of the authentically medieval, it parallels the use of the images of the original *Beowulf* manuscript, and the more extensive decorative use of carefully rewritten Old English text, in Raven and Howe.

In many instances Foreman's two-page illustrations are almost wholly obscured by the large blocks of text on each page, leaving just a half-inch sliver of colour around each text block. The picture is implied to be a landscape, with a hint of the land-sky line often present, and the colour palette reflects the mood of the story, usually featuring dark greys or browns[25] but breaking into bright blues when the mood is victorious.[26] A little more than half of the two-page spreads (twenty-five out of forty-four) feature these large dual-pane text boxes, and all of these include a smaller boxed illustration inside one of the larger rectangles of text; two include a smaller interior illustration in both text boxes.[27] In a little under half of the two-page spreads (nineteen out of forty-four), there is a text box on only one page, often significantly smaller than the full page, and the illustration on the facing page becomes prominent, at times obscuring a small portion of the interlace border,[28] and twice even disturbing the words within the border.[29]

The ninety-two-page text is divided into three chapters, each focused on a monster: "Beowulf and Grendel, the Monster of the Night" (7), "Beowulf and the Sea-hag" (41), and "Beowulf and the Death-dragon of the Deep" (67). The text stays fairly close to the poem in story and tone, holding to a more serious, even sonorous style, and utilizing some alliteration. It is told by an unnamed narrator, like the original. Some elements are condensed and small details changed (Beowulf's father Edgetheow lives, for example, and joins the chorus seeking to persuade the hero not to go after Grendel), but many other elements that might be cut remain: Scyld's ancestry is there, and the coast guard's challenge, and the opening exchange of speeches first with the coast guard, then Wulfgar, and Hrothgar, are all there, pretty much in full. However, digressions are cut – Unferth's confrontation becomes a veiled reference to some who cast "envious looks" and even challenge the hero (24), and the Finnsburg episode is elided into a scene of general feasting, although Wealhtheow's following speeches, albeit condensed, are largely intact (40). Interestingly, Unferth is not wholly absent as a character, emerging to lend and receive again Hrunting upon Beowulf's fight with Grendel's mother, appearing only in his positive guise. Perhaps the contradiction between Unferth's two manifestations in the text, both challenger and helper to the hero, was too much ambiguity for this interpretation. The sole exception to the cutting of digressive material is the Lay of the Last Survivor (70), which, unlike the stories of Sigemund, Hildeburh, Freawaru, Modthryth, Heremod, and the like, can be seen as more vital to the tale of *Beowulf* given the integral nature of the treasure to the story and the linking of the last survivor to the cursed nature of the treasure (88), a much less ambiguous link than the original poem describes. There is little added material of any note. The book ends with an addendum to the summing up of Beowulf's character, an explanation from the narrator in large and less modern-looking type: "which is why, all these years later, I have told this tale" (92).

Where in the Raven and Howe *Beowulf* the sense of disjunction comes from the modern, colloquial text coupled with illustrations that suggest grandeur and antiquity, here the disjunction is reversed: The text evokes the seriousness of the original, sealed off in its interlace border, while the illustrations do not contribute to an ambient sense of the old. As Charles McGrath notes, while praising Morpurgo for preserving "much of the oddness and complexity of the original, and, though his text is in prose, even some of the poetry," the illustrations "are a little pallid and storybookish, with [some] ... apt to elicit snickers rather than shudders."[30] The illustrations belong to a text for children younger than is suggested by Morpurgo's more serious, expressive prose, which "retains the power and authority of the original."[31] Note, for example, the poetic image of the following: "He knew, as they all did, that outside in the falling dark, which would very soon drown the world, the dreaded monster was leaving his lair again, was already gliding through the brooding shadows toward Heorot" (25). Alliteration is present throughout, though never in too heavy-handed a way, and Morpurgo even gets the sound of the Old English compound in moments of increased tension, as in his narration of the "terror-tyrant" Grendel's approach to Heorot, where the warriors lie "turn-tossed" waiting as "Grendel came gliding through swirling moorland cloud-mists, death-dealing in his hate-filled heart" (27) until he, "Rage-wracked, on wreckage bent, ... ripped open the iron-studded doors" (28). In the brief acknowledgments, Morpurgo notes his lack of familiarity with Old English and credits his inspirations as Seamus Heaney, Rosemary Sutcliff, Kevin Crossley-Holland, and Michael Alexander. Three of these writers have authored translations of the poem for an adult market rather than adaptations for children,[32] which may help explain the closeness of Morpurgo's adaptation and his strong sense of an ancient and high tone. It is through his text, blocked off in interlace borders, that the book seeks to appeal to readers who desire a taste of an older, distant world.

The books by Raven and Howe and by Morpurgo and Foreman are both for children or young teens who are not afraid to read; Raven's text is densely typeset and long, while Morpurgo's is stylistically more sophisticated than might seem uniformly appropriate to the identified age group. But whereas in Raven and Howe it is the visual program that invites curiosity about arcane areas of knowledge, in Morpurgo and Foreman's work the text itself, with its tone, gravity, and subtlety of diction, and separated from the more modern-looking visual program by interlace borders, draws readers into a fascination with the old and difficult. Szobody and Gerard's 2008 *Beowulf, Book One: Grendel the Ghastly* achieves, by and large, more consistency between image and text than either of the books so far considered; the visual and the verbal cooperate to produce a sense of an older world.

Like Howe's work, Gerard's illustrations evoke Tolkien, though more subtly. Gerard is a frequent illustrator of fantasy for a children's/ YA audience and his work also shows an abiding interest in Tolkien, including a 2012 exhibition of *The Silmarillion* at Gallery Nucleus and a series of Sketchbooks featuring his interpretation of scenes from Tolkien's works. His description on Gallery Gerard, the gallery he co-owns with his wife and fellow artist Annie Stegg Gerard, proclaims both J.R.R. Tolkien and C.S. Lewis as "constant sources of inspiration."[33] Though not as strongly associated with Tolkien as Howe, and not featured in the marketing of the book as a Tolkien illustrator as Howe is, Gerard does have a public identity as an illustrator influenced by Tolkien.[34] The book covers only the episode with Grendel, ending with Wealhtheow's words; the final page promises *Beowulf, Book Two: The Monster's Mother*, though it seems never to have appeared.[35] At just twenty-six pages and with large print, *Beowulf, Book One* seems aimed at a younger audience than the other two and can be better described as a "picture book,"[36] but it also includes an appendix, consisting of a glossary and a map, as well as a "Letter to Parents and Educators." This book's appeal to the new Tolkien generation is holistic, with text, image, and paratextual apparatus working in harmony to evoke a sense of an ancient world.

Where the Raven and Howe and the Morgurgo and Foreman books appear busy by contrast, the Szobody and Gerard book is often spare, with just a few lines of text and nothing else (e.g., p. 8). The cover has elements similar to both of the other books. The design of the title is reminiscent of the titles of Jackson's Tolkien films, though not as clearly as the Raven and Howe cover. The whole image is surrounded by an interlace border à la Foreman; however, the image is so dark, like those by Howe, that some elements of it may be missed. All the full-page images within the book (there are eight, including one that spreads over two pages [22–3]) are enclosed in an interlace border, but in each instance the border is coloured similarly to the image it encloses so it blends rather than standing out, creating connection rather than separation – quite different from the effect of the interlace borders enclosing the text in the Morpurgo and Foreman *Beowulf*. Interlace patterns appear not only in the nearly obscured borders, but also in the world depicted, featured in the women's clothing, tapestries, and the like (e.g., on pp. 18, 27).

Along with the eight full-page, full-colour illustrations there are smaller illustrations all tinted sepia and enclosed in a circular or oval border that fades to the page, creating a look rather like that of an old photograph.[37] Most show figures in isolation, such as Wealhtheow holding the cup (18) or the defeated, shrunken Hrothgar on his throne (17). Many aspects of the illustrations recall Howe's work. The colour images are dark with the exception of the first and the final ones. These show a Danish kingdom bathed in light and free from the grip of the monster Grendel: the first featuring smiling, even laughing Danes outside Heorot, mostly villagers (7), the final one of Hrothgar presenting Beowulf with a sword, Wealhtheow at his side holding the cup as a row of Danish warriors looks on (27). More serious in tone than the first illustration of the book, this final one is nonetheless similar in its use of light as the group standing outside Heorot's doors is illuminated, with both images favouring brown tones. The green banners featured here could be from Rohan and the image as a whole calls to mind Tolkien's Meduseld, and especially Jackson's visualization of it.

The six intervening full-page illustrations are dark, with what light appears often working to suggest the small bright world of humans being increasingly threatened by the dark wild – very similar to Howe's approach. The second shows a fearful peasant leading his nervous-looking horse through a dark forest as the light from his lantern fails to penetrate the dark around him (9); the only elements of the world of men besides the man and his horse are what appear to be grave markers in the foreground. The accompanying text contains the first reference to the monster (unnamed), asserting his location in "the dark marsh" and his hatred of the world of the hall (8). The illustration of the aftermath of Grendel's first attack on Heorot is almost entirely in grey, with the little light there is resting on a fallen Danish warrior surrounded by destruction as Hrothgar looks on with Wealhtheow, her face in her hands (13). The same colour palette is seen in the following illustration, but now the scant light illumines the proud figure of Beowulf as he stands before the coast guard, the light glinting off the weapons and the blond hair of both Beowulf and the coast guard (15). A brown-tinted scene of men drinking and laughing is next as Wealhtheow crosses in the foreground looking solemn and in shadow (19); her figure is emphasized, however, by being presented in almost the same guise and posture in isolation on the facing page (18). The only two-page illustration is downright scary, as the glowing eyes of the monster Grendel draw focus as he creeps among the sleeping Geats through a blackened hall, though Beowulf's watchful eye can be identified (22–3).

The images of Grendel show him to be unquestionably a monster. Unlike many that stress the humanoid features of the creature, Gerard's illustrations emphasize Grendel's monstrous, animalistic qualities. His face is dragonish and he is usually shown bent over, close to the ground, almost reptilian. He appears only four times, three times creeping towards his prey and once fighting Beowulf and the Geats. Only in the last is he illuminated, and the light shows him in his most humanoid appearance, revealing muscular tattooed arms adorned with bracelets and arm rings as he stands, trying to force Beowulf to release his grip on his arm (25). His mouth is open, one imagines roaring, and his tusk-like teeth are prominent. His eyes glow as they do in all four illustrations. The other three show him hunched over, emphasizing his hairiness and obscuring or rendering invisible the elements of culture like the tattoos and arm rings (11, 20–1, 22–3).

Szobody's text is a much simplified version of the story (no digressions, no series of challenges from the coast guard and door-ward, no Unferth, no long speeches, no Finnsburh or Sigemund), but it goes to some pains to evoke the tone of the original. It begins with an invocation in three lines of all-caps that recalls the original: "NOW HEAR: LONG, LONG AGO WHEN MONSTERS ROAMED THE EARTH, MIGHTY KING HROTHGAR WAS WELL-KNOWN FOR WAR-DEEDS" (6). Szobody also makes free use of alliteration and utilizes compounds that recall the Old English: "To heighten his name, he set about to build a broad, bright feast-hall in Denmark. There, he swore to reward his loyal warriors with wealth. Soon the hall was built. Hrothgar named it Heorot, which means stag, and at the first feast he kept his word. The king gave his fighters sweet mead-drink and ring-riches" (6). As one reviewer notes, "This adaptation is reminiscent of the poem's Old English origins in meter and vocabulary, the boldface heraldic introduction, and the simply stated conclusion."[38]

Like Raven and Howe's *Beowulf: A Tale of Blood, Head, and Ashes*, Szobody and Gerard's book contains an appendix (pp. II–IV); this one consists largely of a glossary and a map. The glossary includes a fairly detailed explanation of epic and its main features as well as definitions of prosody, metonymy, litotes, kenning, and *hwæt* (III). The definition of prosody includes two lines in Old English and explanations of alliteration vs. rhyme, the four-stress line, and the way the verbal balance is reflected in meaning (III). Also present is a letter to parents and educators that retells the story of the manuscript and asserts Szobody's attempt to use "modern vocabulary that stems from Germanic roots wherever feasible" (I). There are even seven footnotes within the main text (6, 8, 14, 18), all guides to pronunciation of names. This apparatus is even more surprising here than in Howe and Raven and seems clearly aimed at adult readers to children. With its discussions of metre and the like it makes explicit what the adaptation is attempting to emulate.[39] The final note to parents and educators makes clear the aims of the book with its claim that "the best ancient books illuminate mysteries of modern culture" (I).

This book is better able to bridge the gulf between the ancient and the modern than the other two books discussed here, as both text and illustrations invoke the older world, yet remain accessible to younger readers. The text recalls the rhythms of Old English metre without embodying them wholly, and its stripped-down narrative focuses attention directly on the tale. This adaptation seeks to invoke the sense of an ancient world through its diction, encouraging explanation of those dictional effects through the educative intervention of librarians, teachers, and parents (perhaps themselves not immune to the attractions of the fantasy and Tolkien resurgence and its visual aesthetics). The illustrations show a world that is older, but recognizable, and the incursions of the monster represent the terror of the dark wild invading the world of human habitation. The images of smiling peasants, drinking warriors, and so on seem familiar, but the details all invoke the antique, from the patterned floor Grendel creeps along (22–3) to the strange engraved stones unnoticed by the fearful peasant (8). The obscured interlace borders around the full-page illustrations encapsulate this tendency, helping to create a sense of the strange alongside the familiar. Even the pages themselves are designed to look old, darkening at the edges with faint lines suggesting tears or crumbling. All these elements – text, image, paratextual apparatus, even the faded look of the pages – work together to appeal to the desire for an ancient world perceived in readers shaped by their experience of Tolkien, both through the books and Jackson's movie adaptations.

These three books reimagine *Beowulf* inventively in text and image, yet each is in its own way deeply respectful of the Old English poem. All are meant to both delight and invite, with the potential to draw young people towards a path of further learning. They are designed to appeal to child readers who like to know things, and who especially like to know that there *are* fields of knowledge beyond their own that, with effort, they might access. But whereas Raven and Howe, Morpurgo and Foreman, and Szobody and Gerard all seem to want children to be stimulated by the possibilities of reaching towards something old and authentic, the 2007 film *Beowulf*, when considered in view of its marketing to educators, looks like a far more cynical attempt to exploit the interests of the new Tolkien generation.

Within a year of the publication of all three books, the Robert Zemeckis film of *Beowulf* was released, and a similar desire to appeal to the audience that loved Jackson's films of *The Lord of the Rings* is evident in that project and its marketing, as also is a negotiation of the modern and the medieval, though here it is less concurrence than elision. A mass-mailed classroom activity kit, addressed "Dear Educator," touts the film as "an excellent opportunity for you to introduce your students to a literary classic," but goes on to conflate the movie with the original, suggesting the equivalency of film and poem. "This timeless story now told onscreen" is described as "an epic that has been passed down for centuries through oral storytelling, written verse, and now film." Teachers are encouraged to engage in various activities with their students focused on the characters, the monsters, and the nature of heroism, all as portrayed in the film, with no reference to an expectation of any textual contact with *Beowulf*. These activities encourage students to make connections between the ancient and the modern, for instance, filling out a chart in Activity 2, "The Age of Heroes," to compare "Heroism in the Age of Heroes" with "Heroism in Our Times"; the "Age of Heroes" side is already filled out with the example of Beowulf – the film's Beowulf – while students are left to fill in the "modern" equivalent as if the movie were not itself a modern reimagining.

This elision is even more apparent in Activity 1, "Epic Lives," where brief character biographies are presented alongside images of characters from the film with the names of the actors portraying them, and students are urged to make a web chart showing Beowulf's relationship to each character, then select a character and write an in-depth character portrait. Similarly, in Activity 3, "Monsters: A Case Study," the guide instructs students to compare the movie's "case study" of Grendel with another example of a monster. Even as it refers to the film's Grendel as a "modern portrayal of an ancient monster," the guide offers this portrayal as a stand-in for the original one, stating in the same section that the "new film *Beowulf* ... tells of a monster who terrified an Anglo-Saxon kingdom in the 8th century." As the guide instructs students to ponder whether "society's view of monsters has changed all that much over the last 1,200 years," it presents the film's version of Grendel *as* that eighth-century monster, stated to be the "son of King Hrothgar and a succubus": a claim deriving from the film – though not quite accurate even to its revision of the story[40] – and having no relationship to the Old English poem.

Not only teachers objected to this conflation of epic poem and film. One writer of the screenplay, Neil Gaiman, and the author of the official novelization of the film, Caitlín R. Kiernan, also protested. In his blog, Gaiman observed that

> the educational pack done for *Beowulf* is simply wrong. Part of the point of the *Beowulf* movie that Roger [Avary] and I wrote is the places it diverges from the story of *Beowulf*, and the ways it explores the relationship between a person and a story about a person. I don't think they should be putting the stuff *we made up* on material intended for schools.[41]

Kiernan expressed similar feelings, giving "a big thumbs-down to YMI, etc. for attempting to pass this film version of *Beowulf* off as the real thing to bolster group ticket sales," and pointing out that the film "diverges significantly from the source material."[42] Both authors recognize and are uncomfortable with the educational packet's attempt to supplant the poem with the film.

The renewed interest in old texts like *Beowulf* piqued by Tolkien and especially the Jackson films of *The Lord of the Rings* includes a desire for the ancient, expressed through attraction to an imagined world that re-calls the depths of former times and cultures. The three books discussed here all demonstrate an attempt to appeal to this, while at the same time contending with the implicit disconnect between attempts to evoke a medieval world and modern sensibilities. The Howe and Raven book arguably succeeds visually with stunning images from a famous illus-trator of Tolkien that clearly echo his images of Tolkien's world, along with its use of the manuscript to call to mind a sense that the old story is being bodied forth in these pages, but the text seems ill-suited to the visual program that compels readers' interest. The Morpurgo and Fore-man *Beowulf* does a much better job of creating an impression of an old poem in its text, staying close to the original in content and echoing ver-bal features of Old English verse. Yet, the accompanying images are a mixed bag. The strongest feature that aligns it with the text's ability to recall the ancient poem is the use of interlace borders to encapsulate the lines of text, serving as an invitation into that ancient world through this feature reminiscent of so much early medieval English decoration. How-ever, the illustrations themselves often seem out of step with the artful, sophisticated text. The Szobody and Gerard book, in spite of its compres-sion, also echoes verbal features of the Old English poem, helping to call to mind an ancient world, and its illustrations bridge the gap between the old and the familiar, tending towards simplicity and accessibility but containing elements that evoke a more mysterious world. Because both text and image contain elements of the ancient and the modern, they work together effectively. Most jarring by far is the Zemeckis film's bid for a youth audience by seeking a place in junior high and high school classrooms as an object of study in lieu of any textual exposure to *Beowulf*.

Tensions between the medieval and medievalism become especially acute when the appeal to the desire for an ancient world promises a genuine experience of *Beowulf*. While the three books I have discussed negotiate this tension differently and with varying degrees of success, all of them allow it to remain visible, exciting readers' imaginations in ways that inform them of further knowledge they may be enticed to pursue. The Zemeckis film with its educational packet, by contrast, resolves the tension misleadingly through a rhetoric of outright substi-tution that loops endlessly back to the modern. The approach of this ostensibly educational supplement could not be more different from Szobody's "Letter to Parents and Educators," which tells the story of the manuscript, describes the poem's content and the verbal qualities of its verse, and argues for its relevance. Rather than beginning and ending as an act of self-promotion (Szobody refers to her book only as an adaptation), *Beowulf, Book One* piques interest in the ancient while arguing for its ties to the modern. The informational paratexts to Raven and Howe's and Morpurgo and Foreman's books likewise gesture towards paths of access to real artefacts of a real medieval world, and in those cases there is reason to believe the paratexts are meant at least as much for their inquisitive child and teen readers as for any adult who might be vetting or mediating the books. Of course all these authors and artists hope their works will sell. But whereas the Zemeckis film sells only itself, using educational structures to gain access to a potentially lucrative demographic of moviegoers, the books by Howe and Raven, Morpurgo and Foreman, and Szobody and Gerard sell entrée to subject matter worthy of the new Tolkien generation's abundant curiosity.

NOTES

1 I would like to acknowledge funding received from Ramapo College to support travel to the 44th International Congress on Medieval Studies, where I gave a paper that was an early version of this project.
2 E.g., Aaron Belz, "Father of Epic Fantasy," *Christian History* 78 (2003), https://www.christianhistoryinstitute.org/magazine/article/father-of-epic-fantasy (accessed 9 July 2019).
3 See, for example, Ed Power, "Sorry, J.R.R. Tolkien Is Not the Father of Fantasy," *Boston Globe* (22 December 2013), https://www.bostonglobe.com/ideas/2013/12/22/sorry-tolkien-not-father-fantasy/pljM6NOC54JmFaqY8bzNSI/story.html (accessed 9 July 2019).
4 Nicky Raven, *Beowulf: A Tale of Blood, Heat, and Ashes*, illus. John Howe (Cambridge, MA: Candlewick Press, 2007); Michael Morpurgo, *Beowulf*, illus. Michael Foreman (Cambridge, MA: Candlewick Press, 2006); Michelle L. Szobody, *Beowulf, Book One: Grendel the Ghastly*, illus. Justin Gerard (Greenville, SC: Portland Studios, 2008). Citations of these three works will be given parenthetically.
5 For more information on Howe, see his website at http://www.john-howe.com/blog (accessed 9 July 2019).
6 This language can be found on most websites selling or reviewing the book (such as Amazon.com, Barnesandnoble.com, and Goodreads.com) and clearly comes from the publisher.
7 Reiner Knizia, game designer, *Beowulf: The Legend*, with art by John Howe (Fantasy Flight Games, 2005). The same image of Beowulf fighting the dragon is used as the cover for both the board game and this book as well as being found inside the book (64–5) and in miniature on p. 7 of the rules booklet for the board game. Further, the two-page illustration of Beowulf about to fight with Grendel's mother (42–3) appears as the front and back

cover of the game's rules booklet, and the two-page illustration of the dragon (56–7) is found in the interior of the rules booklet running beneath the text on pp. 4–5 as well as a section in miniature on the lower right-hand corner of p. 3. The board itself includes the image of Beowulf pulling off Grendel's arm (19), a version of Heorot (5), Grendel (17), the men peering into Grendel's mere (36–7), the dragon (56–7), Beowulf engulfed in flames (65), and Beowulf's funeral (70–1). Even the embossed shield depicted in the book (72) is previewed as a part of the playing board.

  8 The final line of his note also serves as the book's epigraph: "Beowulf may be a tale from the so-called Dark Ages, but would that our own age of enlightenment could provide flames as bright" (i).

  9 John Gardner, *Grendel*, illus. Emil Antonucci (New York: Alfred A. Knopf, 1971); J.R.R. Tolkien, *"Beowulf*: The Monsters and the Critics," *Proceedings of the British Academy* 22 (1936): 245–95.

10 Candlewick Press is a publisher of children's books. Amazon gives the age range as ten and up; Barnes and Noble specifies the age range as 10–14.

11 Seamus Heaney, trans., *Beowulf: An Illustrated Edition*, illustrations ed. John D. Niles (New York: W.W. Norton, 2007).

12 This was a Borders in Middletown, NY.

13 Even the DVD packaging of Jackson's films show this tendency, as they look like books and open in a similar manner, and the special features are called appendices.

14 Ian Chipman, rev. of Raven, *Beowulf: A Tale of Blood, Heat, and Ashes*, *Booklist Review* (15 November 2007), http://www.booklistonline.com /Beowulf-A-Tale-of-Blood-Heat-and-Ashes-Nicky-Raven/pid=2309150 (accessed 17 September 2016).

15 On page 12 "wasa" should be "was a" (line 6) and on page 50 is found the misspelling "councelors" (line 8).

16 My references to the Old English *Beowulf* are from R.D. Fulk, Robert E. Bjork, and John D. Niles, eds., *Klaeber's Beowulf*, 4th ed. (Toronto: University of Toronto Press, 2008).

17 The first pages featuring the strips of text (20–1) show the beginning of the lines on the left and the end of the lines on the right. The next set of pages (24–5) with such strips, however, shows what would be the second strip of letters on the left and the fourth strip on the right. The third and last set of pages (28–9) provides on the left a strip of letters almost identical to the fourth but a little more to the right, while the right-hand side gives a fifth strip. Put all together, they do not reproduce they entire text, but enough to make out whole words.

18 The first set (54–5) gives the beginning on the left and follows with the next section on the right with an overlap of about a letter and a half. The next set (58–9) continues where the previous one left off with an

overlap of about half a letter; the right side again continues with an overlap of about a letter and a half. The final set (62–3) continues on with larger overlap (two or more letters) on the left and about one letter on the right.

19 For example, the Sindarin "A Elbereth Gilthoniel" Frodo hears in the Hall of Elrond (*The Fellowship of the Ring*, 2nd ed. [Boston: Houghton Mifflin, 1965], II, i, 250) and that comes back to Sam before he faces Shelob (*The Two Towers*, 2nd ed. [Boston: Houghton Mifflin, 1965], IV, x, 338–9). Galadriel's song of farewell is in Quenya, though unlike "A Elbereth Giltho-niel," it is translated in the text (*Fellowship*, II, viii, 394).

20 In addition to adapting *The Snow Queen* (Dorking, Surrey: Templar, 2005), *Dracula* (Dorking, Surrey: Templar, 2009), and *Robin Hood* (Dorking, Surrey: Templar, 2012) for a children's/YA audience, Nicky Raven is known for his works *Vampireology: The True History of the Fallen Ones* (Somerville, MA: Candlewick 2010) and a series of erotica; he is editor for the House of Erotica book imprint.

21 Included as well in these italicized passages is Wiglaf's account of Hand-scio's rescue from bandits by Beowulf; it is the only element similar to the digressions or songs of scops, so frequent in the original poem.

22 Danish "Preben" means "first battle."

23 Both Morpurgo and Foreman are award-winning British creators of children's books with long and illustrious careers. Morpurgo was Children's Laureate from 2003 to 2005; his best-known work is perhaps *War Horse* (1982). See his website, https://www.michaelmorpurgo.com, for more information (accessed 9 July 2019). Michael Foreman has won numerous awards including the Kate Greenaway medals and his career spans decades; for more information see his webpage on the British Council Literature site, https://literature.britishcouncil.org/writer/michael-foreman (accessed 10 July 2019).

24 Both Amazon and Barnes and Noble give the age range as 8–12.

25 See pp. 8–9, 12–13, 16–17, etc.

26 See pp. 36–7, 58–9, 60–1, etc.

27 On pp. 46–7 and 66–7.

28 As on pp. 10, 48, 56, 68, 76, 80, and 84.

29 See pp. 48, 68.

30 Charles McGrath, "Children's Books," Sunday Book Review, *New York Times* (17 June 2007), http://www.nytimes.com/2007/06/17/books /review/McGrath-t.html?_r=0 (accessed 10 July 2019).

31 Board of Studies, New South Wales, "Part B: Lists of Texts with Summaries," *Suggested Texts for the English K-12 Syllabus* (Sydney: Board of Studies NSW, 2012), https://syllabus.bostes.nsw.edu.au/assets/global/files /english-k10-suggested-texts.pdf (accessed 10 July 2019).

32 For adults, see Michael Alexander, trans., *Beowulf: A Verse Translation* (Harmondsworth: Penguin, 1973); Kevin Crossley-Holland, trans., *Beowulf* (New York: Farrar, Straus, and Giroux, 1968); and Seamus Heaney, trans., *Beowulf: A New Verse Translation* (New York: Farrar, Straus, and Giroux; London, Faber and Faber, 1999). Crossley-Holland and Sutcliff also produced *Beowulf* adaptations for children: Kevin Crossley-Holland, *Beowulf*, illus. Charles Keeping (Oxford: Oxford University Press, 1982); Rosemary Sutcliff, *Beowulf*, illus. Charles Keeping (London: Bodley Head, 1961).

33 See Gallery Gerard, https://www.gallerygerard.com (accessed 10 July 2019).

34 The marketing copy for the book speaks of "Justin Gerard's luminous paintings [that] create empathy for a time when despair meant defeat and only courage could win the day" (dust jacket, front inside flap).

35 As of July 2019, *Beowulf, Book One* is Szobody's only book publication listed in WorldCat, and the publisher, Portland Studios, appears to be defunct.

36 Barnes and Noble gives the age range as 9–11 years, which is similar to the 8–12 range for Morpurgo and Foreman and the 10–14 range for Raven and Howe. However, the large size of the book coupled with the large size of the font suggests a younger readership than the other two.

37 A few of these occupy a page without any text (11, 17), one covers the bottom half of a two-page spread with text on the upper half (20–1), and a couple are smaller and accompany a page of text (14, 18).

38 Susan Scheps in the *School Library Journal,* as cited for instance at https://www.amazon.com/Beowulf-Grendel-Michelle-L-Szobody/dp/0979718309.

39 This is equally clear in the marketing copy for the book: "With battle-bold words ancient poets sang the clash between Beowulf and Grendel. This modern retelling preserves the splendor of those Old English poetic conventions, while the taut, restrained phrasing captures Beowulf's original aural experience" (dust jacket, front inside flap).

40 This is not the only place the educational packet fails to get correct even the film's own details. For instance, the film, like the poem, concerns a monster in Denmark, not in "an Anglo-Saxon kingdom" as claimed in the quotation given above. Quite apart from the wrongheadedness of the activities, such easily avoided errors join with occasional misspellings (e.g., "loose" for "lose" in Activity 3) to undermine any claim of the packet's educational rather than promotional intent.

41 Neil Gaiman, "Pretty Much a Test Post," *Neil Gaiman's Journal* (6 November 2007), http://journal.neilgaiman.com/2007/11/pretty-much-test-post.html (accessed 10 July 2019). Italics in the original.

42 Caitlín R. Kiernan, "Howard Hughes Ponders the Perplexing World (Pt. One)," *Dear Sweet Filthy World* (12 November 2007), https://greygirlbeast.livejournal.com/404454.html (accessed 10 July 2019).

10 The Practice of Adapting *Beowulf* for Younger Readers: A Conversation with Rebecca Barnhouse and James Rumford

BRITT MIZE

MIZE: Thank you all for being here at today's final session of the *Beowulf* for Younger Readers symposium, hosted at Texas A&M University and sponsored by the Melbern G. Glasscock Center for Humanities Research, the Department of English, the Creative Writing group within that department, and the Critical Childhood Studies Working Group. We're recording.

Dr. Rebecca Barnhouse, videoconferencing with us from Youngstown, Ohio, is a successful author of medieval-themed youth novels. After her critically acclaimed debut, *The Book of the Maidservant*, Rebecca turned to the *Beowulf* story as inspiration for her next two excellent novels: *The Coming of the Dragon*, which we'll focus on today, and its sequel, *Peaceweaver*.[1]

We're joined here in person by James Rumford, who was kind enough to send us in advance many copies of his book *Beowulf: A Hero's Tale Retold*.[2] If anyone here hasn't picked one up yet, there's a stack here in front, and you can take one to keep. Jim is both author and illustrator of this beautiful picturebook, and – oh, Rebecca's got one! [*Barnhouse holds up a copy of Rumford's book.*]

RUMFORD: She's a good advertiser! [*Audience laughter.*]

MIZE: And Jim also published a second *Beowulf*-themed book, *Beo-Bunny*, which is a dual-sourced adaptation of *Beowulf* and Beatrix Potter's *Tale of Peter Rabbit*, complete with Jim's watercolours precisely mimicking the style of Potter herself.[3] Thank you both for being with us today.

BARNHOUSE and RUMFORD: Thank you.

MIZE: I'd like to start by asking you both to talk about what motivated you to create *Beowulf* adaptations in the first place. Jim, as a prolific writer and illustrator of children's books, how do you choose the stories that you want to tell, and how does a project like *Hero's Tale* take shape in that process?

RUMFORD: Well, it's kind of funny. I have lots of ideas in this head, but they often don't find their way out. A friend of mine said, "You know, you ought to do *Beowulf*!" I didn't want to tell her I'd never read it, because she's really literary. And she caught on and said, "Oh, so you haven't read it?" She said, "Why don't you listen to Seamus Heaney reading his translation? See what happens." And so I did, and after I listened to that, I was really inspired. And then another friend of mine said, "Why don't you tell the tale using only Old English words?" And I thought that sounded fun, because I like languages. And so that's how it came about.

BARNHOUSE: I came to this project after tenure, and that freed me up to write about things I hadn't been able to before. It was a story that I had long thought about and wondered about, how I could turn it into a novel. After I'd written *The Book of the Maidservant*, or actually, as I was revising *The Book of the Maidservant* – as always happens, you know, there's always another project that gets into your head, and you're anxious to do that – I finally thought, "By golly, I want to do this," but I didn't know how. And then I read Cinda Williams Chima's *The Warrior Heir*, and I thought, "Okay, she did it," something like what I was thinking my book might be like. In the end mine isn't at all like hers, but it gave me sort of this impetus to say, "All right, let me see if I can write a boy hero," and voila.

MIZE: It sounds like it came more out of your experience working on *The Book of the Maidservant* than out of your academic training as a medievalist. You are, of course, *Doctor* Barnhouse.

BARNHOUSE: It came out of both, because, you know, *The Book of the Maidservant* is about Margery Kempe's teenage servant. I had been writing fiction that was not about the Middle Ages, and at a conference one time I was talking to an art director who knew a lot about the Middle Ages, and he said, "You ought to try writing fiction about the Middle Ages." That was a terrifying thought to me at the time, but it started to seep into my brain, and I started thinking, "All right, could I?" So it's a combination of two interests.

MIZE: There are literally scores and scores of *Beowulf* retellings for younger readers. It's a very large category of production. In terms of quality, those the two of you have written are certainly of the first order – everyone agrees on that – and one can say that even in a crowded field there is always room for the very best. But besides having a sense that you could do it well, what was it that each of you considered to be the "special something" that was going to set your *Beowulf* reworkings apart from others, or the thing you believed you could achieve that people really hadn't done before?

RUMFORD: Well, I think my idea in the beginning was that I wanted to take
something very, very complicated – the more I read about it, the more
complicated I saw that it was – and then make it accessible to children.
How could I make it accessible even to adults, let alone children? On
the book it says, "Ages: strong-hearted and up." So that was my feeling
about the challenge that I wanted to take on. Also, I had in my mind
pictures that I thought I wanted to bring out. I had seen some others,
but I had not seen as many as I've seen today [in prior sessions of the
symposium]. I am totally amazed that there are that many out there.

MIZE: So you were partly attracted to this story by your visual imagination.

RUMFORD: Right, it's the visual as well as the linguistic aspect to the story.
I read it in Old English and I read it in English, and I kept thinking,
"How do I put those two together? How do I make that sound, in some
small way, like the original?" Without the alliteration, without a lot of
other things, it's more of a vocabulary choice. So it was a little different
than anybody else's, I think.

MIZE: Rebecca, what did you think, at least prospectively, was going to be
different about yours?

BARNHOUSE: [*Laughs.*] I did feel that way with *The Book of the Maidservant*.
I felt like I could do something special. I'm a medievalist! and by golly,
I could do something that other people hadn't done. I'd been reading all
these books for kids set in the Middle Ages, and I felt very strongly that
we had, basically, modern characters in medieval garb. Not in all books,
of course, but I saw that more often than I liked. And so I thought, "I'll
show them! I'll write a book that shows what it's really like to be a kid in
the Middle Ages." Then I found out how hard it was.

And so having been humbled by that experience, with my *Beowulf*
book I didn't go in with any feeling that I was going to do something
special. I just wanted to try to tell the story. I hadn't had any fiction
published at this point, and so I didn't really know whether this would
end up being published. I was just trying to tell this story that was really
interesting to me, but not in the sense that I could bring something
special to it. I had read all these other *Beowulf* adaptations, but that
wasn't what I was thinking of.

MIZE: Both of you are unusual, among writers of children's and YA versions
of *Beowulf*, in having a good knowledge of the Old English language.
Rebecca, you learned Old English the same way I did, in graduate
school – and from the same people! But can you say something about
how that background in language study influenced your sense of how
you might respond *creatively* to the poem?

BARNHOUSE: Well, it's sort of like like what Jim was saying about the
language itself. There were all these words that I loved and wanted to try

to bring into it, all these compounds, in particular. Yet on the other hand I had to pull back a lot of times, and say, "Wait. That appeals to you, but it doesn't appeal to anyone else, except maybe Britt Mize" [*audience laughter*], or people like the ones in this room. So it was fun just to play around with the language, but a lot of times I had to remind myself that a novel and an Old English poem are not the same thing.

MIZE: Jim, when and how did you learn Old English?

RUMFORD: I went to the library and got a book. I'm a self-motivated language learner. I really like languages. So I don't know, I started when I started this project, maybe a little bit before. This book took eight years to do, so it wasn't like it just fell out. I wrote a manuscript – here's part of it [*holds up a packet of handwritten sheets of paper*] – probably within the first couple of weeks. But as I went over it, and over it, and over it, and then looked up every word in the dictionary etymologically, and discovered what a mess English is [*audience laughter*], I realized that this was not going to be that easy.

And besides the language aspect of it, there's also the juxtaposition of the pictures and the words. So how do I take that special stuff that's going on in Old English and translate that into the visual? I made this whole series of [M.C.] Escher-style drawings to show the interplay of foreground and background. I thought visually that might appeal to children, and that's sort of what's going on in Old English, what's something going on with those kennings and other things. I made a lot of them, but there's only, in the book, I think one that survived.

MIZE: Is it the ravens?

RUMFORD: It's the ravens! But they're not just ravens. You've got to take a good look at them. Here it is.[4] If you look at it ... Just look at them.

MIZE: Is there a wolf face in there?

RUMFORD: That's it. Because in the very last part of the story, the woman comes out, and she says – where is it? – yes: "A woman came forward singing a sorrow-song – of the foes who would come upon them like ravens, like wolves, now that Beowulf was gone."[5]

MIZE: So you've got a visual riddle built in.

RUMFORD: Right, and I wanted to do that. I had a lot more, as I said, but I got rid of them.

MIZE: *Beowulf* is in some ways a story that you would not think would lend itself to retelling for a younger audience. Its protagonist dies. There's no prominent child character. The poet notoriously overleaps a fifty-year gap in the linear narrative in about three lines of verse. Many adaptors of *Beowulf* in any genre seem to find that last feature – the fifty-year gap – particularly intractable, and a typical response is to omit the dragon episode altogether and just conclude with Beowulf's return home after defeating the Grendelkin.

Rebecca, your approach in *The Coming of the Dragon*, in which you liberally create new story elements around and behind what the poem provides, lets you solve several of these difficulties with a couple of strategic choices. You begin the story late in Beowulf's reign, making the unusual choice of starting *after* the fifty-year discontinuity in the poem's narrative,[6] and you recentre the whole narrative on the perspective of Beowulf's younger kinsman Wiglaf, whom you were thus able to present as a teenager in a coming-of-age story. That had been done once or twice before, but in lavishly illustrated formats,[7] whereas yours really is a text-novel for older kids and teens. You got around those obstacles very gracefully. But I'm curious whether there were other things that you did find especially hard to work with for a younger audience. Your ending is much more optimistic about the fate of the Geats than the Old English poem is, I notice, and your Wiglaf is much more forgiving of the retainers than the poet's Wiglaf. Did those decisions have to do with feeling like the original poem gave you material that was hard to deal with in the literary form and type you wanted to produce?

BARNHOUSE: Yes, it was that exactly. First of all, I had to age down my main character. He's not the warrior that he is in the poem; he's a kid.

And then, I had originally intended this novel to go up to the death of Beowulf and Wiglaf's being named his successor. That was it, you know, the novel was over. But my first reader said, "No, that's the end of Beowulf's story. That's not the end of the story that you have started us with, with *this* main character." That was a struggle for me – "Oh my gosh, I've got to keep going with this story, so now what?" So I made up all these things that I was sure would really annoy people who are purists about *Beowulf*. And then there was the stately pace, and all those connections back and forth in the poem, and the fact that I was losing the first part of it, so I tried to get little bits of it in – the things that I liked a lot – and some of them I saved for *Peaceweaver* and snuck them in there in various ways. But I think the biggest shift of what is in *Beowulf* was the fact that I was really changing things radically by making him so young, and then giving it a happy ending. I'm a sucker for happy endings. I'm way too nice to my characters.

But I will say this: Jim's is an adaptation of *Beowulf*. Mine is "inspired by *Beowulf*" – it says so right on the cover!

MIZE: There's a lot of debate about what that word "adaptation" means, right? Maybe your definition would be more restrictive, but certainly *The Coming of the Dragon* is a rather close adaptation of *parts* of *Beowulf*.

BARNHOUSE: Parts of it, yes.

MIZE: Your freedom in revising and adding to the received story really works in this case.

Jim, your version accepts all those elements we've already mentioned that are potentially difficult to handle for a kid audience. You follow the poem's presentation of the main storyline closely. How would you characterize your strategies for doing this? And were there other things about the poem that you found awkward or hard to deal with creatively?

RUMFORD: When I realized that he aged fifty years – my first reading through the poem, it went right over my head, I don't know why – I thought, "Oh my God. What am I going to do about that?" And I realized I couldn't do away with the dragon, because there's some kind of religious aspect to the story. We don't know what the point of this story was, we don't know who wrote it, but we do know that when Beowulf is asked to kill Grendel, he says, "I won't do this alone. This will be up to God." When he gets old, he says, "I'm going to do this myself, all by myself," so he has to fail. He *has* to fail. You can't change that.

I read once that there are three levels of spiritual interpretation in medieval literature, and there are three parts to this story. I decided I was going to make – as you can see – green here [as the background color in the first portion of the book], blue here [in the second portion], and yellow here [in the third portion], to show this. It's very subtle. But the poem is subtle.

MIZE: You mention your sense of what can't be changed. There are all kinds of other adult opinions about what a children's book can or should be – grownups' opinions about what is appropriate or desirable, for instance – and I imagine that successful writers in the genre have to be mindful of that to some extent. Could you both talk about how aware you are, when working on projects like these, of the need to "cross-write" for adult readers, who of course have some power to control the availability and visibility of your work?

BARNHOUSE: At first, when I was writing this book, I wasn't thinking of that. I was just writing to see if I could tell the story. Later on, when it was going through the editing process, there was a question raised about audience. Rather than "YA," the publisher calls it "middle-grade." And so, then, for *Peaceweaver* – which I was already in the midst of a draft of at the time that that decision got made that they were going to market *The Coming of the Dragon* as middle-grade – now suddenly the second book had to be middle-grade as well. And so those kinds of considerations came in.

But when I'm actually in the process of drafting, they do not enter my mind at all. I'm just in the story, trying to figure out how to tell the story. It's later on, in revision, or in dealing with an editor, that those kinds of questions come up.

Were you also thinking of librarians and teachers, or …

MIZE: Yes, parents, everybody.

BARNHOUSE: No, I never think of them. It's just editors!

MIZE: That's an important class of adults who have control over visibility!

BARNHOUSE: Maybe I *should* pay more attention to them!

MIZE: The YA versus middle-grade question is interesting in your case, because the writing is very sophisticated. That's a real achievement, if the editor still thought that it would be accessible to younger readers than you had in mind.

BARNHOUSE: Well, that's always an argument that one has with editors. I was just listening recently to some other authors talking about having lost that fight with the marketing people, who said, "This is going to be marketed this way," even though the writer felt very strongly he could go for older kids. It's a constant battle. I don't know, Jim, if you've ever had anything like that?

RUMFORD: Yeah, I have to agree with you 100%. Because first of all, it *is* a battle. It's a battle with editors who are afraid of the lexile number, or whatever it's called, and all these other foolish things. I call them "foolish" because a hundred years ago ... you should look at children's books a hundred years ago, and the words that were used a hundred years ago. Why dumb things down?

As for who I think about when I write this story: I think about me as a kid. I think about what it is that I would have wanted to know about that poem. That poem is not accessible to me as a child. Then I think, this poem is also not accessible to me if I'm an uneducated adult: let's say I only went to high school. Let's say I want to read this book to my kids. For this book, because I changed everything to words that have an Old English origin, it turns out to be pretty simple. "He went in," you know? He didn't "enter," he didn't "ingress." He just "went in," you know? [*Audience laughter.*] So that helps a lot.

MIZE: I want to come back to that diction choice in just a minute, because there's an element of play in it. I have a question for you, too, Rebecca, about play, or at least something I interpret as play. Among all the moves that retellers of stories make, there's a phenomenon sometimes of adaptational displacement: an element from the original is taken, is accepted and sort of recycled, but in a different way or in a different context, maybe utterly unconnected from the way that it originally appeared, and you've already said that you do that a little bit. You've got, for instance, the motif of a child found adrift on the sea, but now as part of Wiglaf's biography rather than Scyld Scefing's. You reuse names from the poem, like Dayraven and Finn, but you apply them to totally different characters from their application in *Beowulf*. Is that a playful dialogue with the poem, or how does this come about in your work with the story?

BARNHOUSE: I love that you give it this important-sounding word, "displacement." For me it's more like, "Here are these really cool things in the text, so how can I use them somewhere?" There are great things about the text that I wanted to be able to use, but here I was just writing about the end of the poem, and so I was taking things from the beginning of the poem that I really liked, like the story of Scyld Scefing, and trying to find a place to use them.

But about the names: right in the middle of Jim's – Jim, you give us a pronunciation guide for "Hygelac," and in mine I had to wait till the *end* of the story. I was aware of this frustration that I had as a kid, with fantasy novels in particular, where I had no idea how to pronounce names, and in writing I struggled with the fact that Old English names are so *hard*. They're hard to say, they're hard to translate, a lot of times. Names like Wealhtheow and Hygd just don't lend themselves to writing for modern kids. So when you come across a name like Finn – "Yes! That's easy, let's use it."

And by the way, Finn is now the go-to name for YA literature. Everybody's named Finn now. I didn't start it.

RUMFORD: Mark Twain did. [*Audience laughter.*]

BARNHOUSE: But Dayraven. Dayraven is the coolest name ever! [*Audience laughter.*] How could I not use his name? And kids have definitely responded to him. He's the one they like the most.

I was really struggling with those names. It's less a sense of play than desperation. Where am I going to get names that people will be comfortable with as they're reading?

MIZE: You really did mine all of Germanic literature for the pronounceable names. [*Audience laughter.*]

BARNHOUSE: Yes. Yes, I did!

MIZE: Jim, staying with the topic of play: let me just say again the title *Beo-Bunny*. [*Audience laughter.*]

For those who don't know, *Beo-Bunny* is actually written in neo-Old English, and the wording and phrasing seem to me to be rather carefully engineered to be comprehensible to the modern ear when read aloud. This is obviously a playful thing. *Beowulf: A Hero's Tale Retold* is a more serious work, but you've already referenced your choice to use only words that are etymologically English, and not loanwords. Would you talk a little more about that choice, but especially whether you found it to be truly limiting in any way? Can you identify particular places in the book where it affected your presentation of the story?

RUMFORD: You know, it was very limiting, and that's why I got rid of some of those subsidiary stories. They became too difficult. It also became difficult when I realized that *they, their,* and *them* are not English, but

Norse. And so I gave up, but those are the only ones. Well, I cheated sometimes. *Score* is a word that goes way back, but its meaning today is not the same as it was a long, long time ago. So there's a lot of differences in that. But I really enjoyed it, because in the end, somehow it sounded to me stronger. Is it just because Old English words are the backbone of our language?

Think about this: "What you have heard before is nothing. I will stir up the waters of the old days and shape the long-ago then into now."[8] I can't use the word *past*; I can't use any of the words that would make this so much easier. It took me years to figure out how I was going to make this crossword puzzle of words work. Let's see, in the part where Grendel's arm is going to be torn off: "All the while, Beowulf's men hacked at Grendel with their swords. Their blades could not harm him, though, for the ogre had weakened their weapons with a mighty spell. But he had no spell over Beowulf's iron grip. A deep wound now opened up on Grendel's shoulder and widened,"[9] and on and on. Part of this is inspired by the way Seamus Heaney chose words. He chose strong, strong words for that act.[10]

It was fun. And this is probably what led to this *Beo-Bunny* book too, at some point. I do not remember how I thought of doing that. All I know is it appeared one day.

MIZE: One thing you both have in common is that you play with runes in these books. Jim, you incorporate runic characters in many of your illustrations, where they represent words and lines of Old English from the original poem. Rebecca, you actually give Wiglaf the nickname "Rune" – that's how he's known for most of the book – and for most of your story he does not know his own true given name or its meaning. You make kind of a riddle of this, because he wears a pendant that spells out "Wiglaf" in runes, and those runes are displayed as early as page 36, but you don't reveal to readers what they say at that time. There are hints at the meaning of his name several times after that, but the word "Wiglaf" is not actually disclosed by you, for readers who do not know runes, until about 175 pages later,[11] so you really make them wait for it.

Of course, some small subset of your readership does understand Old English and will be able to read runic characters. The incorporation of elements that require specialized training to understand implies an awareness of that audience, and also a desire to communicate with them in some way. How do you understand your relationship to some kind of insider audience, and what role does this have in your creative projects?

RUMFORD: You know, I like the image you just gave of trying to communicate with other beings. When you sit there and you write a book, yes, it's supposed to be for children, but you know, you could put all kinds of stuff in there. And it's for you guys, you know? You're the ones. The bottle has come to your beach; you get to open it. You get to read the message, and you will see that I've written lines from the poem. You'll also see that I wrote in Old English that James Rumford made this book,[12] and a couple of other things. And it doesn't stop there, because on one of these pages if you look on the table, there's a jug, and on that jug is my name, written in Arabic, in Kufic, a special form of Arabic that would be probably around the seventh, eighth century.[13] I like Arabic calligraphy, so there you go. These are little messages to readers. Again, this whole thing is complicated, so why not?

MIZE: Rebecca, what do you have to say about that?

BARNHOUSE: Well, ironically, my runes are there *for* the kids. They were the one thing that I put in thinking in terms of presenting in schools. You know, I loved runes as a kid. My best friend and I used to send special messages to each other written in runes. [Audience laughter.] And it turns out of course that kids do respond to them. I show a runic alphabet, and have them write messages, or have them write their names in runes. So even though it may appear that I'm appealing to a specialist audience there, in that case, I'm not. Here, can you see that? [*Holds up a handwritten card.*] That's a thank-you note [written in runes] that I got from a kid. I get that kind of stuff, you know? It's the runes that they really remember from a presentation. They're appealing.

It's true that I am aware of the fact that only a specialist audience will get some things, and if they do, that's fine. I'll write something and then be aware that the only person who will get this is somebody who has specialist training. But I'm not doing it *for* them, necessarily. I'm not thinking about that.

RUMFORD: I agree with you. I'm thinking about me being seven, eight, nine years old, looking at a book, and going, "How'd this person know that? I want to know what that is all about." I once did a book about [Jean-François] Champollion, the guy who deciphered the Egyptian hieroglyphs. I wrote the whole story in hieroglyphs, in Egyptian, at the beginning.[14] No one has ever – I'm spilling it, because it's over with, now [*audience laughter*] – no one has ever told me what it was, or even thought it *could* mean anything. This is a problem with children's books: people think, "It can't be that serious. It can't really be true. He just made that up." It's the same thing, Rebecca, with your runes. That's *something*. It *says* something, you know. But children's books aren't given enough credit.

MIZE: And it says something that's crucial to Wiglaf himself, right? What the runes say will be a critical piece of his coming-of-age story eventually.

BARNHOUSE: Yes. Let me add too, Britt, that this also goes back to the names. Wiglaf is a silly-sounding name. I had to do something with that! And I wanted to put runes in there, so there it was.

MIZE: Interesting things like that start to happen when audience boundaries, and genre boundaries, and media boundaries get crossed. I'd like for us to talk about the movements of story across boundaries of medium and literary type. Rebecca, as you transplanted the fictive world of *Beowulf* into the newer soil of the novel, what kinds of options did that make available to you? And was there anything that you felt the genre-change in itself ruled out, or sent you toward?

BARNHOUSE: Well, obviously, I get to get into the mind of my main character in a way that you just don't in *Beowulf* itself. That gave me an opportunity, but it also gave me the problem of verisimilitude. You know, I had this character who I was trying to make not sound like a modern kid, but still be appealing to modern kids. I struggled with just trying to decide what kinds of things he would think, what kinds of things I could get away with him thinking.

MIZE: Jim, thinking especially about media in your case, since you're both a writer and an artist – text and image are co-primary in *Hero's Tale*, a single whole – can you think of one or two moments in the development of this book when you found that an exceptionally attractive creative possibility opened up for you as you went from a solely linguistic medium to a complex text-and-image presentation? Or was there anything about that process that was surprising to you, or caused difficulty?

RUMFORD: There always is [*laughs*]. I always start with the words, and when I like the words, then I start doing the pictures. I always have that moment, "How am I going to do this, now? How am I going to draw those pictures? What *is* this thing?" If you take a look at my books, if you go to my website, you will say, "Those all look like they were drawn by somebody else, some different person." This is because I think differently about each one of the books, and they call to mind different kinds of pictures.

For this book, I did a lot of pictures [*begins flipping through a notebook of draft images*]. Here's some crayon ones that I did in the beginning, and some pen and ink, and just general ideas and scribbly pictures. Then I got more serious. I was in New York, and I saw some window with all this weird silk in it, and I thought, "Oh, that's a good idea, I'll draw silky-like things." And on and on it went, and the years passed, and I finally decided that [Arthur] Rackham, you know, a great illustrator of the twentieth century, really inspired me.

And also, when I saw that window in New York, on Fifth Avenue, I realized that one way to tell this story about that dragon, and to bridge

that fifty-year gap, was to have the dragon come from the very beginning
and wind his way around through the book, so that he becomes
ominous. Something's going to happen: fate is there. It will happen. In
this notebook you can see the beginning of it. Some of these pictures look
like the *Alien* kind of monster, because I got inspired by [H.R.] Giger.

So those were some moments that gave difficult problems of taking the
text and marrying it to pictures that I saw in my head. I saw, today, such
wonderful examples of pictures I didn't even think of, you know, some
of those pictures that people have shown today in their presentations.

MIZE: Your reference to the dragon winding its way through the book is
a good segue, because I wanted to ask you too about book design. You
control many aspects of that in this book. You've already mentioned
what I think of as a wallpaper-like backdrop that's on each page of
the book, upon which the framed text blocks and framed images are
set or superimposed. It's a sinuous, serpentine pattern – it's evocative
of medieval interlace – and then its colour changes, as you pointed
out earlier, from green to blue when we go into the Grendel's mother
episode, and then to gold when we go into the dragon episode; and the
dragon is already there from the beginning, creeping across the page,
behind the pictures and text for the most part. But when we get into the
dragon episode, the dragon makes its way out of the backdrop and into
the foregrounded images.

That complexity of design is part of what makes this a very striking
children's book. Would you say more about how you think those kinds
of choices affect the experience of the audience you're going for here?

RUMFORD: You know, a children's book, to me, is like a movie. A book is one
of the few art forms that you control timewise, but a children's book, a
picture book, can be different.

I'll explain that. When you go to see a movie, you don't get to control
the time. It's going to play in its own time. But a book, you turn the
page, and you physically control it. It's really annoying when you see
adults who go into a children's book store and always look at the end
first. Children never do this. Now do you play your movies backwards?
[*Audience laughter.*] You know? Children *never* do that. So for a kid, this
[the cover] is like the poster on the outside of the movie house. This [title
page, copyright page] is the title, the credits. And then the story is going
to unfold. They start at page one, and the younger they are, the better
they do it. That's part of the idea of book design for me, and it's part of
how I chose these elements and how I wanted to make them work in the
book.

Given all that, every time I do this, I sometimes wish I could make it
move. I'd really like that dragon to move around, but it can't, so I have

to have the imagination be in the children. And so then I say, "Well you know, I could have the dragon jump into the picture just at the right moment to wreak havoc on all of the people."

MIZE: I think the dragon motif there is really brilliant, because to me, it captures something about the original poem that I think is a very subtle effect, which is that when Beowulf and the dragon meet, finally, it's as if they're made for each other. I mean, this is going to be a mutual destiny.

RUMFORD: Right. I just want to add, too, that the other thing is the monk. He's there early and then he shows up again at the very end. I don't know who told this story, as I said before, but he's watching the whole thing.

MIZE: One more design question, Jim. You dedicated *Hero's Tale* to Sid Berger, whose collection of more than twenty thousand samples of decorated paper is archived in Cushing Library, about three hundred yards from where we're sitting.[15] Were some elements of your design for this book, like the beautiful backdrop designs, an homage to him, connecting to his interests as a collector?

RUMFORD: No, not like that, although I have seen his collection and been to his house many times. The reason for the dedication is that he helped me read this story, because he knows the poem backwards and forwards, and I thought I needed somebody. Unlike you, Rebecca, I can't vet myself, you know [*audience laughter*]. But our connection goes back farther in the past, when I was a papermaker, and a typesetter, and a bookbinder, and made my own handmade books and stuff like that. That's how we got to know each other.

MIZE: My last question for the two of you is prompted by Perry Nodelman's characterization of children's literature as "an adult practice with intentions toward child readers."[16] How would you describe your own intentions toward the children who pick up your work? What is it that your practice of remaking a story like this for younger readers can bring about for them, or in them?

BARNHOUSE: I'm just trying to give my readers an immersive experience, because that's what was so much fun for me about books as a kid: you know, totally diving into a book and losing the entire world. Though I know it's getting harder and harder for kids these days to have that kind of experience, I hope that that's what I can give them. If I can also introduce them to something, like runes or the Old English language or *Beowulf*, then that's an added bonus. I don't expect that to happen, but that would be great, if it did.

RUMFORD: You know, I try and present things so that children will be inspired. These books – your books, Rebecca, every author's book – is a stepping stone to something else, and I try and keep that in mind. How can I make this be a springboard so that somebody will go and find out more? Wouldn't it be great if somebody who reads your books, or my book, turns out to be a great scholar? That's all we can hope for.

As an author I had to realize at some stage that I'm only writing a book for one person in this world. And that one person, if I'm really lucky, I might get to meet. Sometimes I have met that one person. It's great if a hundred thousand million people buy it and I become filthy rich [*audience laughter*], but I'll settle for one, because the real intent is to teach somebody something about something that I'm interested in.

NOTES

1 Barnhouse, *The Book of the Maidservant* (New York: Random House, 2009); Barnhouse, *The Coming of the Dragon* (New York: Random House, 2010); Barnhouse, *Peaceweaver* (New York: Random House, 2012).
2 Rumford, *Beowulf: A Hero's Tale Retold* (Boston: Houghton Mifflin, 2007).
3 Rumford, *Beo-Bunny* (Honolulu: Mānoa Press, 2012).
4 Rumford, *Beowulf: A Hero's Tale Retold*, [35]–[45].
5 Rumford, *Beowulf: A Hero's Tale Retold*, [44].
6 A rare precedent is Tessa Potter (writer) and Simon Noyes (illus.), *Beowulf and the Dragon* (Crystal Lake, IL: Rigby Education, 1996).
7 Welwyn Wilton Katz (writer) and Laszlo Gal (illus.), *Beowulf* (Toronto: Douglas and McIntyre, 1999); Nicky Raven (writer) and John Howe (illus.), *Beowulf: A Tale of Blood, Heat, and Ashes* (Cambridge, MA: Candlewick Press, 2007).
8 Rumford, *Beowulf: A Hero's Tale Retold*, [4].
9 Rumford, *Beowulf: A Hero's Tale Retold*, [14].
10 "The monster's whole / body was in pain, a tremendous wound / appeared on his shoulder. Sinews split / and the bone-lappings burst" (Seamus Heaney, trans., *Beowulf: A New Verse Translation*, dual-language edition [New York: Farrar, Straus and Giroux, 2000], 55, ll. 814–17).
11 Barnhouse, *Coming of the Dragon*, 212.
12 Rumford, *Beowulf: A Hero's Tale Retold*, [43].
13 Rumford, *Beowulf: A Hero's Tale Retold*, [16].
14 James Rumford, *Seeker of Knowledge: The Man Who Deciphered Egyptian Hieroglyphs* (Boston: Houghton Mifflin, 2000); hieroglyphic version of the text on pastedowns and endpapers.
15 The Berger-Cloonan Collection of Decorated Papers, Cushing Memorial Library and Archives, Texas A&M University.
16 Perry Nodelman, *The Hidden Adult: Defining Children's Literature* (Baltimore: Johns Hopkins University Press, 2008), 4.

11 Children's Versions of *Beowulf*:
A Bibliography

BRUCE GILCHRIST

This book began with my discovery of a *New York Times* review by Charles McGrath[1] of not just one, but three versions of *Beowulf* adapted for children[2] published in 2007, that annus mirabilis for Beowulfiana. Once I purchased these, and, in particular, saw James Rumford's intelligent and moving adaptation of the poem in watercolours, I decided to become a collector. From there, I bought illustrated versions of the poem as I found them in Syd Allan's rich online catalogue of *Beowulf* translations,[3] with its chronological listing and cover and frontispiece reproductions, and then moved on to methodical searches through the scanned volumes of archive.org, listings of online vendors, and the scholarly bibliographies of Stanley B. Greenfield and Fred Robinson,[4] Marijane Osborn,[5] and John William Sutton.[6] I am greatly indebted to each of these archives, and more recently, to the pilot version of the *Beowulf's Afterlives Bibliographic Database*.[7]

The primary purpose of the following bibliography is to catalogue adaptations of *Beowulf* with children as their intended audience. This includes traditional picture books with illustrations, Edwardian-era anthologies of Nordic and medieval English legends that favour short retellings in nationalist context, comic book and graphic novel versions appropriate for younger audiences, didactic materials such as plays and songbooks performed by children, and even a colouring book. One set of texts not included is the assigned schoolroom anthology, which typically features a heavily abridged version of the poem, or simply a brief excerpt for historical purposes. The sheer profusion of such anthologies over the past century is untraceable without systematic effort beyond my means, as a reworking of *Beowulf* in one can be a mere half-page in a volume of five hundred pages or longer, and not be listed in any bibliographical record. To track these down and assess them is nevertheless a valuable future project.

The listings include adaptations of the poem not identified at first as written for a children's audience, such as Gareth Hinds's 1999 three-part graphic novel, later reissued by a children's publishing imprint, Candlewick, then reviewed by McGrath in 2007, so canonizing it as a children's book. In reverse fashion, William Ellery Leonard's 1923 verse translation, for "Fireside and Classroom," was reprinted in subsequent editions with remarkable lithographs by Rockwell Kent for Random House and Lynd Ward for the Heritage Press; these prestigious reworkings of Leonard's text are included in the bibliography, even though they elevate his original edition from the classroom to the presses of serious book collectors, for not only are they in the lineage of that version for younger readers, they are part and parcel with the poem's reception and cultural work in the modern era. If I have a bias, it is to aesthetically pleasurable retellings, not to highbrow or lowbrow distinctions; the entries run from a turn-of-the-century pennybook, to deluxe, gilt-edged art nouveau treasures, to mass-produced readers keyed to particular grade levels in the United Kingdom, even to a multilingual series of translations for teaching English as a foreign language rendered with fantastical illustrations.

Each bibliography entry marks subsequent reprintings with new publishers, reworkings, and translations with use of an indentation; if there is a further edition based on a change made at the second level, such as an excerpting or a new set of illustrations, this is marked by a second indentation to show the two levels of its derivation. I have not tried to reflect every unaltered reprinting of a source adaptation; instead, I aim to record change of publisher, new page assignment, new illustrator (or illustrator removed), and so on – in general, any information that reformats or recontextualizes the original edition, and whose lineage I can be sure of. In a very few cases, where I am uncertain of date or place of publishing, especially where WorldCat[8] and the HathiTrust Digital Library[9] are not of help or seem unreliable, I include the estimated date or location in square brackets, e.g., [1903]. The illustrator for a larger anthology is only noted if the adaptation of *Beowulf* within the anthology is itself illustrated.

1820   N.F.S. Grundtvig, trans., *Bjowulfs Drape: Et Gothisk Helte-Digt fra forrige Aar-Tusinde af Angel-Saxisk paa Danske Riim* (Copenhagen: Seidelin, 1820).

Excerpted in many Danish school songbooks.[10]

1871   Josef Arnheim, *Inhalt des Beowulfliedes*, Bericht über die Jacobson-Schule zu Seesen (Hanover, 1871).

1873   Eleanora Louisa Hervey [née Montagu], "Roderic's Tale," *The Children of the Pear Garden* (London: Frederick Warne and Co., 1873), 57–67. Illus. Kate Greenaway.

1875   Ludvig Schrøder, "Heltesagnet om Bjovulf," *Om Bjovulfsdrapen* (Copenhagen: Karl Schønbergs Forlag, 1875), 30–47.

1881   John Gibb, "Beowulf," *Gudrun and Other Stories from the Epics of the Middle Ages* (London: Marshall Japp & Co.; New York: Scribner and Welford, 1881), 133–68. Illus. unknown.

Reprinted *Gudrun, Beowulf, and Roland, with Other Mediæval Tales* (London: T. Fisher Unwin, 1884).

Reprinted *Stories of Legendary Heroes. The Children's Hour*, vol. 4 (New York: Houghton Mifflin, 1907), 3–30. Ed. Eva March Tappan; illus. E. Pollak.

1881   Gustav Schalk, *Nordische-Germanische Götter- und Heldensagen: Für Jung und Volk* (Oldenburg, n.p., 1881).

Reprinted *Deutsche Heldensagen für Jugend und Alt* (Berlin: Neufeld und Henius, n.d.), 362–76. Illus. Hermann Vogel.

Reprinted and simplified *Roland und Beowulf, Zwei Heldengeschichten* (Oxford, 1920), 25–47. Ed. H.E.G. Tyndale.

1881   Wilhelm Wägner, "Beowulf," *Deutsche Heldensagen für Schule und Haus* (Leipzig: Otto Spamer, 1881).

Translated into English *Epics and Romances of the Middle Ages* (London: W. Swan Sonnenschein, 1883), 347–64. Ed. W.S.W. Anson; trans. M.W. MacDowall.

Reprinted (New York: Fords, Howard & Hulbert, 1887).

Reprinted *Romances and Epics of Our Northern Ancestors: Norse, Celt, and Teuton* (London: Norroena Society, 1906), 266–85.

Reprinted "The Legend of Beowulf," *Swords and Sorcerers: Stories from the Worlds of Fantasy and Adventure* (New York: Thunder's Mouth, 2003), 135–50. Ed. Clint Willis.

1881   T.H. Ward, "The Story of Beowulf," *Milly and Olly, or A Holiday Among the Mountains* (London: MacMillan and Co., 1881), 159–87.

1887   Adolf Lange, "Beowulf," *Deutsche Gotter- und Heldensagen für Haus und Schule* (Leipzig: Verlag von B.G. Teubner, 1887), 376–96.

Reprint, 2nd ed. (Leipzig: Druck und Verlag von B.G. Teubner, 1903), 349–65.

1895   Mara L. Pratt, "Beowulf," *Stories from Old Germany*, vol. 1 (Boston, New York, Chicago: Educational Publishing, 1895), 139–53. Illus. unknown.

1896   H[élène] A[deline] Guerber, "Beowulf," *Legends of the Middle Ages: Narrated with Special Reference to Literature and Art* (New York: American Book Co., 1896), 9–21. Illus. F. Cormon.

Revised *Myths and Legends of the Middle Ages: Their Origin and Influence on Literature and Art* (London: George C. Harrap & Co., 1909), 1–17. Illus. Count Harrach, Evelyn Paul, and F. Cormon.

Translated into Dutch *Mythen en Legenden uit de Middeleeuwen: Hun Oorsprong en Invloed op Letterkunde en Kunst* (Zutphen: W.J. Theime & Cie., 1911), 1–17. Ed. H.W.Ph.E. v. d. Bergh v. Eysinga; illus. Evelyn Paul, Count Harrach, and F. Cormon.

Reprint (London: George C. Harrap & Co., 1913). Illus. Evelyn Paul and F. Cormon.

Reprint (London: George C. Harrap & Co., 1922). No illus.

1898   A[lfred] J[ohn] Church, "The Story of Beowulf," *Heroes of Chivalry and Romance* (London: Seeley, Service & Co. Limited, 1898), 1–63. Illus. George Morrow.

1898   Zenaïde A. Ragozin, "Beowulf: The Hero of the Anglo-Saxons," *Tales of the Heroic Ages: Siegfried, the Hero of the Norse, and Beowulf, the Hero of the Anglo-Saxons* (New York and London: G.P. Putnam's Sons, 1898), 211–330. Illus. George T. Tobin.

Reprinted *Beowulf, The Hero of the Anglo-Saxons* (New York: William Beverley Harison, 1900), 213–332.

Reprinted in part "Beowulf Conquers Grendel," *Hero Tales from Many Lands* (New York: Abingdon, 1961), 88–99. Ed. Alice I. Hazeltine; illus. Gordon Laite.

1899   Andrew Lang, *The Red Book of Animal Stories* (London: Longmans, Green & Co., 1899), 33–48. Illus. H.J. Ford.

1899   C[lara] L[inklater] Thomson, *The Adventures of Beowulf: Translated from the Old English and Adapted to the Use of Schools* (London: Horace Marshall and Son, 1899).

Second ed. (1904). Illus. unknown.

1900   Eva March Tappan, *In the Days of Alfred the Great* (Boston: Lothrop, Lee & Shepard Co., 1900), 8–9. Illus. J.W. Kennedy.

1900   [Robert S. Wood?], "The Story of Beowulf," *Tales of Long Ago. 1. Childe Horn 2. Beowulf and the Dragon,* Books for the Bairns 51 (London: The "Review of Reviews" Office [May 1900]), 36–60. Ed. W.T. Stead; illus. Brinsley Le Fanu.

Reprinted (London: Ernest Benn, 1926).

Paraphrase-translated into Dutch "Beowulf," *Robin Hood en zijn vrolijke makkers, en andere ridderverhalen* (Hilversum: Bowu, [1956]), 87–108. Trans. Herman Broekhuizen and Jan van den Berg.

1901   Thomas J. Shahan, "Beowulf," *A Book of Famous Myths and Legends* (Boston: Hall and Locke, 1901), 335–49.

Reprinted *Legends That Every Child Should Know: A Selection of the Great Legends of All Times for Young People* (New York: Doubleday, Page & Co., 1906), 9–21. Ed. Hamilton Wright Mabie.

Reprinted *Stories of Great Adventures (Adapted from the Classics),* Children's Hour Series (Springfield, MA: Milton Bradley, 1919), 86–98. Ed. Carolyn Sherwin Bailey.

Reprinted *Beowulf: A Scandanavian Folk Tale,* Baba Indaba Children's Stories (London: Abela, 2016).

1904   Georg Paysen-Petersen, *Beowulf: Älteste Deutsche Heldendichtung Nach Dem Angelsächsischen* (Stuttgart: Loewes Verlag Ferdinand Carl, 1904). Illus. Hans W. Schmidt.

Reprinted (Klett-Cotta, 1971). Illus. Dietrich Ebert.

1905   Florence Holbrook, "The Story of Beowulf," *Northland Heroes* (Boston: Houghton Mifflin, 1905), 73–111. Illus. unknown.

Reprinted (London: George Harrap and Co., 1909).

1905   Eva March Tappan, "Beowulf," *A Short History of England's and America's Literature* (Boston: Houghton Mifflin, 1905), 3–6.

1906   E[theldreda] M[ary] Wilmot-Buxton, "The Story of Beowulf," *Britain Long Ago* (London: George G. Harrap & Company, 1906), 6–24. Illus. Evelyn Paul.

Reprinted E[theldreda] Wilmot Buxton [*sic*], *Stories of Early England* (New York: T.Y. Crowell, 1907), 8–34.

1908   Thomas Cartwright, *Brave Beowulf*, Every Child's Library (London: William Heinemann; New York: E.P. Dutton & Co., 1908). Illus. Patten Wilson.

1908   H[enrietta] E[lizabeth] Marshall, *Stories of Beowulf: Told to the Children* (London: T.C. & E.C. Jack; New York: E.P. Dutton & Co., 1908). Illus. J[oseph] R[atcliffe] Skelton.

Reprinted in condensed form "Beowulf," *Myths and Legendary Heroes*, vol. 2 (of 12) of *Young Folks' Treasury* (New York: The University Society, 1909), 289–301. Ed. Hamilton Wright Mabie. No illus.

Reprinted (London: Thomas Nelson and Sons, 1929).

Reprinted *The Story of Beowulf* (New York: Dover, 2007).

1909   H[enrietta] E[lizabeth] Marshall, "The Story of Beowulf," *English Literature for Boys and Girls* (London: T.C. & E.C. Jack; New York: Frederick A. Stokes, [1909]), 60–5. No illus.

1909   Charles Henry Sylvester, "Beowulf and Grendel," *Journeys through Bookland: A New and Original Plan for Reading Applied to the World's Best Literature for Children*, vol. 3 (Chicago: Bellows-Reeve, 1909), 478–94. Illus. D.A. Peterson, Milo Winter, and Frank H. Young.

Reprinted in New Ed., vol. 3 (Chicago: Bellows-Reeve, 1922), 350–64. Illus. Arthur Henderson.

1909   Eva March Tappan, "The Story of Beowulf," *European Hero Stories* (Boston: Houghton Mifflin, 1909), 68–71. Illus E. Pollak.

Reprinted *Heroes of the Middle Ages: Alaric to Columbus*. Ed. Eva March Tappan (London: George G. Harrap, 1911), 81–4.

1910   John Harrington Cox, *"Beowulf," the Anglo-Saxon Epic, Translated and Adapted for School Use* (Boston: Little, Brown and Company, 1910). Illus. Frank T. Merrill.

1910   John Harrington Cox, "Beowulf," *Knighthood in Germ and Flower: The Anglo-Saxon Epic, Beowulf, and the Arthurian Tale Sir Gawain and the Green Knight, Translated from Original Sources and Adapted for Use in the Home, the School and Pupils' Reading Circles* (Boston: Little, Brown and Company, 1910). Illus. Frank T. Merrill.

Reprinted in *Hero Tales*, The New Junior Classics, vol. 4 (New York: P.F. Collier and Son, 1919), 271–302. Ed. Mabel Williams and Marcia Dalphin; illus. Henry Pitz.

1910   M[aud] I[sabel] Ebbutt, "Beowulf," *Hero-Myths and Legends of the British Race* (London: G.G. Harrup, 1910), 1–41. Illus. J.H.F. Bacon.

1910   Theodor Mühe, "The Story of Beowulf," *Five Stories from English Literature, Arranged for Beginners* (Frankfurt: Moritz Diesterweg, 1910).

1912   Joyce Pollard, "Beowulf and Grendel," "Beowulf and the Fire Dragon," *Stories from Old English Romance* (New York: Frederick A. Stokes, 1912), 1–15.

Reprinted *Myths and Legends of All Nations*, ed. Marshall Logan (Philadelphia: John C. Winston, 1914), 164–78. Illus. unknown.

1913   H[élène] A[deline] Guerber, "Beowulf," *The Book of the Epic: The World's Great Epics Told in Story* (Philadelphia: J.B. Lippincott, 1913), 222–9.

Reprint (London: George G. Harrap & Co., 1916), 272–80.

Reprint (New York: Biblio & Tannen, 1966), 272–80.

1914   Thora Konstantin-Hansen, *Bjovulf: Et Angelsaksisk Heltedigt, frit gengevet for born* (Copenhagen: Gyldendalske Boghandel Nordisk Forlag, 1914). Illus. Niels Skovgaard.

Altered reprint Thora Constantin-Hansen, *Bjovulf: Et Angelsaksisk Heltedigt, frit gengevet for born* (Copenhagen: Rosenkilde og Bagger, 1952).

1916   Christine Chaundler and Eric Wood, "The Story of Beowulf," *My Book of Beautiful Legends* (New York: Funk and Wagnalls, 1916; London: Cassell, 1917), 11–19. Illus. A.C. Michael.

Reprinted *Famous Myths and Legends: Children's Folklore from around the World* (London: Bracken, 1986), 11–19.

1921   Olive Beaupré Miller, ed., "How Beowulf Delivered Heorot: Retold from the Old English Epic, *Beowulf*," *From the Tower Window of My Bookhouse*, vol. 5 (of 6) of *My Bookhouse* (Chicago: The Bookhouse for Children, 1921), 413–22. Illus. Donn P. Crane.

Reprinted with additional volumes (1925).

Revised in vol. 10 (of 12) of new edition of *My Bookhouse* (1937), 80–8. Newly illus. Donn P. Crane.

1923   R.K. Gordon, *The Song of Beowulf* (London: J.M. Dent and Sons, 1923).

Reprinted "Beowulf," *Anglo-Saxon Poetry* (London: J.M. Dent and Sons, 1926), 1–70.

1923   William Ellery Leonard, *Beowulf: A New Verse Translation for Fireside and Classroom* (New York: The Century Company, 1923; New York: Heritage Press, 1923).

Reprinted *Beowulf* (New York: Random House, 1932). Illus. Rockwell Kent.

Reprinted *Beowulf* (New York: Heritage Press, 1939). Illus. Lynd Ward.

Reprinted (New York: Limited Editions Club, 1952).

1923   R[ichard] A[ugustus] Spencer, *The Story of Beowulf and Grendel, Retold in Modern English Prose* (London and Edinburgh: W. and R. Chambers, 1923).

1924   Harriet Buxton Barbour, "Beowulf," *Old English Tales Retold* (New York: Macmillan, 1924), 1–14. Illus. Rodney Thompson.

1925   Eleanor Farjeon, "Grendel the Monster," "Beowulf the Goth," *Mighty Men: From Beowulf to William the Conqueror* (New York: Appleton-Century-Crofts, 1925), 1–11. Illus. Hugh Chesterman.

Reprinted *Mighty Men* (New York: Appleton-Century-Crofts, 1926), 101–11.

Reprinted in part "Grendel the Monster," *Horror Stories* (London: Kingfisher, 1995), 76–84. Ed. Susan Price; illus. Harry Horse.

Reprinted *Dark Side: Truly Terrible Stories* (London: Kingfisher, 2007), 77–83. No illus.

1927   Otto Bruder, *Beowulf: Ein Heldisches Spiel*, Münchener Laienspiele 37 (Munich: Chr. Kaiser Verlag, 1927).

Reprinted (1931).

Translated into English, "Bruder's *Beowulf: Ein Heldisches Spiel*," *In Geardagum: Essays on Old and Middle English Literature* 26 (2006): 19–52. Trans. Marijane Osborn.

1927   Hermann Eicke, *Beowulf: Nordlandsage*, Hillgers deutsche Bücherei 284 (Berlin: Hermann Hilger, 1927). Illus. Maximilian Klewer.

1928   J. Crowlesmith, "Beowulf and the Monster," "Beowulf and the Dragon," *Wonder Tales of the Middle Ages* (London: Goodship House, 1928), 7–16. Illus. H.S. Grieg.

1928   Arthur Wallis, "Beowulf," *Tales of the Norsemen*, The Children's Library: 4th Series (London: Jonathan Cape, 1928), 118–36. Illus. Paul Rotha.

1930   Foeke Sjoerds, *Helden der Menschheid* (Utrecht: Uitgeversmaatschappij W. de Haan N.V., 1930). Illus. Anton Pieck.

1933   Strafford Riggs, *The Story of Beowulf Retold from the Ancient Epic* (New York and London: D. Appleton Century Company, 1933). Decorated by Henry C. Pitz.

   Reprinted (New York: The Junior Literary Guild, 1934).

1934   Manuel Vallvé, *Beowulf* (Barcelona: Araluce, 1934).

1937   John O. Beatty, *Swords in the Dawn: A Story of the First Englishmen* (New York: Longmans & Green, 1937). Illus. Henry C. Pitz.

1940–1   Enrico Basari, "*Beowulf*: Legenda cristiana dell'antica Danimarca," *Il Vittorioso* IV/44–51, V/1–4 (1940–1). Illus. C. Caesar.

   Translated into Portuguese *O Monstro do Caím. Epopeia* 30 (Brazil, 1955): 1–35. Trans. unknown.

1941   E.V. Sandys, *Beowulf* (New York: Thomas Y. Crowell, 1941). Illus. Rolf Klep.

1946   Agnes Rothery, "Beowulf and Bohuslän," *A Scandinavian Roundabout* (New York: Dodd, Mead, and Co.), 198–207. Illus. George Gray.

1947   Dorothy Hosford, *By His Own Might: The Battles of Beowulf* (New York: Holt, Rinehart and Winston, 1947). Illus. Laszlo Matulay.

   Excerpt reprinted "How Beowulf Rules the Geats," *Myths and Legends* (Chicago: Spencer Press, 1953), 97–102. Ed. Marjorie Barrows; illus. H.M. Brock and Walter R. Sabel.

1951   Charles Francis Bricknell Smith, *The Story of Beowulf Retold*, The Young Readers Library (Exeter: A. Wheaton, 1951). Illus. L.H. Bennett Collins.

1951   Olivia E. Coolidge, "The Song of Beowulf," "Beowulf and the Fire Dragon," *Legends of the North* (Boston: Houghton Mifflin Co., 1951), 159–70, 171–6. Illus. Edouard Sandoz.

1951   Eugen Heberle, "Beowulf," *Deutsche Heldensagen* (Heidelberg: Keyser, 1951), 185–203. Illus. Gustel Koch.

1953   Vicente Garcia de Diego, "La leyenda de Beowulf," *Antología de las leyendas de la literature universal* (Barcelona: Labor, 1953), 1077–87.

1953   Henriëtte L. Janssen van Raay, "Beowulf, Koning Hrothgars Kampvechter," *Grote sagen en legenden der mensheid* (Utrecht: Uitgeversmaatschappij W. de Haan, 1953), chap. IV. Illus. H. van der Stok; ed. E. Menten-van Essen and M. Stibbe.

1954   Ian Serraillier, *Beowulf the Warrior* (Oxford: Oxford UP, 1954). Illus. [Mark] Severin.

Reprinted 1st American Ed. (New York: Henry Z. Walck, 1961).

Reprinted *Beowulf The Warrior: A Tale of Monsters* (New York: Scholastic, 1968). Illus. Bill Pesce.

Reprinted (Bathgate, ND: Bethlehem Books, 1994 and 2000).

Excerpts reprinted in Elizabeth Alder, *The King's Shadow* (New York: Farrar, Strauss, Giroux, 1995), 207.

1956   Rosemary Sutcliff, *The Shield Ring* (London: Oxford UP, 1956). Illus. C. Walter Hodges.

1959   Jane Leighton, *The Story of Beowulf*, "It's Fun to Read" series (Frankfurt am Maine: Verlag Moritz Diesterweg, 1959). Illus. Gerhard Steffen.

1959   Anne Terry White, "Beowulf," *The Golden Treasury of Myths and Legends* (New York: Golden Press, 1959), 68–81. Illus. Alice Provensen and Martin Provensen.

Translated into French *Mythes et légendes* (Paris: Éditions des Deux Coqs d'Or, 1961). Trans. Aimé Gabillon.

1960   Dorothy Heiderstadt, "Beowulf, Hero of the North," *Knights and Champions* (New York: Thomas Nelson & Sons, 1960), 27–37.

1960   Morris Schreiber, "Beowulf and the Dragon," *Gods and Heroes: Famous Myths and Legends of the World* (New York: Grosset & Dunlap, 1960), 74–5. Illus. Art Seiden.

1961   Charles A. Brady, *The King's Thane* (New York: Doubleday, 1961). Illus. Henry C. Pitz.

1961   Barbara Leonie Picard, "Beowulf," *Tales of the British People* (New York: Criterion, 1961; London: Kaye and Ward, 1961), 51–71. Illus. Eric Fraser.

1961   Rosemary Sutcliff, *Beowulf* (Oxford: The Bodley Head, 1961; New York: E.P. Dutton, 1962). Illus. Charles Keeping.

Reprinted *Beowulf: Dragon Slayer* (Oxford: The Bodley Head, 1960s).

Reprinted *Dragon Slayer: The Story of Beowulf* (Harmondsworth: Puffin, 1966).

Excerpt reprinted "Beowulf and Grendel," *Tales of Magic and Enchantment* (London: Faber, 1966). Ed. Kathleen Lines; illus. Alan Howard.

Translated into Polish (Warsaw: Nasza Księgarnia, 1966). Trans. Anna Przedpełska-Trzeciakowska; illus. Józef Wilkoń.[11]

Translated into Japanese 英雄ベーオウルフ [*Eiyū Bēōrufu*] (Tokyo: Shōhakusha, 1966). Trans. Shigeru Tokonami and Yoshiharu Ida.

Translated into Afrikaans (Kaapstad: HAUM, 1969). Trans. Chris van Lille.

Translated into Italian *Beowulf e la morte del drago* (Bergamo: Janus, 1970). Trans. Anna Maria Speckel.

Translated into Dutch "Beowulf de Drakendoder," *Helden en monsters* (Amsterdam: Leopold, 1975) [pp. unknown]. Trans. Ruth Wolf; illus. Tonke Dragt.

Translated into Japanese ベーオウルフ [*Bēōrufu*] (Tokyo: Chusekisha, 1990). Trans. Itsuji Akemi.

Reprinted ベーオウルフ: 妖怪と竜と英雄の物語 [*Bēōrufu: Yōkai to ryū to eiyū no monogatari*] (Tokyo: Hara Shobo, 2002). No illus.

Translated into German *Beowulf der Drachentöter* (Stuttgart: Verlag Freies Geistesleben, 1994). Trans. Astrid von dem Borne; illus. Victor Ambrus.

Excerpt reprinted "Beowulf: Dragonslayer," *The Kingfisher Book of Classic Boy Stories* (London: Kingfisher, 2000), 130–7. Ed. Michael Morpurgo; illus. Michael Foreman.

Reprinted *The Kingfisher Treasury of Classic Stories* (London: Kingfisher, 2002), 236–43. Ed. Rosemary Sandberg and Michael Morpurgo.

1962   Gladys Schmitt, *The Heroic Deeds of Beowulf* (New York: Random House/Legacy Books, 1962). Illus. Walter Ferro.

Reprinted (London: Frederick Muller, 1971).

1963   Antonio Urrutia Raspall, "El Poema de Beowulf," *Leyendas Nórdicas*, Colección Auriga, serie púrpura (Barcelona: Instituto de Artes Gráficas, 1963), 133–71. Illus. Vicente B. Ballestar.

1965   J.L. Herrera, *Beowulfo* (Madrid: Aguilar, 1965). Illus. Julio Castro.

1966   Gillian Paton Walsh, *Hengest's Tale* (London: Macmillan; New York: St. Martin's, 1966). Illus. Janet Margrie.

1968   Kevin Crossley-Holland, *Beowulf* (New York: Farrar, Straus, & Giroux, 1968).

Reprinted (London: Folio Society, 1973). Illus. Virgil Burnett.

Excerpt reprinted "Beowulf fights the Dragon," *The Faber Book of Northern Legends* (London: Faber & Faber, 1977), 98–107. No illus.

1968   Robert Nye, *Beowulf: A New Telling* (New York: Hill and Wang, 1968). Illus. Alan E. Cober.

Reprinted *Beowulf: A New Telling* (New York: Bantam Doubleday, 1982). No illus.

1968   Robert Nye, *Bee Hunter: Adventures of Beowulf* (London: Faber & Faber, 1968). Illus. Aileen Campbell.

Reprinted *Beowulf* (London: Random House UK, 1986).

Reprinted *Beowulf* (London: Orion, 1995).

1970   Vladimir Hulpach, Emanuel Frynta, and Václav Cibula, "Beowulf," *Mec a písen: Hrdinské báje staré Evropy* (Prague: Artia, 1970), 10–19. Illus. Miloslav Troup.

Translated into English *Heroes of Folktale and Legend* (London: Paul Hamlyn, 1970). Trans. George Theiner.

1970   Roger Lancelyn Green, "Beowulf and the Dragon," *The Hamilton Hamish Book of Dragons*, ed. Roger Lancelyn Green (London: Hamilton Hamish, 1970), 45–53. Illus. Krystyna Turska.

Reprinted *A Cavalcade of Dragons* (New York: Henry Z. Walck, 1970), 45–53.

Reprinted *A Book of Dragons* (London: Puffin, 1973), 53–60.

1973   Marney Worden, *Beowulf* (Silver Spring, MD: National Association for the Deaf, 1973). Ed. John R. Olson.

1975   Anonymous, "Beowulf and Grendel," *The Magic of Words: The 1975 Childcraft Annual* (Chicago: Field Enterprises Educational, 1975), 76–81. Illus. Brian Froude.

1975   Hannes Hüttner, *Beowulf* (Berlin: Kinderbuchverlag, 1975). Illus. Ruth Knorr.

1975–6   Michael Uslan and Ricardo Villamonte, *Beowulf: Dragon-Slayer*, 6 vols. (New York: DC Comics, 1975–6).

1979   June Oldham, *The Raven Waits* (London: Abelard-Schuman, 1979).

Reprinted (London: Hodder Children's Books, 2001).

1979   Tony D. Triggs, "Beowulf," *The Saxons* (London: MacDonald Educational, 1979).

1980   Gordon Ball, "The Story of Beowulf," *Wonders: Writings and Drawings for the Child in Us All*, ed. Jonathan Cott and Mary Gimbel (New York: Summit, 1980), 72–9.

1980   Brenda Ralph Lewis, "Beowulf," *The World of Myth and Legend* (Cambridge: Brimax, 1980), 28–36. Illus. Rob McCaig.

Reprinted *Myths and Legends* (Newmarket, UK: Brimax, 1985), 32–41.

Reprinted James Riordan and Brenda Ralph Lewis, *An Illustrated Treasury of Myths and Legends* (London: Hamlyn Young Books, 1987; New York: Bedrick, 1991). Illus. Victor Ambrus.

1982   Kevin Crossley-Holland, *Beowulf* (Oxford: Oxford UP, 1982). Illus. Charles Keeping.

Translated into Slovenian (Ljubljana: DZS, 1996). Trans. Marjan Strojan; illus. Irena Majcen.

Reprinted (St. Louis: Turtleback/San Val, 1999).

1983   Halldóra B. Björnsson, *Bjólfskviða* (Reykjavík: Fjölvaútgáfa, 1983). Ed. Pétur Knútsson Ridgewell; illus. Alfreð Flóki.

1985   Anthony Horowitz, "The Grendel," *Kingfisher Book of Myths and Legends* (London: Kingfisher, 1985), 164–70. Illus. Tom Stevens.

Reprinted (2007), 181–7.

1986   William Russell, "Beowulf's Fight with Grendel," *More Classics to Read Aloud to Your Children* (New York: Crown, 1986), 132–7.

1988   Margaret Berrill, *Beowulf and the Monsters*, Great Tales from Long Ago (London: Methuen Children's Books in association with Belitha Press Ltd., 1988). Illus. Paul Crompton.

1988   Mary Pope Osborne, "Beowulf," *Favorite Medieval Tales* (New York: Scholastic, 1988), 8–17. Illus. Troy Howell.

1989   Maurice Saxby, "Beowulf," *The Great Deeds of Superheroes* (Newtown, Australia: Millennium Books; Limpsfield, UK: Dragon's World; New York: Bedrick, 1989), 120–9. Illus. Robert Ingpen.

1989   Clare Scott-Mitchell, *Beowulf: A Traditional Collection* (Auckland: Shortland and Rigby Education), 2–17. Illus. Bryan Pollard.

1992   Gerard Benson, "Beowulf," *This Poem Doesn't Rhyme* (London: Puffin, 1992), 142.

1993   David Passes, "Beowulf and the Fire Dragon," *Dragons: Truth, Myth, and Legend* (New York: Golden, 1993), 20–1. Illus. Wayne Anderson.

1994   Michael Rosen, "The Mere," *A World of Poetry* (London: Kingfisher, 1994), 32–3.

1995   Maria Fernanda Cano, *Beowulf: La Leyenda de Las Dos Criaturas* (Buenos Aires: Ediciones del Eclipse, 1995). Illus. Oscar Rojas.

1995   Thomas O. Jones, *Lord of the Geats* (Unionville, NY: Royal Fireworks, 1995).

1995   Neil Philip, "Beowulf," *Illustrated Book of Myths: Tales & Legends of the World* (New York: D.K. Publishing, 1995), 106–7. Illus. Nilesh Mistry.

1995   Tessa Potter, *Beowulf and the Dragon* (Oxford: Heinemann, 1995). Illus. Simon Noyes.

Reprinted (Crystal Lake, IL: Rigby Interactive Library, 1996).

1996   Georgía Galanopoúlou, Μπέογουλφ [*Béögoulf*] (Athens: Ekdoseis Delfini, 1996). Illus. Panagiótis Beldékos.

Reprinted (Athens: Ekdoseis Patáki, 2002). Illus. Markos Karpoúzas.

1996   Anita Ganeri, "Beowulf's Last Battle," *Dragons and Monsters* (London: MacDonald Young Books, 1996), 15–19. Illus. Alan Baker.

Translated into French "Le Dernier Combat de Beowulf," *Histoires de Dragons et Autres Monstres*. (Paris: Gründ, 1997), 15–19. Trans. Marie-Josée Lamorlette.

1997   Stewart Ross, "Beowulf the Monster Masher," *The Best Tales Ever Told: Gods and Giants* (Brookfield, CT: Copper Beech, 1997), 18–19. Illus. Francis Phillipps.

1997   Brad Strickland, *Wishbone: Be a Wolf!* (New York: Scholastic, 1997). Illus. Don Punchatz.

1999   Jeff Suess, "Brainwulf," *Animaniacs Featuring Pinky and the Brain* #49 (New York: DC Comics, June 1999). Illus. Walter Curzon and Horacio Ottolini.

1999   Gail Gibbons, *Behold the Dragons* (New York: Morrow Junior Books, 1999), 20–1. Illus. Gail Gibbons.

1999   Brian Patten, *Beowulf and the Monster* (Scholastic, 1999). Illus. Chris Riddell.

1999   Marcia Williams, "Grendel," *Fabulous Monsters* (Somerville, MA: Candlewick, 1999), 14–19. Illus. Marcia Williams.

1999   Welwyn Wilton Katz, *Beowulf* (Toronto: Douglas & McIntrye, 1999). Illus. Laszlo Gal.

Translated into Spanish *Beowulf* (Mexico City: Artes De Mexico, 2008). Trans. Rafael Vargas.

1999–   Gareth Hinds, *Beowulf: With Grimmest Grip*; *Beowulf: Gear of*
2000   *War*; *Beowulf: Doom of Glory*, 3 vols. (n.p.: TheComic.com, 1999–2000). Text excerpted from Francis Gummere, 1910.

Reprinted as 1 vol., *The Collected Beowulf* (n.p.: TheComic. com, 2000).

Revised *Beowulf* (Cambridge, MA: Candlewick Press, 2007). Text excerpted from A.J. Church, 1898.

2000   Lorna MacDonald Czarnota, *Medieval Tales That Kids Can Read and Tell* (Little Rock, AK: August House, 2000), 51–60.

2000   Phil Page and Sandra Woodcock, *Beowulf*, Livewire Myths and Legends (London: Hodder Education, 2000).

2001   David Calcutt, *Beowulf: A Play Based on the Anglo-Saxon Epic Poem* (Cheltenham, UK: Nelson Thornes Ltd, 2001). Illus. Richard Johnson and Peters & Zabransky.

2001   Rebecca Tingle, *The Edge on the Sword* (New York: G.P. Putnam's Sons, 2001), 8–15, 28–31, 57–74.

2001   I. Tokmakova, "Беовульф" ["Beowulf"], *Legends of Medieval Europe*, vol. 1 of 6 (Moscow: Olma, 2001), 7–46. Ed. Natalia Budur; illus. Olga Yonaytis.[12]

2002   Beverly Rees, *Beowulf: A Narrative Verse Drama: Presented in Fifteen Drama Workshops and Incorporating Activities for Teaching and Learning Key Skills* (White Heron Educational Productions, 2002). Illus. Anne Bernasconi.

2004   Henriette Barkow, *Beowulf* [printed bilingually in any of eighteen languages alongside English] (London: Mantra Lingua, 2004). Illus. Alan Down.

2004   Nancy Farmer, *Sea of Trolls* (New York: Atheneum Books for Young Readers, 2004), 43–52.

2005   Eric L. Kimmel, *The Hero Beowulf* (New York: FSG Kids, 2005). Illus. Leonard Everett Fisher.

2005   M.A. Roberts, *Beowulf* (Clayton, DE: Prestwick House, 2005).

2006   Michael Morpurgo, *Beowulf* (Cambridge, MA: Candlewick, 2006; London: Walker, 2007). Illus. Michael Foreman.

2007   John Green, *Beowulf* (New York, Dover, 2007). Illus. John Green.

2007   John Harris, *The Geat: The Story of Beowulf and Grendel* (Chelmsford: NotReallyBooks, 2007). Illus. Tom Morgan-Jones.

2007   Penelope Hicks, *Beowulf* (London: Kingfisher, 2007). Illus. James McLean.

2007   Ralph Mason, *Beowulf: Retold for Children Aged Eight and Above* (Children's Classical Library: Books for Learning, 2007).

2007   Stefan Petrucha, *Beowulf* (New York: HarperTrophy, 2007). Illus. Kody Chamberlain.

2007   Nicky Raven, *Beowulf: The Legend of a Hero* (London: Templar, 2007); *Beowulf: A Tale of Blood, Heat and Ashes* (Cambridge, MA: Candlewick, 2007). Illus. John Howe.

Translated into French *Beowulf: un héros de légende* (Paris: éditions Quatre fleuves, 2008). Trans. Frédérique Fraisse.

2007   James Rumford, *Beowulf: A Hero's Tale Retold* (Boston: Houghton Mifflin, 2007). Illus. James Rumford.

Translated into Korean 베오울프 [*Be-o-ulpeu*] (Seoul: Bomulchango Publishing Co., 2008). Trans. Hwang Yunyeong.

2007   Paul D. Storrie, *Beowulf: Monster Slayer, A British Legend* (Minneapolis: Graphic Universe, 2007). Illus. Ron Randall.

2007   Michelle L. Szobody, *Beowulf: Grendel the Ghastly* (Greenville, SC: Portland Studios, 2007). Illus. Justin Gerard.

2008   Tony Bradman, "Terror in the Night: The Story of Beowulf the Hero," *The Orchard Book of Heroes and Villains* (London: Orchard Books, 2008), 34–44. Illus. Tony Ross.

Reprinted *Beowulf the Hero*, The Greatest Adventures in the World (London: Orchard Books, 2010). Newly illus. Tony Ross.

2008   Julia Green, *Beowulf the Brave* (London: A&C Black, 2008). Illus. Tom Percival.

2009   Rob Lloyd Jones, *Beowulf* (London: Usborne Young Reading, 2009). Illus. Victor Tavares.

Translated into Swedish (Stockholm: Bergh, 2011). Trans. Birgit Lönn.

2009   Martin Waddell, *Beowulf and Grendel,* Hopscotch Adventures (London: Franklin Watts, 2009). Illus. Graham Howells.

2010   Rebecca Barnhouse, *The Coming of the Dragon* (New York: Random House, 2010).

2010   Mick Gowar, *Treetop Myths and Legends: Beowulf, Grendel and the Dragon* (Oxford: Oxford UP, 2010). Illus. Paul McCaffrey.

2010   Jacqueline Morley, *Beowulf* (New York: Barron's, 2010). Illus. Li Sidong.

2011   Simone Kramer, "Beowulf," *Van Parcifal tot Beowulf*, Verhalen uit de middeleeuwen 1 (Amsterdam: Ploegsma, 2011), 280–304. Illus. Els van Egeraat.

2011   Joseph Madden, *Beowulf for Kids* (Shamrock Eden, 2011), E-text. Illus. J[oseph] R[atcliffe] Skelton, 1908.

2011   Tóngqù Publishing Company, «贝奥武甫» [*Bèi'àowǔfǔ*] (Beijing: The People's Posts and Telecommunications Press, 2011). Illus. unknown.

2012   Rebecca Barnhouse, *Peaceweaver* (New York: Random House, 2012).

2012   Julia Golding, *Beowulf and the Beast* (Harlow, Essex: Pearson Educational, 2012). Illus. Victor Rivas Villa.

2012   Julia Golding, *Beowulf Meets His Match* (Harlow, Essex: Pearson Educational, 2012). Illus. Victor Rivas Villa.

2012   Joshua Gray, *Beowulf: A Verse Adaptation with Young Readers in Mind* ([n.p.]: Zouch Six Shilling, 2012). Illus. Sean Yates.

2012   James Rumford, *Beo-Bunny* (Honolulu: Mānoa Press, 2012). Illus. James Rumford.

2013   Anita Ganeri, *Beowulf* (London: Collins Educational, 2013). Illus. James Ives.

2013   Joseph McCullough, *Dragonslayers: From Beowulf to St. George,* Myths and Legends, vol. 2 (Oxford: Osprey, 2013), 19–35. Illus. Peter Dennis.

2013   Kim Smith, *Beowulf* (Cambridge: Pegasus Eliott MacKenzie, 2013). Illus. Kim Smith.

2014   Claire Hibbert, "Beowulf," *Terrible Tales of the Middle Ages* (London and Sydney: Franklin Watts, 2014), 22–5. Illus. Janos Jantner.

2014   J.R.R. Tolkien, "The Lay of Beowulf," *Beowulf: A Translation and Commentary together with Sellic Spell* (Boston: Houghton Mifflin Harcourt, 2014), 415–25. Ed. Christopher Tolkien.

2014   N.D. Wilson, *Boys of Blur* (New York: Random House, 2014).

2016   Heather Forest, "Beowulf," *Ancient and Epic Tales: From Around the World* (Atlanta: August House, 2016), 55–62.

2016   Melissa Niemann, *Beowulf* (Maricopa, AZ: Little Literary Classics, 2016). Illus. Melissa Niemann.

2016   Oakley Graham, *Beowulf the Brave* (Newport, New South Wales: Big Sky, 2016). Illus. Emi Ordás.

2017   Steve Barlow and Steve Skidmore, *Beowulf*, I Hero Legends (London: Franklin Watts, 2017). Illus. Andrew Tunney.

2018   3EB [children of Canary Wharf College, Glenworth], *Battles & Beasts: A Collection of Beowulf Stories* (London: 3EB, 2018). Illus. 3EB.

NOTES

1 Charles McGrath, "Children's Books," *New York Times Sunday Book Review*, 17 June 2007. https://www.nytimes.com/2007/06/17/books/review/McGrath-t.html (accessed 18 December 2020).
2 Gareth Hinds (2007), James Rumford (2007), and Michael Morpurgo and Michael Foreman (2007).
3 Syd Allan, "BeowulfTranslations.net" http://www.paddletrips.net/beowulf/html/bibliography.html (accessed 18 December 2020).
4 Stanley B. Greenfield and Fred C. Robinson, *A Bibliography of Publications in Old English Literature to the end of 1972* (Toronto: University of Toronto Press, 1980).
5 Marijane Osborn, "Annotated List of *Beowulf* Translations" (2003), formerly published online by the Arizona Centre for Medieval and Renaissance Studies but removed in 2019. Osborn's list is being republished in *Medieval Perspectives* 35 (2021).
6 John William Sutton, "Beowulfiana: Modern Adaptations of *Beowulf*," formerly available publicly through the library website of the University of Rochester.
7 Britt Mize (author) and Bryan Tarpley (web developer), *The Beowulf's Afterlives Bibliographic Database*, pilot version (2018), beowulf.dh.tamu.edu (accessed 18 December 2020).
8 https://www.worldcat.org (accessed 18 December 2020).
9 https://www.hathitrust.org (accessed 18 December 2020).
10 The long, complex history of this version in Danish public schools is surveyed in Busbee's chapter in this volume.
11 I wish to thank Dr. Daria Izdebska, Liverpool Hope University, for her help in purchasing a copy of the Polish translation of Sutcliff's *Beowulf*.
12 My thanks to Dr. Ilya Sverdlov, Core Fellow at Helsinki Collegium for Advanced Studies, University of Helsinki, for his help in locating this Russian book and representing it correctly.

Index